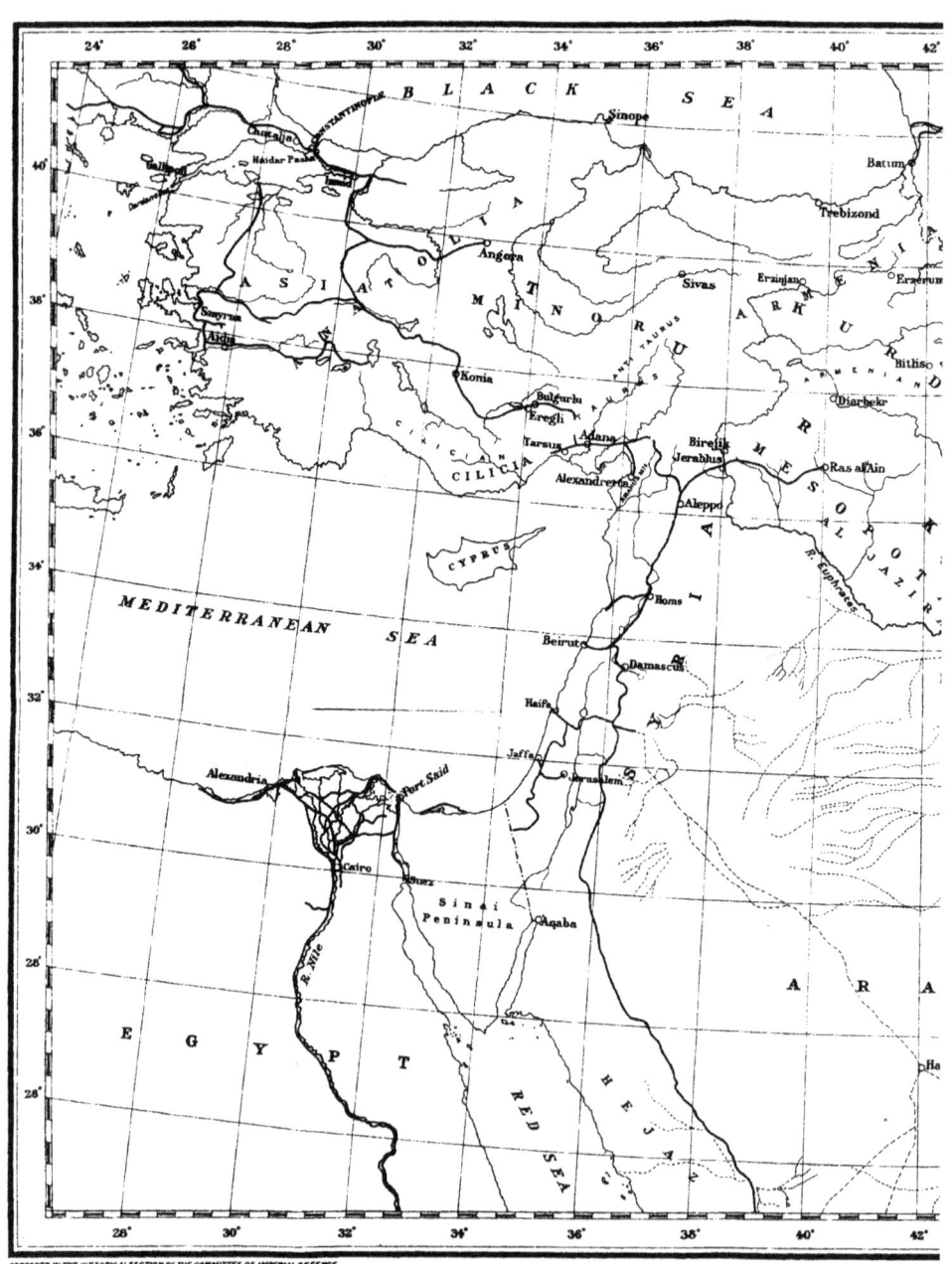

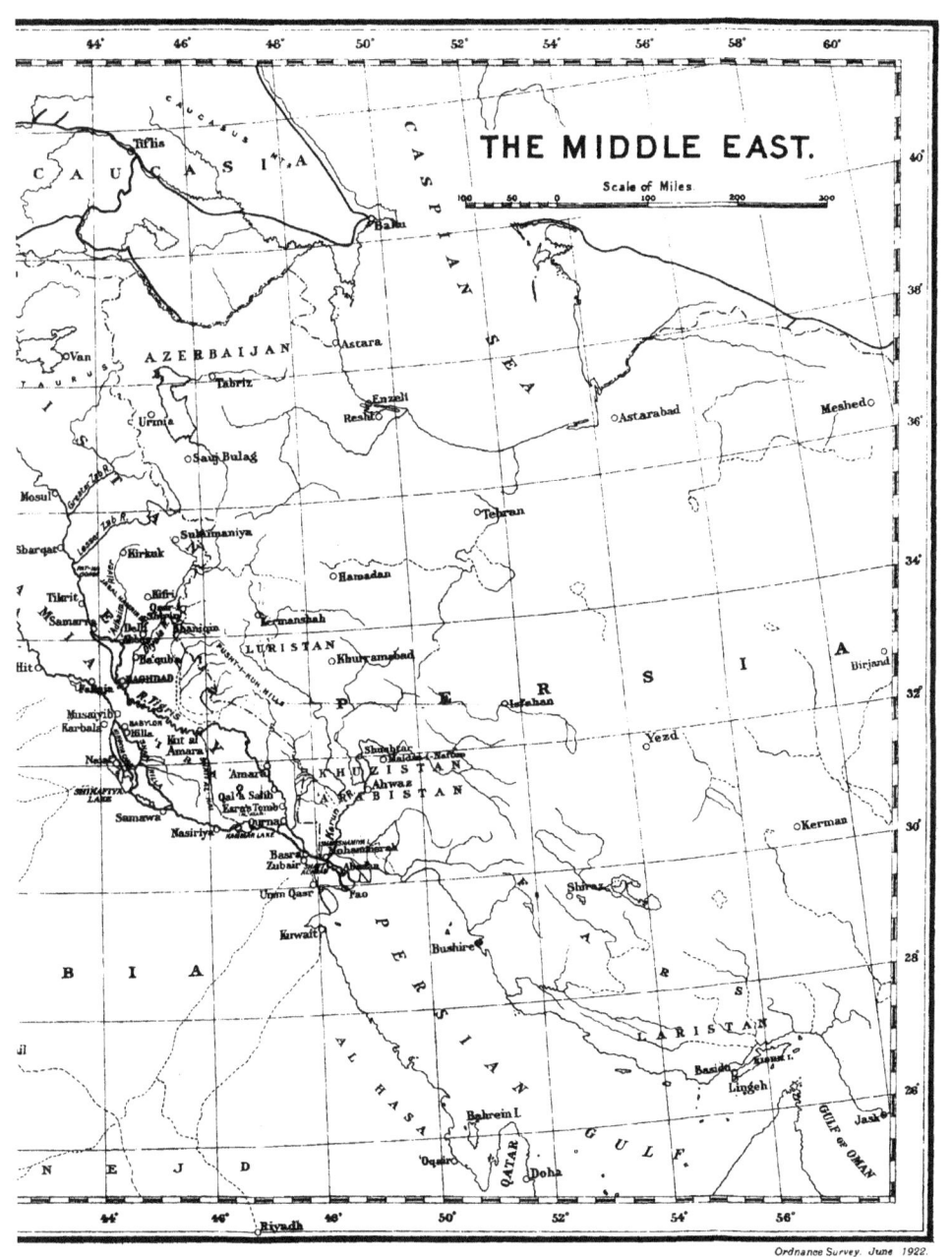

HISTORY OF THE GREAT WAR
BASED ON OFFICIAL DOCUMENTS.

THE CAMPAIGN IN MESOPOTAMIA

1914 - 1918.

Compiled, at the request of the Government of India,
under the direction of the Historical Section
of the Committee of Imperial Defence,

BY

BRIG.-GEN. F. J. MOBERLY, C.B., C.S.I., D.S.O., p.s.c.

VOLUME I.

The Naval & Military Press Ltd

Published by

The Naval & Military Press Ltd
Unit 5 Riverside, Brambleside
Bellbrook Industrial Estate
Uckfield, East Sussex
TN22 1QQ England

Tel: +44 (0)1825 749494

www.naval-military-press.com
www.nmarchive.com

Cover image:
Turkish prisoners after General Brooking's victory at Ramadi, September 1917.

In reprinting in facsimile from the original, any imperfections are inevitably reproduced and the quality may fall short of modern type and cartographic standards.

LIST OF MAPS.

The Middle East	*Frontispiece.*
Map of Lower Mesopotamia	
Map 1.—To illustrate operations described in Chapter VI	
Map 2.—To illustrate fighting near Qurna	
Map 3.—To illustrate fighting round Shaiba ..	
Map 4.—To illustrate operations in Persian Arabistan	*In pocket.*
Map 5.—To illustrate operations in the Akaika channel; 27th June to 5th July 1915	
Map 6.—To illustrate operations near Nasiriya; 6th to 24th July 1915	
Map 7.—To illustrate the battle of Kut; 28th September 1915 .:	

In pocket maps not included in this reprint.

ILLUSTRATIONS.

Qurna	..	..	..	..	..	..	..	*to face p.* 152
Ahwaz	..	..	..	..	..	..	..	,, 225
Nasiriya	..	..	..	..	..	..	..	,, 298

BIBLIOGRAPHY.

Official War Diaries, Army Headquarters, India.

Official War Diaries of the Headquarters Staff, Formations, Units, etc., of the Mesopotamia Expeditionary Force (Force " D ").

Official Records of the Government of India, India Office, Foreign Office, War Office, Admiralty, Committee of Imperial Defence.

Official Handbooks of Mesopotamia issued by the Admiralty, General Staff, India, and the Foreign Office.

Official Despatches on the Operations.

"Handbook of the Turkish Army "; War Office, 1915.

"Report on the Administration of Mesopotamia "; by Miss Gertrude Bell, 1919.

The Report of the Mesopotamia Commission and its appendices, containing the evidence given before it, and papers submitted to it.

Army in India Committee Report.

Persian Gulf Committee, 1909 (Committee of Imperial Defence).

"Naval Operations," Vols. I and II. Sir Julian Corbett.

Cyclopedia of India, 1907. (Thacker & Co.)

"Foundations of Reform." "The Times" Military Correspondent.

"British Campaigns in the Near East, 1914-1918." Edmund Dane.

"My Campaign in Mesopotamia." Major-General Sir C. V. F. Townshend.

"The Long Road to Baghdad." Edmund Candler.

"In Kut and Captivity." Major E. W. C. Sandes.

"The Navy in Mesopotamia, 1914 to 1917." Conrad Cato.

"A History of Persia, 1921." Brigadier-General Sir Percy Sykes.

"Mesopotamia, 1914-1915." Captain H. Birch-Reynardson.

"The Oxfordshire and Buckinghamshire Light Infantry Chronicle."

"On the Road to Kut." Black Tab.

"Besieged in Kut and After." Major C. H. Barber.

"The Turco-British Campaign in Mesopotamia and Our Mistakes." Staff Bimbashi Muhammad Amin; published by the Turkish General Staff.

"The Turkish Empire: Its Growth and Decay." Second Edition. From 1288 to 1914 by Lord Eversley; from 1914 to 1922 by Sir Valentine Chirol.

"Memories of a Turkish Statesman, 1913-19." By Djemal Pasha.

Diaries and private correspondence of numerous individuals, including several high officials.

Various magazine and newspaper articles (given in text).

PREFACE

THIS narrative of the operations of 1914-18 in Mesopotamia is based mainly on official documents. Criticism has been omitted and only such comment has been made as seemed desirable to place certain situations in a clearer light; and to obviate controversy extracts from the records have frequently been quoted at length. The official records, however, do not contain all that was required and the writer has received much assistance from numerous individuals, who have given him access to their private papers or have assisted him from their recollection of events. The writer desires to take this opportunity of acknowledging with gratitude the assistance he has thus received. His researches among the records of the different Government Departments in England, India and Mesopotamia have cast a good deal of extra work on their officers and officials, and he desires also to acknowledge gratefully the ready and cordial assistance he has obtained from them, especially from those in the Historical Section of the Committee of Imperial Defence and his own assistant, Colonel F. E. G. Talbot. The writer is also indebted to the headquarters of the Royal Air Force in Mesopotamia for several photographs, three of which are reproduced in this volume.

The fighting in Mesopotamia was generally dwarfed by the greater issues in Europe, except when it was brought into unusual prominence by some particular success or disaster. For this reason, and owing to the fact that the operations were carried out under conditions which were unique—even in an Empire like ours—few people were able to follow them systematically throughout their course. Since a thorough grasp of these conditions is necessary for a proper appreciation of the operations, the first few chapters of the history have been devoted to their description.

This first volume deals with the operations up to the 5th October 1915, which were practically an unbroken success; the second volume will treat of the first and ill-fated attempt to capture Baghdad, culminating in the surrender of Kut; the third and fourth will show how final victory was achieved.

The spelling of names is according to the latest* rulings of the Permanent Committee on Geographical Names of the Royal Geographical Society, to whom the writer is also indebted.

---

*Some further alterations have been received too late for inclusion, as the maps had already been printed.

CONTENTS.

PART I.
BEFORE THE OUTBREAK OF HOSTILITIES.

CHAPTER I.
GENERAL DESCRIPTION OF THE COUNTRY.

Boundaries — River system — Rainfall and floods — Roads — Climate — Products — Supplies — Upper Mesopotamia — Population—Characteristics of the Arabs—Religion—Turkish administrative system—The oilfield in Persian Arabistan—Kuwait—Al Hasa .. .. **PAGE 1–15**

CHAPTER II.
THE TURKS IN MESOPOTAMIA.

Historical summary up to 1875—Turkish administration under Abdul Hamid (1876–1908)—Turkish revolution, 1908—The Pan-Islamic and Pan-Turanian movements—Aggressive Turkish policy, 1908–1912—Turco-British Agreements, 1913–14—German influence—Railway construction—Relations of Turks with their neighbours—Turkish army: reorganisation after 1882; administrative system; strength at outbreak of the war; organisation and distribution; defences in Mesopotamia—Turco-German plans of operation **16–34**

CHAPTER III.
BRITISH PRE-WAR POLICY.

Strategic effect of the Baghdad railway—The religious factor—Turco-British relations until end of 19th century—Decline of British and rise of German influence—Enver Bey; his anti-British and pro-German proclivities—The Baghdad railway, 1871–1914—British rights of navigation on Mesopotamian rivers—Political relations of Britain with the Persian Gulf from 1622 onwards—British relations with Persia **35–48**

CHAPTER IV.
THE ARMY IN INDIA AND PRE-WAR MILITARY POLICY.

The Army of the East India Company—Reorganisation in 1858 and 1879—The Russian menace—Imperial Service troops—The "Curzon policy"—Reorganisation between 1900 and 1908—Lord Kitchener's scheme—Recommendations of the Army in India Committee of 1912—The tradition of economy—Strength of the army in India—Relations of India with Afghanistan—The tribes of the North-West Frontier—The internal situation in India—Organisation of the army on the outbreak of the Great War—Difficulties of expansion under Indian conditions—Assistance of India to the Empire **49–74**

vi   CONTENTS

CHAPTER V.   PAGE
INCEPTION OF THE OPERATIONS.

Dominating position of the Germans in Turkey—Arrival at Constantinople of the *Goeben* and *Breslau*—Turkish mobilization—Disquieting news from Mesopotamia, August, 1914—Admiralty urges despatch of troops for protection of oil-works at Abadan—India Office and the problem of British military action in Mesopotamia in event of war with Turkey—Musalman feeling in India—Question of Arab co-operation—Turkish action in Mesopotamia at the beginning of September—British naval movements—General Barrow's "appreciation" of 26th September—Further demands for troops made by Great Britain upon India—British Government's decision to despatch a brigade to the head of the Persian Gulf, and its departure from Bombay—Britain starts hostilities against Turkey 75–98

PART II.

THE CAMPAIGN IN LOWER MESOPOTAMIA.

CHAPTER VI.

THE LANDING IN MESOPOTAMIA OF FORCE "D" AND THE OPERATIONS LEADING TO THE OCCUPATION OF BASRA.

Mobilization of 6th Division—Instructions for the advanced force—Alternative plans—Armament and equipment of General Delamain's force—Departure from India—Arrival at Bahrein on 23rd October—Information regarding Turkish forces in Mesopotamia—Orders for operations in Mesopotamia, issued 31st October—Capture of Fao, 6th November—British landing at Sanniya, 8th–10th November—Abortive Turkish attack on British outposts, night 10th/11th November—Arrival of Lieutenant-General Sir A. Barrett, commanding 6th Division—British *communiqué* regarding outbreak of war with Turkey ; Indian Mahomedan sentiment—Orders to General Barrett—Arrangements for despatch of remainder of 6th Division—Disembarkation at Sanniya on 14th–16th November of second *echelon* of 6th Division—Affair of Saihan, 15th November; defeat of the Turks—Mirage—Attitude of local Arabs—Affair of Sahil, 17th November ; defeat of the Turks—Reconnaissances 18th–20th November—Turkish evacuation of Basra 99–126

CHAPTER VII.

THE OCCUPATION OF BASRA AND THE CAPTURE OF QURNA.

British reach Basra, 21st November—Description of Basra—Ceremonial entry into Basra on 23rd—British proclamation—Sir P. Cox suggests advance to Baghdad—Views of India and the India Office—India Office vetoes advance to Baghdad, but authorises advance to Qurna—General Barrett's "appreciation" of 29th November—Arab co-operation ; question of announcing permanent British occupation of Basra—Naval reconnaissance towards Qurna—Arrival at Basra of third and last *echelon* of

CONTENTS

6th Division—Preparations for advance on Qurna—First action of Qurna : the fighting at Muzaira'a, 4th December ; despatch of British reinforcements ; the fighting in vicinity of Muzaira'a, 7th–8th December ; surrender of Qurna, 9th December—Qurna—Close of first phase of the operations 127–153

Chapter VIII.
COMMENCEMENT OF THE TURKISH COUNTER-OFFENSIVE.

Results of capture of Qurna—General Barrett's request for river craft and aeroplanes—Turks on Tigris reinforced ; reported impending Turkish advance from Nasiriya against Basra—General Barrett reinforces Qurna : rise of waters in the vicinity —Effect of Russian victory over Turks in Caucasus—Reinforcements for General Barrett mobilized in readiness in India —Sir P. Cox's views on unsatisfactory political situation—The attitude of Ibn Saud—Turkish activity on Tigris near Qurna increases—Affair of 20th January 1915—Intelligence regarding the Turks—General Barrett asks for reinforcements on 26th January—Turco-Arab move into Arabistan—India arranges to reinforce General Barrett—*Comet*, with small infantry detachment, goes up the Karun river—Disquieting news from Ahwaz—India Office views on protection of oilfields and pipe-line : Viceroy's views : necessity of bringing Force " D " up to strength of two divisions—General Barrett reinforces Ahwaz —Turkish strength and dispositions in Mesopotamia at beginning of February—Lord Hardinge's visit to Basra—Pipe-line breached by disaffected tribe in Arabistan—Ahwaz further reinforced—Rising floods affect situation—Cavalry skirmishes west of Shaiba and growth of enemy strength there—Difficulty of providing reinforcements from India—Death of Major Shakespear ; effective assistance from Ibn Saud not to be expected—General Barrett reinforces Shaiba and reduces garrison of Qurna —Situation in Arabistan grows worse—Question of mobility of Force " D "—Cavalry affair near Shaiba, 3rd March—Affair near Ahwaz, 3rd March—India arranges for reinforcements for Mesopotamia 154–188

Chapter IX.
DEVELOPMENT AND DEFEAT OF THE TURKISH COUNTER-OFFENSIVE.

British dispositions on 7th March—Reinforcement of an infantry brigade from Egypt—Turkish dispositions at the end of March—Main Turkish force's intentions against Shaiba —The " Euphrates Blockade " force—Unfavourable situation in Southern Persia—Arrival of British reinforcements—Imminence of a Turkish offensive—Reorganisation of Force " D " into an Army Corps under General Nixon—General Nixon arrives Basra, 9th April—His instructions—British dispositions on 11th April—Effect of floods—Arrangements to meet Turks at Shaiba—Battle of Shaiba 12th–14th April—Simultaneous minor Turkish activity at Qurna and Ahwaz—Results of the battle of Shaiba—General Nixon undertakes operations to clear Arabistan—His request for reinforcements refused—Turkish dispositions at end of April—British dispositions 189–223

Chapter X.

OPERATIONS IN ARABISTAN AND THE CAPTURE OF AMARA.

General Gorringe to conduct operations in Arabistan—Concentration of his force up the Karun river—Cavalry reconnaissance of 29th April—Concentration at Ali Ibn Husain—Crossing of the Karkha river—Affair of Khafajiya, 14th–16th May—Reconnaissance to Umm Chir—Trying climatic conditions—March of a detachment to Amara—Punitive action against Arabs, 9th June—Close of operations and reduction of force in Arabistan—Discussion in regard to policy governing operations—Advance to Amara sanctioned, but a cautious policy laid down by India Office—Reduction of British force at Shaiba; establishment of new post near Old Basra—Naval reconnaissance of Hammar lake and water approaches towards Nasiriya—Arrival of General Townshend at Qurna, 24th April—Situation at Qurna—Plans and preparations for advancing up Tigris on Amara—Definite orders for offensive up Tigris issued by General Nixon on 11th May—Preparations for the advance energetically carried out—General Townshend's operation order of 28th May—Second action of Qurna, 31st May; complete British success—The pursuit up the Tigris—Occupation of Amara, 3rd June—Brilliant success of the operations 224–266

Chapter XI.

OPERATIONS ON THE EUPHRATES AND THE OCCUPATION OF NASIRIYA.

British distribution after the capture of Amara—Changes in organisation—River craft—Aeroplanes—Effect of climate—Turkish dispositions—Policy: General Nixon prepares to advance on Nasiriya; he recommends occupation of Kut al Amara; advance on Nasiriya sanctioned on 22nd June; consideration of question of advancing to Kut; India asks General Nixon for "appreciation" thereon—Deterioration of situation in Persia—Responsibility for defence of Bushire placed on General Nixon—Movements of German emissaries in Persia—General Gorringe to conduct operations against Nasiriya—His instructions, 23rd June—Topography—Concentration of force at Qurna and commencement of operations, 26th–27th June—Action in the Akaika channel, 5th July—Occupation of Suq ash Shuyukh, 6th July—Advance up the Euphrates—Reconnaissance of enemy's position—General Gorringe requests reinforcements, which arrive 11th–13th July—The fighting of 14th July: failure of attack on the "sandhills"—General Gorringe requests further reinforcements, which arrive on 19th–20th July—Arrival of British aeroplanes—Gorringe's dispositions on 23rd July—His orders for attack next day—Action of 24th July: defeat of the Turks—Occupation of Nasiriya, 25th July 267–298

Chapter XII.

THE BATTLE OF KUT AND OCCUPATION OF AZIZIYA.

Minor operations on Tigris above Amara, June and July—British dispositions end of July—Turkish dispositions—Policy: question of an advance to Kut: protection of the oil supply—

CONTENTS

Operations near Bushire—Situation in India, August and September—Proposed withdrawal of Indian divisions from France : question of advance to Baghdad : General Nixon's memorandum of 30th August—Preparations for the advance —The Turkish position covering Kut—Preliminary movements on 26th and 27th September—Battle of Kut, 28th September : victory and pursuit : Aziziya reached on 5th October— Developments in organisation of Mesopotamian Force, June to October—Distribution of British force at beginning of October 299–343

APPENDICES.

Appendix		Page
I.	Extracts from the Diary of Dr. Zugmayer	344–5
II.	Embarkation strength of General Delamain's Force and of the reinforcements under General Barrett	346–7
III.	Composition of Force "D" on 1st December 1914	348–9
IV.	Reorganisation of Force "D" as decided upon by the Government of India on 1st April 1915	350–1
V.	British forces in Arabistan on 1st May 1915, under the command of Major-General G. F. Gorringe	351–2
VI.	Summary of a pamphlet "The Turco-British Campaign in Mesopotamia and our Mistakes," by Staff Bimbashi Muhammad Amin; published by the Turkish General Staff	352–5
VII.	Distribution of Mesopotamian Force at the beginning of October 1915	356–7

INDEX 359

CHAPTER I.

GENERAL DESCRIPTION OF THE COUNTRY.*

THE area known as Mesopotamia consists, generally speaking, of the lowland regions of the basin of the Euphrates and the Tigris. The term Upper Mesopotamia is usually applied to the northern portion reaching almost as far south as Baghdad. Lower Mesopotamia, or Iraq, stretches thence, roughly southward to the sea. The boundaries of Mesopotamia are on the north the Armenian plateau and Kurdistan; on the east Persia; on the west the Arabian tableland and the Syrian Desert; on the south the Persian Gulf and the deserts of North-Eastern Arabia.

The line of demarcation on the south and west between the authority of the Turkish Government and the spheres of the various Arab tribes has been at all times indefinite. On the east, the Turco-Persian frontier was demarcated in 1914; it emerges from the mountains east of Baghdad through the foot-hills some forty miles from the Tigris and, passing west of Mohammerah, joins the Shatt al Arab.

The whole zone may be regarded as a former northern extension of the Persian Gulf, which at one time probably reached almost to the Mediterranean. In the north the plain has a fall in three hundred miles of some fourteen hundred feet to near Baghdad, whence to the south it is nowhere more than one hundred feet above sea-level.

The sole access from the sea is through the channel formed by the confluence, at Kurmat Ali, of the Euphrates and the Tigris and known as the Shatt al Arab. This is a fine river, about one and a half miles wide at the mouth, narrowing at Basra, sixty-two miles up-stream, to about six hundred yards. Up to this point it is navigable by any vessel that can cross the bar at the entrance.†

The Karun river enters it about forty-five miles upstream at Mohammerah. This is navigable for vessels of two and a half to five feet draught, according to the season of the year,

---
* See Frontispiece and Map of Lower Mesopotamia.
† In 1914, to cross the bar, vessels drawing more than eleven feet had to wait for the flood. At high water spring tides, vessels of twenty to twenty-two feet could enter; but at neaps the draught was only seventeen feet.

and forms the principal means of communication with Arabistan and the Anglo-Persian oilfields. The delta below Mohammerah is navigable by only one arm and for six months in the year is generally a swamp caused by the melting of the snows and occasionally by the action of the autumn rains.

At Kurmat Ali, five and three-quarter miles above Basra, the Euphrates enters from the west by its new channel; while its old channel comes in at Qurna, forty miles further up. The course of this river is nowhere clearly defined in its lower reaches; for, in addition to the old and new channels of the main stream, there are many subsidiary watercourses and tracts of water. Navigation is consequently complicated, especially during the flood season. The Hammar lake, about thirty-five miles west of Qurna, offers the chief obstacle owing to its shallowness and narrow entrance. In 1914 this lake was navigable only by vessels of three feet draught and that only during the high water season: in the time of low water all navigation was suspended except for *bellums*.*

From Qurna to this lake and beyond it to some seven miles downstream of Nasiriya the channel runs through extensive swamps. There is then some cessation of these to Samawa (209 miles from Qurna), though the country adjoining the river is liable to floods in the spring. Here two channels come in. These are the branches into which the Euphrates divides a short distance below Musaiyib (155 miles up-stream) and are generally known as the Hindiya canal and Shatt Hilla. The Hindiya barrage, one of the Willcocks irrigation projects, is situated at the point of diversion of the two channels and regulates the distribution of water between them. Between the barrage and Samawa are considerable tracts of water and marsh, including the Shinafiya lake.

From Musaiyib to Falluja, a distance of fifty-six miles, the average width of the river is 270 yards. The depth of water in this stretch averages six and a half feet at its lowest and the stream-level is then some ten feet below the river-banks. In the spring the floods increase the depth of water from six and a half to about eighteen feet, and the country on the right bank for some twenty miles upstream of Musaiyib is then liable to flooding if the marginal *bunds* are not well looked to.

---

* Country sailing boats of one to seventy-five tonnage (freight) and with a draught of one to five and a half feet when fully laden. On the Shatt al Arab this term is applied to small rowing boats, while the larger boats are termed *mahailas*.

GENERAL DESCRIPTION OF THE COUNTRY

Generally speaking, the river from the Hammar lake to the Hindiya barrage and from the Hindiya barrage to Falluja was, in 1914, navigable by vessels of three feet draught, but only during the high water season. Above Falluja, navigation was confined almost entirely to downstream traffic by flat-bottomed country boats, called *shakturs*. Experiments by the Turks with small steamers and motor-boats had met with little success.

The Tigris, the main line of communication between the sea and Baghdad, begins above Kurmat Ali.

The seasons of high and low water, on which navigation depends, follow usually a recognised sequence: about mid-November, rain causes the first rise and from January to March keeps the river fairly full, although frost in the mountains may lower it; in March, the melting of the snows causes the water to rise and in April and May the river is at its highest; it falls gradually in July and August, and from then to November the water is at its lowest. During September, October and November, however, navigation is easier, as the channels have become known. The table below gives further main details of the factors affecting navigation :—

Section of river.	Length in miles.	Average width in yards.	Average depth in feet.	
			Low water	Flood.
Basra to Qurna	46	600–270	10	45
Qurna to Ezra's Tomb	29	270–65	9	19¼
Ezra's Tomb to Qala Salih "The Narrows"; vessels cannot pass one another unless the up-bound one is banked in. Darkness, fog, or sand-haze stop navigation.	28	70	5	13
Qala Salih to Amara	29	197	6¼	13
Amara to Kut al Amara	153	330	6¼	26
Kut al Amara to Baghdad. At low water navigation is impeded by shoals with shallow and winding channels.	213	380	6¼	26

The strength of the current is an uncertain factor, varying with seasons and localities; about one and a half miles an hour at low water, it may attain six miles an hour or more during floods, and averages then four miles an hour.

Although it is the best port for transhipment from ocean-going steamers to river craft, Basra in 1914 had many disadvantages as a base for operations. Owing to the total lack of wharves or quays, vessels had to be unloaded in midstream into native sailing craft by primitive methods. Although to some extent our men were billeted in the houses, there were few buildings suitable or of sufficient size for the accommodation of stores or animals; and roads were equally lacking. The river-banks to a depth of about a mile were planted with date trees, and, as these plantations are below the level of high water, they are flooded to a depth of one to two feet for a considerable portion of the year. This fact limited greatly the amount of dry ground available for camps or stores. The surrounding country is flat and swampy, and many irrigation channels or creeks (unbridged for the most part) enter the main stream here. Basra was in no sense a modern civilised port and possessed no resources or facilities which would assist materially towards the development required to meet the sudden increase of traffic.

Above Baghdad, navigation is usually only downstream by rafts, though small steamers can go 50 miles up, to Samarra.

Connecting the Tigris and Euphrates is the Shatt al Hai, a branch of the first-named river which it leaves at Kut al Amara; but thirty miles above Nasiriya it diverges into many small channels which waste themselves for the most part in the Hammar marshes. It is navigable throughout a portion of its length from February to June and is used mainly by country craft which draw up to five feet of water. At other seasons it is not navigable, and the bed is dry in many places from July to November.

The navigation difficulties of the country, naturally considerable, were much aggravated in 1914 by the lack of proper water conservancy arrangements under the Turkish Government.

Between Baghdad and Qurna, the country contained by the Tigris and Euphrates is the ancient Babylonian plain, once of great fertility but largely uncultivated through the long period of Turkish misrule up to 1914 owing to lack of proper control of the waters. Practically the whole of Lower Mesopotamia is beneath the water-level of these two main rivers during the high flood season; and the rivers are only kept within their banks by means of slight dams of loose earth heaped up at the edge of the rivers. These dams are a constant source of anxiety, as an unnoticed break in them is apt to put miles

GENERAL DESCRIPTION OF THE COUNTRY. 5

of country suddenly under water. Owing to the low-lying nature of the country there are large areas of marsh and shallow lakes, which may extend to twenty miles in width and fifty miles or more in length. Curiously enough, these areas are frequently not contiguous to the rivers, but may be anything from half a mile to four miles away, the land between being dry except during prolonged bad weather. These dry belts between river and marsh are flat and without cover ; and they are intersected by numerous creeks and irrigation channels which are generally sufficiently deep and broad to require bridging. In the low water season, when most of the marshes dry up to a greater or less extent, wide cracks occur constantly in the ground.

The actual positions of these lakes are affected greatly by the direction and force of the wind ; and they have been known to extend on one side or contract on the other for as much as one or two miles, when a strong wind from the north has succeeded a strong wind from the south. These changes, moreover, do not take place gradually ; in one case the edge of a lake approached a camp at a rate of between twelve and fifteen yards a minute, necessitating a rapid change of site.

The average annual rainfall of the Mesopotamian plain* is only about six and a half inches, of which about five-sixths falls between October and April. A slow steady fall is almost unknown and the rain occurs generally in sudden storms, frequently of great violence and accompanied by hail and strong winds. Although they do not last long, these storms occasion considerable damage. It should be noted that the so called "flood season" has little to do with the rains and owes its being almost entirely to the melting of the winter snows in the Caucasus and the highlands of Asia Minor. Snow falls occasionally in the Mesopotamian plain, and as many as four days of snow were recorded in January 1912 at Babylon. The effect of water on the soil, which in Lower Mesopotamia is everywhere a sandy loam, is to convert it into a thick, tenacious mud which impedes all military movement until it has dried. When dried, the surface is capable of supporting temporarily all but the heaviest military traffic.

From the foregoing, it will be realised how adversely floods caused by a broken dam or a sudden rise of the river level, rain, or a shifting lake, may effect military operations. Troops may find themselves unable to stir from a camp, dry and

* The rainfall is moderately plentiful in or near the mountains.

sufficiently remote from water the night before, until they have constructed causeways, possibly some miles in length, along which they can defile. It becomes, therefore, an ordinary precaution to surround camps or trenches by protective dams or other earthworks. Unfortunately, moreover, the flood season occurs at the best time, climatically, for military operations. The weather from March to May is better than at any other time; there is little rain and a reasonable temperature prevails; but the subsidence of the floods is followed immediately by the extreme heat of June, July and August.

Nor does the subsidence of the floods help towards the water supply of moving troops. Floods generally recede wholesale, leaving few if any pools behind them; any water remaining such as in marshes or lakes, is usually brackish and unfit for human consumption.

Trees are scarce, being limited practically to a few date-palms, and consequently all wood for building has to be imported. There is also an almost total absence of stone; consequently, such roads as existed before 1914 were unmetalled and for the greater part without bridges. Tracks across the desert soon cut up and become heavy under artillery and transport traffic. Caravans were accustomed to pass from point to point by the line which circumstances might make the easiest at the time, and a caravan route may have many possible variations, great and small. Land communication was so unsatisfactory and the rivers so universally regarded as the best means of travel, that, up to 1914, little attention was paid to the location and condition of roads and our information relating to them was imperfect.

The principal roads before the war were in Northern Iraq, where well-used routes radiated from Baghdad. The following, practicable under favourable conditions for wheeled transport, were the main routes; wheeled transport was not used extensively, however; camels, donkeys and—in the hilly country—mules being the principal means of transport :—

Basra to Nasiriya.
Baghdad to Najaf via Musaiyib and Karbala.
Baghdad to Hilla.
Baghdad to Falluja (for Damascus and Aleppo).
Baghdad to Samarra (for Mosul).
Baghdad to Delli Abbas via Ba'quba (for Kifri, Kirkuk and Mosul).
Baghdad to Khaniqin (for Kermanshah).

GENERAL DESCRIPTION OF THE COUNTRY

There were also well-used caravan routes from Baghdad via Kut al Amara and Amara to the Persian border and from Basra to Kuwait and Nejd via Zubair. Along those of the above routes traversing country away from the main rivers water supply is always a difficulty in the dry season.

There are tracks across most of the marshes in the dry season, but they are little used: the ground remains soft and any regular traffic soon makes them deep in mud: they are consequently unsuitable for military purposes except in an emergency for small bodies of men.

The rivers of Lower Mesopotamia were crossed at a number of points by boat bridges. Most of these consisted of a roadway on pontoons or native boats (*safinehs* or *danaks*), some portion of which could usually be swung open to let vessels pass. While some of them could take light-wheeled carts, many were fit only for pack animals. In a high flood most of the bridges had to be removed temporarily. In Northern Iraq many of the roads crossed canals by brick bridges; and there was an iron bridge four miles from Baghdad on the road to Najaf. With these exceptions, the bridges in the country were few.

The climate is one of extremes, as shown in the accompanying table.

TEMPERATURES (FAHR.) OF DIFFERENT CENTRES IN MESOPOTAMIA.

	Jan.		Feb.		Mar.		April.		May		June	
	Max	Min	Max	Min	Max	Min	Max	Min	Max	Min	Max	Min
Basra ..	80·1	23·7	83·3	31·1	91·9	39·7	99·9	52·3	114·2	59·1	111·4	70·3
Babylon..	75·4	20·8	81·7	25·9	95·7	32·9	105·3	41·7	114·1	57·7	120·7	61·3
Baghdad	79·9	20·8	84·8	29·8	98·8	33·5	99·1	43·8	109·9	50·0	119·2	62·8
Mosul ..	62·6	4·3	66·4	5·2	71·1	34·5	87·6	37·6	103·5	53·2	110·3	61·9

TEMPERATURES (FAHR.) OF DIFFERENT CENTRES IN MESOPOTAMIA—*contd.*

	July		Aug.		Sept.		Oct.		Nov.		Dec.	
	Max	Min	Max	Min	Max	Min	Max	Min	Max	Min	Max	Min
Basra	114·4	70·7	113·9	68·7	109·4	59·7	101·4	52·5	92·4	35·7	76·6	29·9
Babylon	119·3	60·1	121·3	63·0	116·1	57·2	104·4	46·0	90·9	27·1	80·8	18·9
Baghdad	120·2	71·1	121·0	68·9	117·2	56·0	108·0	47·5	95·3	29·5	81·0	18·6
Mosul	118·8	71·2	117·7	67·1	113·9	58·3	97·0	48·9	86·5	29·1	71·8	27·9

The hot weather begins in May and ends about the beginning of October, the hottest period being from June to September. In November the weather is usually cool and from December to February it is decidedly cold, especially in Upper Mesopotamia, where the temperature falls not infrequently to below freezing point. March and April are warm and unsettled, with occasional thunder and sandstorms. The prevailing winds are from the north and north-west and the *Shamal* comes from the latter direction. It begins normally about the middle of June and blows intermittently for about forty days: its velocity occasionally reaches forty miles an hour and it has the effect of drying the atmosphere and of affording some relief from the great heat. The east wind is accompanied usually by high temperature, and the south wind is oppressive and accompanied by dust. Sandstorms are most common in the spring months.

Mesopotamia is a hot-bed of ravaging diseases. Plague, small-pox, cholera, malaria, dysentery and typhus, if not actually endemic, are all prevalent.

Most of the buildings and houses in the country are indifferent structures of sun-dried brick, without verandahs. They have no sanitary arrangements of any sort, and are hot and badly ventilated. They have been found generally unsuitable—except in a few cases such as Baghdad and Amara—for use by a military force.

GENERAL DESCRIPTION OF THE COUNTRY 9

The staple products of the country are dates, rice, barley and wheat, wool and goats' hair, hides and skins. The principal date-producing areas are the banks of the Shatt al Arab, the lower Euphrates, the Hilla-Karbala area, and on the Tigris about Baghdad. In Iraq agriculture depends mainly on irrigation and in Upper Mesopotamia on the rainfall. Transport difficulties and the attitude of some of the Arab tribes rendered impossible the collection of local supplies in adequate quantities. Grain, salt, *ghi* and straw were produced in sufficient quantities if they could have been collected. Cold storage is necessary to store and preserve potatoes and vegetables for any but the shortest period. Meat could have been obtained in ample quantities if it had been possible to induce the Arabs to bring in their cattle or to allow sheep to come down from the Persian hills. Grazing for horses exists in places, but it cannot be depended upon for long and rarely grows where it is most wanted.

In Upper Mesopotamia the plains are generally more or less undulating, though there are several wide expanses of flat country. Here and there they are traversed by low ranges of hills, whose general trend is eastward to westward. The surface of the plains is open and treeless. The soil is generally of a better surface to stand military traffic than in Iraq. In the north, where numerous streams carry water for half the year, large tracts are covered in the spring with rich grass ; but to the south, the plain becomes increasingly arid, being in many places a hard desert. There are also large areas in which water from *wadis** collects and on evaporation leaves an incrustation of salt.

Northward of Baghdad, the Euphrates and the Tigris have cut for themselves shallow valleys one to five miles wide bordered by low hills or cliffs, where stretches of alluvium occur, being the deposit of the rivers in flood time. Along the banks of the upper reaches of these rivers there is often considerable cultivation. To the east the plains slope from the Kurdish hills to the Tigris ; they are crossed by the Adhaim, the Lesser Zab and the Greater Zab (tributaries of the Tigris), and in the spring are generally clothed with grass. The southern portion of these plains is traversed from south-east to north-west by the rocky sandstone and conglomerate range of the Jabal Hamrin—rising to four hundred to six hundred feet above plain level—which is pierced by the Diyala (another tributary of the Tigris) near Delli Abbas, by the Adhaim about

---
* Watercourses or valleys.

thirty-five miles farther north-west and by the Tigris at the Fat-ha gorge about sixty-five miles above Samarra. In the region of the two Zabs there is much cultivation.

The Kurdish mountains rise to heights of 11,000 to 14,000 feet and form a difficult and intricate barrier. To the south-east they merge often into rolling downs and lower hills, where in spring grass is frequently plentiful. Along the Persian frontier the ranges run generally north-west and south-east and the tracks for pack animals which cross them are all more or less difficult. The passes in winter are usually blocked by snow.

West of the Euphrates the country is generally an arid desert, though towards the north it becomes gradually less so.

The above necessarily brief description of a country, difficult to visualise even in general terms—because it is rarely the same for more than a few weeks together—shows that " all military problems therein, whether strategical, tactical or administrative, are affected by local conditions to an extent rarely met with in any theatre of war. Nearly all the conditions combine to create difficulties; there is little to alleviate them, and most may be ascribed either to a lack of water or a surfeit of it. Far away from the rivers want of water makes operations impossible, while near them the excess of water is almost as great a source of trouble."*

The population has been estimated at between two and two and a half millions; but, as there are no accurate statistics on which to base such an estimate, it may be very wide of the truth. The Arabs form the great majority of the population in the plains, where other races are hardly found except in the towns or on the northern and eastern fringes of the plains—Armenians and Kurds form the majority of the latter category; but there is a sprinkling there, in the hills and especially in the towns, of Persians, Jews, Christians of different races and sects, Yezdis, Chabaks, Circassians, etc.

The Arabs have emigrated from the Arabian deserts and their establishment in Mesopotamia dates back very many years. Probably caused by the pressure of an increasing population on a soil growing steadily poorer, they have taken the opportunity offered by the weakness of neighbouring northern states to occupy land and pastures. The weakness of past administrations has not assisted to accelerate their transition from a nomadic to a settled life. It seems probable, however, that in a reconstituted Mesopotamia the surplus population of

---

* Field Notes, Mesopotamia, General Staff, India.

Arabia will find not only an abundant means of livelihood but far-reaching possibilities of social and intellectual advance.*

The Arabs are not found in the east beyond the Tigris above Mosul—a predominantly Arab city—but south of there they share with the Kurds the plains east and north of the Jabal Hamrin to where it is pierced by the Diyala river, where the Jabal Hamrin forms the dividing line between the two races. Arabs meet Kurds at the foot of the Pusht-i-Kuh hills, and in Arabistan they hold the greater part of the plains.

If united, the Arabs would constitute a factor of the highest importance in the general situation : but differences of religion, character, pursuits and interests have prevented any enduring combination. About one half of them are nomads or semi-nomads, and it is this fact which has hitherto placed insuperable obstacles in the way of the development of the country. Most of the nomads are found in Upper Mesopotamia, the western desert and Arabistan. They are pastoral tent-dwellers and possess a tribal organisation. Each tribal unit has certain pasture grounds which it visits according to the state of pasture and water, and their movements are frequently far and wide. Some of the nomad Shaikhs have more or less recognised claims over cultivated lands, which are worked for them by negroes or fellahin. But disputes and strife over all lands are common and add to the complexity of administration.

The semi-nomads consist generally of tribes living in various intermediate stages between pure nomadism and the condition of settled cultivators. But reversion to the nomad stage is frequent. They are, as a rule, mainly dependent on their live-stock, and in the spring, when there is abundant pasture in the open desert and steppe, the majority of them range over the plains with their flocks and herds. Some of them live in tents all the year round even when they raise their crops ; others have villages of mud or reed huts near their fields. Among them also tribal organisation still holds sway, though having taken partly to agriculture as a means of livelihood they have lost caste with the true Bedouin.

Amongst both nomads and semi-nomads tribal law and customs reign and tribal blood feuds continue. The Turks exercised only a limited authority over them and the Turkish administration was wont deliberately to foster tribal jealousies from sheer inability to exercise effective control.

The settled Arabs who are cultivators still keep more or

* Readers interested in this question are referred to the Report on the Administration of Mesopotamia by Miss Gertrude Bell. 1919.

less to their tribal organisation, but in many cases the tribal bond is weak or absent. The town Arab is often of very mixed blood and is generally in bad repute.

The marsh Arabs who are found on both banks of the Tigris between Qurna and Amara and along the Lower Euphrates are non-Arab in origin. They live mainly by fishing and the produce of their buffaloes, but here and there they cultivate a little rice. They generally bear rather a bad reputation.

The Arab is generally intelligent, quick and impressionable; often he has a certain subtlety of mind which is capable of a high state of cultivation. But he is slovenly and uncreative in practical matters and is lacking in the power of co-operation and of sustained labour in the face of difficulties. He has a natural bent for intrigue, is much under the sway of personal ambitions and jealousies, and is very much of a time-server. His word is generally easily broken unless given under certain forms or in certain circumstances which make it a point of honour with him to keep it. For many of them blackmail and thieving are normal and proper ways of earning a living. At the same time, the Arab ideal of conduct is humane and includes courtesy, generosity and hospitality and may express itself finely in action if it is not stifled by the desires of the moment.

The Arab is used to continual warfare of a guerilla type. He frequently commits acts of treachery and is generally ready to rob or blackmail a weaker neighbour. In warfare against regular troops he confines himself as a rule to raiding and harassing of retreats; and his offensive operations are rarely of a very determined and sustained character. During the war, the tribes were found to be well provided with modern rifles, especially in Lower Mesopotamia, and were usually possessed of ample ammunition. They are, however, poor marksmen.

Owing to the way in which the old tribes and tribal groups have scattered, as a result of their former invasions, it is difficult to give any adequate description of the tribal system in brief or general terms. The largest unit is the group or confederation of tribes. Some of these are of considerable size, such as the Muntafik in Southern Iraq, the Anaiza in the Syrian desert, and the Shammar who are the predominant group in Upper Mesopotamia and extend southwards to the country between the Tigris and the Persian hills. The greater groups may contain sub-groups, and the tribes again are divided into sub-tribes and clans ; and the composition of all of them is liable to continual fluctuation. As the authority of the tribal " Shaikhs " was always greater than that of Turkish law and administration and as their number and extent of authority fluctuated with the composition of the various tribal units, it will be realised that Arab administration is sufficiently difficult and complex on this score alone. In practice, tribal government depends generally on the free consent of the tribesmen, and that consent has to be obtained in councils where the Arab love of intrigue and argument produce interminable and tortuous discussion.

The Kurds predominate in the hills, and their lawlessness has occasioned much trouble in the past. They have not the subtlety and imagination of the Arab, but are more industrious and capable workers ; they are steadier and cooler in danger and possess a better physique ; but being more callous they are extraordinarily reckless about taking life. On the other hand, they are often good-humoured, hospitable, and in some ways frank and loyal ; though in war and brigandage they are little hampered by scruples of good faith. As fighters they are generally brave and determined and many of them are admirable horsemen. They are good marksmen.

Religion in Mesopotamia is for the most part a question of race ; with few exceptions, all Arabs, Kurds, Turks and Persians are Musalmans ; all Armenians and Syrians are Christians ; and Jews, Yezdis, Sabians and Chabaks have their own distinctive religions. Of the Musalmans, the Turks, Kurds and Arabs of Upper Mesopotamia are Sunnis ; the Persians and most of the Arabs of Lower Mesopotamia are Shiahs. There are many shrines—both Sunni and Shiah—in the country, and the strife and differences between the two sects are frequently a cause of serious embarrassment to the administration.

Under the Turks, the country was divided into *vilayets*, each under a *Vali* or Governor. The area we are concerned with consisted of the three *vilayets* of Mosul, Baghdad and Basra ; each *vilayet* was again sub-divided into *sanjaqs*, and these into still further sub-divisions. The administration was thoroughly inefficient and was only effective in certain limited areas—chiefly in some of the larger towns. Each tribe was assessed at a certain revenue and so long as that was paid the tribe was practically exempt from Turkish authority. The collection of this revenue gave constant trouble and not infrequently led to open rebellion, when traffic was held up, crops destroyed, and the banks of the rivers broken down.

Before concluding this chapter it is advisable to refer briefly to some relevant factors concerning the adjoining states and principalities.

Persia, for reasons which are well known, was practically impotent during the campaign to resist any but minor aggression from without.

The Anglo-Persian oilfield is at Maidan-i-Naftun, about twenty-six miles south-east of Shushtar in Bakhtiari territory. In this oilfield the British Government before the war had obtained a predominant interest in order to secure a controlled supply for the needs of the navy. The Bakhtiaris had a financial interest in the oilfields and were under a definite agreement to protect them and the pipe-line within their territory. This pipe carries the oil for over one hundred and forty miles to the refinery in Abadan island on the Shatt al Arab: for the greater part of its length it passes through the country of the Shaikh of Mohammerah, who, although paramount in Southern Arabistan, had not much power over the tribes west of the Karun river and had practically no power at all over the Arabs of Northern Arabistan. The principal means of communication in Arabistan is by the Karun river and the tracks that exist are usually only practicable for pack transport. The physical and climatic conditions in the greater part of this area are generally similar to those prevailing in Lower Mesopotamia.

Kuwait is an Arab State, south of Basra, extending about one hundred and ninety miles from north-north-west to south-south-east, but with indefinite and fluctuating boundaries to westward. It possesses a fine bay and was at one time considered as a possible terminus for the Baghdad railway, due mainly to exaggerated ideas of the difficulty of navigating the Shatt al Arab. The Shaikh of Kuwait has independently contracted obligations from time to time with the British Government and when war broke out he was definitely under our protection.

Stretching south-east from Kuwait towards the territory of the "Trucial" chiefs and inland to the frontiers of Nejd is the province of Al Hasa. The Turkish garrisons, whose effective control had never extended beyond the immediate vicinity of their posts, were ejected from this province by Ibn Saud, Emir of Nejd, in 1913. This ruler had since then entered into more or less intimate relations with the Indian Government which led, shortly after war broke out, to his espousing definitely the cause of Great Britain against the

GENERAL DESCRIPTION OF THE COUNTRY 15

Turks. During the early part of the 18th century Nejd was the centre of the extensive Wahabi* empire which extended from Mecca to near Baghdad. Originally ruled by one Emir, it had gradually resolved itself into two main zones of influence : that centering round Riyadh to the south under Ibn Saud and that centering round Hail to the north under Ibn Rashid of the Shammar dynasty. The latter, together with the Shaikhs of the Muntafik confederation and of the Bani Lam tribes† of Mesopotamia, took up arms on behalf of the Turks when war broke out.

The hostility of the Bedouin to the Turk has always been extreme, but in the war many Arabs fought on the Turkish side against us. They were not, however, trustworthy, and there were many occasions on which, when the Turks had been defeated, their Arab allies turned on them and harassed their retreat.

It should be borne in mind that the above description of the country contains much information that was only obtained by our forces in Mesopotamia after months of actual experience.

---

* A section of Musalman reformers of a bigoted and puritan type.

† A large and powerful group of semi-nomad tribes occupying the country above Amara.

CHAPTER II.

THE TURKS IN MESOPOTAMIA.

FROM 3000–4000 B.C. till A.D. 1258, when the Mongols invaded Iraq, captured Baghdad, massacred the inhabitants and ruined the system of irrigation in the country, Mesopotamia was a centre of dominion and civilising influence. Many great powers have in the past obtained riches from the land of the two rivers. Sumerian, Assyrian, Babylonian, Macedonian, Parthian, Saracen, Roman, Persian, Arab and Turk all had their turn.

A second invasion under Tamerlane in the fourteenth century completed the depopulation of the country; and for the next two hundred years it practically disappears from history. Between 1520 and 1566 the Ottoman Turks captured Mosul and Baghdad; and the Tigris and Euphrates became the Turco-Persian frontier. In 1603 the Persians overran Mesopotamia and twenty years later occupied Baghdad.

In 1638 the Ottoman Turks under Sultan Murad IV recaptured Baghdad from the Persians and from that date till 1917 it remained continuously in Turkish hands. Till the middle of the eighteenth century, however, their supremacy was frequently contested by the Persians, who on two separate occasions were in occupation of Basra for a series of years. Until 1834 the government of the country rested with the Pashas of Baghdad and Basra, who were supported by forces of Janissaries and were generally appointed by the Sultan from the ruling families of the country. The Sultan himself was regarded rather in the light of suzerain than of ruler and his authority was constantly defied. In 1834, attempts were commenced to centralise the administration of the empire by substituting direct control by the Porte for the semi-independent rule of the Pashas: but the efforts of the Governors—sent from Constantinople to replace the Pashas—to fill the public purse by a stricter collection of the revenues aroused dissatisfaction amongst the Arabs and rebellions were of frequent occurrence. Midhat Pasha, who was sent to Baghdad as Governor in 1869 to introduce the *vilayet* system of government, was an enthusiastic and vigorous reformer. He made great

THE TURKS IN MESOPOTAMIA

and honest endeavours to develop the country and if he failed it was chiefly due to lack of foresight and of the requisite technical knowledge.

During the reign of Abdul Hamid (1876-1908) the Turkish administration on the whole effected some progress, in spite of its mistakes and crimes. The Kurds were brought under some measure of control; cultivation and trade developed to some extent in the valleys; and a considerable proportion of the nomads were compelled or induced to adopt a more settled way of life. Though the Sultan unjustly converted into his private property about thirty per cent. of the best cultivated land in the *vilayets* of Basra and Baghdad and a considerable amount in the northern provinces, it has been pointed out that his action was probably of economic benefit to the country, for his estates were comparatively well managed through his private staff, and law and order were enforced within his limits. Nevertheless, the methods of his government—its corruption, fraud and violence—aroused great discontent throughout Mesopotamia.

Under the *vilayet* system, the *Valis*, or governors, had no power over the Imperial departments of Public Justice, Revenue, and those relating to the convenience of the public. The local directors of these departments corresponded direct with Constantinople. The *Valis*, however, were the political representatives of the Ottoman government and, as such, conducted all dealings in their *vilayets* with foreign consular officers and with the chiefs of the semi-independent tribes. One of their most important duties was the collection of taxes; these they farmed out, with the results that bribery and corruption were rife and that a very large section of the people escaped taxation altogether. The *Valis* had no authority over the regular troops but could call upon their commander for support; in practice, however, this division of authority constantly paralysed attempts at effective action.

The gendarmerie who were responsible for the maintenance of law and order were distributed as military police under the orders of the *Valis*, but they were under the control of the Turkish War Office. These military police, or *zaptiehs*, were commanded partly by regular military officers and partly by civilians; about half of them were mounted and the remainder on foot. As a rule they were dispersed in small detachments and were employed on all kinds of miscellaneous work besides their regular duties. Though not smart in appearance they were useful and hardy. In the larger centres of population and in places of administrative importance there existed a small number of purely civil police, whose authority, however, did not extend beyond their own centres. Every Turkish official, from the *Vali* downwards, was assisted by a civil administrative council, of which he was *ex officio* president, composed of officials and non-officials. These councils had only advisory powers and met but seldom. In certain towns also there were municipal committees, who had no more power than the administrative councils. Secret service agents, or spies, abounded and reported direct to Constantinople.

In considering this centralised system of government it has to be borne in mind that the Turkish constitution, brought into being in 1856 after the Crimean War, had been completely nullified in 1878 by Sultan Abdul Hamid II. He then prorogued Parliament indefinitely and governed through the Palace and the Porte for over thirty years. Although the laws of Turkey guaranteed freedom of religious worship and perfect equality among all Ottoman subjects, in the greater part of their dominions Christians and Jews were without the security which the intervention of the Shaikh-ul-Islam and the College of Ulemas obtained for the Sultan's Moslem subjects. In Mesopotamia, however, there appears to have been little persecution of Christians or Jews: this was probably due to a great extent to the fact that animosity between the two chief Moslem sects—Sunnis and Shiahs—was more marked than between Moslems and non-Moslems. Relations with Persia were indifferent, owing chiefly to boundary disputes, which were a constant source of strife; and the hostility between Sunnis and Shiahs became invested with a political character, aggravated by the attitude of the Turkish authorities towards Persians in Turkish territory, particularly the pilgrims to Karbala and Najaf, the holy cities of the Shiahs.

The Turkish revolution of 1908 was welcomed by the majority of the population; but the chauvinist policy of the Young Turks disappointed the hopes that had been entertained. They governed by putting the Chamber of Deputies under the shadow and terrorism of the secret court martial. The proceedings of this Court were manipulated by the central office of the irresponsible Committee of Union and Progress, who established branches in all the provincial centres to control the action of the official local authorities. As the Central Court Martial was composed of officers who—either from having studied in Germany or for other reasons—were under German influence, the German Ambassador and his military attaché gained considerable power in the central and provincial administration of the country. There was thus little amelioration in the condition of Mesopotamia. The unsuccessful wars with Italy in 1911 and with the Balkan States in 1912-1913 made matters worse ; and the Arab disaffection in Mesopotamia was brought into connection with the anti-Turkish movement in Arabia. Opposition to the Government grew even in Basra and Baghdad ; the Muntafik under Ajaimi Ibn Sa'adun were reported to be planning an attack on Basra ; the waterways between Baghdad and the Persian Gulf were rendered insecure by the prevalent disorder ; a general rising of the southern Mesopotamian Arabs was feared ; and lawlessness was increasing in Kurdistan, where a number of chiefs were entering into relations with Russia. The whole situation was still uncertain when the European War broke out.

During recent years much has been heard of the Pan-Islamic and Pan-Turanian movements and it seems advisable to give here a brief *résumé** of these movements and their objects. Pan-Islamism, the older of the two, is based on the ideal of a union of all Moslem countries looking to Turkey as their liberator from alien control, their protector from outside interference, and their nominal or actual head. Abdul Hamid, theoretically (as Caliph) the religious head of all Musalmans, exploited this movement to the utmost. Nominally a religous movement, it has actually become a political weapon, first in the hands of Abdul Hamid and then of the Committee of Union and Progress, who suggested, on the principle of political independence for Islamic states, a Triple Alliance of Turkey, Persia and Afghanistan. Its advocacy by the Turks has militated against its chance of becoming a religious movement, for the Arabs who have been responsible for most of the modern religious revivals in Islam regard the Turks as little better than infidels. On the other hand, it has appealed to Musalman communities under European government who are not sufficiently in touch with Turkey and Turkish affairs to realise the true state of affairs ; to some among them it appeared to offer hopes of obtaining the benefits of self-governing institutions for themselves, whilst to others its religious ideal has undoubtedly been a goal to be striven for. The Ottoman empire is the only Musalman power of modern times which has dealt on equal terms with the naval and military powers of Europe, a factor of great importance to Musalman communities

---

* For much of the information here the historian is indebted to " The Round Table," December 1917, and " The Times," 3rd and 5th January 1918.

elsewhere, who were often apt to overlook the fact that the Turks owed this status mainly to their possession of subject European provinces. The defeat of Turkey in the Balkan war, however, brought this point of view into prominence and had a considerable effect in the Musalman world, leading to movements in many parts for the regeneration of Turkey; and the Committee of Union and Progress seized on the Pan-Turanian movement as the best available political weapon for their purpose.

The term Turanian was first applied by philologists to a group of Asiatic languages and subsequently to the peoples who spoke these languages, thus confusing linguistic and racial affinities.* This in turn was extended by the Turkish advocates of the movement to include all the racial elements that can be inferred from the Turanian group. The original Pan-Turanian movement had for its aims the purging of the Turkish language and culture from foreign (chiefly Arabic) influences, the strengthening of Turkish nationality in Anatolia by education and social reform, and the changing of the political ideal of the Ottoman Turk from Imperialism to Irredentism.† On the other hand, the Committee of Union and Progress desired to use it to purge the Turkish state from foreign (chiefly European) influences, to exterminate the non-Turkish nationalities scattered through the country and to give their lands and houses to Musalman refugees from the provinces lost in 1912-1913, and to compensate for losses in Europe by gains in Asia and Africa. The abolition of the Capitulations,‡ the language ordinance making the use of Turkish obligatory, the race war against Albanians, Armenians, Greeks and Arabs and the whole policy of forcible Turkification within the boundaries of the Empire were manifestations of Pan-Turanian activity under the rule of the Committee of Union and Progress.

Although the two movements are antagonistic in principle, the Committee of Union and Progress exploited both at once—Pan-Islamism best met their requirements in Persia, Afghanistan

---

* " The ' people of Turan ' are the nomads of many different languages and races who constantly overran Persia from the north-east till the Russians pacified Central Asia half a century ago." " The Round Table," December 1917.

† " The Turkish nation abandoned the tradition of being a dominant race in Europe, resolved to develop its own latent possibilities in Anatolia, and conceived the ambition of making up for lost alien subjects by attracting to itself the scattered branches of the Turkish race outside the Ottoman frontiers." " The Round Table," December 1917.

‡ Old Treaties on which were based the relations of foreign governments and of foreigners resident in or doing business with Turkey.

and India, while Pan-Turanianism was better suited to the Ottoman territory and to Central Asia.

From 1908 till 1912, i.e., from the accession to power of the Young Turkish party till the Balkan war, Turkish policy in Mesopotamia and the Persian Gulf was markedly aggressive and inimical to British interests, and it is noteworthy that this was coincident with the efforts of Germany to strengthen her commercial position in these areas. Attempts were made to induce the Shaikh of Kuwait to accept Turkish nationality, in direct contravention of the agreement of 1901 between the British and Turkish governments to maintain the *status quo* there; intrigues against the Shaikh of Mohammerah culminated in 1910 in the use of force and were only tided over by the diplomatic pressure of the British and Russian governments; aggressive claims to the peninsula of Qatar, adjacent to Bahrein, and parts of the " Trucial " coast were advanced; and objections were raised to various long-standing British privileges at Baghdad and on the Tigris. In 1912, however, the attitude of the Turks towards the British underwent a marked change for the better and led to a series of negotiations and agreements between the two nations in 1913–1914. These negotiations comprised twenty-three different subjects and illustrate well the widespreading and long-standing questions of great complexity which had for many years dominated the relations of the two countries. They established complete guarantees against discrimination in respect of British or Indian merchandise on any railway, present or prospective, in Asiatic Turkey; they brought about an acceptable compromise regarding navigation on the Tigris and Euphrates; they secured improved conservancy, with British expert assistance, of the Shatt al Arab, for the equal advantage of all nations; they contributed to the final settlement of the Turco-Persian frontier; and they led to the definite recognition of the political *status quo* on the shores and on the waters of the Persian Gulf. At the same time the British Government agreed to a number of fiscal changes and economic reforms, as well as to British co-operation in the revision of judicial procedure, to which British assent—necessary under existing treaties and conventions—was desired by Turkey in order to promote her commercial development.

It is impossible when discussing Turkish policy at this period to avoid reference to the factor of German influence, for Germany brought Turkey into the war against us; and one is forced to the conclusion that for many years previously

German endeavours had been directed towards shaping Turkish action to provide the necessary means, when opportunity offered, of striking at British power and British commercial prosperity in the East. Indeed her own writers have admitted as much.* German intervention in Turkish affairs dates back to 1875, when she failed to achieve a grouping of the European powers which would permit her to declare war on France. For nearly forty years German diplomacy has worked to obtain complete ascendancy in the Turkish dominions and whether, as at first, their efforts were mainly to foment distrust between Great Britain and Russia in regard to Turkey, Persia and India, or, as latterly, to create discord between Turkey and Great Britain in regard to Egypt, Arabia, Mesopotamia and the Persian Gulf, their policy has been continuously detrimental to British interests. German diplomacy and German finance worked hand in hand. Their banks were supported by diplomatic action and the whole policy was controlled and co-ordinated from Berlin. There are many reasons for supporting the statement that it was the consistent German policy to weaken Turkey in order to secure her greater dependence; and it was probably due to this that German influence has tended to aggravate, rather than to modify, those political and administrative vices which have been the main cause of the Turkish downfall. The "*Drang nach Osten*" visualised a German Empire extending from the North Sea to the Persian Gulf, with Austria, the Balkan States and Turkey as mere dependencies. Admiral Mahan, in "The Problem of Asia," has shown how such an extension would affect the security of Egypt and Great Britain's eastern possessions.

The concessions for railway construction in Asia Minor and Mesopotamia obtained by Germany are specially relevant to this history. While in Syria French capitalists have from the first taken a predominant interest in railways, such enterprises in Asia Minor were at the outset entirely in British hands; and the first proposals for a railway in Mesopotamia connecting the Mediterranean and the Persian Gulf were made by a British company who, in 1857, obtained a concession from the Ottoman government for its construction. In 1914, the Smyrna-Aidin railway was the only British concern

---

* Much has been written on this subject, and reference thereto is hardly necessary. The author has found the articles " German Methods in Turkey " and " The Baghdad Railway Negotiations " in the " Quarterly Review," October 1917, particularly useful summaries.

remaining, the Euphrates railway concession had lapsed, and German interests were predominant in the Anatolian and Baghdad railways. The reasons for this were largely financial, but these again were dependent on the difference between British and German financial methods and on the fact that the alignment of the railways had been carried out on strategical and political lines rather than with a view to early commercial profit. In 1888* two *irades* were issued at Constantinople conveying to a nominee of the Deutsche Bank the right of working the existing Haidar Pasha-Izmid line and a 99 years' concession for an extension of that line to Angora. In 1893 the German group received two further concessions, one of which—for an extension to Konia—was completed in 1896. The lines from Haidar Pasha to Angora and Konia now form the Anatolian railway. The next development was the Convention signed in 1899 which conceded in principle to the Anatolian Railway Company the right to extend from Konia to the Persian Gulf; this was succeeded in 1902 by a further convention which served in turn as the basis for the elaboration of the definitive scheme—the Baghdad Railway Convention of the 5th March 1903. There are a few points to notice in regard to the above. The concession of the right to extend to the Persian Gulf was obtained when Great Britain's attentions were concentrated on South Africa; the original intention that the line should go from Angora via Sivas, Diarbekr, Mosul and Kirkuk was rejected in favour of the route via Konia, ostensibly on account of engineering difficulties, but really because of the opposition of Russia, who had constant suspicions of German designs in Asiatic Turkey; it was argued at the time that the Turks were in no position financially to provide the revenue required as a guarantee for building the line; and the British Government declined to assist or participate in the project until, as will be explained in the next chapter, just before the war.

The Konia-Eregli section of the line was opened in 1904 and was extended to Bulgurlu, but owing apparently to lack of funds no further progress was made till 1908, when it was resumed. By the outbreak of war the line had been completed to Ras al Ain, with the exception of the portions where the line passes through the Taurus and Amanus mountains; and from the Baghdad direction the line had been completed as far as Samarra. This delay in building, whether due to the

---

* Direct railway communication had just then been established between Berlin and Constantinople.

British refusal to participate or not, was fortunate for us, as the two serious gaps in the line between Haidar Pasha and Baghdad were a grave hindrance to Turkish plans throughout the operations. The gap in the Taurus–Amanus section meant five days' journey by motor lorry; the distance by road from Ras al Ain to Mosul was about 200 miles; and from Mosul to Samarra about 165 miles by road or 190 miles by river: the latter route, which was the one generally used by Turkish reinforcements, took anything from two to ten days, according to the state of the river, wind, etc., for the journey was carried out on rafts (*keleks*) which could each transport about one hundred men.

The relations of the Turks in Mesopotamia with their neighbours were generally discordant and have to be borne in mind as affecting more or less directly the general situation there. In consequence of a series of frontier incidents and other disputes, relations between Turkey and Persia became so strained in 1842 that war appeared imminent. The frontier itself presented an extraordinary difficult problem as it passed through unmapped territories frequented by nomadic and semi-independent tribes, where tradition, racial and religious prejudices, the conflicts and ambitions of rival chiefs and their shifty allegiance all combined to delay and obstruct any attempts at settlement; protection for Persian pilgrims to the Shiah shrines in Mesopotamia was hard to ensure, and there were serious difficulties over the civil and judicial rights of Persians residing in Turkish territory; and there were urgent counter-claims by both nations for the possession of Mohammerah. Under British and Russian mediation a settlement was apparently arrived at in the Treaty of Erzerum signed in 1847; but, when attempts were made to carry out in practice the settlement arrived at, no agreement was found possible. Negotiations were delayed and in 1876 delegates of the four powers again met in Constantinople, but with no more satisfactory results. After that, matters remained relatively quiescent till 1905, when Turkish aggression in the Urmia region revived the question in an acute form and occasioned fresh disputes, which were not settled finally till 1913. Theoretically, therefore, when war broke out there seemed no reason why Persia should be likely to have any great sympathy with Turkey. It rapidly became apparent, however, that the Persians' hatred of Russia was such as to lead them to regard the latter's adversaries with considerable favour and the public attitude was definitely pro-German, if not pro-Turk. Persia, therefore, afforded a useful centre and fruitful field for the activities of Turkish and German agents. On the other hand, the pro-British attitude of the Shaikh of Mohammerah, suffering from many years of Turkish aggressive action, was never in doubt.

The Arabs had little love for the Turk, but the latter's policy of fomenting inter-tribal disputes had left many Arabs whose self-interest bound them to the Ottoman Government. In 1818, the Turks undertook a successful expedition against the Wahabi power in Nejd and Turkish garrisons remained there till driven out in 1831. The Ottoman Government, however, continued to regard the ruling Emirs of Nejd as tributary to their authorities at Basra and in 1871, Midhat Pasha, *Vali* of Baghdad, gave a fresh impetus to this claim by his support of one of the claimants to the Emirate. His expedition there in 1871–1872 resulted in a rather ineffective military occupation of the province of Al Hasa, where Turkish garrisons remained till evicted by Ibn Saud, Emir of Nejd, in 1913. By this time whatever vestige of Turkish authority there may have been in Nejd at any time had completely disappeared and both Emirs (Ibn Rashid and Ibn Saud) enjoyed an altogether independent status. The dominating factor was the rivalry between the two and in the war the former, dependent on the Turks, espoused their cause, while the latter declared for the British and against his rival.*

Prior to Midhat Pasha's expedition, there were on the Arabian coast of the Persian Gulf " no symbols of Turkish authority, no Turkish jurisdiction, effective or ineffective," south or east of Oqair, the port of Al Hasa; and a Turkish claim to Bahrein in 1850 had been successfully resisted as unjustifiable. There were well-founded rumours in 1871 that Midhat Pasha meant to extend his enterprise in Arabia to cover the occupation of Bahrein, Qatar and part of the " Trucial " coast; and, in spite of the assurances of the Turkish government to the contrary a few months earlier, in July 1871 a Turkish deputation succeeded in obtaining local assent to the establishment of a small Turkish garrison in the town of Doha on the east coast of the Qatar peninsula.

In 1871 the Shaikh of Kuwait, then independent, co-operated with Midhat Pasha in the latter's intervention in Nejd and,

* A Turkish General Staff pamphlet recently issued regarding the Mesopotamian operations, emphasises the fact that their Headquarters at Constantinople did not realise this. Ibn Rashid is said by them to have given them no assistance and they had not grasped the enmity felt towards them by Ibn Saud. See Appendix VI, p. 352.

in return for his services, received a grant of land at Fao and an annuity. This fact—put forward by the Turks as implying their suzerainty over Kuwait—led till recent years to various unsuccessful attempts by the Turks to exercise pressure to obtain what they professed to be their rights in this area. Thus, when war broke out, his interests had forced the Shaikh of Kuwait into a definitely anti-Turkish attitude.

To turn to the Turkish Army, the following summarised description is based upon information collected before, during and after the war and may not be wholly accurate. In 1914, the effects of the Balkan war of 1912–1913 were still manifest in grave deficiencies in organisation and equipment and added to the disorganisation caused by the declaration of war; during the war many new formations were called into being, some of them to replace others captured or decimated, and there was often consequent confusion as to title numbers of units and formations. The numbers and armament of the Turkish forces at any fixed time cannot be estimated with entire accuracy; their own figures, obtained during and after the war, are often unreliable; desertions were rife, and disease was constant and often of an epidemic nature, causing sudden and considerable reductions; casualties were frequently not reported; and fraudulent returns were not unknown.

The Musalman Turk is courageous, enduring and obedient, and makes an excellent private soldier. Although in 1914 his prestige had been somewhat lowered by the events of the Balkan war, in the Dardanelles, Palestine and Mesopotamia he proved to be a formidable opponent.

The reorganisation of the Turkish army was undertaken by Germany in 1882. Colonel Köhler, who commenced the work, died in 1883 and was succeeded by Lieutenant-Colonel von der Goltz. The latter " was appointed sub-chief of the General Staff as well as Inspector-General of Education, and in this double capacity effected all that was, humanly speaking, possible in a country like Turkey, where the reformer usually finds more obstacles than encouragement."*

The system introduced by von der Goltz held good, with certain modifications, up to the year 1911, when a fresh organisation was adopted on the advice of the same officer, under which the Empire, excluding the Red Sea provinces and Tripoli in Africa, was divided into four *Ordus* or Army Inspections.

---

* " Foundations of Reform," by the Military Correspondent of " The Times."

At this period was introduced a new policy regarding recruitment, under which the liability to compulsory service, hitherto limited to certain classes of Moslems, was extended to include practically all subject races, whether Christian, Jew or Moslem. The introduction of this law caused much controversy and met with considerable opposition in Kurdistan and Arabia. It was a change from a policy which had, in the past, invested wars waged against Christian powers with a religious character;* it was disliked by the majority of Christians and Jews, who feared attempts at conversion during the period of colour service and displayed no enthusiasm at the idea of serving in the army and, moreover, whose martial qualities were considered by their Moslem fellow-subjects as of a low standard; it seemed likely to interfere with the liberty of some of the semi-independent subject races; and it was a departure from custom, a sufficient reason in an oriental country to invoke distrust and obstruction. Although in the Balkan war the Armenians had fought well, in contradistinction to the Greeks and Slavs who had proved unreliable, the experiment so far failed that, in 1914–1915, the great majority of the Christians and Jews who had been enrolled were drafted into unarmed labour battalions, used for road-making, etc.

The Sultan was the supreme head of the army, whose administrative chief was the Minister for War,† controlled nominally by Parliament. He was assisted by a Superior Military Council with consultative and advisory duties, of which the Vice-President was Field-Marshal von der Goltz Pasha, who, in 1914, still retained this position although for three or four years previously he had carried out few of the duties attaching to the appointment. Early in 1915 he returned to Turkey. From 1913 a military mission of some seventy German officers, under General Liman von Sanders Pasha, had instituted a system of more intensive training.

The army was divided into :—
 (i) Active Army (Nizam) ;
 (ii) Active Army Reserve (Ihtiyat) ;
 (iii) Territorial Army (Mustahfiz).

The actual numbers in the forces at the outbreak of war are

---

* " Everyone in Turkey, every Turkish officer, will at once inform you that the reason for their defeat by the Bulgars was because all religious element had been stupidly disregarded by the " Young Turk " party . . . and without the religious ' touch ' the Anatolian soldier . . . . would not fight."—" My Campaign in Mesopotamia," by Major-General Sir C. V. F. Townshend.

† When war broke out this post was held by Enver Pasha.

difficult to ascertain. They have been estimated at just over 200,000, though the Turkish General Staff after the war stated that they were nearer 150,000. By September 1914 some 800,000 men are said to have been mobilised, and these numbers, according to the Turkish General Staff, rose during the war to a total of 2,850,000, of whom, according to the same authority, 1,900,000 had by 1st May 1917 become casualties, including all counts. The pre-war organisation and distribution was as follows :—

Army Inspection.	Head-quarters.	Area.	Composition.
I.	Constantinople	Constantinople, Thrace, Western Asia Minor and Anatolia	Ist, IInd, IIIrd, IVth and Vth Army Corps each consisting of one cavalry brigade* and three infantry divisions, with a varying number of heavy artillery and other units.
II.	Erzinjan	Kurdistan	IXth, Xth and XIth Army Corps each consisting of one cavalry brigade and three infantry divisions with certain heavy artillery and other units.
III.	Damascus	Syria and Cilicia	VIth and VIIIth Army Corps each consisting of one cavalry brigade and two infantry divisions with certain artillery and other units.
IV.	Baghdad	Mesopotamia	XIIth and XIIIth Army Corps of which the former had one cavalry brigade and two infantry divisions and the latter one cavalry regiment and two infantry divisions. They were both under strength in artillery batteries and other units.
Outside Inspection Areas		Yemen	VIIth Army Corps of two infantry divisions.
		Asir	21st Division.
		Hejaz	22nd Division.

* The Ist Army Corps had two cavalry brigades.

THE TURKS IN MESOPOTAMIA

In peace time there was a total of thirty-six infantry divisions; early in the war these were increased to forty-five,* and during the course of the war seventy divisions in all were raised, though there were never this number " in being " at the same time. The Turkish General Staff estimate that the strength of their army reached its maximum in May 1916.

The normal composition of a cavalry brigade was ten to fifteen squadrons (1,400 to 2,000 sabres), twelve machine guns, and eight horse artillery guns; and of an infantry division three regiments of three battalions and a machine gun company each, sometimes a rifle battalion, and a varying number of field or mountain batteries, pontoon sections and sanitary detachments; the nominal average strength of a division was 8,000 to 9,000 rifles, 12 machine guns and 24 to 36 field or mountain guns.

Cavalry regiments were organised in peace in five squadrons, of which, on mobilization, one squadron formed a depôt to supply reinforcements for four squadrons in the field. They had a nominal war strength of 647 of all ranks (472 sabres) and were armed with Mauser carbines and swords; they carried sixty rounds of ammunition per carbine on the man and were for the most part mounted on undersized country horses; they had been trained mainly in patrol and piquet duties and not in shock tactics, for which their horses were unfit. The militia raised from Kurdish and Arab tribes, known as the Hamidieh cavalry, had practically ceased to exist; but the material remained and large bodies of Arab horsemen were used against us at times.

The artillery was organised in regiments, each infantry division being allotted nominally one field gun regiment of two or three battalions, each of three four-gun batteries; each corps cavalry brigade should have had a battalion of two four-gun horse artillery batteries; and each corps should have had two mountain battalions, each of three four-gun batteries and one howitzer battalion of three six-gun batteries of field and heavy howitzers. But in October 1914 there were insufficient quick-firing guns in the country to arm these numbers, and the corps in Mesopotamia were known to be very short of artillery. The Turks had lost the greater part of their guns in the Balkan war and had only been able to replace part of them. During the first part of the war,

---
* The Intelligence Department, Cairo, in their Handbook of the Turkish Army dated 1.3.15, estimated that the Turks might be able to raise nine or ten divisions of full strength in addition to the thirty-six peace divisions.

however, and also subsequently, guns of many types and calibres were supplied to Turkey from Central Europe.

Infantry battalions consisted of four companies, each with a nominal war strength of 266 of all ranks; in common with the rest of the army they were clothed in khaki. They were equipped on modern lines and were armed with Mauser rifles. These were of two patterns: the 9·5 mm. of the 1887 pattern, with which the Mesopotamian Corps was armed, and the 7·65 mm. of the 1903 pattern. They were short of rifles in 1914, and they had to depend on Germany to a great extent for their supply. One hundred and twenty rounds of ammunition per rifle were carried in the men's pouches and thirty rounds in the knapsack; an additional hundred rounds per rifle were carried in the first line pack transport with a further supply, up to four hundred rounds per rifle, in carts or on pack animals.

The machine gun companies which most regiments possessed were armed with Hotchkiss or Maxim guns and consisted of 120 to 160 of all ranks.

Under the reorganisation scheme there should have been an engineer pontoon section and a field battalion and telegraph company to each army corps. These however, did not exist and the two army corps in Mesopotamia were reported to have had only one independent company of engineers each, numbering about 225 of all ranks.

The air service had made no real progress, though in 1913 several flights were made by Turkish officers in front of the Chatalja lines and a number of German aeroplanes had been sent to Turkey at the commencement of war.

The medical organisation, though complete on paper, was actually insufficient and inefficient; and the supply and transport arrangements, though fairly well organised in the areas round Constantinople, were indifferent in the outlying portions of the Empire, such as Mesopotamia, being generally left to local improvisation.

There were gun, small arm, ammunition and carriage factories round about Constantinople, but their out-turn was limited and the Turks depended throughout the campaign on German supply for a great part of their requirements.

There were many schools and colleges for the military education of boys, training of cadets and for the staff. In 1908, the Military Correspondent of " The Times "[*] described the system of military instruction as very complete and observed

---

[*] " Foundations of Reform."

that the percentage of school-trained officers in the army had risen to fifty. But after that date training undoubtedly suffered owing to the different expeditions and campaigns in which the Turkish army became involved.

There were no modern land defences in Mesopotamia and the only Turkish vessel of war in these waters was the gunboat *Marmariss*, armed with four 9-pounder Q.F. and two one-pounder guns, also with one eighteen-inch torpedo tube : there were also a certain number of armed motor and other launches, mounting small guns.

The reserve system of the Turkish army had broken down completely in the Balkan war and a new scheme had only been introduced in 1914. Preferably to detailing this, it has been considered better to describe very briefly the actual arrangements carried out, as ascertained from our Intelligence reports and from accounts subsequently given by the Turkish General Staff. On the 3rd August 1914, the date on which general mobilization had been ordered to commence, the younger classes of reservists, i.e., men of from twenty-three to thirty years of age, were mostly drafted into active units, while men of from thirty to thirty-eight years of age were sent to depôt formations for training. Some men in the *Mustahfiz* category (i.e., thirty-eight to forty-five years of age) were embodied for a few weeks of rudimentary training and then sent home with instructions to be ready to rejoin at twenty-four hours' notice, while others were sent to garrison and detached duties, road-making, etc. ; and considerable numbers, especially of non-Musalmans, obtained exemption on payment of the exoneration tax. Mobilization arrangements proceeded rapidly on the whole, though without much enthusiasm and with a maximum of discomfort to the civil and foreign population owing to drastic requisitioning and lack of regard for the rights of property or for the ordinary conditions of life of the country. This system of requisitioning destroyed the nation's agriculture and its economic equilibrium, and led to the starvation of hundreds of thousands and to the financial ruin of many. The following depôt formations were organised with a view to maintaining units in the field at their proper strength : for every infantry regiment a depôt battalion was formed ; for each cavalry regiment the fifth squadron became the depôt squadron ; and depôt batteries of artillery, battalions of engineers, companies of signallers, battalions of transport personnel and field hospitals were formed at certain centres. In Mesopotamia, Palestine and the Caucasus reserve training camps were at times substituted for the above depôt formations and the commanders in those areas were warned that they were to keep the units up to strength by local recruitment.

At the end of August 1914 many of the depôt battalions were turned into regular battalions (forming in some cases new divisions) and new depôt battalions were formed (in some cases three depôt battalions for each regiment). In 1915 certain changes took place in the system : all the reserve organisations were placed under an Inspector-General ; new depôt units were raised, training camps were formed and reserve regiments created from them, enabling the organisation of more new divisions ; and many of the depôt regiments were sent to various parts, among them the 11th being sent to Mosul. Between 1915 and 1918 there was apparently no great change in system.

Turkey's strategical situation was such as to render her a valuable ally to either side in the great war. The diplomatic history of August to October 1914 shows that Germany, however confident of the result she may have appeared, attained no easy success : to ensure it she probably found herself obliged to involve Turkey in those definite acts of hostility which eventually precipitated the crisis. If it is permissible at this stage of history to hazard such an opinion it is that, in any circumstances, Turkey would not—owing to her geographical position—have been able to maintain her neutrality throughout the war. Securely astride the most important ice-free sea access of Russia to Europe and her allies, thus depriving both of the means of drawing on the other for supplies, reinforcements or munitions, Turkey at the same time threatened Great Britain's main line of communication with India and Australasia.

The Turco-German plans of operations in special relation to the Mesopotamian campaign can still only be surmised from the insufficient material as yet available, and deductions or conclusions now arrived at can consequently not be regarded as in any way final or accurate. The initial main concentrations of the Turkish army appear to denote that no operations on a large scale or of decisive importance were expected in Mesopotamia.*

---

* The 1st Army of five army corps was around Constantinople in European Turkey ; the 2nd Army of two army corps was in Asia Minor but also partly round Constantinople ; the 3rd Army of three army corps was concentrating towards the Caucasus ; the Yemen army corps and the Asir and Hejaz divisions remained in their usual areas ; and of the two army corps normally in Mesopotamia, the bulk was withdrawn to Syria and to Erzerum. See Appendix VI, p. 352.

THE TURKS IN MESOPOTAMIA 33

Mesopotamia affords the most direct avenue of approach from South or Central Europe and Turkey to South-Western Asia. Lying between the desert plateau of Arabia on the one hand and the intricate mountain ranges of Armenia, Kurdistan and Persia on the other, it affords a natural covered way to Persia and the Persian Gulf, immune throughout its length from danger from the sea. The one marked natural gateway through the flank is the depression in the Persian ranges near Qasr-i-Shirin, about 110 miles north-east of Baghdad; this gives a route by which it is possible to outflank the Caucasus and to enter North Persia and thence Afghanistan.

The main drawbacks, from a Turco-German point of view, to the utilisation of Mesopotamia for military operations were the great distances involved; the indifferent land communications, including the incomplete state of the Baghdad railway; the lack of local manufactures or supplies; the difficulties of navigation of the Euphrates and Tigris and the want of adequate shipping; the climatic extremes; the want of a sufficiently decisive objective to compensate for the detachment of forces from a more important theatre of operations; and the vulnerability of Basra from the sea.

The advantages on the other hand were not negligible and offered considerable possibilities of embarrassing Great Britain and obliging her to retain forces in the East which would otherwise be diverted to more important theatres of war. The great distances involved would operate more to the disadvantage of the British than of the Turks; navigation downstream was easier and required an inferior class of vessel than navigation upstream and—in the absence of good land communications—traffic of any volume was limited practically to the waterways; the inhabitants were for the most part Moslems and their religious susceptibilities could, it was expected, be turned against the infidel invaders; the lack of communications, the shortage of local supplies, the climatic difficulties, and the fact that Great Britain had not a large army ready or available, would all tend to render unlikely any but minor enterprises and these could be met and countered by comparatively small Turkish forces*; finally, Baghdad, through which passed most routes to the East, formed an ideal centre for German propaganda in Persia and Afghanistan.

The position of Great Britain in India—her main base in the East—is only assailable by land, from the north or north-west, through the deserts of Persia or the mountains of Afghanistan;

---
* See Appendix VI, p. 352.

and her flanks are invulnerable as long as she possesses command of the sea. In the Persian Gulf Great Britain had great interests, especially in the Anglo-Persian oilfield, and she had always been particularly susceptible of the slightest attempt at interference in those regions. In South Persia she had also acquired a special position in view of its situation towards India. It might, therefore, be expected that Great Britain would take steps to secure at least her naval position in the Persian Gulf.

In these subsidiary factors in the East, the Turco-German alliance apparently sought to find their opportunity and that at but little cost in man-power to themselves. The " national " movement in India, the constant unrest on the North-West Frontier, and the natural tendency of the Persian, the Afghan and the Arab to intrigue were all to be exploited for the purpose. A large proportion of the populations concerned were Musalman and the religious factor was to be expected to exert a considerable influence.

What expectations lay beyond this it is impossible now to say, nor is it necessary; for the plans were doomed to failure.

CHAPTER III.

BRITISH PRE-WAR POLICY.

FOR the military student, one of the chief interests in the study of the relations of one country with another lies in the strategical results which have been achieved by statecraft or—as is more generally the case—which have been brought about by circumstances beyond the control of statesmen. Such results are often of no obvious military significance; they may arise from physical, political, or economic conditions, whose direct or indirect influence on the strategical situation may not be immediate nor even immediately apparent; they may occur in regions remote from the area to which they will apply; their influence may vary with different periods; and their bearing is constantly affected by the happenings in the different dominions of the nations to whom they apply. The systems of government of the different countries, their resources, their needs, the motives and sentiments which sway their governments and the different races under those governments, besides their potential military strengths, are all factors in the problem. It will be seen, therefore, how complex and comprehensive any really adequate narrative of our past relations with Turkey would have to be. For these have covered many regions and many subjects. Moreover we are not as yet in a position to know the whole truth concerning them. All that can be attempted here is to epitomise those salient facts, which, by the prominence they have attained during the course of the world war, appear to be specially relevant to this history.

So long as it was traversed only by indifferent communications, Mesopotamia—the most direct route from south-eastern Europe to the Persian Gulf—was of minor strategic importance to Great Britain; but, as the construction of the Baghdad railway progressed, the significance of this avenue of approach became more and more apparent. At the same time, Turks and Germans were displaying an active and increasing interest in this area and in adjacent territories, where British influence had for years been predominant and where intervention by aggressive powers was not compatible with the security of our Eastern possessions. Our influence in most of these territories was, however, based on moral, rather than actual, power, owing to our unselfish policy in the past ; and the loosely held strings of authority were susceptible of disruption unless closely watched and attended to. The religious factor was an ever present menace and one of which the effects were impossible to gauge with any exactitude. Musalmans were everywhere predominant and although divided into warring sects and tribes, lacking organisation or visible means of co-operative action, the effect on them and their co-religionists in India of a strong religious movement had always to be considered. The power of the Turco-German combination to originate, organise and direct such a movement against us was accordingly one of the main dangers against which we had to guard.

Our differences with Russia in regard to western Asia generally had been settled amicably by the agreement of 1907, and our subsequent good relations with her had assisted in our negotiations after that period with Turkey and Germany. At the same time, this agreement brought disadvantages owing to the dislike and distrust of Russia by Turkey and Persia and was to have its effect at the outbreak of war.

Till the latter portion of the nineteenth century Great Britain's relations with Turkey had been friendly in the extreme. " England had backed Turkey to the verge of war in 1878, and, during the Crimean War, England, France and Sardinia had supported her in arms.* But the blood-stained history of the Turkish autocracy showed no signs of improvement despite the friendly influence of British support, and under the magnetic touch of Gladstone's withering oratory the cause of Turkey in England crumbled to dust. England broke with the religious head of sixty millions of her Musalman subjects and regarded not at all the day of reckoning. It was magnificent but it was not diplomatic war. The question for us has always been whether Turkey should be on our side or on the side of our rivals and potential enemies. Mr. Gladstone and the Liberal party, unwarned by any British Moltke, decided the question in the latter sense. The warm and generous sympathy of our people with suffering races overbore the cold and calculating prudence of diplomacy which weighs beforehand the consequences of its acts.

" For Germany the Turkish alliance was an excellent *trouvaille*. Magnificently placed astride three continents,

---

* " Foundations of Reform," by the Military Correspondent of " The Times."

inveterately hostile to Russia, whose overwhelming numbers lay upon the soul of the German strategist like a nightmare, embittered with England on account of the atrocity campaigns and the loss of Cyprus and of Egypt, and capable of serving as a weapon against Russia, Austria or England at will, the warlike Empire of Othman appealed with irresistible force not only to the soldier-heart of a military State, but to the common-sense of German statesmen and to the pocket of the German merchant."

During the first few years of the twentieth century there are only two factors in the general political situation in Turkey that stand out with any clearness. The first was the pose of the Sultan as the benefactor of the Musalman world by his construction of the Hejaz railway, and the other was the maintenance of the friendliest relations between the Sultan and the German Emperor. The other European powers had in many ways shown their displeasure at Turkish methods of government and the relations between Great Britain and Turkey were little more than tolerable. The main reason why the Sultan preserved any show of friendliness was that he believed that eighty per cent. of his subjects were friendly to Great Britain, being mindful of the benefits rendered by us in the past. At the same time, the British Government was taking an increased interest in the development of British enterprises in Turkey. The constitutional movement of 1908 let loose all the friendship and respect for Great Britain that had been lying dormant in the country and it looked as if the new Turkish Government would be much guided in future by the advice tendered by Great Britain, especially as, concurrently, German political influence had waned owing to their implication in the late corrupt regime. In Mesopotamia, although the revival of the constitution was generally welcomed, the year 1908 was marked by more than the usual degree of insecurity and lawlessness.

The counter-revolution of 1909 achieved little but the deposition of Abdul Hamid and the confirmation of the power of the Committee of Union and Progress. By the end of 1910 the Turks generally were disappointed because their extravagant expectations of immediate reform had not been fulfilled. Although Parliamentary government had obtained in name, martial law existed alongside; and financial improvement was nowhere apparent. Constitutionalism had to a great extent vanished and with it the enthusiasm for Great Britian. There was disappointment that we had not given more moral and material assistance towards the regeneration of the country; British criticism of Turkish methods and British policy as regards Crete, Egypt and Persia combined to lower our influence; the Anglo-Russian agreement of 1907 had alienated the sympathies of many elements in Turkey; the idea that Great Britain distrusted the movement on the part of Turkey to enter into more direct and intimate relations with their co-religionists in Egypt, Persia and India; and our attitude with regard to the Persian Gulf and to the Shaikhs of Mohammerah and Kuwait all helped to lessen confidence in us. Germany, on the other hand, gained influence. She allowed no unfavourable public comment on Turkish affairs; she gained power in the army;* she sold Turkey two naval cruisers after Great Britain and France had refused to do so; she assisted Turkey by a loan of money which had also been refused by Great Britain and France; and she was not suspected of any ambition to occupy any Turkish province. Politics were now crystallising into a struggle between the moderate party, who favoured intimate relations with Great Britain and France, and the extremist section, whose main attention was directed to army reform and who, depending on Neo-Pan-Islamism for its policy, leant towards Germany.†

In Mesopotamia the Turkish authorities took practically no preventive measures to deal with the prevailing disturbances, but both the *Valis* of Baghdad and Basra by their actions showed their determination to strike at British interests and prestige both in Mesopotamia and the Persian Gulf.

From 1911 onwards the guiding influence of the Committee of Union and Progress became more and more apparent and culminated in the *coup d' état* of 1913, which, led by Enver Bey and Talaat Bey, caused the downfall of the Cabinet, ostensibly on the ground that they were making an ignominious peace with the Balkan powers. The Government had not been successful, either internally or externally; they had not carried out any real internal reforms; the wars with Italy and the Balkan Powers had lowered Turkish prestige and

---

* The continually increasing number of Turkish officers who returned after attachment to the German army had a widespread and important influence on Turkish opinion.

† The German Ambassador at Constantinople from 1897 till 1912 was Baron Marschall von Bieberstein; and in the circumstances his country could have had no more effective representative. Possessing a most impressive personality, his character and ability enabled him to wield a greater influence in Turkey than any other foreign Ambassador. It was due to him that after the revolution of 1908 German influence in Turkey, which had seemed to have been destroyed, was so quickly re-established.

deprived her of territory ; and their foreign policy had pleased no European Power. Curiously enough, while Germany incurred a considerable loss of prestige owing to the failure of the German trained and equipped Turkish armies and to her own failure to give more material assistance to Turkey against Italy and the Balkans, she actually increased her activities politically and commercially during this period. She realised that the methods of the Committee of Union and Progress were the same as those of Abdul Hamid, and she utilised this knowledge to gain ground and to become a power behind the Government as the friend and supporter of the Committee. As the Germans lost ground with the Turks, many of the latter turned their thoughts to obtaining assistance from Great Britain and, though the conduct of the Turkish Government towards Great Britain had not been marked by any great friendliness, our unsympathetic attitude after the Balkan reverses was much felt. The situation disclosed the fact, however, that the country as a whole had still strong sympathies towards us and we were able in consequence to carry through the successful negotiations of 1912–1914 which have been alluded to in the last chapter.

Enver Pasha became Minister of War in December 1913 and from the outbreak of war was our main opponent in the Turkish Government. Though his influence as one of the secret group which governed Turkey after the revolution of 1908 was great, he was content to remain in the background till 1913. Quiet and reserved, he was a man of capacity and great energy, daring to an unusual degree, but unscrupulous and vain. About 35 years of age in 1913, small and attractive in appearance and married to a Princess of the Imperial Family he was stated to have had the ambition of becoming a second Napoleon, whom he considers that he resembles and for whom he has a great admiration. Though without private means, he lived in a palace on a lavish scale and was always attended in public by four or five General officers and Aides-de-Camp. His sympathies, education and methods were German and his residence in Berlin as military attaché had a strong influence on his character and career. There are good reasons to believe that, before the war, he was subventioned by the German Government. He was the first Minister for War in Turkey who had the courage to make a clean sweep of inefficients in the Ministry and he showed considerable activity in introducing administrative reforms. In 1913–1914 he was a man to be counted upon and likely to make his mark.

The Baghdad Railway question received for many years sustained and careful consideration by the British Government. In 1871–1872, a select Committee of the House of Commons was appointed " to examine and report upon the whole subject of railway communication between the Mediterranean, the Black Sea, and the Persian Gulf," with the result that the " Euphrates Valley Railway Company " project fell through owing to the inability of the Imperial or Indian Governments to give the necessary financial guarantee. The German concessions for the Baghdad Railway were—from the nature of the agreements with the Turkish Government under which they were granted—unacceptable to Great Britain and were the cause of many negotiations. The whole question was fully considered in its strategical, political and commercial aspects by the Committee of Imperial Defence in 1908–1909 and on their report was based the British policy which appeared in August 1914 to have succeeded, by friendly negotiation with Turkey and with Germany in bringing the question to a satisfactory conclusion. The policy of this country was one in which substantial unanimity of opinion existed and was perhaps most clearly expressed in Parliament in March 1911 by the Lord President of the Council and by Lord Curzon of Kedleston. On that occasion, after laying great stress upon the importance of securing equal treatment for British goods on the Baghdad Railway; giving a brief review of our historical position in Mesopotamia and the Persian Gulf; and quoting with approval a statement of policy made in 1903 by Sir Charles Dilke, Lord Curzon made the following pronouncement :—

> " It is a foundation principle of British policy that we cannot allow the growth of any rival or predominant political interest in the waters of the Gulf, not because it would affect our local prestige alone, but because it would have influences that would extend for many thousands of miles beyond. I venture to think that the assertion of this principle, even in its most emphatic form, is not, and need not be, antagonistic to the interests of any other Power in that part of the world. I imagine that it would be frankly accepted by Germany, and I have no knowledge that it has ever been disputed by her. I believe it to be compatible with a full and generous recognition of the sovereignty of Turkey in those parts. When we come to the upper end of the Gulf, and to the district between Fao and Baghdad, to my mind a strong, prosperous, and independent Turkish Government, able

to consolidate its power, to keep in check the unruly tribes on the bank, to guarantee the safety of the waterways, and to develop the immense potential resources of the delta, is an object that ought to be one not merely of anxious solicitude, but of paramount necessity to a British Government. I can imagine nothing that is more essential to ourselves than a strong Turkish Government in these regions, and I am sure that this House would commend any steps taken to fortify the authority of the Turkish Government in that quarter, and that whether we enter into negotiations with Germany or with Turkey, there is nothing in our present position that is likely to be detrimental to the successful issue of any such negotiations.

" My Lords, quite frankly, if I were to speak this afternoon as an Englishman alone, I do not think that I should be anxious to see the Baghdad railway carried down to the Gulf . . . I have never convinced myself that it is desirable to continue the building of the railway beyond Baghdad, and certainly not beyond Basra, up to which I believe, even if a railway be there constructed, the trade will still go in boats . . . . But if the Turkish Government is resolved on the building of the railway in so far as it lies within its own territory, and if the railway can be built without serious financial risk, then I think His Majesty's Government are entirely entitled and are bound to enter into a discussion with them in a reasonable spirit, with a view, it may be, to arriving at some conclusion . . . ."

In replying to this speech Viscount Morley spoke with emphasis of the past services and present position of Great Britain in the Persian Gulf, agreed with much that Lord Curzon had presented, and went on to say :—

" His Majesty's Government cannot legitimately object to the construction of any railways in Turkish territory, but they cannot directly or indirectly facilitate the construction of those railways if their completion is to alter the existing position in Mesopotamia to the detriment of British interests and to the exclusion of British participation on reasonable terms. It is undeniable that His Majesty's Government are in principle favourable to the construction of railways in Turkey ; they appreciate how important this construction is, among other purposes, for the consolidation of the new *régime*, and the new *régime* in

Constantinople we cordially wish will continue and prosper. If, therefore, we could look forward to a settlement on terms acceptable to the country of the railway question in Mesopotamia . . . . the principal objection now entertained to an increase in the Turkish customs duties, which are, of course, the instrument by which we have a hold upon these affairs, would at once fall to the ground."
And he concluded :—

"Here is no Alexander going from Europe to Asia—it is a very different thing you have to think of ; here are great rival international interests and a great movement more difficult to adjust in all its elements. It is not merely military ; the military and strategic aspects are among a whole congeries of elements that go towards the complication of questions of enormous importance both to the political and commercial future of this country, and therefore to the world."

It had been freely stated in Parliament and the Press that the Baghdad Railway could not be built without access to the financial markets of Great Britain and France, but after careful investigation of this point the British Government arrived at the conclusion that these assertions were too unqualified and that the assent of the Powers to the increase of the Turkish customs duties was not an indispensable condition of the ultimate completion of the line.

After prolonged negotiations, the British Government intimated in July 1912 to the Ottoman Government that, as the question of British participation on terms acceptable to them was likely to cause embarrassment to Turkey, and as they were anxious to reach a comprehensive understanding without delay or controversy, they were prepared to withdraw their request for British participation, if all British interests were safeguarded by a satisfactory agreement on other points enumerated. These included the following :—

(a) An arrangement for the exclusion of differential treatment on all railways in Asiatic Turkey.
(b) The admission of two British representatives, agreeable to His Majesty's Government, to the Board of the Baghdad Railway Company.
(c) The terminus of the Baghdad Railway to be at Basra.
(d) No railway to be continued beyond Basra in the direction of the Persian Gulf without prior agreement with His Majesty's Government and on conditions acceptable to them.

(e) Long-standing British rights of navigation on the rivers of Mesopotamia to be confirmed and extended.

(f) A Settlement to be made in regard to the Turco-Persian frontier, and a convention to be concluded, on the basis of proposals submitted, for the future conservancy of the Shatt al Arab.

(g) A complete adjustment to be reached of all questions relating to the Persian Gulf, so as to ensure the recognition and continuance of the political *status quo* of a hundred years, and the consequent maintenance of peace and development of trade in those regions.

All these points were settled satisfactorily and were on the point of ratification when war broke out. Concurrent negotiations were pursued by Great Britain and Germany on the one hand and by Germany and Turkey on the the other, the British object being to reconcile the great and manifold interests of both countries and to substitute mutual co-operation for suspicion and distrust. The ensuing Anglo-German convention was also on the point of ratification in August 1914.

With the possible exception of the Turco-Persian boundary question, there is perhaps no single subject so complicated, no correspondence so voluminous in the archives of the Foreign Office, as that respecting British rights of navigation on Mesopotamian rivers during the past eighty years. Before then no serious difficulties arose and nothing but a friendly welcome was extended to the British flag. All through the latter half of the eighteenth century the East India Company's ships assisted the Pasha of Baghdad in his operations against the Arabs above and below Basra; in 1774, British-built vessels, each carrying fourteen guns, were supplied for the Pasha, who, finding himself unable to man them, said he must rely upon the British Resident to employ them as he might think best for Turkish interests; in 1775, the naval defence of Basra against the Persians was entrusted to Englishmen, who in 1778 aided in regaining the town for Turkey and re-established order on the rivers. Nor was the association of British ships with these waters confined to naval operations: the first attempt of the East India Company to trade with Basra was made in 1639, and in five years' time this place was described as one of the Company's most important centres of exchange. By the end of the seventeenth and throughout the eighteenth century the Company's ships navigated the Euphrates and Tigris; and although by the beginning of the nineteenth century regular sailings on the Euphrates by

British vessels had ceased owing to its inferiority as a trade route, the situation on the Tigris was very different ; for there, British vessels, whether British-built, British-owned, or British-protected, navigated regularly and the only subject of dispute was the dues payable on the vessel or her cargo.

In 1834, the British Government considered it expedient to obtain a special *firman* authorising the placing of two steamers on the Euphrates, and in 1841 a further *firman* was issued to the Pasha of Baghdad instructing him to assist Captain Lynch of the Indian Marine in the navigation of the Euphrates with the steamers of the British Government.

In 1845, local disputes arose as to the payment of dues by British vessels on the Tigris and the next year a *firman* was issued giving British-built vessels the right to navigate the Euphrates and the Tigris under their own flag, subject to payment of agreed dues. In 1864 local opposition was raised to the placing of a second steamer on the Tigris by Messrs. Lynch[*] of the Euphrates and Tigris Steam Navigation Company ; and, although this opposition was eventually withdrawn, constant disputes arose till 1883, when matters culminated in the sudden and forcible stoppage of British navigation, the immediate object being to secure the profits exclusively for Ottoman steamers. A vigorous protest by His Majesty's Government resulted in the rights hitherto enjoyed being respected ; and thenceforward Messrs. Lynch's steamers have been allowed to navigate the river, but with restricted facilities, with the result that it was found impossible to cope with the increasing trade from Basra to Baghdad. Finally, under the agreement[†] reached with Turkey just before the war, a compromise was arrived at under which the right of navigation, under the Ottoman flag, would be conferred upon a British subject, nominated by His Majesty's Government, who would form a new Ottoman Navigation Company.

The complex physical conditions of the Shatt al Arab, combined with the anomalies of the Turkish legal status, rendered the situation in that river very difficult. During the eighteenth and nineteenth centuries protective and punitive measures on the estuary were alone carried out with any effect by His Majesty's ships and it had been through British agency

---

[*] This Company held a special position in virtue of a Vizierial letter of 1861, confirming, in respect of their steamers allowed to navigate the Tigris, the right to navigate and under the British flag. This letter was subsequently twice confirmed and the rights so conferred were recognised as permanent in the negotiations of 1913.

[†] See para. (e) on p. 43.

BRITISH PRE-WAR POLICY 45

that the approaches to, and the upper reaches of, the river have been charted and periodically surveyed and that for over sixty years buoys have been maintained to mark the channel. This was the situation with which we were faced: a river of which the waterway was owned by Turkey; where Persia had freedom of navigation and ninety per cent of the ocean-going vessels were British; where Great Britain alone had maintained order and thus rendered navigation possible in the past and where she had great interests, not only on account of her close and intimate relations with the Shaikh of Mohammerah but also owing to her larger responsibility for peace in the waters of the Persian Gulf; a river of which the importance must increase immeasurably with the advent of the Baghdad Railway and the development of internal trade and navigation; a river which presents exceptional difficulties to the hydrographer and the engineer, where unskilled intervention may effect great damage both to irrigation and to navigation, and the technical works, undoubtedly necessary to meet the requirements of modern shipping, can only be executed by means of continual expert supervision and at very substantial cost. This situation was also rectified by a convention* with the Turkish Government for the establishment of a " Commission " to improve the conditions of navigation on the Shatt al Arab. This Commission was to consist of two members only, one of whom was to be of British nationality nominated by the British Government.

The political relations of Great Britain with the Persian Gulf date from the year 1622, when under an agreement with the Shah of Persia the East India Company undertook " to keep two men-of-war constantly to defend the Gulf " and at the same time, despatched a fleet to aid the Persians in expelling the Portuguese, who had established and maintained a close monopoly of trade. This undertaking to patrol the Gulf became a permanent obligation which has been fulfilled for three centuries.

At a very early date, the Arabs, who had shown a superiority at sea over the Persians—who at all periods of their history have abhorred that element—possessed themselves of the harbours and islands of the Gulf and there maintained a rude independence. Their aggressive character came into special prominence at the end of the seventeenth and at the beginning of the eighteenth centuries, when they spread their fleets over the entire seas surrounding the peninsula of India causing great

* See para. (f) on p. 43.

losses, especially on the Madras side, while they were so numerous and powerful in the Persian Gulf that the Shah asked for naval aid from Bombay. While these depredations were for many years a source of anxiety to the British authorities, and protective measures taxed to the utmost the limited naval resources of the East India Company, it was not till the end of the eighteenth and the beginning of the nineteenth centuries that the lawlessness in the Persian Gulf reached its height. Several of the East India Company's trading vessels and some of their cruisers had been attacked and even captured; and punitive measures had to be undertaken. No fewer than three expeditions were necessary for the final subjugation of these pirate tribes. In the last—that of 1819—a fleet of twelve ships-of-war and over three thousand troops were engaged. This long-drawn conflict, which was conducted entirely by British agency and means, resulted in the establishment of treaty relations with the great majority of the Arab chiefs (afterwards termed the Trucial Chiefs) under which they bound themselves to abandon piracy against any nation whatever, to observe perpetual peace, and to refer all disputes to the British Resident at Bushire. The *Pax Britannica*, which has ever since, with rare exceptions, been maintained, is the issue of these arrangements and is the exclusive work of this country. Three results of capital importance have been achieved by British intervention in the Persian Gulf: the suppression of piracy; the cessation of war between the Arab chiefs; and the approximate extinction of the slave trade.

" If England has become, in any sense, the arbiter and the guardian of the Gulf . . . . it has not been through a restless ambition urging her on to the control of the waste places of the earth, but in obedience to the calls that have been made upon her in the past to enforce peace between warring tribes, to give a free course to trade, to hold back the arm of the marauder and the oppressor, and to stand between the slave dealer and his victim.

* * * * * * * *

" Although England . . . has at no time enjoyed, or even asked for territorial acquisition in that region, she has for centuries borne burdens there which no other nation has ever undertaken anywhere, except in the capacity of sovereign. She has had duty thrust upon her, without dominion. She has kept the peace amongst people who are not her subjects; has patrolled, at intervals, waters over which she has enjoyed no formal lordship : has kept, in strange ports, an open door through which the traders of every nation might have as free access to distant markets as her own."*

While our political relations with Turkey and Persia were conducted by our Foreign Office in London, those with the Persian Gulf were to a great extent controlled by the Government of India.† The British Consular representatives in Mesopotamia under the Foreign Office were the Consul-General at Baghdad and the Consuls at Mosul, Karbala and Basra. The Political Resident in the Persian Gulf who was under the Indian Government was also Consul-General at Bushire, and to that extent he was under the Foreign Office ; he received His Majesty's Commission as Consul-General for the provinces of Fars, Khuzistan and Luristan and the district of Lingeh and for the coasts and islands of the Persian Gulf, being within the dominions of Persia. He resided at Bushire and the cost of his establishment was divided between Great Britain and India. His judicial powers and jurisdiction were exercised by virtue of his commission as Consul-General, under the Persian Coast and Islands Order in Council. He exercised an undefined but considerable influence upon the political affairs, more especially external, of Muscat, the Trucial States, Bahrein and Kuwait, at which places the representatives of the Indian Government were under him.

Before concluding this chapter it is necessary to refer briefly to Persia. Situated, as she was, astride the one main outlet to the east from the Mesopotamian plain, some parts of northern Persia suffered during the war somewhat severely from the Turco-Russian operations. The whole country, moreover, was traversed by Turco-German emissaries and at one time their activities appeared to indicate them as the advance agents of an invading force with an objective still further east ; but their efforts were either frustrated or died out for want of support. British relations with Persia have been of a friendly and intimate character for many years and owing to her geographical situation we have special reasons to regard with

---

* Mr. Thomas Jewell Bennett's paper on " The Past and Present Connection of England with Persian Gulf," read before The Society of Arts on 8th May 1902.

† This arrangement was the reason for the division between the General Staffs at the War Office and in India of the pre-war duties for the collection of Military Intelligence described in the next chapter. Collection of such intelligence in peace-time is intimately connected with our political relations with the areas in question.

care any foreign activity there. Military operations of a minor nature, by British detachments, had to be undertaken from time to time in the south and east of Persia but these, comparatively speaking, had little effect on the main operations in Mesopotamia and, although it may be necessary, subsequently, to refer to these at times, they are beyond the scope of this history.

Although it was no doubt partly due to the physical difficulties attending all military movements in her territory and to the general poverty of the country, it was in the main owing to our successful invasion of Mesopotamia that Persia did not suffer more real interference with her independence.

CHAPTER IV.

THE ARMY IN INDIA AND PRE-WAR MILITARY POLICY.

FROM early in the seventeenth till the middle of the eighteenth century, the East India Company entertained armed followers as guards for their different settlements and as personal escorts for their agents. The majority of the personnel consisted of Portuguese locally recruited and of native irregulars, the few European soldiers maintained being employed solely for purposes of defence.* After the declaration of war with France in 1744, however, and till the end of the century the East India Company's obligations extended so rapidly as to require considerable augmentation of their military forces and statutory authority from Parliament to wage war.†

By 1808, the military forces in the three Presidencies of Bengal, Madras and Bombay had reached a total, in round numbers, of 24,500 Europeans and 130,000 natives; and by 1856 they had further increased to 39,500 British and 311,000 Indian troops. Nearly half of this army belonged to the Bengal Presidency, where the Indian portion consisted mainly of Brahmans and Rajputs recruited in Oudh and from beyond Benares. The risk attending this policy of recruitment from one area was exemplified in the mutiny of 1857, which was almost entirely confined to Bengal troops; the Bombay army proved generally true to their salt and only one cavalry regiment of the Madras army gave any trouble, while the Punjab Frontier Force rendered invaluable services against the mutineers.

In 1858, on the assumption of government by the Crown, the East India Company ceased to exist and a general reorganisation of the army ensued. The British Army had increased to about seventy thousand and has remained approximately at that strength ever since. The "irregular" system of the Punjab Frontier Force and other Indian units raised about

---

* The first English military garrison in India was that of the factory at Armegon, which in 1628 consisted of twenty-eight soldiers with twelve pieces of ordnance."—" Cyclopedia of India," 1907.

† 13 Geo. III, cap. xiii.

that time was taken as a model for the Indian portion of the army and brought about a considerable reduction of British officers in each unit and, except in a few minor instances, the total abolition of the system of having British non-commissioned officers in units. Recruitment was spread over larger areas and an Indian Staff Corps was formed, with a system of time promotion, to provide British officers for the various appointments on the staff, in units and in departments—military, civil or political.*

In the next twenty years there were various minor operations on the frontiers, and expeditions were despatched to China, Abyssinia and Perak; and in 1878-1879 the Afghan war, in which comparatively large forces were employed beyond the frontier, proved a great strain on India's military resources and showed many defects in organisation and administration. The different Presidency armies had, from force of circumstances,† grown up apart. Under this system, the Central Government, though nominally the head of the army, had actually little authority over the British troops in the different Presidencies and no authority at all over the Indian troops; a situation so anomalous as to constitute a real danger in time of war. This had been foreseen by the Indian Government, who had endeavoured, but without success, to impress their views on the Home authorities.

The Army Organisation Committee of 1879 went into the whole question of the strength, composition and distribution of the army and made many recommendations. Extensive reductions in public expenditure were rendered imperative at that time owing to the unfavourable state of Indian finances, and the Committee were required to give their opinion as to what would be the smallest permanent military organisation which should be maintained. The aims and objects of Indian military policy, as stated by them, were threefold, namely the prevention and repelling of attacks, or of threatened aggressions, from foreign enemies beyond the border; the power of immediate repression of armed disturbance or of rebellion within British India, or its feudatory states; and the watch and domination over the armies and peoples‡ of

---

* Civil and political appointments were, and are, open to a limited extent to military officers.

† The reader who is not well acquainted with India is recommended at this stage to study the map of India, and specially to note the distances in miles between the main centres and between them and the different frontiers.

‡ These amounted at that period to 381,000 and 53,000,000 respectively.

ARMY IN INDIA : PRE-WAR MILITARY POLICY 51

feudatory native states. At that time war with Russia was not considered a likely contingency; the danger on the frontiers was negligible; and the requirements of internal control were paramount. They recommended certain reductions in the army which were carried out; and they advocated its division into four Army Corps (Punjab, Bengal, Madras and Bombay). The latter reform was not carried out till 1895, for the Home authorities were at first averse to the proposal; and when their approval had been obtained, it was found that statutory authority was necessary. Its inauguration had been so long delayed that it had ceased to be adequate. The areas had been defined mainly by consideration for their geographical position without regard to the formations, units or numbers of troops located in them; in other ways the arrangement was unsuitable; and moreover, in the meantime, circumstances had brought about a considerable change in the factors determining military policy.

The imminence of war with Russia in consequence of her sudden attack on Afghan troops in 1885, followed by increased Russian activity in the improvement of communications up to the Afghan and Persian borders; our responsibility—incurred by treaty—for repelling unprovoked foreign aggression on Afghanistan; the annexation of Upper Burma; the occupation of Baluchistan, Gilgit and Chitral; and the measures taken with the purpose of strengthening the hold of the Government over those outlying portions of the North-West Frontier which had been recognised as falling within their control by the Durand Frontier Agreement of 1893 with Afghanistan, had all rendered the possibility of foreign aggression more apparent and had accentuated the importance of frontier military control. At the same time any danger from the feudatory states which might have been anticipated in former days had disappeared. The chiefs had come into close contact with the Government of India. Their position had altered both as regards the strength and equipment of their forces, and the Imperial Service Troops system had been inaugurated on a satisfactory basis.

Regarding these Imperial Service Troops a short explanation is necessary. Certain of the Ruling Princes had sent contingents to assist the British forces in the Afghan war of 1878–1879, and at the time of the Russian incident of 1885 most of them had come forward with offers of assistance in men, horses and money. Most of their armies were then large, ill-trained and undisciplined and constituted a source of potential danger.

All the principal Ruling Princes, therefore, were invited to reorganise their forces by reducing their numbers and forming corps with improved discipline, better training and more efficient armament and equipment. These corps were to remain under the complete control of their own rulers during peace and British officers (serving under the Foreign Office of the Government of India) were appointed to supervise their training under their own officers ; in time of war they were to be placed at the disposal of the Government of India. The scheme proved acceptable and has been a distinct success ; the Ruling Princes who adopted it have taken a great pride and interest in these forces ; and the greater part of them have rendered valuable services on the frontier and overseas.

In the summer of 1897 there occurred on the North-West Frontier an extensive fanatical outburst against the British which spread in succession right along the border and called for the employment of considerable military forces* before peace was restored in the following spring. Large detachments had, however, to remain in occupation of advanced positions under field service conditions for some time until the whole question of frontier policy could be reviewed. In the meantime, the Russians had completed the Merv-Khushk railway to the boundary of Afghanistan, constituting so grave a menace to his independence as to cause the Amir to consult with the Government of India regarding measures for counteracting its influence. The danger of locking up large numbers of the most efficient troops on the frontier, whence it would be dangerous, if not impossible, to withdraw them for operations in Afghanistan, was thus accentuated.

The first question that confronted Lord Curzon upon assuming the Viceroyalty in January 1899 was that of framing the principles for a new and definite frontier military policy. The main principles which had been laid down by His Majesty's Government for the guidance of the Government of India were : that no new responsibility should be undertaken on the frontier which was not rendered obligatory by actual strategical requirements ; that unnecessary interference with the tribes was to be avoided ; and that concentration of the troops should be effected. The ensuing review covered the whole frontier and the principles enunciated have been termed the " Curzon Policy " as being mainly due to that statesman's personal intervention. Whatever drawbacks may have been ascribed to them, to them have been attributable the generally

---

* It was found necessary to mobilize nearly 70,000 troops.

peaceful conditions which endured on the North-West Frontier from 1900 till the outbreak of the world war and after.* The general aims and principles were stated by Lord Curzon in his budget speech of 30th March 1904 as being " not so much to prevent war by preparing for it, as to produce peace by creating the requisite conditions," and in the official despatches they were summarised somewhat as follows :—

(a) to avoid locking up regular garrisons in costly fortified positions at a distance from our base, where the troops themselves are practically lost to the offensive strength of India, and in time of emergency would probably require additional forces to be detached from the Indian army for their protection ;

(b) inasmuch as positions or districts, which had been taken under a greater or less degree of control by the Government of India, could not be left without military protection, to interest, as far as possible, the inhabitants of the locality in their own defence, and at the same time to establish a lien upon their loyalty by enrolling them in varying systems of organisation as a tribal force to supply the local garrisons ;

(c) to maintain movable columns of regular troops at bases within or contiguous to the administrative frontier of India, ready to march at a moment's notice to the relief or defence of the advanced positions : further to connect the cantonments in which the movable columns are quartered with the military resources of India by means of light railways joined to the main railway systems.

In the next seven years the army was to be reorganised, redistributed and re-equipped. The necessity of such reforms had become and continued to be increasingly apparent until the Anglo-Russian Convention of 1907 placed the relations of the two countries on a more friendly basis. This necessity was due to the closer proximity to our North-West Frontier which Russia attained ; to the growing power of Afghanistan ; and to our increased responsibilities on the North-West Frontier. Moreover, in the Budget Debate of 1903 in the Indian Legislative Council, Lord Curzon drew attention to the world changes that were affecting Asia and which would, as he said, " have

---

* Although to a certain extent this policy failed in 1919 and, owing to its having contributed in part to our difficulties in 1915–1919, has had to be reversed in some particulars, the causes of the failure could in no way have been foreseen in the period under review.

an effect upon India that is at present but dimly discerned." He pointed out how India was being brought more into touch with European nations and Asiatic empires and states and that consequently it could no longer be said that the foreign policy of India had little to do with any other foreign nation. He continued " The geographical position of India will more and more push her into the forefront of international politics. She will more and more become the strategical frontier of the British Empire. All these are circumstances that should give us food for reflection, and that impose upon us the duty of incessant watchfulness and precaution. They require that our forces shall be in a high state of efficiency, our defences secure, and our schemes of policy carefully worked out and defined."

It may appear unfortunate that this point of view was not kept more in mind after 1907 and in 1912, when the " Army in India Committee " was appointed to consider and report whether any measures for the reduction of military expenditure were compatible with the efficient maintenance of the army having regard to the obligations it might be called on to meet during the next few years. But the Russian menace had disappeared for the time; the Amir Habibulla of Afghanistan was not unfriendly; the foreign relations of the Empire gave little warning of the world calamity to come; India was a poor country, whose form of government necessitated a small budget with low taxation; and there was great need for increased expenditure on social and economic reforms and development. In 1885, the Russian attack on Afghans had brought about a large increase of military expenditure, but in the following years the operations in Upper Burma, the financial crisis owing to the depreciation of the rupee, the series of expeditions on the North West Frontier from 1895-1898 and the famine of 1896 had caused the reduction of all the ordinary military estimates to the lowest practicable limits. The South African war and the increasing Russian menace showed clearly, however, by 1900 that reorganisation and re-equipment could not be delayed; and funds, at first not available, accrued by reason of the savings due to the loan, for Imperial service in South Africa and elsewhere, of a part of the Army from India, and then for a period became annually available owing to the exceptional prosperity enjoyed by India.

The reorganisation and redistribution undertaken during the period 1900-1908 remained practically unaltered till the outbreak of war, and it is necessary to refer to some of these reforms to allow of a proper understanding of the military

ARMY IN INDIA : PRE-WAR MILITARY POLICY 55

situation in India in 1914. During the years 1900-1903 every branch of military policy and every part of the army were submitted to exhaustive examination with a view to putting matters on a more efficient basis. Some of the most pressing deficiencies were rectified forthwith, but most of the larger questions, with the material collected for their proper consideration, were kept pending the arrival of Lord Kitchener, who had been nominated as Commander-in-Chief in India as soon as his services could be made available after the South African war.

Shortly after his arrival Lord Kitchener intimated officially his disagreement with the system of military administration and suggested radical changes; but within a few days he withdrew his memorandum and continued his investigations for the reorganisation and redistribution of the army. A year later, however, he returned to the charge and his scheme and memorandum on the subject were communicated to His Majesty's Government in the summer of 1904 by Lord Curzon when he proceeded home for some months before assuming his extension of office as Viceroy. The question was raised on Lord Curzon's return to India by the Secretary of State and resulted in a complete change of system. As the Government of India considered that to avoid a military autocracy it was essential that they should possess a second expert opinion upon matters of military importance and as in the system decided upon by His Majesty's Government there was no such provision, Lord Curzon found himself unable to undertake the responsibility of introducing a system which he considered unsuitable and mischievous; and he resigned.

The Mesopotamia Commission Report considered this system as contributing to the errors of judgment and shortcomings in the conduct of the operations and their opinion is to some extent supported by the evidence of the two General Officers who succeeded Lord Kitchener as Commanders-in-Chief—Sir O'Moore Creagh and Sir Beauchamp Duff. The Report describes the position as follows : " The whole of the administrative and executive work of the army became concentrated in the hands of one man, who has a duality of responsibility, for he is both Military Member of Council and Commander-in-Chief. Being the only military representative on the Viceroy's Council it is his duty to be present at the meetings of the Executive Council. The two Army Departments, namely, that of which the Commander-in-Chief in his capacity as such is the head and that of which the Commander-in-Chief in his capacity as Military Member of Council is also the head, are both permanently located in Simla;" and in their "Recommendations" they say, " It is clear that the combination of the duties of Commander-in-Chief in India and Military Member of Council cannot adequately be performed by any one man in time of war and that the existing organisation is at once over-centralised at its head and cumbrous in its duality below." It is no part of this history to discuss the merits and demerits of this question, but it may be stated confidently that the higher military authorities at home and in India have been, and are still, averse to any reversion to the former arrangement which had been stigmatised by Lord Kitchener as one of dual control and divided responsibility; and they consider that by amending procedure and by relieving the Commander-in-Chief of some of his responsibilities, the system can be placed on a proper footing. The Mesopotamia Commission appear to have had some difficulty in understanding the question and they have included in their report a curious inaccuracy with regard to the location of Army Headquarters at Simla.*

Just before Lord Kitchener's arrival, the Government of India accepted the following principles put forward by General Sir Power Palmer, then officiating as Commander-in-Chief, to form the basis of the reorganisation of the army: " The object that should be aimed at is a redistribution of troops followed by a fresh grouping of Districts and Commands, which would enable each military area to provide its definite *quota* to the field army with the least possible dislocation, with districts and brigades, if possible, taking their places in the field under the commanders who had trained the various units in peace, and leaving sufficient troops in obligatory garrisons to hold the country in rear." Lord Kitchener's scheme presented in 1903 was framed in accordance with these principles, with a Divisional instead of a District organisation, as being better suited to meet field service conditions on or across the North-West Frontier. He considered existing

---

* " Simla, as is well known, is a hilltop in the Himalayas on the borders of Nepal," and they continued to animadvert on its remoteness and inaccessibility. In point of fact, Simla is 400 miles from the Nepal border and it is connected by a railway line 58 miles long, as well as by a good motor road, with the main broad gauge railways of India ; and, *as distances go in India*, it is within an easy railway journey of Delhi, Lahore, Bombay and Calcutta, while it is nearer Lahore, Rawalpindi, Peshawar and the main military cantonments of Northern India than any of the other large centres. Moreover it is essential in a country like India that military headquarters should be at the same centre as the chief civil government.

ARMY IN INDIA : PRE-WAR MILITARY POLICY 57

arrangements unsatisfactory in the following main respects : the field army was insufficient having special regard to the fact that the Home authorities could give no guarantee as to the date of arrival of reinforcing troops* from England and overseas ; the numbers of troops allotted for internal security were considered excessive in consideration of the improved communications and the assistance that should be got from the volunteers and police ; the distribution of troops was unsatisfactory, the number of small stations being too great and the concentration of field army brigades being desirable, while each divisional area ought to contain not only the field army division but also the troops required for the internal security of the area ; and munitions of war should be increased, by the establishment of more local manufactures and the accumulation of adequate reserves, to render India independent of England for several months.

The scheme was drawn up primarily to meet the contingency of war with Russia on or beyond the North-West Frontier, and it marked a distinct advance in the organisation, command and training of the army. It was never completed. The Anglo-Japanese alliance, the Russo-Japanese war, and the Anglo-Russian convention altered the whole situation, and Lord Kitchener himself, before he left India, acquiesced in, if he did not initiate, a considerable reduction in military expenditure and a relinquishment of part of the increases and additions he had advocated in men, buildings, munitions and stores.

The " Army in India " Committee of 1912 again reviewed the whole military position having regard to the altered situation, and their " Majority Report " defined the conditions governing the upkeep of the military force in India as follows :—

" (i) Maintaining internal security and tranquillity.

" (ii) Being in a position to deal with the States and frontier tribes which adjoin India, in so far as they may be likely to be hostile.

" (iii) Being able, in the event of war with a great outside Power, e.g., Russia, to hold our own pending reinforcement from Home."

They went on to reject† the idea that it was " the duty of the Government of India to maintain forces out of Indian

---

* This applied also to munitions.
† It is to be remembered in considering this question that India does not enjoy the same unrestricted privileges of membership of the Empire as the self-governing Dominions.

revenues, in readiness for Imperial service outside India, in excess of the forces required for self defence;" and, after alluding to the many precedents for the employment of Indian contingents for Imperial purposes at Imperial expense, they continued, " Indeed, in the event of a grave emergency arising which threatens the integrity of the British Empire, all parts of the Empire must be prepared to run risks in support of the forces operating at the decisive point. We are therefore of opinion that, while the army in India should not be specifically maintained for the purpose of meeting external obligations of an Imperial character, it should be so organised and equipped as to be capable of affording ready overseas co-operation, when the situation in India allows of it, in such direction as His Majesty's Government may determine." They recommended that the field army should consist of seven divisions, five cavalry brigades, and certain army troops, as being the force they considered necessary* to deal with a combination against India of Afghanistan and the tribes on the North-West Frontier;† and they further recommended that the annual military expenditure should be limited to 19·5 million pounds sterling.

The Committee consisted of Field-Marshal Lord Nicholson (President), Lieutenant-Generals Sir Percy Lake and Sir Robert Scallon, and Sir William Meyer, the Finance member of the Governor-General's Council. The Majority Report (drawn up by Lord Nicholson and Sir William Meyer) did not meet the views of the other two members and they submitted a separate report, disagreeing in several particulars with the Majority Report, the main difference that we are here concerned with being that they considered "that there are strong grounds for the conclusion that a field army of less than nine divisions and five cavalry brigades will not be adequate to deal satisfactorily with a combination against us of Afghanistan and the tribes on the North-West Frontier, if any hope is to be entertained of bringing the operations to a reasonably rapid conclusion."

---

* The Committee had placed the maintenance of internal security and tranquillity as the first condition governing the size of the army and they stated that they considered that Lord Kitchener had been unduly optimistic in relegating it to a position of minor importance and in reducing the size of the force allotted to that duty. In their review of the question they increased the latter force again and this *ipso facto* led to a reduction of the field army.

† Their contention was " we hold that in present conditions, if we provide a field army fully adequate to deal with the maximum external danger to which India is now exposed, i.e., a war with Afghanistan in combination with the tribes, this army will also suffice to meet any minor contingency arising elsewhere."

ARMY IN INDIA : PRE-WAR MILITARY POLICY 59

The Secretary of State accepted generally the recommendations of the Majority Report, asked for a general assurance from the Government of India that the limits within which military expenditure in the immediate future would be confined would be on similar lines to the recommendations of the Majority Report, and stated that until they were in a position to give such an assurance he would find it difficult to deal with any separate proposals, involving expense, on measures recommended by the Committee. The whole question was still under discussion when war broke out.

The outstanding point to be noted in connection with the above is that, with the annual expenditure so limited, the field army recommended could not be equipped on a scale which would render it fit to meet a European army on equal terms; for at that period all European Powers had increased, or were increasing, their military expenditure, in order to equip their armies with the latest scientific and mechanical inventions. The result was to be seen in Mesopotamia. Economy had become a tradition, and the inherent military risks attaching to such a policy had also become a tradition; risks, moreover, which were generally undertaken successfully and which, amid general plaudits, had built up the British Empire; and consequently British officers have always been found ready to take the risks, whose dangers as professional soldiers they thoroughly understood, in the firm belief that it was a necessary part of their British birthright.

The total strength of the army in India had varied from 74,000 British and 139,000 Indian ranks in 1890 to about 76,000 British and 159,000 Indian ranks in 1914. The strength of the field army had, however, varied considerably in the same period, and although nominally it amounted, under Lord Kitchener's scheme, to nine divisions and eight cavalry brigades, in 1913 only six divisions and six cavalry brigades were fully equipped, plans had only been made out for the movement of five divisions and four cavalry brigades, and it was admitted that it would take months before the whole of the field army could be placed on the frontier in readiness for active service.*
The Commander-in-Chief, Sir O'Moore Creagh, in his evidence before the Mesopotamia Commission shows that he was well aware of these deficiencies and stated that his representations on the matter had no result. Sir Beauchamp Duff, who succeeded him, had not been long enough in the country†

---

* Army in India Committee Report.
† Although in the Indian Army, he had been employed in the India Office at Home for about four and a half years.

when war broke out to have had time to investigate, or cope successfully with, the question; and he had to make the best of matters as he found them.

By August 1914, the different factors which govern the employment of the army had developed so that Afghan and tribal aggression combined with internal unrest had become the chief dangers. The Anglo-Russian convention had stood the strain of great divergency of interests in Asia, especially in Persia and Afghanistan,* and our mutual relations had much improved. It was, indeed, to the interests of both nations that this should be the case; for the German-Austrian alliance, its policy in the Balkans, the increasing German influence in Turkish affairs, and the Young Turks' exploitation of the Pan-Islamic and Pan-Turanian movements were likely to be equally harmful for both nations. In consequence the Russian menace had for the time being ceased to be a governing factor.

The Amir Habibulla of Afghanistan was frankly displeased at the Anglo-Russian convention and in consequence he had at first grown much less friendly towards us. He reversed the policy of his father by facilitating the acquisition of arms by his own tribesmen and by those in our sphere of control, over the latter of whom he exercised a considerable influence both in religion and politics. But by 1914 he had begun to realise that there were dangers to his own independence in the policy he had at first pursued; and our frontier officials understood that, as he had a difficult game to play to hold his own among his own subjects, it was safer to judge him by his actions rather than by his words.

There was a strong anti-British section in the country headed by the Mullahs (Musalman priests) and also, it was generally believed, backed by the influence of the Amir's brother Nasrulla, who since his return from England in 1895 had shown strong anti-British tendencies; and this party—in touch with the Pan-Islamism of the Young Turk party—had always a popular grievance against us in the territories on our North-West Frontier, which are inhabited by Pathan tribes and which many Afghans profess to claim as rightly pertaining to Afghanistan. There were the usual intrigues against the throne and there were continuous opportunities for friction along the frontier where our respective frontier tribes were under loose and inadequate control. For some years the Afghan army had been training under Turkish instructors; they were possessed of

---

* The Amir of Afghanistan had declined to subscribe to the convention, but Russia had agreed to waive the point.

ARMY IN INDIA : PRE-WAR MILITARY POLICY 61

nearly four hundred guns—about one hundred being of European manufacture—and the arms factory at Kabul was turning out an unknown* number of guns, modern rifles and ammunition. The strength of the Afghan army was estimated at about 60,000 regulars, backed by a number of irregulars varying, according to the locality, to a maximum of about 100,000 at any one time. The whole situation was full of uncertainties and consequently gave rise to considerable anxiety.

Within the area in our sphere of control the Amir kept up regular pro-Afghan agencies—for some years Nasrulla had control of these—and subsidised many of the principal men among our tribes ; although, with two or three exceptions, the tribal militias fufilled their purpose, there were at times signs that our system of non-intervention and of allowances paid to the tribes for their pacific co-operation did not really afford adequate control ; so that the general view among our frontier officials was that in the event of hostilities with Afghanistan we should have most of our own frontier tribes also against us.

Inter-communication among the tribes themselves had also improved, and in consequence there was always the possibility that, were their susceptibilities to become affected by any considerable religious movement, we might have to face a large and partially organised rising along the whole frontier. Many of the tribesmen had received a full military training in the ranks of our regular or irregular units and were well acquainted with our principles and methods of warfare ; this knowledge, added to their own natural aptitude for fighting and with their martial qualities kept alert by constant tribal fights and blood feuds, constituted them rather formidable opponents. Their fighting strength was estimated at about 350,000 of whom about a quarter possessed modern rifles. In considering the potential dangers of the situation, the inaccessibility and remoteness from main railways and roads of these frontier areas must be borne in mind ; for these facts and the warlike capacity of the tribesmen had in the past compelled us to employ forces disproportionate to the armed strength and military resources of the territories we had to deal with ; moreover, we had, except in a few minor instances, never inflicted such a crushing defeat on them as to leave the memory of it long in their minds; and it is a necessity, arising from the nature of our rule and

---

* This was owing to the strict secrecy maintained by the Amir and to our deliberate policy of non-intervention and abstention from *espionage*.

existence in India, that we should from the outset carry the war into the enemy's country. Any permanent occupation of tribal territory was at this stage considered to be unjustifiable and all that could be done was to keep military forces in readiness to act at the shortest notice.

Internally the situation had passed into a new phase. The loyalty to British suzerainty of the feudatory states had grown as it became increasingly apparent to them that their interests and ours were identical and that we had no desire or intention to interfere with their independence. British rule in India depends on the firmness, justice and impartiality of its administration, and its success is due to a great extent to our capacity for governing Asiatic peoples and to our military superiority. Although it is alien rule, no government of India—owing to its size and its diversity of races and creeds—can be other than alien and any government must be as dependent as we are on the personal self-interest, or hereditary connections, of its indigenous agencies of administration.

Up to the present there is no definite national feeling among the majority of its three hundred odd million inhabitants— of whom about one three-hundredth part are really literate ; but it has commenced to grow. Improved communications (internally and externally), the spread of education, the Japanese victories in Manchuria, emigration to British dominions, the increasing number of cheap vernacular newspapers, and the extended use of the English language all help to this end. In the process of evolution, agitators found their opportunity and —though, in 1914, the majority of the population were contented and were likely to be only passive spectators in case of trouble— unrest, agitation, attempts to corrupt the Indian army and sedition have created a feeling during the last six or seven years that at times has caused the Government some anxiety and led our enemies to believe that India was ripe for revolt. The Army in India Committee in their review of the question in 1913 had come to the conclusion that a considerable proportion of the army had to be allotted for the purposes of internal control and security ; and in this connection it must not be overlooked that the number of male Europeans and Anglo-Indians in India, including aliens and males of all ages, amounted in 1914 only to 144,000, of whom 118,000 belonged to the army or volunteers.

On the outbreak of war the army was organised in two armies of ten divisional and four brigade areas and provided a field army of seven and one-third divisions, five cavalry brigades

ARMY IN INDIA: PRE-WAR MILITARY POLICY 63

and certain army troops. A field army division* contained three infantry brigades (each consisting of one British and three Indian infantry battalions†), one Indian cavalry regiment,‡ one brigade field artillery (armed with 18-pounder quick-firing guns), two mountain batteries (armed with 10-pounders), two companies of sappers and miners, one pioneer battalion, one divisional signal company and many other ancillary units; and a cavalry brigade comprised one horse artillery battery with ammunition column, one British and two Indian cavalry regiments. In addition to the above there were about 23,000 Imperial Service Troops, 40,000 Volunteers (of whom more than half were cadets or railway employés) and 34,000 Frontier Militia, Levies and Military Police.

The field army was deficient of certain equipment; it was equipped and organised for warfare on the frontier of India and "was not well found for an expedition overseas"; § there was only sufficient clothing and boots for six divisions and six cavalry brigades; motor transport, though ordered from Home for experimental purposes, had not arrived; there was no reserve of the new short rifles (in fact only the field army units had these, the remainder of the army having still the old rifle); there was only sufficient material for the manufacture in the country of four million rounds of small arms ammunition; aviation was in an initial and experimental stage and there were only four aeroplanes in the country; there was no wireless telegraphic apparatus and the telephone equipment was not sufficient for warfare against European troops. The British units were dependent on drafts from England to replace casualties on any but a very minor scale; the Indian army reserve of about 33,000 was inefficient; the reserve of British officers for the Indian army only numbered forty; and the

---

* Combatant strength about 13,000.

† Infantry battalions were each organised in four double companies, with sixteen British and sixteen Indian officers; British officers commanded the battalion and the double companies and held the appointments of adjutant, quartermaster, signalling, scout and transport officers, and Indian officers commanded companies and half-companies, bearing the titles of Subadar and Jemadar respectively; the senior Subadar had the rank of Subadar Major with certain additional duties and privileges and one of the Jemadars was Indian adjutant. Shortly after the outbreak of war the British organisation of companies and platoons was adopted, the commands being held by British and Indian officers respectively.

‡ Cavalry regiments were organised in four squadrons, with sixteen British and seventeen Indian officers. The former commanded the regiment and squadrons and the latter "troops." There was one Risaldar Major, three Risaldars, four Ressaidars and nine Jemadars.

§ Sir Beauchamp Duff's evidence before the Mesopotamia Commission.

number of British medical officers had been recognised for many years as being quite inadequate for mobilisation requirements. Some of the deficiences were on the point of being made good ; but in the main reliance had been placed on obtaining what was required from England on the outbreak of hostilities. The contingency that the Empire would be involved in a world war at the same time that India would require her deficiencies to be made good had not been allowed for ; the question was in fact under discussion when war broke out.

Conditions in India rendered it impossible to expand her military forces and to supplement deficiencies in munitions and equipment without assistance from the United Kingdom, and from there for many months after the outbreak of war no appreciable assistance was forthcoming. It is difficult for those who have not spent some years in India to realise the complexities of the situation, and consequently some digression is made here to attempt a very brief summary of the main directions wherein lay the difficulties. India is not one country, but is a collection of countries, kept together by their common British government and comprising a variety of races with different creeds and languages which offer as distinct separate nationalities as any continent. The prominence and importance of the *caste* system limits recruiting for the military services to certain races and demands an almost universal adhesion to hereditary employment or occupation. It was estimated, after an exhaustive enquiry during the war, that, of the three hundred odd million inhabitants, the total number of males of military age fit and suitable for military service did not exceed ten million. Many of the people are still in a quasi-aboriginal state ; a still larger number, owing to climatic conditions, have failed to attain normal development or have degenerated ; another vast section comprises the so-called depressed classes who are generally below normal development and are, moreover, so looked down upon by the military classes as to render their employment together in equal positions in any military unit quite impossible ; there are several races whose religion prohibits, under pain of eternal damnation, the taking of life in any form ; and, finally, there are those peoples whose martial traditions have faded through long years of peace and growing prosperity.

" In the days prior to British rule, armies were little more than bands of mercenaries or adventurers assembled for some enterprise and attracted by the hope of plunder, rather than

ARMY IN INDIA : PRE-WAR MILITARY POLICY 65

an organised force maintained for the protection of the State. . . . . The Indian army of the eighteenth and the early part of the nineteenth century was an army of adventurers . . . . The Company's troops, which were purely mercenary in character, disappeared in the convulsion of 1857 with few exceptions, and thereafter recruitment was limited to those castes and races which had proved their worth and steadfastness." (Records of the Government of India.)

After the mutiny, the Hindustani sepoy—hitherto the mainstay of the Bengal Army—was condemned in the mass ; the ensuing experiment of recruiting from the lower classes proved disastrous ; and the need for efficiency, financial considerations and the policy of maintaining a definite proportion of British to Indian troops led more and more to recruitment only of the material considered best. Consequently, and as a sudden expansion on a large scale was never anticipated, until the world war the exploitation of the full man-power of India for military purposes had not been considered. The idea of a short service system with a large active reserve had been considered as unsuitable to the conditions of the country and to some extent politically undesirable ; and the long service organisation with the small—and as it happened inefficient—reserve was not calculated to meet the wastage of modern warfare. Compulsory military service has never yet been imposed in India, and as it would affect only a small part of the population could not be regarded as equitable.

Another of the difficulties is the diversity of languages. Recruits can usually only talk their own dialect, and have to be taught to read and write in the regimental schools, where it was not always possible or politic to confine the teaching to Hindustani* ; in consequence the army speaks many dialects and the British officer serving with it must have a working colloquial knowledge of Hindustani and at least one other dialect. The Indian soldier possesses admirable military qualities ; hardy and courageous, he is most amenable to discipline and when war broke out there was almost universally a spirit of *camaraderie* between British officers and their men that the efforts of agitators had done little to loosen and which in the war itself induced the Indian soldier, time and again,

---

* There is no *lingua franca ;* Hindustani, the most common language, is in two dialects, Urdu and Hindi, each with a different script after its parent Persian and Sanscrit respectively.

to follow his British leaders under unaccustomed conditions to almost certain death.*

The war proved what has been always urged in India, namely, that to get the best out of the Indian soldier, it is essential that he should be commanded and led in action by a British officer who knows and understands him.† For any expansion of the Indian army, therefore, British officers who knew the language by which the men had to be trained were required in considerable numbers; and they were extraordinarily difficult to obtain. The War Office had at the outset taken 10 per cent. of the whole number in the Indian army for the European war and they recruited for the same purpose many others who by past experience and linguistic qualifications would in most cases have been more useful to the Empire if they had been sent to India. British civilians in India in peace time are only employed to a limited extent and those generally in the supervising ranks of essential occupations or industries, from which, therefore, only a small percentage could be spared in war time. Indian officers, even if they had been forthcoming in sufficient numbers, had not the necessary education, training or prestige to take the place of British officers to any appreciable extent. Most of them had been promoted from the ranks and only a very small percentage knew English. Attempts before the war to increase the

---

* Message from H.M. the King-Emperor to the Indian Army and the Imperial Service Troops, delivered by H.R.H. the Duke of Connaught in laying the foundation stone of the All India War Memorial at Delhi in February 1921 :—

" The great war from which our Empire has emerged victorious involved the most powerful nations of the earth and spread over vast seas and continents. From the crowded record here and there certain features stand clearly out, arresting the attention and admiration of the world to-day and claiming with confidence the verdict of posterity. In this honourable company the Indian Army has an assured place.

" Scattered far and wide under alien skies, in adversity and in triumph, the Indian troops played their part with stout and gallant hearts. True to their traditions, they answered the Empire's call with soldierly discipline and fortitude, and staunch in the loyalty they have ever displayed to the Throne and person of their King-Emperor, they made this cause their own and willingly laid down their lives for their Sovereign.

" Gratitude for loyalty such as this lies deep in my heart and is beyond the power of words. They did their duty."

† It is true that there were many occasions in the war when young Indian soldiers followed gallantly British officers they hardly knew, and other instances where they were rallied and held positions before fierce attacks by the action of individual British N.C.Os. and soldiers posted among them from some neighbouring unit. But the writer has discussed the question with many officers of Indian experience who served with their units in the field during the war, and their almost unanimous opinion is that it was only the officers who knew and understood their men who obtained the finest results.

numbers of direct commissions to Indian gentlemen of higher education had not been very successful, as the best of this class preferred the higher emoluments and greater prizes of civil employment. The Indian officer commanded a troop or platoon* and in practice the interior economy of the unit was to a great extent in their hands, owing to the social and religious questions affected; and much of the value of the Indian army was due to their loyalty, ability and training. It has often been asked why Indian officers were restricted to the lower grades and before the war it was a matter of considerable controversy for some time, which lack of space forbids us to discuss here. It must be acknowledged, however, that whatever the Indian gentleman of modern times may attain to in this direction, it is an unquestionable fact that had not his predecessors been less efficient leaders of men than the British officer, we should not now occupy the position in India which we do; and it must always be questionable policy to officer alien oriental races with any but the best available material.

As regards medical arrangements, although there was sufficient equipment for hospital units for a field army of seven and one-third divisions and five cavalry brigades for frontier operation conditions, there was a deficiency of some three hundred to four hundred medical officers and two hundred assistant surgeons for even this standard; and the medical institutions in the country were not of a nature to be able to give much assistance†. Lord Kitchener had relied, in the event of war, on obtaining the necessary additional trained personnel from overseas and he had altered the organisation of the Army Bearer Corps from an active strength of 6,000 to an active strength of 1,500 with a reserve of 4,500, which was unfortunate, as it never reached a strength of more than one hundred;‡ and while Lord Nicholson's Committee had recommended an

---

* The Indian officer commanded a company under the old "double-company" organisation; when the British organisation of companies and platoons was introduced into the Indian infantry, he commanded a platoon.

† The medical colleges in India train and give degrees to assistant and sub-assistant surgeons who are generally Indian born and educated and in most cases in Government employ. The former, usually of European or mixed parentage, get four years' training and are qualified for practice in India, those in military and civil employ being under a definite obligation to serve overseas. The latter, mostly Indians, get three years' training and are qualified as Indian doctors, those in civil employ being under no obligation to serve overseas, which in the majority of cases they declined to volunteer for during the war.

‡ The men who form this corps in India are a special race dating from the days when most people in India travelled in "*palanquins*"; nowadays these men are few in number and require continual practice to keep them efficient in the performance of their duties.

increase of the active strength of the Army Bearer Corps to 4,500* they considered that the deficiency in trained medical personnel should, in case of mobilization, be obtained from Great Britain or, if she was at war, by improvised arrangements or from the Dominions and, under the Geneva Convention, from neutral nations.

India's industrial development was so backward that it was said that it was not possible for her to equip completely from her own resources even one infantry soldier. Her annual out-turn of rifles was only nine thousand, of shell twenty-four thousand, of quick-firing field artillery only the very small number of guns required to replace ordinary wastage and of small-arm ammunition fifty-two million rounds; machine guns, heavy artillery and many classes of shell were not made in the country at all. For expansion, men, machinery, tools and material had to come from Home, where already there was a shortage; and the same applied to railway, telegraph and telephone material and in fact to practically every article of military equipment, except clothing and boots. At the outbreak of war all the pilots and students at the aviation school were sent home and given up to the War Office, and when the latter were able many months afterwards to send out the first two aeroplanes, aviators had to be borrowed from the Dominions. And so it went on. From the very commencement India denuded herself freely, and that she could not give more was due to her conditions and to the same fact that hampered operations in Europe, namely, the lack of national organisation of the resources of the United Kingdom and the Empire for purposes of war.

During the period that the danger from Russian aggression appeared greatest, His Majesty's Government had accepted the responsibility of providing reinforcements for India from overseas in the event of war. About 1911, when war with Germany appeared a possibility, the thoughts of the General Staff at the War Office turned to the assistance that India might be able to render the Empire in time of need. There is evidence to show that during the next two years some members of the General Staff both at the War Office and at Army Headquarters, India, were discussing this question among themselves, but apparently without the knowledge of the higher civil authorities in either country. In December 1912 this discussion resulted in the preparation by the General Staff at the War Office of a draft letter from the Army Council to the India Office asking

---

*When war broke out the active strength was 3,150.

ARMY IN INDIA: PRE-WAR MILITARY POLICY 69

definitely the extent to which India would "be prepared to co-operate with the Imperial Forces by the despatch and maintenance of reinforcements in the event of a serious war breaking out in Europe in which Great Britain is involved." At that time, however, the Army in India Committee was still conducting its investigations and the draft was held over pending the publication of its report, which was considered likely to throw some light on the subject; the letter was finally despatched to the India Office on the 31st July 1913 and forwarded by them to the Government of India, for an expression of the latter's views, on the 22nd August 1913. After long and careful consideration, the Government of India replied on the 30th July 1914 saying that under normal conditions the Army Council could rely on getting two divisions and one cavalry brigade from India, which might be increased under abnormal conditions and at some risk to India by another division, but that such increase could not be counted on with any degree of certainty. This reply was not received in London till after the outbreak of war.

When war broke out with Turkey, the General Staff at the War Office was fully occupied with the operations in Western Europe—the main theatre of operations. The number of officers trained and qualified to deal with plans of operations, involving large political and strategical issues, was strictly limited. Most of them had accompanied the army in the field, whose demands were generally the first to be met. A reserve of such officers was almost totally lacking owing mainly to the fact that a General Staff, in the modern sense of the word, was a comparatively recent institution. Consequently, it may be said that the conduct of a co-ordinated campaign against Turkey under the proper auspices of a General Staff was not possible, without recalling to London several officers whose services were at the time required urgently in the field, unless there were specially cogent reasons for such a course.

The duties of the General Staff in peace time include the collection and collation of information concerning probable theatres of operations and the preparation of projects, or plans, for possible military operations in these theatres. Before the war an arrangement had been come to between the General Staff at the War Office and the General Staff at Indian Army Headquarters allotting certain areas for which each would be responsible as regards the collection and collation of information (implying inferentially also the preparation of plans for operations). Under this arrangement the General Staff in India was responsible for the Persian Gulf including the port of Basra and for a portion of Arabia ; and the General Staff at the War Office was responsible for the rest of Arabia and Mesopotamia.

There was no pre-war plan* for operations in Mesopotamia ; and the reasons for this are quite clear. There are very few parts of the inhabited globe in which British military operations are not possible. But as the army is the national weapon for enforcing its policy, military preparatory plans are limited strictly, by financial and political considerations, to areas where in the opinion of our statesmen the national policy seems most likely to require military support. Turkey was not such an area, and, even if it had been one, Mesopotamia was not regarded as a suitable avenue of attack for any but the most subsidiary movement.† Anyone experienced in pre-war public affairs has only to visualise the effect of an announcement, or even a hint, that money from the military budget was being devoted to the preparation of a plan of campaign against Turkey to realise the correctness of the above view. The idea of hostilities with Turkey occurring as a mere incident in a world war, in which national service in the United Kingdom and the Dominions would bring into the conflict a great part of the manhood of the Empire, was at that time certainly not considered.

As the probability of hostilities with Turkey became imminent the question received its due attention and consideration.

The apparent reasons, speaking broadly, why Germany brought Turkey into the war were to create a diversion against Russia and to sever her direct communication with the Allies, to threaten British communications with the East, and to create such a menace to our Eastern possessions as would oblige us to retain forces there which would otherwise be available for utilisation in one of the main or subsidiary theatres of the war outside Eastern limits. The view of the General Staff, speaking in a similarly broad sense, was that Russia had sufficient forces to deal adequately with any

---

* The General Staff in India had drawn up a plan for the occupation of Basra, but for nothing beyond that.

† An interesting sidelight on this question is the fact that a few years before the war the students at the Staff College in India were given, as an academic study to be worked out, the problems arising from a possible war with Turkey. In the results it was found that the majority of students had arrived at the conclusion that operations in Mesopotamia, via the Tigris and Baghdad, should form an important part of any such operations. The directing Staff of the College, however, decided that the distances and difficulties of communications involved, with the lack of attainable decisive objectives and the forces that would be available, ruled such an operation out, having regard to other possible avenues of attack.

Turkish offensive; that, having regard to the general principles of strategy, the main theatre of operations in the West required all available forces and that consequently detachments for subsidiary purposes should be limited strictly to an absolute minimum; and that maintenance of security in the East was legitimately and primarily a question for the Indian Army, whose personnel were in many respects not too well adapted, even if available, for employment in Europe.

In Europe and Asia Minor, operations against Turkey were rendered difficult in the extreme owing to the absence of communications in Thrace and Anatolia and to the lack of suitable ports as bases of large operations, as well as to the fact that the considerable Turkish forces grouped in these areas would require the employment of a force larger than we or the French could spare from the main theatre of operations. The forcing of the Dardanelles, a project carefully considered by the Admiralty and War Office some eight years earlier, was then held to be a most difficult and dangerous operation requiring action by a considerable combined naval and military force for any measure of success; and it was therefore ruled out. The General Staff favoured an attack on, and occupation of, Alexandretta as the best means of defending Egypt and helping Russia. Such an attack would be a direct stroke at Turkish communications with Syria and a menace to their communications with Mesopotamia; combined with feints elsewhere and the spreading of false reports, it was considered that such an operation would oblige the Turks to retain large forces about Constantinople and the Dardanelles. This project, for which a scheme was worked out, was at first agreed to by Lord Kitchener, but was abandoned when it became the definite war policy to attack the Dardanelles and when further military operations against Turkey in the west were limited to a local defence of the Suez Canal, where the natural physical difficulties, the absence of good communications and the distances involved all combined to our advantage and to the disadvantage of the Turk.

With regard to Mesopotamia, the main corridor or line of approach from Turkey to Persia and the Persian Gulf and via Persia to Afghanistan and the North-West Frontier of India, the principal broad results to be anticipated from Turkish action were, firstly, an indirect menace to Egypt and the Suez Canal from the Arabs; secondly, interference with naval oil supply from the Anglo-Persian oilfields; thirdly, the embarrassment likely to arise from any disturbance of the *status quo* in the Persian Gulf (where, however, there was little doubt of our being able to retain command* of the sea); and, lastly, the menace to the security of India by the raising of a *Jahad*, which would combine Afghanistan and the Musalman tribes of the North-West Frontier of India with a possible rising in India itself. The last mentioned was the most serious and raised all sorts of minor issues, connected mainly with Persia and the intervening territory. Not the least among such minor issues was the effect on unrest in India that might be produced by military inactivity in face of grave provocation. It was, however, felt that this part of the question was one primarily for India to solve as being well within her capacity. It had been a long-established custom for the Government of India to control and direct military operations based upon that country, and in the conduct of such operations to act independently of the War Office; with such general control by H.M. Government as was required being exercised through the medium of the India Office. In consequence, when the first proposals for operations at the head of the Persian Gulf were put forward, the War Office, overweighted already by their commitments elsewhere, welcomed the idea that they should be controlled by the India Office and conducted by the Government of India.

The India Office and War Office were both represented in the Cabinet and the records show that the staffs of both offices had frequent intercourse concerning the general progress of the operations; and although, as stated by the Secretary of State for India in the House of Commons (on the 12th July 1917), the India Office was not organised to conduct military operations, there appeared at first to be no reason for the necessity of direct intervention by the Chief of the Imperial General Staff; and it was not till the failure to reach Baghdad, the investment of Kut al Amara, the evacuation of Gallipoli and the growth in importance of the Egyptian operations, that it became increasingly apparent that a more closely co-ordinated measure of control was essential. The reasoned statement of the 31st January 1916 submitted by the Chief of the Imperial General Staff to the War Committee recommending such central co-ordination will be dealt with hereinafter in its chronological order.

Although there was no pre-war plan for operations in Mesopotamia, the possibility that troops from India might be

---
* The occupation of Basra preventing its use as a submarine base perfected our command of the Gulf and adjacent waters.

ARMY IN INDIA: PRE-WAR MILITARY POLICY 73

employed there had been considered. Lord Haig, when Chief of Staff in India, put forward a memorandum in 1911 suggesting that India might have to furnish an expeditionary force, armed and equipped, to meet a European army, and he instanced the possibility of a war with Turkey either alone or supported by Germany. Lord Hardinge, then Viceroy, did not approve of the suggestion that such an eventuality should form part of the basis for fixing the strength of the army in India; although, as he stated in his evidence before the Mesopotamia Commission, he had arrived in India with the conviction that war with Germany was inevitable, he considered that India was not likely to be implicated to any considerable extent and that the state of her finances was not such as to permit of the additional military expenditure involved in such a policy as was adumbrated; and he was also aware that H.M. Government did not approve of the principle of maintaining troops in India for anything but local offence and defence. At the end of the same year the unfriendly attitude of the local Turkish officials in Mesopotamia led to a consideration of the measures that the Government of India would be prepared to suggest for the vindication of the position of the British Government *vis-à-vis* Turkey in the Persian Gulf, and the question was referred to a Committee of four officials in India: The naval Commander-in-Chief, East Indies (Admiral Sir E. Slade), the Chief of the General Staff, India (Lieutenant-General Sir P. Lake), the Foreign Secretary, India (Lieutenant-Colonel Sir H. McMahon), and the Political Resident in the Persian Gulf (Sir P. Cox). This Committee, among other recommendations in their report of 15th January 1912, advocated the occupation of Fao and Basra. The Government of India, however, did not concur in these proposals, although in the case of widespread hostilities with Turkey they considered a descent on Basra might in certain circumstances be useful; and they considered that to hold Basra effectively would require more than the one division suggested by the Committee. Sir O'Moore Creagh in his evidence before the Mesopotamia Commission referring to this question said that at that time he could get little reliable intelligence of the military position in that part of Turkish Arabia, and that he advised that to occupy Basra three divisions would be required, one of them being kept in reserve in India. As our relations with Turkey continued to improve, the matter was dropped, but came up again in January 1914 in connection with the defence of the Anglo-Persian oilfields and led to a request from the India

Office to the Government of India in July 1914 for their considered views on the matter. War intervened to prevent a reply.

CHAPTER V.

INCEPTION OF THE OPERATIONS.

ON the 4th August 1914, Herr von Jagow telegraphed from Berlin to Constantinople : " England will possibly declare war on us to-day or to-morrow. In order to prevent the Porte breaking away from us at the last moment under the impression of the English action, the declaration of war by Turkey on Russia, if possible to-day, appears of the greatest importance."*

War was not so declared and the exact stage at which Germany determined to force Turkey's hands and bring her into the war is not yet quite clear.† The battle of the Marne, the Russian successes in Galicia, the Balkan situation, the slowness of Turkish mobilisation and the reluctance of the majority of the Turkish cabinet—voicing general Turkish sentiment—to undertake hostilities against the Allies were all essential factors. The outstanding point is that the dominating position acquired by the Germans in Constantinople, as the result of the passage through the Dardanelles on the 10th–11th August of the *Goeben* and the *Breslau*, combined with the great influence they exercised over the Minister for war and in the Turkish Army, rendered the Turkish Government and the Turkish nation impotent to avert the catastrophe.

Although the German Emperor is said to have informed the Greek Minister at Berlin on the 4th August that Germany had concluded an alliance with Turkey, there is sufficient evidence to show that the inference of an imminent declaration of war on the part of Turkey was at least premature. For, though Enver and Talaat Pashas had known by the middle of July of Germany's intention to make war and had used this knowledge to prepare the great Arab chiefs and the

---

* Karl Kautsky, " Official Publication of German Documents." (No. 836.)
† This chapter was in print before the publication of Djemal Pasha's book : " Memories of a Turkish Statesman." According to him the Turco-German alliance was signed on the 2nd August, but the Turks decided to take no active part in the war till their mobilisation was complete.

Although this information stultifies much that has been written below, it has been decided to let it stand as originally written.

Governors in Mesopotamia—and possibly elsewhere—for such intervention as circumstances might permit to further the plans of the Young Turk party, the general sentiment in Turkey was pro-British rather than pro-German. The Sultan, the Heir-apparent, the Grand Vizier, and the majority of the Cabinet were opposed to war with Great Britain or her Allies, while Djemal Pasha, the Minister of Marine, was Francophile rather than pro-German. Djemal was one of the triumvirate who exercised the main power in the Turkish Government, but he had little authority after mobilisation had been decreed, when the Minister of War became supreme in naval as well as in military matters. The other two of the triumvirate were Enver and Talaat. Enver was whole-heartedly for joining in the war on the side of Germany, and as mobilisation proceeded his power increased greatly in every direction, and that of Talaat waned. Before mobilisation, Talaat, as Minister of the Interior, was the most influential member of the Government, and at first he appears to have fallen in with many of Enver's actions under the impression that they could use Germany to further Turkey's aims without losing control of the situation. There are grounds for thinking that he realised his error when it was too late to retrieve the position.

It was unfortunate for us that, on the outbreak of the war, we were obliged to retain the two Turkish "Dreadnoughts" building in this country, for we thereby gave the Germans a handle for anti-British agitation in Turkey, which they exploited to the utmost ; and, though our action was justified by the subsequent Turkish behaviour in regard to the *Goeben* and the *Breslau*, it accentuated the difficulties against which our diplomatists had to strive. The loss of these ships by Turkey was deeply felt and widely resented. One of them had been paid for by money borrowed at usurious interest and the other by millions of public subscribers, as the country looked on them as affording the one chance of retrieving the national position *vis-à-vis* Greece.

The mobilisation of the Turkish Army, ordered on the 31st July to commence on the 3rd August, and explained by the Turkish Government as a precautionary measure requiring some months to complete, was, in reality, initiated, controlled and carried out by German agency. The fact that the German military mission was remaining in the country and that their officers employed hitherto in instructional establishments were taking up active posts in the field army was counterbalanced by the repeated and emphatic assurances

INCEPTION OF THE OPERATIONS 77

of the Grand Vizier to our representative that Turkey intended to observe strict neutrality. Events were soon to prove, however, that these assurances could not be relied upon. The Turkish military authorities maintained a hostile attitude and acted in many ways in violation of international obligations; in addition to the retention of the crews of the *Goeben* and the *Breslau*, there was a continuous stream of German officers and men into the country for the Turkish army, navy, and munition factories, and of consignments of arms and ammunition; and there were many reliable reports of the despatch of Turkish and German emissaries to carry out anti-British agitation in Egypt, Arabia, Persia, Afghanistan and India. Sir Louis Mallet, the British Ambassador in Constantinople, had gauged the situation accurately at an early stage and in his reports throughout August, September and October, although he expressed frequently the hope that a rupture of relations could be avoided, he did not minimise the critical nature of affairs, and—two months before it happened he had foreseen the actual operation by which Germany ultimately brought about hostilities.*

The news that reached the Government of India on the 12th and 14th August from Mesopotamia was most disquieting; and it came when India was making arrangements to send more than half of her field army westwards to meet the Empire's call. In Baghdad, the mobilisation of the XIIIth Army Corps had commenced, and reservists up to the 45th year had been called up; official Turkish circles were openly pro-German (though the local population was pro-British); martial law had been proclaimed; and the rights of domicile of British subjects had been violated, animals and cloth having been seized without payment. The Turks hoped to recruit 30,000 men at Basra and Baghdad and another 30,000 at Mosul; and they also, it was said, hoped for a rising of Moslems in Egypt, India and the Caucasus. Our consular representative at Baghdad, reporting the above on the 11th August, gave it as his opinion that the local population, exasperated at the mobilisation measures, might give serious trouble under the influence of anti-British agitation, and he added " the situation appeared to responsible residents as having more serious possibilities in it than any former one within their recollection." The Political Resident in the Persian Gulf, who was at Bushire, telegraphed, on the 13th, reports emanating from Basra three

---

* His telegram of 27th August, 1914, to Sir Edward Grey. " Events leading to the Rupture of Relations with Turkey. (Cd. 7628.)

days previously, showing the existence there of strong anti-Russian and anti-British feeling ; he also stated that the Turkish gunboat *Marmariss* was deep down in water, steam up and coaled ready for a long voyage, and that the *Vali* of Basra had notified British merchants that he might commandeer all supplies of coal and oil. On the 15th, the Secretary of State telegraphed a report of the despatch of Turkish emissaries to rouse Pan-Islamic anti-British feeling in India ; and in the next two days the Political Resident in the Persian Gulf reported that the oil company's settlement at Abadan was nervous of being attacked by the Turks and asked for the protection of a British war ship ; that all Moslems were very anti-British ; that emissaries might go from Basra to stir up trouble in India ; and that the Turks had requisitioned the coal at Basra belonging to the Euphrates and Tigris Navigation Company (Messrs. Lynch), whereby mail steamers were prevented from running.

The situation appeared to call for precautionary action and the Government of India at first made arrangements with the Naval Commander-in-Chief for a warship and one hundred sepoys from the Indian infantry detachment at Bushire to proceed to Abadan for defensive purposes in case of attack by the Turks. The local officers pointed out, however, that such action was likely to precipitate a collision with the Turks and would be disliked by the Shaikh of Mohammerah. In the meantime reports showed that the attitude of the Porte had slightly improved ; and as it appeared to the Government of India to be of the highest importance that the responsibility for any hostile action should lie with Turkey even if it were to entail some military disadvantage or loss, on the 21st they referred the question to the Secretary of State for the consideration of His Majesty's Government and requested instructions. On the same date they sent the Secretary of State a further telegram saying that Germans of the Hamburg-Amerika liner *Ekbatana* were reported as busy filling an old Turkish lightship with sand preparatory to taking her down the Shatt al Arab and sinking her in the fairway.

In London the situation was already engaging the attention of the Admiralty and the India Office, where Admiral Sir E. Slade, as representing the Admiralty, and General Sir E. Barrow, the Military Secretary at the India Office, held several conferences on the subject. On the 18th, the Secretary of State had telegraphed to the Viceroy asking him to consider, in view of the possibility of an early rupture with Turkey, what political and other measures could be taken in the Persian Gulf, Nejd and Yemen to create immediate diversion and secure our ultimate position ; and on the same day the Admiralty had sent telegraphic orders for H.M.S *Odin* to watch the *Marmariss* closely and to be prepared to engage her on receipt of orders. The *Odin* and the *Lawrence* were then the only two British Government vessels in the Persian Gulf and though the *Lawrence* was a wooden paddle vessel with a few small guns, the *Odin* was quite capable of dealing with the *Marmariss*. The question was discussed by the India Office with the Foreign Office and the Admiralty and resulted in the issue of orders, on the 25th, to the Naval Commander-in-Chief, East Indies, to " be prepared to send *Odin* and *Lawrence* at short notice to Shatt al Arab in order to prevent any attempt at blocking and if necessary stop transport of Turkish troops and stores by water." At the same time, the Admiralty recommended that an expeditionary force should be prepared at Karachi to move up the Gulf at the shortest notice and that a portion of this force—they suggested two battalions of infantry and a mountain battery—should be sent to a position in the Persian Gulf whence they could be moved into the Shatt al Arab in forty-eight hours and would thus provide ample force for safeguarding the oil refinery against attempts to interfere with it. The matter was brought up at a Cabinet meeting, but it was still hoped that the Turks would not precipitate hostilities and, in view of the demand for men in France, it was considered premature to divert troops from India for this purpose, so long as all the force that could be spared from there were likely to be more urgently required elsewhere ; and no final decision was arrived at.

The news from Mesopotamia continued to be disquieting. Some 2,000 Turkish troops were arriving at Basra and the intention was, it was said, to send many towards Kuwait, while the anti-British talk of Kuwaiti and other Arabs in Basra— who were spreading reports of the revolt of Musalmans in India and of an Afghan* invasion there—accentuated the dangers of a situation which was leading the local consular officials to consider arrangements for sending British women and children away from Baghdad. Unfortunately this was the season that the date crop was usually shipped, and the unusual absence of British ships was causing unfavourable

---

* As a matter of fact, the Amir had by this time written to the Viceroy— expressing friendship for Great Britain and giving an assurance of his intention. to maintain neutrality.

comment, not lessened by the fact that a failure to despatch the crop would affect the pockets of many of the Arab chiefs and local notables. Earlier in the month, the Foreign Office had issued a warning to British ships to avoid Turkish waters and ports; there had been a misunderstanding as to the extent that ships proceeding up the Shatt al Arab could be covered by war insurance; the reports regarding mines and the intention of the Turks to block the fairway had acted as a further deterrent; and the British India Steamship Navigation Company had been obliged by the demands for shipping in other directions to take most of their regular ships off the run.

On the 29th, Admiral Slade urged on the India Office that troops should be despatched as suggested by the Admiralty for the protection of the oil works at Abadan, to which they attached great importance; and on the 1st September, the Viceroy telegraphed Home expressing doubts as to the sufficiency of our naval strength in the Persian Gulf. The next day the Political Secretary at the India Office, Sir A. Hirtzel, raised the whole question on political grounds. He wrote " though it may be true that, so far as Turkey's power of offence in Europe is concerned, we can safely leave her till a later stage in the war . . . . in the meantime the political effect in the Persian Gulf and in India of leaving the head of the Gulf derelict will be disastrous, and we cannot afford, politically, to acquiesce in such a thing for an indefinite period while the main issues are being settled elsewhere. From the military point of view a Turkish diversion in that region is doubtless negligible —though under German officers it may not be wholly ineffective: but it will be worked for all it is worth for the sake of the political effect which the Turks and Germans hope to produce through it on Moslem feeling in India. Moreover . . . . we cannot begin by sacrificing the Shaikh of Kuwait."

In minuting on the above, General Barrow pointed out how the Turkish menace had altered the military problem, as far as India was concerned; and he continued: " That problem resolves itself into the extent to which we can employ Indian troops outside India with a due regard to the defence of India and the direction in which these troops can best be utilised. The Government of India have concurred in the employment of :—

(a) Three infantry and one cavalry divisions in Europe.*
(b) A force consisting of a mixed regular brigade and of Imperial Service troops in East Africa.†

---

* Known as Force " A." † Known as Force " B."

INCEPTION OF THE OPERATIONS

(c) Certain other small detachments such as a battalion for British East Africa and a battalion for Mauritius.

(d) Certain Imperial Service forces for Egypt and British East Africa.

This leaves us in India with only just sufficient troops to form three infantry divisions and one cavalry brigade for the defence of the Frontier. The Viceroy on the advice of the Commander-in-Chief says this is sufficient for that purpose. Personally I think this force is too weak, but they are responsible and we must accept their estimate.*

It is clear from the above that India cannot spare another man and therefore it only remains to consider how we can best use the troops lent to the Imperial Government. Directly war is declared we shall have a ferment in Egypt and at the head of the Persian Gulf. As regards the former, we are all right (here followed a statement of the troops reaching Egypt). As regards the head of the Persian Gulf the position is very different. The oil tanks and installations in Abadan island and the pipe-line from the oilfields are exposed to instant destruction. British interests at Baghdad and Basra will be swept out of existence. Our allies the Shaikhs of Mohammerah and Kuwait will be threatened and may consequently be either attacked or seduced, in which case all our prestige and all our labours of years will vanish into air and our position in the Gulf itself will become precarious. Can we avert this?"

He concluded that we ought to try; and he suggested that Force "B," consisting of one regular infantry brigade (one British and three Indian infantry battalions) one Indian pioneer battalion, three Imperial Service battalions and a mountain battery, which was then ready to sail from Bombay for East Africa, should be diverted to Abadan or Mohammerah.

There are some points in the above memoranda which require at this stage certain consideration. At this period of the war the Franco-British armies in France were still retiring before the Germans, the naval situation was obscure, and there was some anxiety regarding Turkish aims towards Egypt. The following note by Mr. Winston Churchill, the First Lord of the Admiralty, of the 1st September, on a minute by the Naval Staff urging the desirability of despatching troops to defend the oil works, is some indication of the attitude of the authorities

---

* Subsequently events on the North-West Frontier, both during and after the war, showed that the Viceroy and Commander-in-Chief accepted fully their share of the great imperial risks at this period.

at that time :—" There is little likelihood of any troops being available for this purpose. Indian forces must be used at the decisive point. We shall have to buy our oil from elsewhere. The Turk also can be dealt with better at the centre. I have told Lord Crewe* that Europe and Egypt have greater claims than we have on the Indian Army."

As regards the effect of a rupture with Turkey on Moslem feeling in India it was difficult then to speak with any certainty. The Musalman community had joined whole-heartedly in the wave of loyal enthusiasm which had swept through India on the declaration of war with Germany and their offers of co-operation and assistance had been no less great or sincere than those of other creeds. But, in the case of war with the Caliph, complicated questions of religion and sentiment came into consideration and the Government of India had by this time felt themselves bound to take into their confidence the leaders of Musalman opinion and to take steps to counteract the effects of mendacious hostile propaganda. For already there was Pan-Islamic agitation at work, instigated from Turkey and Egypt, where Musalmans in India were regarded as a depressed people with no political or religious liberties and as being ripe for a *Jahad*—a manifestation of extraordinary ignorance which did Turkey little good. It may be said at once that subsequent results showed that Indian Musalmans regretted almost universally the rupture of relations with Turkey, that they were quick, however, to realise that the fault lay with Germany, and, as they came to see that their religion was in no way threatened, held fast to their loyalty to Great Britain ; and many thousands of Musalman soldiers were found ready to lay down their lives for the Empire of which they and their fathers were members. That there were exceptions was of course to be expected, but these were mainly to be found among the tribes beyond our administrative border on the North-West Frontier and they were generally swayed by other than religious motives.

As regards the military forces from India mentioned in General Barrow's minute, Force " A " consisted ultimately of two infantry and two cavalry divisions, which left India for service in France at different dates between 24th August and 19th November, 1914. Force " B " was for operations against German East Africa and the official correspondence shows that the Indian authorities and the India Office were somewhat averse to its despatch there, so long as there was a chance of troops having to be despatched to the Persian Gulf. For

---

* Then Secretary of State for India.

reasons which do not concern us here, its despatch was decided on by the Cabinet and it left India for East Africa in the middle of October. It will be for the strategist of the future, viewing the world war and its results as a whole, to consider the effect, in Mesopotamia and elsewhere, that a different decision might have brought about.

It was thus becoming clear that the Foreign Office, the naval authorities at the Admiralty and the political and military authorities in India and at the India Office considered that some action of a precautionary nature, at the head of the Persian Gulf, was a pressing requirement. But the Cabinet had still to be convinced of its necessity. It was of paramount importance to avoid any semblance of hostilities against Turkey, the question of whose joining in the war was beginning to tremble in the balance. On the 4th September, the Viceroy telegraphed a reply to the enquiry of the 18th August by the Secretary of State regarding political measures which could be taken in the Persian Gulf, etc.,* saying that he considered we could rely on assistance from the Shaikhs of Mohammerah and Kuwait, and on a friendly, or at all events, a correct attitude towards British interests on the part of other Arab potentates in the Gulf ; that it was difficult to foresee exactly how far the Turks would be able to appeal successfully to the Arabs ; and that an Arab rising against the Turks would not be difficult to start—there was in any case a considerable likelihood of such a rising—but that unless we were in a position locally to maintain order, all civilised interests and the safety of Europeans would be endangered by such a rising. He considered that for these and other reasons the presence of another warship in the Gulf besides the *Odin* was of great importance ; and although, of course, the assumption by us of control at Basra would be the most effective and far reaching measure, it was then impossible to say if we could, at any particular juncture, spare sufficient troops to seize that place in the face of armed Turkish opposition ; finally, the Shaikhs of Kuwait and Mohammerah and Ibn Saud could not do much to assist us in such an operation.

The question of Arab co-operation, in the contingency of hostilities with Turkey, was at this period being discussed and considered. The Egyptian authorities had been approached by a representative of an Arab Committee in Mesopotamia, asking for British support to help them to form a united Arabian state. The Arabs in Mesopotamia and Northern Arabia were said to be ripe for revolt and looked for active assistance from

---
* See p. 78.

the Syrian Christians and the Druses; and those in Southern Arabia, although, owing to their tribal feuds, not to be depended upon for any sustained united effort, might be relied on to sympathise with any general rising against the Turks. Although it was, of course, impossible to accede to this request, it was felt that it would be unwise, in view of Turkey's attitude, to ignore the advantage that Arab co-operation would afford and that would at the same time deprive the Turks of a means of declaring a *Jahad* against us.

Between the 5th and 9th September, the news from Mesopotamia was far from reassuring. The military authorities at Baghdad were sending troops to Basra as fast as steamer facilities would allow, two thousand having left up to the 1st September; and it was said that six thousand more were to follow. The Turks had taken soundings and had posted four guns on the Shatt al Arab at Shamshamiya, about four miles above Mohammerah, and had notified the Consul at Basra that they intended these guns to prevent navigation past the spot where they were posted, between sunset and sunrise. Owing to the confiscation of their coal at Baghdad and Basra, Messrs. Lynch had taken all their steamers off the Tigris and had sent them to Mohammerah; and the Consul-General at Baghdad was much exercised regarding the safety of the British women and children there, with no British steamers available to take them away. The Foreign and India Offices were of opinion that the British women and children should be sent down to Basra at once and arrangements were made with Messrs. Lynch to send a steamer specially up the river for that purpose. On the 8th, General Barrow gave it as his opinion that if Turkish reinforcements as stated were being sent to Basra, the two brigades detailed for Force " B " would not suffice to dominate the situation, and that for this purpose a whole division would be required. At this time the battle of the Marne had checked the German advance in France, and it appeared likely that, if this success was maintained and if Russian successes in Galicia were repeated, there would be a very good chance of Turkey remaining neutral. Moreover, it was considered likely in some well-informed quarters that the Turkish reinforcements for Basra were directed rather against possible Arab risings than against us. On the 10th, the Admiralty answered the request for a further display of naval force by ordering the *Espiègle*, *Odin* and *Lawrence* to proceed to the Shatt al Arab, to patrol from Mohammerah to the sea, to prevent any interference with the navigation by the Turks, and, in the event of war with Turkey, they were to stop the Turks from attacking the refinery at Abadan ; if this place had to be abandoned, the British and Indian population were to be removed if practicable and the telegraph station at Fao was to be held as long as possible. On the 11th, Sir L. Mallet telegraphed from Constantinople saying that reports from Baghdad were more reassuring and that the *Vali* had given the Consul-General strong assurances that, whatever happened, he would protect British subjects from injury. As responsible British people did not want to leave Baghdad and as Turkish steamers were still taking passengers for Basra, the Consul-General deprecated any general departure of British subjects. In consequence, on the 14th, Messrs. Lynch were told that a special steamer would not be required.

On the 16th, the *Odin* arrived at Mohammerah and the *Lawrence* at Abadan, and on the 18th the Admiralty received the following telegrams repeated to them by the Naval Commander-in-Chief, East Indies :—

(i) From S.N.O. Persian Gulf : " As a result of recent Reuter telegrams, behaviour of populace of Basra shows signs of improvement. There are eight thousand troops at Basra, normal number should be approximately one thousand. A certain amount of movement of troops up and down river noticeable. Apparently throwing up earthworks at Kiln on right bank ten miles distant from Fao, commanding long stretch of river both ways. *Vali* of Basra has protested against violation of neutrality caused by *Odin* remaining in Shatt al Arab. Matter has been reported to Constantinople. Am not patrolling owing to difficulty of communication ; blocked lighter is in position sunk four miles above this. It would not appear to be intention to attempt to block channel below Mohammerah at present."

(ii) From Political Resident, Persian Gulf : " *Vali* of Basra has raised formal protest to Consul against *Odin* entering Turkish waters without giving notice of leaving within twenty-four hours and without having W/T sealed."

On the same day Sir L. Mallet telegraphed to Sir E. Grey : " Following sent to Basra : Turkish authorities have of course no right to interfere with wireless on men of war." On the 25th Sir L. Mallet was informed that in view of the equivocal conduct of the Turks in the case of the *Goeben* and other matters H.M. Government were justified in ignoring the complaints of the Turkish local officials about the *Odin*, and on the 29th he was informed that the Turkish Ambassador in London, who had raised the question under instructions from his government, had been told that as long as Turkey persisted in her then unneutral attitude, H.M. Government did not consider that she could appeal to the rules of neutrality, which she had violated on her own initiative. In the meantime news continued to be received of Turkish hostile preparations in the direction of Egypt, of the Turkish intention to lay mines in the Persian Gulf, Aqaba and Alexandretta, and of their arrangements to spread Pan-Islamic propaganda in Mesopotamia, the Caucasus, Persia and India ; and the Viceroy had telegraphed to the Secretary of State pointing out that if action had to be taken at the head of the Gulf the Government of India saw no possibility of sending a third infantry division to Europe, except at the cost of reducing the internal defence troops or the three frontier divisions, which must at any rate be kept intact.*

On the 26th General Barrow wrote the following appreciation of the situation :—

"*The role of India in a Turkish war.*"

"All the omens point to war with Turkey within a few weeks or even days. Such a contingency need not alarm us unless the Turks succeed in drawing the Arabs to their side. In that case they will proclaim a *Jahad* and endeavour to raise Afghanistan and the frontier tribes against us, which might be a serious danger to India and would most certainly add enormously to our difficulties and responsibilities. This shows how important it is to us to avert a Turco-Arab coalition.

It is known that Turkey has been intriguing right and left to win over the Arabs, and it is even said that Ibn Saud, the leading Arab chief, has been induced to join the Turks † If this is true we may expect serious trouble in Mesopotamia and in Egypt.

I have discussed this aspect of the question with Major Shakespear,‡ and he feels sure that Ibn Saud has not yet fully committed himself, as his hatred of the Turks is too pronounced to admit of an easy surrender to their blandishments. Moreover he is convinced that we have only to give some sure sign of our intention to support him and the Arabs generally against the Turks to turn the balance in our favour. How

---

* On the 18th September a Mahsud Wazir *Jirga* had advocated an attack on the frontier, as British forces were so weakened.

† This report was shortly afterwards found to be untrue.

‡ An officer of the Indian Political Department who had been on a former mission to Ibn Saud and who had an intimate knowledge of him and of the local conditions.

INCEPTION OF THE OPERATIONS

can we give the sign ? My solution of the problem is that we must give the signal *before* war breaks out or it may be too late, and that the best way of doing so is to send a force from India to the Shatt al Arab *at once*. We can easily do so at the present moment without arousing any suspicion. Troops and ships are in readiness at Bombay. The navy can convoy them to the mouth of the Gulf, and the expedition, if despatched under sealed orders, could arrive at the mouth of the Shatt al Arab without a soul knowing anything about its despatch for this purpose.

On arrival the troops could be landed on Persian soil at Mohammerah or at Abadan island, ostensibly to protect the oil installation, but in reality to notify to the Turks that we meant business and to the Arabs that we were ready to support them. So startling and unexpected a sign of our power to strike would at once determine the attitude of the Shaikhs of Mohammerah and Kuwait as well of Ibn Saud, and the support of the Arabs would utterly destroy all prospect of Turkish success either in Mesopotamia or in Egypt. With the Arabs on our side a *Jahad* is impossible, and our Indian frontier is safe from attack.

The force that we might thus despatch in the first instance need not be large, as it will be perfectly secure from attack by the Basra division in its position on the left bank of the Shatt al Arab. I am of opinion that it might be limited to :—

One brigade of the 6th Division.*
Two mountain batteries.
Two companies of Sappers.

If war breaks out it will be necessary to occupy Basra at once, and this force might not be sufficient for such a purpose if the Baghdad troops had also been brought down. This contingency might be provided for by bringing the necessary reinforcements later on to Basidu (Kishm†) where they would be within two days sail of the Shatt al Arab. We should thus have a force more than sufficient to deal with any Turkish opposition south of Baghdad itself . . . . (Here follow some details regarding the 6th Division which it was proposed to employ).

This seems the psychological moment to take action. So unexpected a stroke at this moment would have a startling effect.

---

* This was the third Indian infantry division, which had been mobilized in readiness to follow the other two infantry divisions to Egypt or Europe.

† Kishm island in the Persian Gulf, where Basidu was a British naval station.

(1) It would checkmate Turkish intrigues and demonstrate our ability to strike.
(2) It would encourage the Arabs to rally to us and confirm the Shaikhs of Mohammerah and Kuwait in their friendly attitude.
(3) It would safeguard Egypt, as without Arab support a Turkish invasion is impossible.
(4) We should effectually protect the oil installations at Abadan.

Such results seem to justify fully the proposed action."

In analysing this appreciation there are certain points which stand out. It was written entirely from the Indian point of view, and, although it touched on the effect on Egypt, it only took into account proposed operations at the head of the Persian Gulf. It foresaw correctly the declaration of war, the proclamation of a *Jahad* and the Turkish endeavours to raise Afghanistan and the frontier tribes against India. Regarded in the light of our subsequent knowledge it was rather optimistic as to the results to be achieved from Arab co-operation. The question of our relations with the various Arab tribes and chiefs is a complicated problem over which there is still much expert controversy, but it now seems clear that lengthy organising efforts, several expert officers and much warlike material would have been required to arrange a rising of sufficient magnitude and sustained vigour to have affected appreciably the result of the Mesopotamian operations. In Mesopotamia—though several Arab chiefs, Ibn Saud, the Shaikh of Kuwait, and especially the Shaikh of Mohammerah, rendered us much assistance at times—we soon came to realise that it was not until we were in a position to make it quite clear to the Arabs that there was no chance of their being liable to suffer from the consequences of a Turkish return to their territories that we could place the slightest reliance on their not turning against us. On the other hand, the Turks were no better off than we were in this respect, and they failed utterly in their attempts to rouse Islam by an Arab *Jahad*. For the Arabs were prompted mainly by their desire for plunder and displayed little or no religious fanaticism against us.*

The appreciation then emphasises the desirability of sending troops to land at once at Abadan or Mohammerah. It will be seen shortly that this part of the proposal was not carried out and one can only conjecture what its effect would have

---

* Turkish Army Headquarters also placed great reliance on their ability to raise the Arabs against us. See Appendix VI, p. 352.

INCEPTION OF THE OPERATIONS

been. The force proposed was only to hold Abadan or Mohammerah, but the reinforcements were considered more than sufficient to deal with any Turkish opposition south of Baghdad. Subsequent events will show to what extent this opinion and that regarding the summarised results to be expected from the proposed action turned out to be correct. It must be borne in mind that the available data on which this forecast was based were meagre in the extreme, that the reservists forming the Turkish forces at Basra had been reported to be ill-armed and mutinous and that all reports on the Arabs were unanimous as to their readiness to rise in revolt against the Turks; while if the physical difficulties of the country were not sufficiently realised, it was felt that reports from the officer commanding the landing force would enable us to rectify matters before extended operations were undertaken.

This appreciation was seen by Lord Crewe and Lord Kitchener and the former authorised the despatch of the following telegram that evening (26th Sept.) to the Viceroy: " The situation as regards Turkey is most menacing and it may be necessary to demonstrate at head of Persian Gulf. For this purpose 6th Division would suit admirably, but this should be kept absolutely secret and no hint given of possible change of destination. Should Cabinet decide to take this action one brigade of the 6th Division with two mountain batteries and Sappers should be shipped at once as if they were urgently required for Egypt, but with sealed orders to proceed to Shatt al Arab. Will communicate further on this subject to-morrow. Pending this take no action."

On the 28th the Viceroy was sent a further telegram referring to that of the 26th and saying, " The situation is still acute but it is decided to take no action for a couple of days. Meanwhile be prepared to act as proposed." On that day a telegram was received from the Viceroy reporting that the Political Resident in the Persian Gulf had obtained copies of telegrams said to have been sent by Enver Pasha in the latter half of July 1914 to Ibn Saud warning him of the despatch of arms and ammunition and of officers for training his Arabs, measures called for by the imminence of war in Europe; and other telegrams of about the same period informing the *Vali* of Basra that the Turkish Government was prepared to help Germany in return for assistance received during Balkan War, that arms and ammunition were being sent to Basra under the German flag and that 32 secret emissaries including German officers* were on their

---

* Appendix I gives extracts from the diary of one of these German emissaries.

way to preach a *Jahad* in Afghanistan, Baluchistan and India. On the same day news was received from Constantinople that the commandant of the Dardanelles—a German officer—had closed the straits on the 27th evening.

On the 29th, with reference to the telegrams from the Secretary of State of the 26th and 28th, the Viceroy asked to be kept fully informed of any new complication with Turkey and was told in reply on the same day that the menacing situation alluded to referred to evidences of military and naval preparations by Turkey which could not be ignored, but that the political situation at Constantinople remained much the same.

In the meantime still further demands for troops had been made on India from Home. Lord Kitchener had asked on the 17th September that thirty-nine of the forty-two regular British infantry battalions remaining in India should be exchanged for territorial battalions from Home. The Government of India felt, however, that they must retain in India the nine regular battalions required for the three frontier divisions, which would only give them sufficient troops to form a containing force on the long North-West Frontier* and afforded no force for reprisals or incursions into hostile territory; they held that for " open " warfare on the frontier it was essential to have trained regular troops. In the end they sent Home or to Egypt in October and November, in addition to the divisions, etc., already mentioned, twenty regular horse, field, and heavy batteries,† thirty-two regular British infantry and twenty Indian infantry battalions; these were replaced in India by twenty-nine Territorial field batteries and thirty-five Territorial infantry battalions, with obsolete and inadequate arms and equipment. The risks which the Empire ran in thus depleting India were constantly apparent to the civil and military authorities there. At this time, there were rumours of frontier risings, several reports of a Turco-German mission on its way to Afghanistan—which eventually proved true—and frequent requests from local administrations for a further allotment of troops to assure internal security.‡

---

* It is over one thousand miles long.

† Those remaining in India were reduced to four-gun batteries to assist in meeting the call for guns from England.

‡ The riot near Calcutta on 29th September, by Punjab emigrants returning from America, causing loss of life to police and rioters, was an indication of subsequent trouble which added to the difficulties in India. Originating in a conspiracy by Indians in America and supported by German agents and German money, some four thousand emigrants returned to the Punjab in the next few months and by their revolutionary actions and propaganda gave considerable trouble, necessitating military action and precautions. In addition, the results of Pan-Islamic propaganda were constantly cropping up in various directions and showed considerable Musalman sympathy for Turkey.

INCEPTION OF THE OPERATIONS 91

A further complication at this period was the presence of the German cruiser *Emden* in the Bay of Bengal, which, irrespective of any other effects, was retarding the despatch of troopships.

On the 29th Sir L. Mallet telegraphed from Constantinople that he had heard on good authority that the Germans were making capital out of the closure of the Dardanelles and were exerting great pressure on the Turks to induce them to attack Russia in the Black Sea, which, so far, they had refused to do. He continued: " Great umbrage has been caused to the Turks by the fact that it was upon the German Ambassador's order that the *Breslau* went into the Black Sea the other day. Grand Vizier is most anxious to re-open the Straits and has again begged me this morning to let him know whether His Majesty's Government would not consent to move British fleet a little further off." On the 30th Sir E. Grey replied pointing out that it was unnecessary to have closed the Straits that the Turkish Government were well aware that we had no aggressive intentions and that the watch maintained by the British fleet outside the Dardanelles could not be withdrawn so long as German officers and men remained in Turkish waters and were in control of the Turkish fleet.

On the 29th the *Odin* left the Shatt al Arab for Bushire, on the 30th the *Espiègle* arrived at Mohammerah, and the British India Steam Navigation Company had arranged to resume their regular sailings to Basra from the 1st October.

On the 2nd October the situation was considered so critical that the Government decided to take precautionary measures and to send a force to the Shatt al Arab to guard our interests. The Government of India was informed of this decision in the following telegram of the same date: " Government have decided to take the action indicated in my telegrams of 26th and 28th September. The force mentioned should be embarked so as to sail on 10th together with Expedition 'A,' its real destination being only communicated by sealed orders after ships have sailed. Suggest your sending a special staff officer with officer commanding force who will be able to communicate your instructions and hand over books, maps, etc. Admiralty consider that no escort is required from Karachi onwards, nor from Bombay if they leave with the main body, but on this point final decision should rest with Naval Commander-in-Chief who as officer on spot has best information. Please telegraph which brigade and commander will be sent, also which mountain batteries. After force has sailed get ready remainder of 6th Division for despatch but with idea that they are destined for

Europe or Egypt. Secrecy can be dropped after leading brigade has reached Shatt al Arab. Will telegraph more precise instructions to-morrow as to action to be taken. Of course all ships utilised should be suitable for Shatt al Arab. Presume you will adopt Expedition 'D' for description of this movement."

On the 3rd, the following more precise instructions were telegraphed to the Viceroy: "Expedition 'D' Please instruct officer commanding that we are at peace with Turkey and on no account is he to land troops on Turkish territory or take any other hostile action against Turks without orders from you except in case of absolute military necessity. He may disembark if convenient to do so either on Abadan island or at Mohammerah but preferably at Abadan. On this point, however, he should work in concert with naval and political authorities. He should endeavour to avoid any action which might cause friction with the Arabs either in Persian or Turkish territory as we may have to rely on their co-operation in the event of a rupture with Turkey. He will of course take all steps to protect the oil tanks and other British interests in Persian territory.

You will doubtless take measures in sufficient time to warn the political officers in Gulf of action contemplated so that necessary communications may be made by them to Shaikhs of Mohammerah and Kuwait and to Ibn Saud in good time so that they may have sufficient previous confidential intimation of approach of expedition. Resident Baghdad should also be warned and directed to communicate with Consul at Basra but it is most important that no information regarding expedition should leak out before it reaches Shatt al Arab. Admiralty are instructing naval authorities. I am communicating with Shakespear and will telegraph further about his movements."

On the same day the Government of India telegraphed saying that Expedition "A" could not sail till the 12th or 14th and that they were sending to the Persian Gulf General Delamain with the 16th Brigade and the 23rd and 30th Mountain Batteries: they concluded "We assume you are sure that this advanced brigade is strong enough for its purpose. We cannot judge of this without knowing its instructions and objective. Do you intend that we should manage this expedition or do you mean to run it direct from India Office?"*

On the 5th in reply to the above telegram and in amplification of his telegram of the 3rd, the Secretary of State wired: "The force under orders is only intended to occupy Abadan,

---

* These two telegrams of 3rd October, to and from India, crossed one another.

INCEPTION OF THE OPERATIONS

protect oil tanks and pipe line, cover landing of reinforcements if these should be necessary and show Arabs that we intend to support them against Turks. With warships at Mohammerah troops detailed are considered ample for above purposes. Should Turkey become a belligerent, management of expedition will devolve on you, but instructions as to scope of operations will of course come from me. Meanwhile you should prepare remainder of division for despatch but we do not propose to send more troops to Abadan till Turkey shows her hand, though it may be advisable to send a first reinforcement to Basidu as a near support. If political situation presages war the whole division would be wanted and land transport would become necessary. With this in view you might think it convenient to move division gradually by rail and sea to Karachi, where presumably you would be better able to equip with mule transport.

Shakespear will leave by next mail for Bombay and I am instructing him to endeavour to communicate with Ibn Saud.

Presume you will detail a political officer to accompany leading troops. Admiralty requested to make arrangements for disembarkation with Naval Commander-in-Chief. Shall be glad to have a full expression of your views."

On the same day and before the receipt of the above telegram in India, private telegrams were exchanged between the Secretary of State and the Viceroy. Lord Crewe told the Viceroy that war with Turkey need not yet be regarded as inevitable and that Force " D," which was contemplated for defence of British interests in the Gulf, was at that stage only a precautionary measure, though it was also necessary to provide for possibility of offensive action being required in the event of a declaration or act of war there or elsewhere on the part of Turkey. The telegram also referred to the issue of a *communiqué* in the event of war which had been prepared to inform the public and especially Indian Musalmans of the attitude adopted towards us by Turkey since the outbreak of war. The Viceroy's telegram ran as follows :—" Expedition to Gulf. I suppose it has occurred to you and the Foreign Office that we cannot land troops at Abadan* without the risk of a protest from the Persian Government and without in the event of war with Turkey violating the neutrality of Persia. Both these results would be regarded

---

* It must be remarked however, with regard to this that the oil concession here was leased from the Persian Government, and though the Shaikh of Mohammerah was responsible for policing it, it was clear that he could not protect it from a Turkish attack and that he would look to us to do so.

unfavourably by Indian Mahomedans. The latter eventuality would present an opportunity to Turkey of seizing Persian territory more to the north where Turks would meet with practically no resistance and from which it might be difficult to dislodge them. Has the question of landing troops at Basidu been considered ? It is only five hundred miles from head of Gulf. Basidu is British territory and Persia could not object. I still maintain that it is desirable that no action should be taken in the Persian Gulf that could be regarded by Turkey as a direct provocation and pretext for declaring war. The works at Abadan can be protected by *Odin* unless artillery is brought up by the Turks from Basra. In the event of a landing at Abadan as suggested it will be necessary to consider what defensive measures should be taken for the protection of Kuwait. When the expedition starts I shall send Cox* to the Gulf to control all political matters."

On the 7th the Government of India telegraphed the full expression of their views which the Secretary of State had asked for on the 5th. It appeared to them that Germany's aim was to create a situation in which it would appear that Turkey was the object of aggression of one or more Christian powers. In consequence they deprecated the despatch of troops to Abadan as being action of a provocative character likely to precipitate hostilities in the manner desired by Germany. While they recognised that nothing could really secure the safety of the oil works except the occupation of Abadan, they doubted whether the value of these was sufficient to outweigh the consequences of an apparent attack by us on Turkey. If, on the other hand, the object in view was merely to demonstrate at the head of the Gulf, they suggested a landing at Bahrein, as the water difficulties at Basidu were almost insuperable.

On the 8th the Government of India was informed that Major Shakespear was leaving England at once with instructions to get into touch with Ibn Saud with a view to securing Arab good-will in the event of war with Turkey and to prevent disturbances among the Arabs as a result of our proceedings. In the meantime, the Government of India were to let Ibn Saud know, through the Shaikh of Kuwait, that German influence was trying to entangle

---

* Lieutenant-Colonel Sir P. Cox was then Foreign Secretary in India. He had been for many years on political duty in the Persian Gulf, and as the Viceroy expressed it, " his knowledge of the Chiefs and of Gulf politics is unique."

INCEPTION OF THE OPERATIONS

England with Turkey, and that it was hoped that he and the Shaikh of Kuwait would use their influence to maintain peace in Arabia. Between the 8th and the 13th, further telegrams were exchanged between Home and India in which the Secretary of State said that for the time being it was not necessary to decide regarding Abadan. The merits of Basidu and Bahrein for the landing were discussed, the decision being left to the Government of India, who selected Bahrein, and informed the Secretary of State that arrangements were being made for Force " D," consisting of two mountain batteries, one company of Sappers and Miners and one infantry brigade, to sail from India about the 15th.

By analysing the above series of telegrams—which were drawn up either at conferences at which the Foreign Office, the Admiralty, the War Office and the Indian Office were represented, or as a result of such conferences—we get the following summary of the intentions of His Majesty's Government : Premature hostile action against Turkey was to be avoided, but the Arabs were to be conciliated and to be shown that we were prepared to support* them against Turkey. For this purpose a force was to be despatched to the Persian Gulf, which His Majesty's Government would have sent to Abadan but for the protests of the Indian Government, who particularly desired that Indian Musalmans should not have any ground for supposing that we had aggressive intentions towards Turkey. In addition to occupying Abadan, the force was to protect the oil tanks and pipe-line and cover the landing of any necessary reinforcements. As the pipe-line extended for over one hundred miles into Arabistan, it must have been apparent that General Delamain's brigade alone could not afford it efficient protection. For this purpose, therefore, reinforcements or assistance from the Arabs would be necessary.

Finally the Government of India were informed that if Turkey should become a belligerent, the management of the expedition would devolve on them, but that instructions

---

* In his evidence before the Mesopotamia Commission, Lord Crewe laid stress on the fact that a failure on our part to support the Arab Shaikhs at the head of the Gulf might ignite a fire which would spread throughout Arabia and even involve Mecca itself, and by setting Islam against us would probably excite risings in Persia, Afghanistan and India ; and he stated that in a private letter to Lord Hardinge of the 9th October he had said, " Of the various objects to be attained by sending a force up the Gulf, I have always regarded the moral effect on the Arab chiefs as the primary, and the protection of the oil stores as the secondary."

as to the scope of operations would come from the India Office.

We shall see in the next chapter how the Government of India interpreted these instructions in the orders they issued to General Delamain and the extent to which they were modified by the India Office when hostilities against Turkey were ordered to commence.

In the meantime, telegrams from Sir L. Mallet reported that Turkish military preparations were being pushed forward everywhere, and it appeared to him that if the *Goeben* attacked the Russian fleet in the Black Sea, or if things should take an unfavourable turn for the Allies, the Turks would have their troops ready for action at a favourable point, and that they would be in a position to cross the Egyptian frontier without much further delay. At the same time, Sir L. Mallet considered that the Turks did not then intend to make war, but that they were falling in with German designs in order to extract as much as possible from Germany—and it was in his opinion an undoubtedly dangerous game for the Turks to play, as he did not see how they could prevent Germany taking matters into her own hand. Our Military Attaché derived the impression from a long interview with Enver Pasha that he had ambitious schemes in the Arab world and in Egypt, and, although he disclaimed any intention of initiating offensive movements, Enver admitted that some of the measures taken were precautionary against Great Britain, and that proposals had been made to the Bedouins to enlist their sympathies as supporters of the Turkish Empire in all eventualities.

At this time the *Vali* of Basra was adopting a most hostile attitude to the presence of our ships of war in Persian waters at and near Mohammerah, and this in spite of an assurance given to Sir L. Mallet on the 7th by the Grand Vizier that the *Vali* had been instructed to avoid all interference with H.M. ships in the Shatt al Arab. The anomalous position in this river has already been referred to in a preceding chapter, but it was impossible for us to acquiesce in a refusal to allow our ships access to Mohammerah, where the Shaikh was dependent on us for protection against the Turks, or to Abadan, on which the Admiralty were dependent for a large part of their oil fuel. In the negotiations of 1913 over the Turco-Persian frontier, when the Persian claim for a mid-channel boundary line in the Shatt al Arab had been abandoned, it was understood that the right of access to Abadan and Mohammerah would remain unimpaired. To have relinquished our claim to free

INCEPTION OF THE OPERATIONS

navigation at this stage would have undermined our relations with the Arabs and put most of them definitely on the side of Turkey, with results that could not but be unfortunate for us. The Turks, moreover, went in other directions far beyond what they must have known would be acceptable, for they claimed that their territorial waters extended for six miles to sea from the furthest projecting point of shore, and they threatened to intern a British ship of war lying in the (Persian) Karun river unless she left within a week. A further complication of the question was the news, from generally reliable sources, that the *Emden* intended to make for Basra. Though the Admiralty considered this an improbable contingency, they could not ignore the repeated reports to this effect, and they had to take precautionary steps to meet such a possibility—more especially in view of the fact that both the *Odin* and the *Espiègle** would be far outranged by the *Emden's* guns. To meet Turkish susceptibilities as far as possible, the Admiralty had issued orders for one ship to remain in Persian waters and for the others to stay outside territorial waters beyond the recognised limit of three miles. More than this could not be conceded, and the Turkish Government were informed that we were prepared to discuss the question in a friendly spirit if they would on their part recognise their international obligations in regard to the German crews of the *Goeben* and the *Breslau*. The first portion of Force "D" left Bombay on the 16th, and its subsequent movements and operations will be dealt with in the next chapter.

Little more remains to be told in this chapter. All reports tended more and more to show that the war party in Turkey were getting the upper hand. The German and Austrian Ambassadors were increasing their efforts to involve Turkey, and their officers, naval and military, were openly conducting preparations for operations against Great Britain, while their emissaries were uniting with those of Turkey in spreading anti-British propaganda in every Musalman country in the East. In Mesopotamia, Arabs friendly to us were convinced that Turkey was bent on war ; mines were reported to have reached Baghdad on their way to Basra, more Turkish guns were posted on the banks of Shatt al Arab, arrangements for blocking the channel were repeatedly reported, and naval and military reinforcements continued to pass unceasingly down the Tigris.

---

* Both sloops were similarly armed with six 4-inch B.L. and four 3-pounder Q.F. guns.

On the 29th, Sir L. Mallet reported a great struggle in progress at Constantinople between the war party and the moderates, but expressed the hope that everything was not yet lost. However, the Germans took the law into their own hands, and on that day several Russian ports were bombarded by the *Goeben* and *Breslau*, which, with some Turkish destroyers, had entered the Black Sea under the command of the German Admiral Souchon. This meant war, and on the 30th the British, French and Russian Ambassadors demanded their passports.

On the 31st the Admiralty and the India Office issued their " war " telegrams, Russia formally declared war on Turkey on the 2nd November, and on the 5th—the day that France also formally declared war on Turkey—a proclamation was issued in London extending to the war with Turkey the proclamations and Orders in Council then in force relating to the war with Germany and Austria-Hungary.

CHAPTER VI.

THE LANDING IN MESOPOTAMIA OF FORCE "D" AND THE OPERATIONS LEADING TO THE OCCUPATION OF BASRA.
(SEE MAP 1.)

THE 6th (Poona) Division had been ordered on the 6th September to mobilize as part of Force "A" (i.e., for service in France). On the 4th October instructions reached Divisional Headquarters to hold the following force in readiness to start overseas on the 10th, under command of Brigadier-General W. S. Delamain, C.B., D.S.O. :—

    16th Infantry Brigade (2nd Dorsetshire, 104th Rifles, 117th Mahrattas and 20th Punjabis).
    22nd Company Sappers and Miners.
    1st Indian Mountain Artillery Brigade (23rd and 30th Mountain Batteries).

To these were added certain medical, supply and transport units, etc.*

On the 10th, General Delamain received his instructions at Bombay from a staff officer sent from Simla. These were in three parts :—

(*a*) Secret instructions for the employment of his force ;
(*b*) Plans of operation for (i) the protection of British interests at the head of the Persian Gulf ; (ii) the support of Mohammerah ; and (iii) operations in Turkish Mesopotamia ;
(*c*) Copies of official correspondence between the Government of India and the Secretary of State regarding the organisation, despatch and employment of Force "D."

General Delamain was told at the same time to place himself in communication at once with the local Naval Commander-in-Chief.

The "secret instructions" were framed on the Secretary of State's orders for disembarkation at Abadan or Mohammerah, and repeated his warning to avoid hostilities with the Turks and friction with the Arabs. The concluding paragraph read : "In the event of hostilities with Turkey, the remainder of the 6th Division is being held in readiness to support your force and will follow as quickly as possible. In the meantime, you

---

* For details, see Appendix II, p. 346.

will take such military and political action as you think feasible to strengthen your position and if possible occupy Basra."

The " plans of operation " prepared by the General Staff in India were based on the latest available information, which it was noted might require revision. Owing to the state of affairs when these instructions were issued, it was impossible to define exactly what the force might have to do, and accordingly three alternative plans were sent. It was, however, stated that it was to be clearly understood that these plans were not intended to fetter the discretion of the officer commanding as to the action he might consider best calculated to carry the intentions of Government into effect.

In addition to a summary of specially relevant portions of the topographical and other information contained in " Field Notes* on Lower Mesopotamia," these plans gave an estimate of the existing Turkish military strength in Mesopotamia. This was placed at about 10,000 regular troops, including 1,200 sabres, with 114 guns and 6 machine guns, which the inclusion of reservists might increase to 15,000 men. It was thought that not more than 8,000 rifles, 500 sabres, 58 guns and 6 machine guns could be concentrated at Basra, in which neighbourhood the latest information indicated the following distribution :—†

> Basra.—Two infantry battalions (belonging to the 26th and 112th Regiments) ;
> Zubair.—One infantry battalion (112th Regiment) ;
> Fao-Hor Abdullah ; Zubair-Kuwait.—Two infantry regiments (113th and 114th Regiments) ;

totalling about 3,600 infantry and, in addition, 1,000 gendarmerie. There were reported to be two batteries of guns on Shamshamiya island (where the Turks had made preparations to block the channel of the Shatt al Arab), one or two batteries at Fao, and four guns at Dabba island near the mouth of the Karun river. The document then went on : " None of the troops in Mesopotamia are well trained. The infantry are hardy and are good natural soldiers. They are armed with Mauser rifles of two or three different patterns. The artillery

---

* This handbook, issued to all units of the force, had been compiled in September 1914 by the General Staff in India from material supplied by the War Office, supplemented by local information. It was subsequently replaced by later editions giving the fuller information that had been obtained locally.

† Information from Turkish sources indicates that the total force available in Mesopotamia comprised about 17,000 rifles, 400 sabres, 44 guns, and 3 machine guns ; of which 4,700 rifles, 18 guns, and 3 machine guns were concentrated in the vicinity of Basra. (See Appendix VI, p. 352.)

INSTRUCTIONS FOR THE ADVANCED FORCE 101

is still mostly equipped with old pattern guns. The only quick-firing guns reported are one mountain battery of four guns at Baghdad and one of four guns at Mosul (July 1912). The cavalry are not well mounted and are barely a match for the local Arab mounted tribesmen."

It was considered unlikly, owing to the Russian menace on the Caucasian frontier, that reinforcements could be spared for Mesopotamia from the IXth, Xth, or XIth Turkish Army Corps, i.e., the 2nd Military Inspection in Eastern Anatolia and Kurdistan; and a description was given of the few small forts between Basra and the Persian Gulf. The principal Arab tribes were mentioned with their supposed armament and they were described as usually hostile to the Turk, but their numbers could not be estimated with any accuracy; the numbers that might be raised by the Shaikhs of Mohammerah and Kuwait, whose interests were bound up with ours, were estimated at 5,000 to 10,000 and 16,000 respectively; and reference was made to Ibn Saud as not being pro-Turk.

The second section of each plan gave a method by which the object desired could, in the opinion of the General Staff, be attained. For " the protection of British interests at the head of the Gulf " a landing on Abadan island, by an advance if possible up the Hor Bahmanshir*—so as to avoid any misunderstanding with Turkey by the use of the Shatt al Arab—was advocated.

For "the support of Mohammerah" it was considered probable that the force sent from India would be directed to occupy Basra. For this purpose not less than a division and a cavalry regiment were likely to be required. In consequence preliminary action as follows was suggested for General Delamain's force: Take measures to secure the co-operation of the Shaikhs of Mohammerah and Kuwait; capture Fao as a preliminary to moving up the river and leave a post there; occupy the oil-works at Abadan, and, leaving a post there, move up to support the Shaikh at Mohammerah; and reconnoitre carefully Umm Qasr—which appeared to offer the best base for the main operations—and the road from there to Basra.

---

* This river formed the original mouth of the Karun river. It runs from near Mohammerah, east of the Shatt al Arab (i.e., in Persian territory), into the Gulf. Its condition at that time was uncertain, but as it was not navigable by vessels drawing more than seven feet, the force would have had to be transported by towing, and its progress would have been difficult and slow, if possible at all.

To meet the contingency of having to use this route, General Delamain endeavoured, without success, to obtain the steam launches which would have been required.

102 HISTORY OF THE WAR: MESOPOTAMIA

For "operations in Turkish Mesopotamia" the object laid down was the occupation of Basra and of the Shatt al Arab up to that place. In the first instance it was important to support the Shaikh of Mohammerah, and for this suggestions had been made as above. Then, if Basra was too strongly held for General Delamain's force to attack it, it was suggested that the remainder of the division should land at Umm Qasr and move on Basra from the south-west.

With regard to the armament and equipment of General Delamain's force: each mountain battery had six 10-pounder guns carried on mules, and 735 rounds of ammunition per gun accompanied the force; the British and two of the Indian infantry battalions had the short ·303 M.L.E. rifle, while the third Indian infantry battalion had the long ·303 M.L.E. charger-loading rifle; 1,000 rounds per rifle accompanied the force and each battalion had two Maxims; clothing was on the Indian winter scale and full field service tentage was taken. The transport consisted only of pack mules, the camel transport at first ordered being detained at Karachi (presumably because the force would not be operating away from the river); and two months' supplies except meat on hoof (obtainable at Mohammerah) were taken. The Officer Commanding Sappers and Miners was directed to obtain at Bombay additional engineering equipment for bridging, rafting, etc.; and for disembarkation, reliance was apparently placed on ships' boats and on craft obtainable locally.

Some departure from the usual procedure on mobilisation was necessary to maintain the strict secrecy which had been enjoined from Home regarding the destination of the force; and owing to this some minor difficulties were experienced by the force during the concentration period and the initial operations in Mesopotamia. But they were generally unimportant and were soon rectified. To show, however, how difficult it is to maintain secrecy in such a case in a country like India, General Delamain reported on the 15th that people in Bombay had deduced his destination a fortnight before; this may have been due to ships having to be selected which were suitable for the Shatt al Arab.

General Delamain was given supreme control of all political matters arising in or connected with the area of operations, with Sir Percy Cox as his chief political adviser; and Commander Hamilton, Royal Indian Marine, went as Marine Transport Officer.

With the exception of the mountain artillery which sailed

from Karachi two days later, the force left Bombay, with part of Force " A " and Force " B," on the 16th in four transports under naval escort. On the 19th, at sea, the convoy met H.M.S. *Ocean*, and Force " D " parted company, steering northwards under escort of the *Ocean*. Next day, the units of the force were informed that their destination was Bahrein, and on the 21st they arrived at their rendezvous to find the R.I.M.S. *Dalhousie* and the transport containing the mountain artillery awaiting them. The strength of the force was just over 5,000 men and 1,200 animals.*

The five transports, under escort of the *Ocean* and *Dalhousie*, then proceeded together, arriving at Bahrein on the 23rd. Here it was found that instructions had been received from the Admiralty that disembarkation was to be suspended till further orders.†

In consequence of these orders, the troops remained on board the transports, and advantage was taken of the delay to practise them in rowing and in disembarking in ships' boats, an experience which proved subsequently very useful to them. For the first few days there was a total lack of breeze and the supply of drinking water obtainable on shore was limited. In consequence, men, and especially animals, suffered severely from the heat.

On the 28th, a conference was held on board the Headquarters transport *Varela* and a plan was issued for a landing at Fao. The presence of the force at Bahrein was now known at Basra and Mohammerah, and in accordance with instructions from the Secretary of State, our representatives there and elsewhere in touch with Arabs gave the utmost publicity to the news. At the same time they announced that the British Government contemplated no aggressive action, but had been obliged to despatch this force for the eventual protection of British interests and of their friends, in view of the continued anti-British military measures taken by the Turks under German guidance.

At this period General Delamain received further information regarding the Turkish forces in Mesopotamia. The two regular divisions of the XIIth (Mosul) Corps had moved westward, the 37th Division of the XIIIth Corps had been reported at

---

* For details see Appendix II, p. 346.

† The Jask wireless station had lost touch with the force after the 22nd and consequently the same order—which had come from the Secretary of State—did not reach General Delamain from India till the 26th. As soon as the difficulty of wireless communication was realised, the Admiralty made arrangements for erection of wireless installations at Bushire and Abadan.

Mosul moving towards Erzerum, and there were left at Baghdad fourteen guns of the 37th Artillery, thirteen model battalions, five hundred men of the 114th Infantry and nine thousand reservists, of whom four thousand were without rifles. This meant that, excluding gendarmerie and new and partly armed organizations, there was only one regular division, the 38th, left in Mesopotamia.

On the 31st, General Delamain received from India the news of the Turkish attack on Odessa, and was warned to be ready to move at the shortest notice; and next day there reached him the Secretary of State's telegram of the 31st, saying that war had broken out with Turkey. At this time, the *Espiègle* was still at Mohammerah and the *Odin* was off Fao, outside the three-mile limit. The orders for the actual operations in Mesopotamia were despatched by the Admiralty and the India Office on the 31st. The telegram from the Admiralty was addressed to the Commander-in-Chief, East Indies, and the Senior Naval Officer, Persian Gulf, and ran as follows: " Commence hostilities against Turkey. *Espiègle* to deal with the guns posted opposite the oil-works and to prevent any attempt to damage them and generally to protect British interests up the river. The expedition has been ordered to proceed from Bahrein to the bar. *Odin* to await the arrival of the expedition at the bar and to accompany it into the river, first dealing with the guns at Fao. *Dalhousie* should remain at Bushire to maintain communications by wireless until Fao is captured and the telegraph cable is working again. Steps should be taken to obtain all the steam tugs in the river and mount small guns so as to assist the troops. The armed launches should be concentrated in the river as soon as possible. *Ocean* to assist in landing the expedition and to supply small guns for the tugs. Although it is not probable that mines have been laid, every precaution should be taken to guard against them.* The Shaikh of Mohammerah must be reassured as to our proceedings and informed that the main object is to keep the river open and trade free to his towns and territories. That his position will be amply secured as we have no quarrel either with him or with any of the Arabs." The *Dalhousie* acknowledged receipt of this order on the 1st November and reported its transmission to the *Ocean, Odin* and *Espiègle*.

The telegram from the India Office was addressed to the

---

* On 1st November, however, the Political Agent, Kuwait, reported that the Shaikh had received reliable information from his man at Fao of the arrival of mines there intended for the mouth of the river.

Viceroy: " Please instruct brigade at Bahrein to proceed at once to Shatt al Arab and to concert measures with naval authorities for immediate attack on Fao. Force will then clear Turks out of the Shatt and its vicinity as far as Shamshamiya if possible.* After which it will await arrival of reinforcements from India.† Admiralty advise that reinforcements may be sent without escort from Bombay unless Naval Commander-in-Chief has any reasons to contrary. *Königsberg* located on African coast south of Equator. Take steps to inform Arab chiefs in Gulf and on Aden side." These orders, received in India on 1st November, were sent on to General Delamain on the same day.

On the 1st, Captain Hayes-Sadler, R.N., the Senior Naval Officer, sent orders to the *Odin* to remain where she was to protect the buoys in the river, and to the *Dalhousie* to meet him with pilots, tugs, etc., on the morning of the 3rd, off Bushire, where he would be arriving in the *Ocean* escorting the convoy from Bahrein. The same day the *Espiègle* had sent the tugs *Sirdar-i-Naphte* and *Sumana* down the river from Mohammerah to try and reach the *Odin* off the bar to assist in sweeping operations. They were both fired on, however, from Fao and only the *Sirdar-i-Naphte* got through, but the *Sumana*, thanks to the lack of initiative on the part of the Turks, managed to return to Mohammerah.

On the 2nd, General Delamain and Captain Hayes-Sadler had a conference on board the *Varela* ; and the launch *Mashona*, which had been armed by the *Ocean*, was sent to take Major Radcliffe of the Dorsetshire Regiment to Kuwait, to obtain information as to where troops could best be disembarked near Fao and to rejoin the force off the Shatt al Arab. Next morning, the *Dalhousie* met the convoy off Bushire, bringing five pilots. That day, at a further conference, the Senior Naval Officer informed General Delamain that the *Ocean* drew too much water to be able to get within effective range of

---

* On the 31st the *Espiègle* had reported that the Turks had sunk two ships in the channel at this place.

† It had been arranged, by telegram on the 30th between India and the India Office, that General Delamain's force was not to advance on Basra till reinforced by another brigade of the 6th Division which was to sail from Bombay about 7th November, and he was told not to move till he got further orders, but to make all preparations, and that the Naval Commander-in-Chief was being consulted as regards co-operation with the navy. This telegram was received by General Delamain at sea on the 2nd, after the convoy had left Bahrein in accordance with the Admiralty instructions ; but the same afternoon he received definite orders from India to carry out the Secretary of State's instructions, followed by further orders from India that his force was not to go beyond Shamshamiya, nor was it to go to Mohammerah.

Fao fort; that it would take about forty-eight hours to arrange for the armament of tugs and launches and to fit the necessary sweeps; and that sweeping would make subsequent progress slow. As the final arrangement for landing at Fao could not be made, however, till the return of Major Radcliffe with the required information from Kuwait, and as he was not expected back till the 6th, the delay was immaterial.

At 4.30 p.m. on the 3rd, the convoy arrived off the outer bar of the Shatt al Arab and met the *Odin*. At 3.50 a.m. the same day, the *Espiègle* had left her anchorage in the Karun river and, apparently unperceived by the Turks, had proceeded with all lights out and anchored in the main channel south of Mohammerah, in order to intercept Turkish launches and to cover Abadan and Mohammerah.

On the 4th and 5th, naval preparations for the attack on Fao were carried out with some difficulty owing to the heavy swell; and bullet-proof cover was provided on the upper decks of the transports to facilitate covering fire for the landing force. On the morning of the 5th, Major Radcliffe arrived back from Kuwait with the information that Fao fort was in ruins, that the Turkish force there was about four hundred strong,* with seven or eight guns of old pattern, and that the landing opposite the fort was bad. General Delamain accordingly decided† that the landing should take place next day at and just below Fao village, about four miles above the fort, after the *Odin* had silenced the Turkish guns at the forts. The transports proceeded to the inner bar at 11 a.m., where orders for next day's operations were issued. To carry these out, a force of a naval beach party, one hundred marines, two mountain guns, a section of sappers, three companies of the Dorsets, the 20th Punjabis and 117th Mahrattas, under Lieutenant-Colonel Rosher of the Dorsets, was to land near the telegraph station under cover of fire from the *Odin* and from guns and rifles on board the transports *Varela* and *Umaria*. But, as there were insufficient boats to land the whole force at one time, four relays had to be arranged.

On the 6th, at 6 a.m., the *Odin* moved up the river, with the armed tug *Sirdar-i-Naphte* and *Ocean's* picket-boat sweeping

---

* Information from Turkish sources indicates the strength as one hundred and ten rifles and four guns (vide Appendix VI, p. 352), but there were probably Arabs as well.

† The Shaikh of Kuwait had suggested landing to the west of the port, via a narrow *hor*. General Delamain rejected this scheme, as not only would previous reconnaissance have been necessary, but also he was too short of steam launches.

three cables ahead ; but owing to the numerous dhows coming down on the ebb-tide progress was slow. No signs of the enemy on shore were observed till just after 10 a.m., when some guns near the fort opened fire. The *Odin* replied, opening at 5,500 yards range and, although some difficulty was at first experienced in directing the fire owing to the enemy's well-concealed position and to the lack of features and colour in the landscape, the hostile gunfire was silenced by 10.45 a.m., after the *Odin* had closed in to 1,700 yards. The Turkish guns, consisting of four Krupp field pieces firing from behind banks about five hundred yards south-east of the fort, had been well served and had hit the *Odin* twice ; and as she approached the shore a heavy rifle fire was opened on her by about three hundred Turks in trenches on the river-bank. This, however, ceased on the *Odin* firing a few shrapnel ; and the enemy were soon observed to be retiring towards Fao village. At 11 a.m., on the news that the enemy's guns were silenced, the transports *Varela* and *Umaria* proceeded to opposite the telegraph station, the two transports and the *Mashona* towing the seventeen boats containing troops, and naval launches towing the detachment of marines. The telegraph station was reached at 2 p.m. and the boats cast off, formed line, and made for the shore. There was no opposition, and by 3.45 p.m. the covering party and first and second reinforcements had landed. At 4 p.m., a company[*] of the 117th Mahrattas landed to form the garrison of Fao and to protect the rear of Colonel Rosher's force, which now proceeded southward to take the fort. This was accomplished without opposition during the night, the four Turkish field guns, which it was impracticable to carry away, being dismounted and thrown into the river ; and the force returned next morning to the telegraph station.

Early on the 6th, in anticipation of a Turkish attack on Abadan while the bombardment of Fao was in progress, the *Espiègle*, leaving the armed yacht *Comet*[†] at Mohammerah, had moved down the river and anchored southward of the oil-works. She also landed on the Turkish bank of the river an armed party, which cut the telegraph and telephone cables

---

[*] Although some little time elapsed after the outbreak of the Great War before the British organisation of companies and platoons was adopted throughout the Indian infantry, the term " company " and not " double company " is used throughout this work to indicate the unit representing one-quarter of a battalion.

[†] She had arrived a short time before from Baghdad, where she had been the official vessel of the Consul-General.

between Basra and Fao. About 1 p.m., the Turks opened a heavy rifle fire from mud walls and trenches on the river-bank opposite Abadan and the *Espiègle* replied with gun and rifle fire. In about half an hour the Turkish defences had been much knocked about and were on fire in places, and the *Espiègle* dropped farther down the river to enfilade the enemy's trenches, the fire from which was completely silenced before 2 p.m. The *Espiègle*, which had two men wounded and whose upper works had sustained some slight damage, continued to search the scrub and houses on the river-bank with occasional shrapnel till it became apparent that the enemy had evacuated the foreshore. It was subsequently reported that the Turks lost forty-six men killed in this engagement.

On the 7th, having re-embarked the landing force and leaving the 117th Company to garrison the Fao telegraph station, the transports proceeded up-stream, anchoring about sixteen miles above Fao, within sight of the oil-works at Abadan. Next day, General Delamain, after reconnoitring with the Senior Naval Officer in the *Odin*, decided to land and form a camp at Sanniya, on the Turkish side of the river about two and a half miles up-stream of the oil-works, where the river-bank, being firm and steep with deep water close inshore, was most suitable for a disembarkation. The troops commenced to land that afternoon and continued throughout the 9th and 10th. The operation was carried out with some difficulty, owing to the wind, strong tide, and the lack of suitable craft.*

From the 8th to the 10th, continual reconnaissances were carried out on land and up the river. These were rendered specially necessary and at the same time difficult by the date plantations which fringe the river-banks everywhere in this area to a depth of one or two miles. These plantations are closely intersected by tidal water cuts, often of some width and depth, and afford excellent cover for concealment, especially from river craft. Beyond occasional Arab snipers, however, no opposition was encountered and no enemy was seen, except by the *Espiègle*, which, in a northward reconnaissance to intercept some Turkish armed launches on the early morning of the 9th, was fired on from the shore near Mohammerah by about one hundred Turks and by a Turkish launch. In reply, the *Espiègle* silenced the enemy's fire and sank one launch

---

* The tugs drew too much water and all the towing had to be done by the two steamboats from the *Ocean* and a small one from the *Odin*. At Bahrein the Sappers had prepared eight ships' life-boats to carry seven or eight mules each, and only four lighters could be obtained from the oil-works. Each ship's boat had a naval coxswain detailed for it.

and damaged another, without sustaining any casualties herself.

General Delamain had thus successfully carried out a great part of his instructions. Thanks to the way in which the Turks had been surprised—or to their apathy—and to the co-operation of the navy, he had effected the usually difficult task of landing on a hostile coast without much trouble and without loss.

On the evening of the 10th, the Shaikh of Mohammerah informed the British Consul of the presence south-west of Mohammerah (eight or nine miles from the British camp) of a Turkish force of six hundred men with seven or eight guns under the command of Sami Bey, who, he said, intended to attack at dawn. Just before 3 a.m. (11th), General Delamain received information from the same source that the Turkish force had started on their way to attack him; and all preparations had been made when the attack came about 5.30 a.m. It was carried out against our outposts in a determined way by about three hundred Turks, being mainly directed against an old mud fort, about seven hundred yards south-west of the camp, which was held by a detached post of a company of the 117th Mahrattas.* The Mahrattas had no difficulty in holding their position, and the Turks were driven off by a counter-attack delivered by the 20th Punjabis, supported by the 23rd Mountain Battery. This counter-attack led to some close fighting among the date-palms, and we had two British officers wounded (Major Ducat, 20th Punjabis, died of his wounds), one Indian killed, two Indian officers and five Indians wounded. Six Turkish prisoners were captured, and the Turks, who left nineteen dead and twelve wounded behind them, admitted officially to eighty casualties. It was ascertained from the prisoners that further Turkish attacks were to be expected from a force which might amount to as many as ten battalions.

General Delamain had intended to advance against the Turks by land to the vicinity of Shamshamiya, but as he could get no news from India of the expected reinforcements (owing to the constant interruption by thunderstorms of the wireless communication)† this intimation of further probable enemy attacks decided him to remain where he was for the time being, in order to safeguard the oil-works. He was further

---
* The camp lay to the south of a bend of the river running nearly east and west. (See Map 1.)
† A telegram sent from India on the 10th informing him of the despatch of reinforcements did not reach him till the 15th.

strengthened in this decision by the heavy rain which fell on the 12th and 13th and which rendered the ground so heavy and muddy as practically to preclude any military movements. The force had thus an early illustration of one of the difficulties of campaigning in Mesopotamia.

On the 13th, transports were reported to have arrived at the bar and a request for news was received from Lieutenant-General Sir A. A. Barrett, commanding the 6th Division, who arrived himself in camp next day and assumed command of the operations.

In the meantime, the following statement had been published in London by the Foreign Office, on 1st November :—

"At the beginning of the war the British Government gave definite assurances that if Turkey remained neutral her independence and integrity would be respected during the war and in the terms of peace. In this France and Russia concurred.

"The British Government have since then endeavoured with the greatest patience and forbearance to preserve friendly relations, in spite of increasing breaches of neutrality on the part of the Turkish Government at Constantinople in the case of the German vessels in the Straits.

"On Thursday, 29th October 1914, the British Government learnt with the utmost regret that Turkish ships of war had without any declaration of war, without warning and without provocation of any sort, made wanton attack on open undefended towns in the Black Sea of a friendly country, thus committing an unprecedented violation of the most ordinary rules of international law, comity and usage.

"Ever since the German men-of-war *Goeben* and *Breslau* took refuge at Constantinople the attitude of the Turkish Government towards Great Britain has caused surprise and some uneasiness. Promises made by the Turkish Government to send away the German officers and crews of the *Goeben* and *Breslau* have never been fullfilled. It was well known that the Turkish Minister for War was decidedly pro-German in his sympathies, but it was confidently hoped that the saner counsels of his colleagues, who had had experience of the firm friendship which Great Britain has always shown towards the Turkish Government, would have prevailed and prevented that Government from entering upon the very risky policy of taking a part in the conflict on the side of Germany.

" Since the war, German officers in large numbers have invaded Constantinople, have usurped the authority of Government, and have been able to coerce the Sultan's ministers into taking up a policy of aggression.

" Great Britain as well as France and Russia has watched these proceedings patiently, protesting against the many acts which have been constantly committed contrary to neutrality, and warning the Government of the Sultan against the danger in which they were placing the future of the Ottoman Empire. Vigorously assisted by the Ambassadors of Germany and Austria, the German military elements at Constantinople have been persistently doing their utmost to force Turkey into war both by their activities in the services of the Turks and by the bribes of which they have been so lavish.

" The Minister of War with his German advisers has lately prepared an armed force for an attack on Egypt. The Mosul and Damascus Army Corps have, since their mobilization, been constantly sending troops south, preparatory to an invasion of Egypt and the Suez Canal from Aqaba and Gaza. A large body of Bedouin Arabs has been called out and armed to assist in this venture, and some of these have crossed the Sinai frontier. Transport has been collected and roads have been prepared up to the frontier of Egypt. Mines have been despatched to be laid in the Gulf of Aqaba. The notorious Shaikh Aziz Shawish has published and disseminated through Syria, and probably India, an inflammatory document urging Mahomedans to fight against Great Britain. Doctor Prueffer, who was so long engaged in intrigues in Cairo against the British occupation and is now attached to the German Embassy at Constantinople, has been busily occupied in Syria trying to incite the people to take part in this conflict. Aggressive action was certain to be the result of the activity of the numerous German officers employed in the Turkish Army and acting under orders of the German Government, who thus have succeeded in forcing the hands of the advisers of the Sultan.

" German intrigue cannot influence the loyalty to Great Britain of the seventy millions of Mahomedans in India and the feeling of the Mahomedan inhabitants of Egypt. They must look with detestation on misguided action under foreign influence at Constantinople, which will inevitably lead to the disintegration of the Turkish Empire, and which shows such forgetfulness of the many occasions on which Great Britain has shown friendship to Turkey. They must feel bitterly the degeneration of their co-religionists, who can thus be dominated against their will by German influences, and many of them realise that when Turkey is pushed into war by Germany, they must dissociate themselves from a course of action that is so prejudicial to the position of Turkey itself.

"The Turkish Government summarily and without notice on Friday shut off telegraphic communication with the British Embassy at Constantinople. This is no doubt the prelude to further acts of aggression on their part and the British Government must take whatever action is required to protect British interests, British territory, and also Egypt from attacks that have been made and are threatened."

A similar statement in India was accompanied by an assurance on behalf of the British Government and her allies that the Holy Places of Islam would be immune from any hostile action on their part. Enquiries on the spot indicated the sentiments of Indian Moslems on the subject.* Their general feeling was one of regret that Turkey had been decoyed into ranging herself on the side of Great Britain's enemies, but they were convinced that Turkey and Germany had committed a grievous political miscalculation if they counted on causing England embarrassment in India through the war. While Indian Moslems were naturally anxious for the preservation of the integrity and independence of Turkey and desired that the Turkish guardianship of the Holy Places of Islam should be continued, the enlightened among them fully understood the character of the present Government in Turkey. The spirit of loyalty and devotion to the Empire which Mahomedans in India displayed in this crisis was described a few days later in a telegram from the Viceroy, in which he referred to the numerous resolutions, telegrams and letters received on the subject and which he said left no doubt as to the feelings which prevailed.

On the 31st October, General Barrett had received orders to hold the following units in readiness to start at short notice under his command to reinforce General Delamain :—

---

* "The Times," 2nd November, 1914.

ORDERS TO GENERAL BARRETT

6th Divisional Headquarters;
10th Brigade R.F.A. (63rd, 76th and 82nd Batteries);
18th Infantry Brigade (2nd Norfolks, 7th Rajputs, 110th Mahratta L.I., 120th Rajputana Infantry);
Divisional Ammunition Column and certain hospitals;
and to these were added in the next few days as it became evident that shipping for them would be available:—
Two squadrons 33rd Cavalry;
17th Company Sappers and Miners;
No. 3 Wireless Troop and 34th Divisional Signal Company (less 17th Brigade Section);
48th Pioneers;
10th and 12th Mule Corps and the Jaipur Imperial Service Transport Corps;
Twelve hundred camels and the usual supply, ordnance and veterinary units, as well as further hospitals.*

On 2nd November, a staff officer from Army Headquarters reached Poona and handed over his orders to General Barrett as well as copies of correspondence (including orders sent) with General Delamain and with the Secretary of State.† In these, General Barrett was instructed to accompany the reinforcements and to assume command of the whole force at the head of the Gulf, as well as political control in the area of operations. His objective would be telegraphed to him subsequently.

The Admiralty and the local Naval Commander-in-Chief having decided that the situation permitted of transports sailing for the Persian Gulf without naval escort, these reinforcements left Bombay and Karachi in eighteen transports on 7th, 8th and 9th November; and on the 10th, arrangements were made for the despatch some ten days later of the 17th Infantry Brigade and the remainder of the division.

Owing to atmospheric disturbances, wireless communication

---

* See Appendix II, p. 347.

† Amongst the orders sent were copies of the "Organisation orders for Force ' D,' " which, besides giving the detail of the whole force which it was intended to send, with the scale of ammunition, equipment, etc., to be taken, stated that all units of the force would move on the field scale of establishment and equipment. This last notification was of special importance as the division had already mobilized on a special scale for service with Force "A." But owing to some misunderstanding and to the short time available, some units had not received notice of this change and in consequence left Bombay without all their proper equipment, the most notable deficiency being the lack of personnel and gear for carrying water. This matter was, however, brought to notice before they left Bombay and was rectified by the early despatch to Mesopotamia of what was missing.

with the force in the Shatt al Arab had been much interrupted. Steps were being taken to remedy this as far as possible, but some days would have to elapse before better communications could be assured. Owing to this and to the fact that General Delamain had as yet little further to report, there was some anxiety at the India Office. The failure of Force "B" to effect a landing in face of opposition at Tanga in East Africa, and the report of an impending attack on Muscat by Arab insurgents had no doubt increased this anxiety; and on the 13th November, when telegraphing to know what instructions had been given to General Barrett and to ask if the Arabs had given any sign of their attitude towards us, the India Office requested further information regarding events in the Gulf. The Viceroy had already wired on that day informing the Secretary of State that General Barrett was being instructed to move on Basra if he considered his force strong enough to do so, and to send a daily telegraphic progress report both to India and to the Secretary of State. General Delamain's situation was described in a telegram from him, despatched early on the 13th before he had received news of the arrival of the reinforcements. He said, "I have received several reports that the Turks are now being reinforced and intend to assume the offensive in combination with the Arab tribes. Very heavy rain has made the country impassable. Military situation is uncertain as I do not yet know date of arrival of remainder of division"; and he went on to say that he had prepared a defensive position at Sanniya and that he proposed to wait there till he got further information about the reinforcements.

On the 13th, on his arrival off the Shatt al Arab and after communicating with General Delamain, General Barrett gave orders for his transports to proceed up the river to Sanniya next day. Any idea of landing at Umm Qasr was abandoned as it was necessary to concentrate at once to meet the reported Turkish advance. As, however, only five river pilots were available and as no lighters or tugs could be spared from the work of disembarking troops to lighten the cargoes of two of his transports, which were too heavy to cross the bar, only a part of his force could be moved up at once. Five transports (containing Divisional Headquarters, 63rd Field Battery, 17th Company Sappers and Miners, Norfolks, 7th Rajputs, half the 120th Infantry, 48th Pioneers, and two squadrons 33rd Cavalry) started up the river at 6 a.m. on the 14th and reached Sanniya just before 11 a.m., when the work of disembarkation commenced. The camp site (sodden by the recent rain) and a field of fire had to be cleared, involving among other work the cutting down of date-palms on all sides; and roads and ramps —constructed mainly of hatch covers from the transports— had to be made for landing guns, wagons and horses. In consequence, only the 17th Company of Sappers and the 63rd Field Battery disembarked that day.

General Barrett now received the following order from India : " Your objective is Basra. If after discussion with and taking over from Delamain you consider your present force strong enough you will move on Basra. Remainder of 6th Division embarks on 19th at Bombay for Shatt al Arab." After discussing the situation with General Delamain, who told him that information from reconnaissances and various other sources indicated that Turkish forces were concentrating about Saihan, only four miles west of the camp, General Barrett instructed General Delamain to reconnoitre next day and to dislodge this hostile gathering without involving his own force too seriously.

For this operation, General Delamain detailed the 30th Mountain Battery, Dorsets, and 104th Rifles under his own command—with the 23rd Mountain Battery and 20th Punjabis held ready in camp to reinforce should an engagement take place—and stated his intention in his orders as " a reconnaissance will be made up-stream to-morrow." On the 15th, this force moved off at 6 a.m. and emerging south of the date plantations marched westwards across the desert at a distance of about 1,200 yards from them. About 7.10 a.m., when the advanced guard consisting of half the Dorsets and two guns of the 30th Battery arrived south of Saihan village and creek, the enemy opened fire on it from two positions on the edge of the plantations with rifles and machine guns and on the main body, 1,200 yards behind, with artillery. The 104th were sent to turn the enemy's left, capture their first position, and then to work through the plantations from the east. By about 8.30 a.m., supported by the 30th Battery which also kept in check the hostile artillery in the Turkish second position, the 104th had captured the first position " in capital style." By this time the 23rd Battery and 20th Punjabis, who had started from camp on hearing the firing, had arrived; and the advanced guard—reinforced by the remainder of the Dorsets and of the 30th Battery—extended to its left to outflank the enemy's second position from the west. Two companies of the 20th were pushed in to fill the gap between the Dorsets and the 104th, while the remainder of the 20th and the 23rd Battery remained in reserve under General Delamain. A general advance was now made against the enemy's second position, supported by the well-directed fire of both batteries. This position was entrenched and, though held by the Turks with determination, was gallantly rushed by the Dorsets about 9.30 a.m., the enemy after some further close fighting making off northwards through the plantations.

In the meantime, the 104th, finding progress difficult in the plantations owing to the thick scrub and the numerous water channels, had met with some opposition. At a fortified village the Turks, with a gun and a machine gun, attempted a serious counter-stroke; and the officer commanding 104th, unable to get into signalling communication with brigade headquarters owing to the mirage, had been obliged to ask the 20th Punjabis on his left for assistance to reinforce his right. Thus reinforced, the 104th and 20th advanced steadily but slowly till they reached the line held by the Dorsets and the rest of the 20th, when the whole line advanced and captured the Turkish camp. The Dorsets now swung round to their right, preparatory to a further advance, but it was about 10.30 a.m. and the arrival of Turkish reinforcements might be expected at any moment. Our force had done considerable damage to rifles, ammunition, stores, etc., found in the Turkish camp and had forced the enemy to retire. General Delamain therefore decided, in view of his instructions not to get too seriously engaged, that he would withdraw to camp. The retirement was ordered to commence at 10.45, but touch had been lost with the right of the line in the plantations and the force did not begin to retire till about an hour later. It returned to camp unmolested.

The *Odin*—joined later in the morning by the *Espiègle*—had steamed up the river parallel to the troops and had endeavoured to co-operate in the fight, but, owing to the impossibility of observing and directing fire through and over the belt of date plantations, the assistance she could render was not very great. General Delamain estimated the enemy's strength at about twelve hundred, with four mountain and three machine guns, but the examination of prisoners showed it to be much stronger; and it was subsequently ascertained to be about 3,100,[*] with

---

[*] 700 of 112th Regiment, 1,400 of 113th Regiment, 800 of new levy (or 26th Regiment), and 200 gunners. Information from Turkish sources, however, gives the strength as 2,000 regular infantry. (See Appendix VI, p. 352.)

four field and four mountain guns. Our force sustained sixty-two casualties,* while the Turks left about one hundred and sixty dead and wounded on the ground. We captured twenty-five prisoners and destroyed two Turkish machine guns.

The Turks had been definitely defeated. Although they could probably have reoccupied the Saihan position if they considered it wise to do so, the reconnaissance had removed the immediate menace to the progress of our disembarkation and had given General Barrett breathing time in which to get his force ashore in readiness for the advance towards his objective. The operations had proved the superiority of our troops over the Turks ; they were bound to affect the attitude towards us of the Arabs ; and they had given the troops a useful illustration of some of the difficulties to be expected in this strange land.

Among the physical disabilities experienced for the first time by most of the force was the mirage, which was to cause our troops endless trouble and misunderstandings in the months to come. Difficult to realise until actually met with, its effects can best be described by quoting from Edmund Candler's able narrative, " The Long Road to Baghdad " : " The atmosphere is most deceptive and in the haze or mirage it is difficult to tell if the enemy are horse or foot, or to make any estimate of their numbers. Everything is magnified. A low-lying mud village becomes a fort with walls twenty feet high, a group of donkeys a palm-grove . . . . There is not a cavalry regiment with the force which has not at some time or other mistaken sheep for infantry. . . . . Often in a reconnaissance the enemy are within six hundred yards before the squadron commander can distinguish whether they are mounted or on foot. . . . .

" The dancing mirage plays one a hundred tricks. My sapper friend put up a direction post for prismatic compass survey, a little mound with a flag on it. When he started back to camp he took down the flag. He had left the mound a mile behind, when, looking back, he saw what he thought was an Arab pursuing him. He lay down and covered the figure with his rifle and called to his orderly to do the same. They lay in wait while the Arab still came on at the same rapid stride, his cloak flying in the wind. Whole minutes passed, yet though he never ceased to move he came no nearer. They approached and found it was the little mound no more than a foot high. . . . ."

---

* Killed : 6 British and 3 Indian other ranks. Wounded : 2 British officers, 35 British and 16 Indian other ranks.

"The first row of duck I saw . . . . I took for a battalion of infantry."

During the 15th and 16th, the disembarkation of the force continued and by the evening of the 16th all the cavalry and infantry had landed, but only one of the field batteries was ashore. General Barrett could now take stock of his position. The difficulties of disembarkation and the small amount of land transport ashore made him dependent on the river transport for the daily maintenance of his force in munitions and supplies. Even for this the available steamboats and lighters were barely sufficient. It consequently became a question how much more of his artillery and auxiliary units he was wise in landing till he had obtained the use of more river craft from Mohammerah and the Karun river. To attempt to get this shipping before he had driven the Turks from the neighbourhood of Mohammerah would have precipitated a Turkish attack on the Shaikh, whom they were even now threatening with reprisals for what they termed his breach of neutrality in harbouring the *Comet*.* On all grounds this was very undesirable. The attitude of the surrounding Arab tribes was still doubtful and there were military and political advantages in obtaining their early co-operation, in deterring them from joining the Turkish forces and in avoiding any semblance of conflict with them. Judging from the fighting on the 15th, there seemed little doubt that General Barrett's force could defeat any Turkish body of troops at and below Basra, as these were still inferior to his own both in numbers and armament. On the other hand, the immobility of his troops, dependent for their existence on the transports in the river, was likely to prevent effective pursuit of a defeated enemy. Thus, unless he were able to neutralise this disability by superior tactics, he would be deprived of decisive results of a victory; and this would tend to delay his occupation of Basra.

At this juncture, General Barrett was informed by his political advisers that the Shaikh of Mohammerah was apprehensive of an immediate attack from a Turkish force on the left bank of the river; and, further, that the British ability to make headway against the Turks without further delay would make all the difference in the attitude of the neighbouring Arabs. He consequently decided that it would be in our best interests to advance at once. This decision was made

---

* To avoid giving the Turks any pretext for attacking Mohammerah, the *Comet* was ordered to pass down the Bahmanshir river if possible, and in this she succeeded.

known to his naval and military commanders at a conference on the 16th, and in a telegram of the same date he informed the Chief of the General Staff in India that he proposed to move his camp eight miles forward on the Turkish bank in order to safeguard the Shaikh of Mohammerah and that he would probably meet with resistance. The remaining field batteries were to be disembarked as rapidly as possible and to follow him as soon as circumstances would permit.

General Barrett's information led him to believe that the Turks were holding positions about Sahil, with their main force at Baljaniya. In his operation order of the 16th, he gave his intention as being to march next day, as light as possible, to a new camp and he stated that opposition might be expected at Saihan and farther north-west. Baggage was to be carried in the ships, infantry were to carry two hundred rounds per rifle on the person, other arms as much ammunition as possible, and only the " bearer sub-divisions " of the field ambulances were to accompany the force. The Senior Naval Officer would co-operate in the movement with the naval ships.

On the 17th, at 5.15 a.m., the force* moved out of camp and advanced in a north-westerly direction across the open desert, parallel to and about fifteen hundred yards from the date plantations.† On the river, the *Espiègle*, *Odin*, the armed yacht *Lewis Pelly* (two 3-pounder Hotchkiss and one Maxim), and the armed tug *Sirdar-i-Naphte* (one 8-cwt. 12-pounder and one Maxim) moved abreast of the advanced parties on land.

To minimise the disadvantages of his immobility, General Barrett intended if possible to turn the right of any enemy position met with, so as to cut the Turks off their line of retreat and to drive them through the plantations on to the river-banks, where they would come under the fire of the ships. The advanced guard was directed accordingly. As will be seen later, circumstances were to prevent this, thus illustrating how

---

* The advanced guard under command of Major-General C. I. Fry, commanding the 18th Brigade, was composed of one squadron 33rd Cavalry, 23rd Mountain Battery, 17th Company Sappers and Miners, and two battalions of the 18th Brigade (Norfolks and 7th Rajputs). The main body's order of march was as follows : one squadron 33rd Cavalry, Force Headquarters, 34th Signal Company Headquarters, 22nd Company Sappers and Miners, two battalions 18th Brigade (110th and 120th, less one company), 48th Pioneers, 63rd Field and 30th Mountain Batteries, two and three-quarter battalions 16th Brigade (Dorsets, 20th, half the 104th and one-quarter of the 117th), bearer sub-divisions of field ambulances, mule second line transport. There was a right flank guard of half a battalion (117th), a left flank guard of one company (104th), and a rear-guard of two companies (one company 104th and one company 117th).

† See Map 1.

it is generally inadvisable to make a definite plan of attack before reconnaissance or contact with the enemy has discovered his dispositions.

About 6.30 a.m., the enemy's former position at Saihan was found to be unoccupied and was passed through by the right of the advanced guard ; and it was not till 7.30 that the cavalry reported hostile patrols near an old mud fort (see Map 1) and about fifteen hundred yards west of it. About 8 a.m. they reported about 1,200 enemy with five guns, distributed in three parties and extending from a position to the east-north-east past the old mud fort to near Sahil. General Fry, commanding the advanced guard, after hearing the report of a cavalry officer sent back to him, decided to continue his advance across the enemy's front at a comparatively safe range, so as to leave room for the main body to deploy on his right. At the same time he ordered up the Norfolks on the right of the 7th Rajputs, who were leading. Turkish artillery near the old fort now opened fire with a few shrapnel and the 23rd Mountain Battery came into action (about 9.15), but found the range too long. About 9.30 a very heavy rainstorm came on which turned the surface of the ground into a quagmire and made the going very heavy. The ships had meanwhile found that, owing to the date plantations and to the shallows and islands preventing a close approach to the shore, the operations could only be observed from aloft. Fire was therefore controlled by an officer with a megaphone at the masthead and at 9.15 this officer saw two of the enemy's guns leave the open and take shelter, apparently as the result of the naval fire.

General Fry had now decided to direct his advance on a mosque, about two and three-quarter miles north-west of the old fort, which would bring him against the enemy's right flank. At 9.45 he was told by Force Headquarters that they were reinforcing him with a battalion, and that the 16th Brigade would operate on his right. At the same time, General Barrett informed General Delamain, commanding 16th Brigade, that the 18th Brigade would attack the hostile right and centre, while the 16th Brigade, linking up with the right of the 18th Brigade, were to attack the old fort, which then appeared to be the enemy's left flank. To carry out this operation, General Delamain gave the following orders to his commanding officers : the Dorsets were to attack (in a north-north-easterly direction) on a frontage of three hundred and fifty yards with their right flank directed on a point about one hundred yards south of the old fort ; the 20th Punjabis were to prolong the line to the left three hundred yards and to keep touch with the right of the 18th Brigade; the 22nd Company Sappers and Miners, were to move echeloned on the right rear of the Dorsets; seven platoons of the 117th Mahrattas, called in from the right flank guard, were to form a reserve behind the Dorsets; and half the 104th Rifles were to form a reserve behind the 20th. General Barrett had retained under his own command, as a general reserve, the 48th Pioneers and the 120th Infantry; and placed the whole of the artillery (63rd Field and 23rd and 30th Mountain Batteries) under his C.R.A.

About 10.30, when the 18th Brigade was moving to its right to lessen the gap between the two brigades, another heavy rainstorm came on. The mist this caused obscured the whole front for a time and caused the 18th Brigade temporarily to lose their direction. The ground was now ankle-deep in slippery, clinging mud, and for a time the advance almost came to a standstill. Men, guns and horses could only move at a slow walk and the artillery wagons stuck heavily and frequently. Moreover, the hand-barrows carrying the telephone cable of the headquarter signal section stuck so badly that attempts to link up headquarters by telephone with the other formations had to be abandoned. Consequently, communication during the rest of the fight had to be carried out mainly by dismounted orderlies; for visual signalling was constantly interrupted by the atmosphere, and the mud and open country militated against the use of mounted men.

Meanwhile, all the artillery had come into action in the open between the two brigades and engaged the enemy's position between the old fort and the mosque, to cover the advance of the 18th Brigade. This brigade was halted at 11 a.m. to enable the 16th Brigade to move up into the same alignment; and then the whole line advanced. Soon after, the enemy opened a heavy rifle fire from his whole line and this disclosed the position of a well-concealed line of trenches north-west of the old fort and at about one thousand yards range from the 18th Brigade firing line. The Arabs forming the main garrison of this part of the hostile line were using black powder and the line of smoke this caused afforded an excellent target. This hostile rapid fire continued for some time, but being generally too high it had little effect on the 18th Brigade; it caused, however, heavy losses to the Dorsets in the 16th Brigade, whose line it partly enfiladed.

The further attack of the 18th Brigade was devoid of special features. Their advance was steadily maintained under cover of our artillery fire, the mountain batteries moving up with the advance in close support and rendering effective assistance. By noon, the artillery had been further reinforced by the arrival of a section of the 76th Field Battery, which, having disembarked, had hurried up to join the force.

The part of the position being attacked by the 16th Brigade was held mainly by Turkish regulars using smokeless powder, and it soon became evident that the enemy's left flank extended for a considerable distance to the south of the old fort, along a series of mounds and banks on the edge of the plantations. The Dorsets, when about a thousand yards from the old fort, moving with two companies in the firing line and two in support, found themselves under a cross-fire, which caused their left to swing round northwards in order to face the trenches north-west of the old fort and at the same time obliged them to reinforce the right of their firing line with a company from the supports. The attack again pushed slowly forward, but the Dorset's left, still under a heavy cross-fire, could not keep pace, across the glutinous and open plain, with their right. The 22nd Company of Sappers now moved into the firing line, extending it to the right, but here also progress soon became slow. In view of this situation, General Delamain now ordered the seven platoons of the 117th and a company of the 104th to make a turning movement round the enemy's left flank. This action was shortly afterwards confirmed by receipt of orders to the same effect from General Barrett.*

The turning movement of the 104th and 117th was checked by enemy detachments thrown back in the plantations on the Turkish left, where the date-palms and the thick scrub among the water channels and banks rendered the position somewhat difficult and obscure. General Delamain consequently found it necessary to put his last reserves into the fight and also to proceed in person with his staff to co-ordinate the movement on the right with the original attack against the old fort. The

---

* In his report, General Barrett says: "After watching the course of the engagement for some time, I came to the conclusion that it would be advisable to abandon my original intention of turning the enemy's right, which extended some distance, and was echeloned back into broken ground and palm-groves. The key of his position appeared to be the old mud fort. I therefore sent word to General Fry with the 18th Brigade to engage the enemy's right and centre with a frontal attack, while General Delamain with the 16th Brigade turned his left flank and captured the fort. At the same time I reinforced General Delamain with a battalion from the Reserve. General Delamain had meanwhile anticipated my intentions and had already commenced the turning movement."

artillery were not supporting this attack.* In any case they experienced great difficulty in observing and directing their fire owing to the featureless monotony of the desert or the screen of palm-trees exaggerated by the mirage.

The disposition of the force attacking the old fort under General Delamain was now : in the firing line, from the left, 20th, Dorsets, 22nd Company Sappers and Miners, 117th (seven platoons), 104th (two and a half companies) ; and in support, 48th Pioneers, half being behind the 104th and the other half behind the Dorsets. The fight to the south-east of the old fort took the form of several separate attacks against Turkish detached parties, and, although these were successful, General Delamain's personal control was required to swing the line round to their left to capture the old fort. This was now done with the aid of the Dorsets—who had rushed the last two hundred yards of open separating them from the plantations —and of the intervening portions of the line. The Turks evacuated the fort, retiring northward at 1.15 p.m., and at the same hour the enemy facing the 18th Brigade—mainly Arabs in white clothing—suddenly rose from their trenches and began a rapid withdrawal, which afforded our artillery and infantry an excellent target. The whole of the Turkish force was now in retreat in a north-westerly direction. Their retirement, covered by their guns, was skilfully carried out under cover of long earthen embankments and through a succession of good positions. The British line advanced everywhere, firing heavily and doing considerable execution, but the state of the ground prohibited rapid movement and thus saved the enemy greater losses. The part of the force under General Delamain destroyed large quantities of ammunition and stores found in the Turkish camp two miles north of the old fort, and the 7th Rajputs, pushing on in pursuit with the Dorsets, captured two Krupp mountain guns which the Turks had abandoned after removing the breech-blocks.

Meanwhile, at 11.20 a.m., in order to obtain more accurate fire, the ships had anchored in the river about one mile northward of the Abadan boat channel, and shortly came under a very heavy rifle fire from the bank. Their return fire, however, caused the enemy to retire and soon afterwards also set on fire

---

* The point is mentioned by General Barrett in his report : " These Turkish regulars were using smokeless powder and were invisible from the point where the guns were in action, the latter being fully engaged with the enemy's artillery and with the long line of entrenchments on the main front Hassanain-Zain."

the Turkish camp. Military officers, both artillery and infantry, had been detailed to proceed on board the ships to assist in inter-communication and fire co-operation, but the intervening date plantations had prevented full advantage being taken of the naval fire.

Just before 3 p.m., General Barrett considered it advisable to issue orders for the pursuit to be broken off. The wet ground preventing rapid movement had allowed the Turks to organise an effective retreat ; a camp had to be selected, occupied, and entrenched ; and a considerable number of wounded scattered over a large area had to be attended to and brought in. While these orders were on their way a violent sandstorm came on, obstructing communication, with the result that some units did not break off the pursuit till 4 p.m. and that the warships could not see the enemy's retirement.

The Turkish force was estimated at 3,500* regular infantry belonging to the 26th, 112th, 113th and 114th Regiments, 200 gunners with 4 Q.F. field and 8 mountain guns, 350 gendarmerie, and about 1,000 Arabs. Their losses were heavy and amounted in killed and wounded to between 1,500 and 2,000 and in prisoners to 150, including six officers. Their guns had been well served and cleverly handled, but their elevation was generally too great and the fusing of their shells indifferent. To this and their rather indifferent rifle fire must be attributed the comparatively low British losses. As it was, these amounted to a total of 489 killed and wounded.†

The behaviour of the troops engaged—British and Indian— had been worthy of their traditions. General Barrett singled out for special commendation the 2nd Dorsetshire Regiment and the 22nd Company Sappers and Miners.

A camp was selected at Sahil on the river-bank, about two miles south-east of the old fort. It continued to blow hard during the evening and in consequence the transports were unable to anchor opposite the camp. It was bitterly cold and though the troops were in excellent spirits after their victory, they spent a comfortless night without greatcoats, blankets or cooking pots, as these had been brought up by river from Sanniya and could not be landed. The storm also hindered

---

* Information from Turkish sources indicates that only 1,200 regular infantry with 8 guns were on the position. (Vide Appendix VI, p. 352.)
† Killed : 4 British officers, 21 British and 29 Indian other ranks. Wounded : 17 British and 4 Indian officers, 186 British and 228 Indian other ranks.

The majority of the British casualties occurred in the 2nd Dorsetshire, whose losses amounted to 2 officers and 21 rank and file killed, and 1 officer and 149 rank and file wounded.

BASRA AS THE OBJECTIVE

the work of bringing in the wounded. This continued far into the night, and was further interfered with by the intermittent firing on our outposts which caused several casualties. In his despatch General Barrett pays a very high tribute to the medical personnel engaged in this difficult and trying task.

The new camp site, although the best available, proved unsuitable for disembarkation owing to the shelving mud shore, much of which was exposed at low tide. The sappers and pioneers did what they could to improve matters by making ramps of palm logs and roadways of palm leaves over the mud ; but there were many sick and wounded to be embarked and there was considerable difficulty in landing sufficient supplies and stores.

The mouth of the Karun river was now practically safe from Turkish attack, and three shallow-draught river steamers (*Mejidieh, Blosse Lynch* and *Malamir*) belonging to Messrs. Lynch were requisitioned from Mohammerah and proved very useful in working between the transports and the shore. But it was evident that these makeshift arrangements for maintaining the force could not suffice for much longer and it was fortunate that the necessity for the attempt did not arise.

From the 18th to the 21st, our troops remained in camp and reconnaissances were carried out upstream by both military and naval forces. These disclosed the fact that the Turks were holding a position at Baljaniya with four guns covering the obstruction in the river channel. But, the *Espiègle*, reconnoitring to within a thousand yards of this, reported that it did not appear to block the channel completely.

The situation was summed up by General Barrett in his telegram to India of the 20th, in which he combined with his daily report for the 19th an answer to a telegram from the Secretary of State forwarded to him from India. The Secretary of State, after congratulating the force on their fight of the 15th, informed the Government of India that the Cabinet had approved the capture of Basra as the immediate objective of Force " D " ; and he presumed that if the political and military situations were favourable, the Government of India would instruct General Barrett to continue his advance. The Commander-in-Chief, India, in forwarding this telegram had left it to General Barrett's discretion whether he would move on to Basra at once or await the arrival, about the 28th, of the third brigade of his division. General Barrett's reply ran thus : " I consider force at my disposal strong enough to move forward and attack enemy's position at Baljaniya and

I am anxious to do so. Great difficulty of landing artillery and stores here has caused delay. But two complete (field) batteries are now on shore with me, but risk and labour is so great that third battery goes back to land opposite Abadan, whence it will cross desert to join us. Owing to obstruction at upper end of Dabba island, ships can go no farther and I am now dependent on them for supplies. Owing to enemy's field guns in position commanding it, *Espiègle* has not been able to approach nearer than one thousand yards so cannot make close examination. As we advance we hope to turn these guns out. For supply purposes I propose to use Lynch's boats as far as Baljaniya. The result of this engagement and report on the obstruction in the river will decide plans as to Basra. There are still three deep-draught transports containing transport and supplies at the mouth of the river beyond the bar. The principal marine transport officer, Hamilton, will try to get them up as soon as possible. I cannot move except with help of river transports as I have only very few mules available.

"Villagers met with during daily reconnaissances appear friendly but the attitude of the Arabs is doubtful as every night they snipe the camp. Yesterday an armed enemy launch was destroyed by *Espiègle* . . . . . The anchorage here is not very safe and is insufficient for all the ships . . . . ."

General Barrett had decided to advance on the 21st against Baljaniya, but on the afternoon of the 20th he told the Senior Naval Officer that he might not be able to do so owing to the difficulty being experienced in landing guns, horses, ammunition, stores, etc. That evening, however, news came in that the Turks had evacuated Basra and were retiring on Amara.

CHAPTER VII.

THE OCCUPATION OF BASRA AND THE CAPTURE OF QURNA

ON the 20th November the Shaikh of Mohammerah brought information of the Turkish evacuation of Baljaniya and Basra and of the retirement of all their forces on Amara. Till then General Barrett had not realized the decisive nature of his victory of the 17th. The news was confirmed the next and following days; and the accumulating evidence of the Turks' severe losses showed that for the time being their demoralisation was great.

Information from Turkish sources indicates that the news of the Turkish defeat at Sahil caused no little dismay at Constantinople, where it was realised that a British occupation of Basra would follow in a few days. Enver Pasha at once resolved that the British should be driven out of Mesopotamia. On the 22nd November he ordered two battalions of the Fire Brigade Regiment to mobilize under Ali Bey for service in Mesopotamia. These battalions started from Constantinople on 3rd and 4th December; and other reinforcements for Mesopotamia were to follow.

On the 21st November the British warships and launches proceeded to reconnoitre and to examine the obstruction in the river channel between Shamshamiya and Dabba islands.* This channel, about 370 yards wide, was partially blocked by three ships sunk athwart the fairway;† but a clear space, about 50 yards wide, remained between the bows of the s.s. *Ekbatana* and Dabba island. Its passage, however, was rendered difficult by the eddies set up by the obstruction and by adjacent wrecks.

About 11 a.m., when the ships were still examining the obstruction, a steam launch bringing some British residents and local notables from Basra came through the obstruction and alongside the *Espiègle*. Confirming the news that the Turks had evacuated Basra, they said that Arabs were looting the town and they asked for a British force to restore and

---
* See Map 1.
† The s.s. *Ekbatana*, the s.s. *John O'Scott* and an old light vessel.

maintain order. Captain Hayes-Sadler at once sent this news by wireless to General Barrett. He then decided to attempt the passage through the obstruction so as to push on to Basra with the ships under his command. The message to General Barrett brought an immediate reply asking whether the warships could assist and saying that he would provide a military detachment to accompany them. It was soon arranged that Major-General Fry should proceed at once with a detachment in two river steamers and that General Barrett should march that evening for Basra with the remainder of the force.

About 2 p.m., when it appeared to be slack water, the *Espiègle* negotiated the obstruction with a little difficulty and was followed at a short interval by the *Odin* and *Lawrence*. They anchored opposite the deserted Turkish battery at Baljaniya and landed a party to dismantle the four field guns abandoned there. At 3.30 p.m., there was no sign of the river steamers with troops, and a cloud of smoke was observed in the direction of Basra, betokening burning buildings. Thereupon, Captain Hayes-Sadler decided to proceed at once with the *Espiègle* and *Odin*, leaving the *Lawrence* to escort the troops. Basra was reached about 5.30 p.m., and the Custom House was seen to be on fire and full of plundering Arabs. These were dispersed by a blank charge and naval landing parties cleared the Custom House and its vicinity. By dark the town was comparatively quiet and the shore parties were withdrawn for the night. Early next morning, however, Arabs recommenced looting and naval parties were again landed. About 9.30 a.m.* General Fry's detachment† arrived in the *Mejidieh* and *Blosse Lynch*, took over the guards on shore and established order without difficulty.

The main force under General Barrett reached the south-western outskirts of Basra about noon. Leaving Sahil at 8 p.m. the day before, their twenty-eight mile march had proved tedious and trying; for movement had been very slow owing to the numerous high banks and irrigation channels which crossed the track and which had to be levelled or bridged. On arrival at Basra the few bridges over the several creeks traversing the area had to be repaired or strengthened; the indescribably filthy condition of the town and its environs showed that quarters for the troops could only be arranged

---

* The delay had been due to the difficulties of embarkation at Sahil and to the necessity for waiting till daylight to pass the obstruction in the river.

† 18th Brigade Headquarters, Norfolks, 110th, two mountain guns, a wireless section, and a section of a field ambulance.

after careful examination ; and men and animals were badly in need of rest and food. General Barrett, therefore, decided to bivouac near the Khora creek south of the town and to postpone his entry till the next day.

The area known as Basra consisted of several distinct parts : the Custom House, the British, United States, and German Consulates,* European mercantile firms' houses and buildings, the Turkish commodore's house, the quarantine station, and a few other buildings, on the river-bank ; the town of Ashar, lying about a quarter of a mile inland to the north of the Ashar creek, with the Turkish barracks adjoining it to the north ; the town of Basra lying about two miles inland to the south of the Ashar creek ; and the wharf and small dock at Maqil, about five miles up the main river. Tidal creeks running into the main river intersected the whole area, which abounded in date-palms. The whole country was waterlogged, but the vegetable and fruit gardens round the town testified to the productivity of the soil. Though there were a few rough and narrow tracks, generally along the banks separating the gardens and plantations, there was only one road which connected the two towns ; and there was no through communication at all along the river-bank. Basra and Ashar towns were a maze of tortuous lanes whose centres were ankle-deep in filth, offal and litter. Many of the houses were comparatively well built and double-storied ; but the total absence of any sanitary system or method and the presence of numerous disease-ridden brothels rendered both towns unsuitable for the billeting of troops. Trade, decayed under Turkish rule, had recently shown signs of revival and the bazaars were well stocked. The population of about thirty thousand was of many races—Arabs, Indians, Armenians, Chaldeans, Jews, Syrians, Persians, and others—and although openly they expressed pleasure at our arrival, their misgivings lest the Turks should ultimately return imbued their welcome with caution.

Facilities for disembarkation were very few. The only jetties were at the German Consulate and Maqil. Ocean-going ships could not come alongside either, and Maqil was for the time being out of the question as it was five miles off by river, and the only practicable land route was a detour through the desert to avoid the many unbridged creeks. Ships had to be discharged in midstream into native craft which then drifted

---

* The head of the German firm of Wonckhaus acted as German consul, though he had no official status as such.

with the current until within poling depth of the bank. In wet weather, the lack of roads and of road metal impeded, if it did not stop, all landing work ashore; and there was a difficulty in obtaining local labour. The native craft used were *mahailas* and *bellums*. *Mahailas* are from thirty to eighty feet long with a beam about one-third of their length. They are generally open with small platforms fore and aft; they carry a lateen sail, but in shallow water they are towed or poled. Their carrying capacity is from ten to seventy-five tons. *Bellums* are long and narrow, somewhat resembling the Venetian gondola; about twenty feet long and three feet wide, they are flat-bottomed, with a small platform at either end. They are used for passengers and small goods traffic.

On the afternoon of the 22nd November, Major Brownlow, the Deputy Judge Advocate-General of the force, was appointed Military Governor, with Mr. Bullard, the late British Consul at Basra, as his civil adviser, and Mr. Tom Dexter* as his personal assistant. He started his work by sending for the *Mulkhtars* (headmen) of the different wards and instructed them to furnish night watchmen from the local population to supplement the military patrols. Proclamation was also made by beat of drum advising the inhabitants to proceed peacefully with their ordinary business, warning them to refrain from looting and directing them to deliver up all arms in their possession.

On the 23rd, the force made a ceremonial entry, advancing through the narrow lanes of Basra town to the Ashar bridge, where the Union Jack was hoisted on the roof of one of the principal buildings under a salute from the naval guns. The troops presented arms and gave three cheers for His Majesty the King, and the following proclamation was read in Arabic by Sir P. Cox, in the presence of the leading notables of the town :—

" PROCLAMATION

issued on behalf of the General Officer Commanding the British Forces in occupation of Basra to the notables and public of the town : 23rd November 1914.

" Let it be known to all that from of old the British Government has had many millions of Mahomedan subjects

---

* For thirty years an engineer in the *Comet*, the son of a bluejacket of the old Indian navy and a Baghdadi lady, he had considerable influence among the river Arabs. He was made prisoner in Kut al Amara when serving under General Townshend and suffered some ill-usage at the hands of the Turks.

more than any other Power in the world—more even than Turkey.

"As is well known, Great Britain has in the past always displayed friendship and regard for Turkey; and a few months ago, when war broke out between certain of the Powers of Europe, the British Government urged most strongly on the Sublime Porte that the Ottoman Government should on no account join in the conflict, as such a course was opposed to the best interests of Turkey. Furthermore, in this connection, Turkey was assured that so long as she refrained from participation in the war, the British Government and her allies would guarantee the maintenance of her independence and integrity. Unfortunately the Turkish Government did not accept or attend to the advice of the British Government in this regard, for the reason that she was misled and tricked by German intrigues to such an extent that she committed numerous acts of hostility which forced the British Government into a state of war with her.

"The British Government has now occupied Basra, but though a state of war with the Ottoman Government still prevails, yet we have no enmity or ill-will against the population, to whom we hope to prove good friends and protectors. No remnant of Turkish administration now remains in this region. In place thereof the British flag has been established—under which you will enjoy the benefits of liberty and justice, both in regard to your religious and your secular affairs.

"I have given strict orders to my victorious troops that in the execution of the duties entrusted to them they are to deal with the populace generally with complete consideration and friendliness. It remains for you yourselves to treat them in the same way.

"In conclusion, you are at full liberty to pursue your vocations as usual and your business as before, and it is my confident hope that the commerce of Basra will resume its course and prosper even more than in the past."

That day, General Barrett, in publishing a telegram from the Commander-in-Chief in India congratulating Force "D" on their success, included his own congratulations to the force on the achievement of their two main objects, viz., the defeat of the enemy's forces in the field and the occupation of this important town; and he expressed his warmest approval of their gallantry in the field and their cheerful performance of the arduous duties inseparable from a campaign of this nature.

During the next few days there was much to occupy everyone. Most of the leading Turkish officials had fled and the few remaining were generally unreliable or useless ; and some form of government had to be improvised. The inhabitants were much impressed by the exemplary behaviour of the troops and relations between the two became and continued very cordial ; but many bad characters—generally from outside—threatened trouble in the town. When the Turks retired, the newly mobilized Arab soldiery had been left to their own devices and many of them had bartered their arms and equipment locally before dispersing to their homes. A few arms were delivered up on demand but many remained concealed, necessitating continual searches. The locally recruited Arab watchmen or police were on the whole not unsatisfactory, but it soon became apparent that for real watch and ward reliance could only be placed on our troops. Two Deputy Military Governors were appointed for Basra and Ashar respectively, and by degrees the civil administration began to take shape, as regulations for the control of taxes, trade, traffic, sanitation, etc., came into force. In the settlement of affairs, the local knowledge and experience of the British local agents of mercantile firms were of much use to us.

The troops were fully employed in cleaning up the extraordinarily dirty surrounding of their camps or billets and in unloading and landing stores from the ships, as well as in reconnaissances and visits to neighbouring villages, etc., for arms. The lack of jetties, roads and bridges kept the sappers and pioneers hard at work ; and the essential work of improving the sanitation of the place was rendered difficult by the presence of water everywhere near the surface of the ground. There was no metal for roads and finally it had to be imported all the way from India for the main communication.

Drinking water was obtainable from the river only. This water was contaminated everywhere near land, and for drinking purposes it had all to be fetched in boats from the centre of the river and then chlorinated before use. Suitable hospital accommodation could not be found till the Shaikh of Mohammerah placed his palace, a mile above Ashar creek, at our disposal for that purpose.*

---

* The Turkish military hospital, though outwardly a handsome building of mud bricks, plaster and wood, was internally dirty and insanitary in the extreme.

SUGGESTED ADVANCE TO BAGHDAD

Owing to the lack of facilities, disembarkation was slow and difficult and the line of ships in the stream waiting to be unladen soon grew to some miles in extent. Moreover, the loading in Bombay had been carried out of necessity in a hurry and the contents of the ships were often not available in the order in which they were required, and even in some cases were not completely known at Basra. Hard work and good will on the part of all concerned, however, overcame these difficulties and before the end of the month General Barrett's force had settled down with their tents and baggage, and the auxiliary services were beginning to function efficiently.

General Barrett had now to consider the situation. Beyond the occupation of Basra he had no orders; and he felt himself at rather a disadvantage in not having received before leaving India some indication of our probable future policy. The Commander-in-Chief in India, however, in his evidence before the Mesopotamia Commission pointed out that he furnished General Barrett with copies of the whole correspondence with the Secretary of State, which afforded all the information that the Government of India themselves possessed of the intentions of H.M. Government. Moreover, Sir Percy Cox had been Foreign Secretary to the Government of India up to a few days before General Delamain's force left Bombay and consequently had intimate knowledge of all that had transpired by then. In a " private " telegram to the Viceroy from Basra of 23rd November Sir P. Cox put the situation to him as follows :—

> " G.O.C. and I are studying the topographical details bearing on the question of advance to Baghdad in case that course be decided on. Will Your Excellency kindly consider the problem. It would be convenient if we could learn the intentions of Government in this connection as soon as possible in order that thorough proposals may be submitted without delay. The local outlook is as follows : According to general reports Turkish troops recently engaged with us were completely panic-stricken and very unlikely to oppose us again. Arab element in Baghdad is already friendly and notables here volunteer opinion that we should be received in Baghdad with the same cordiality as we have been here and that the Turkish troops would offer little if any opposition. There remain the tribes between here and Baghdad. From among this element the well-known Muntafik Shaikh, Ajaimi, who was

ostensibly co-operating with the Turkish troops, has just sent in an emissary to convey his submission and intimate his wish to come in and hand over four thousand rifles received or seized by him from the Turks and it is hoped that the neutrality if not the active co-operation of the tribes can be secured by judicious diplomacy. Effect of the recent defeat has been very great, and if advance is made before it wears off and while cool season lasts Baghdad will in all probability fall into our hands very easily. After earnest consideration of the arguments for and against I find it difficult to see how we can well avoid taking over Baghdad. We can hardly allow Turkey to retain possession and make difficulties for us at Basra; nor can we allow any other Power to take it; but once in occupation we must remain, for we could not possibly allow the Turks to return after accepting from Arabs co-operation afforded on the understanding that the Turkish *regime* had disappeared for good. It is also a matter for consideration that there are some thirty British subjects detained there whom we need to release. I may mention that I sent Major Shakespear to Ibn Saud with instructions to get him to come north and to remain with him in case we wanted him to assist us with the tribes beyond Basra. I shall report officially in due course arrangements we are making for administration of Basra."

General Barrett approved of the despatch of this telegram, thinking that in view of the possibility of a later advance up the Tigris there were obvious advantages in ventilating the subject as soon as possible. The resulting reply was likely to show the intentions of H.M. Government and both General Barrett and Sir P. Cox were anxious to know these, to help them in their military and political plans and policy. As General Barrett was led to believe that Arab co-operation and support would be forthcoming to the desired extent, he considered at that time that an advance to Amara would be both feasible and expedient. It was not till nearly two months later that force of circumstances* brought home to him that his force would be compelled to remain on the defensive.

---

* As will be seen later these were: the failure of the Arabs to afford the expected co-operation and support; the increasing strength of the Turks; the lack of aeroplanes and light draught gunboats; and the indications that the threatening frontier and internal situations in India were likely to interfere with the despatch of reinforcements.

The Viceroy, repeating this telegram to the Secretary of State on the 25th, added, " Before giving you my views I am consulting the Commander-in-Chief and will formulate them as soon as I know how far the proposal is feasible from a military point of view." On the 25th, the Chief of the General Staff, India, sent orders to General Barrett to consolidate his position at Basra and the head of the Persian Gulf, and he asked for General Barrett's appreciation of what he required to hold Basra securely and to keep the control of the river as far up as was necessary for that purpose. He also asked for further information, on that and the next day, regarding the enemy, the attitude of the Arab tribes, the number and capacity of available steamers and lighters, the supplies and transport locally procurable, and the state of the roads. In the meantime and before he received General Barrett's replies, he had written a short appreciation from the military point of view of Sir P. Cox's proposal to advance on Baghdad. In this he estimated that the disposable Turkish troops about Baghdad did not exceed fifteen thousand, of whom not more than four thousand would be properly armed, organised and equipped, and that they would have sixteen to twenty guns. He pointed out that it was essential that the Arabs should co-operate, and that if they did so it might be possible for the one brigade with horses and guns—which the available river transport was believed to be capable of carrying in one trip—to seize and occupy Baghdad if sent promptly. The round trip would probably take fourteen days, so that this brigade would have to maintain itself unsupported at Baghdad for a fortnight. He considered that eventually a division would have to be kept in Baghdad " to make the position even moderately safe " ; and another division would be required between Baghdad and Fao, to secure the line of communication and provide a reserve for Baghdad. This second division could only be found by diverting a brigade from Egypt, sending one brigade from the North-West Frontier* and making up a composite brigade of troops from Muscat, China, Mauritius, and from the Territorial Force. After taking into consideration the distance of Baghdad from Mosul and the Russian operations in the Caucasus, he came to the conclusion that these two divisions might be sufficient so long as Russia occupied the Turkish armies in Armenia. In the event, however, of a Russian repulse or snow in the Caucasus closing

---

* At this time it had been found necessary to reinforce the Waziristan area owing to an attack by a large body of tribesmen from across the frontier.

operations, it seemed possible that Turkish forces from there would be diverted against Baghdad. " If this happened, as we should be unable to reinforce them further, we should have either to withdraw or run the risk of a considerable disaster." He was of opinion that the ultimate strategical value of Baghdad was doubtful, while it was clear that the addition to our military responsibilities by its occupation would entail the diversion of more troops to what was, after all, only a secondary objective. He concluded : " It will thus be seen that, however desirable politically the seizure of Baghdad may be, the military considerations indicate that even success would result in our general strategical position being weakened rather than strengthened."

On the 27th, General Barrow, the Military Secretary at the India Office, was also considering Sir P. Cox's proposal, and in his minute of that date he analysed the situation on the following lines. A policy of passive inactivity was to be deprecated if we were to continue to impress the Arab and Indian world with our ability to defeat all designs against us. Within the next week or so the third brigade of the division would have arrived in Mesopotamia, and General Barrett and Sir P. Cox would be able to form a sound appreciation of the position with regard to the Arabs. If this was favourable a forward move would be safe, though it was premature to embark on any such ambitious project as the occupation of Baghdad. A suitable objective was Qurna, up to which warships like the *Odin* and ships of fifteen-feet draught could proceed. No obstacle to such an advance was known and no opposition seemed likely, so that probably a brigade of infantry with a proportion of other arms would suffice. The object of going to Qurna was to secure a strong strategical point and a dominating position. Situated at the junction of the Tigris and the old channel of the Euphrates, it covered and controlled all the rich cultivated land along the Shatt al Arab. Immediately to the north of Qurna was the arid country between it and Amara and both flanks were practically unassailable ; on the right the Hawiza marshes reaching to near the Persian frontier and on the left the Euphrates. The advantages of the position were :—

(1) Its commanding military value.
(2) The control it would give us of the whole navigable water-way to the Gulf.
(3) The possession of the whole of the rich cultivated area from Qurna to the sea.
(4) The fact that it completely covered Persian Arabistan and safeguarded it from Turkish intrigues or incursions.

(5) The moral effect on the Arabs.
(6) The control of the telegraph up to this point and also of the passage of the Euphrates.

He concluded, "When we have reached Qurna and fully established ourselves there it will be time enough to consider whether we should go farther. We should know by then the attitude of Ibn Saud and of the Arabs as a whole. We shall know the political situation at Baghdad and whether the Turks are in a condition to resist us. We shall have fully established ourselves in a military sense at Basra. I see no object in doing more than this at present. When we have consolidated ourselves in the Shatt al Arab region we shall be in all the better position to take another step forward with Baghdad as its objective, but let nothing be done in haste. Time is on our side. It would be unwise to decide on going to Baghdad till we can frame a policy for the future, and this we cannot do till we see clearer the general trend of events and the inward attitude of the Arabs. But whatever we do, let us not stand still. Let us move on to Qurna directly General Barrett gets his third brigade and is ready for the move."

As a result of the above the Secretary of State replied on the 27th to the Viceroy's private telegram of the 25th as follows : " We are not disposed to authorise an advance to Baghdad at present as there are grave international considerations involved, but as soon as General Barrett is ready to do so we sanction an advance to Qurna with a brigade or such portion of his force as may be necessary for the operation.* Presumably he will await the arrival of his third brigade, for Basra and the whole region from Qurna will have to be controlled by us in both a military and a political sense, and on such considerations it will probably be desirable to keep the bulk of the division at Basra, which should for the present be regarded as the headquarters."

This telegram was repeated on 3rd December to General Barrett, who had already decided of his own accord to occupy Qurna. The Viceroy, writing to Lord Crewe on 2nd December, said : " You did not give me time to send you our views on

---

* These " grave international considerations " were subsequently explained in answer to a query by the Viceroy as follows : " But setting aside difficulty of force necessary to occupy and hold Baghdad, because if we once were there it would be unfortunate to retire under menace of superior force, I consider that it is premature to take action, which appears to oblige consideration both by Allies and by Arabs of ultimate settlement regarding Mesopotamia and other parts of the Turkish Empire. It will be a most complicated matter, and we are not at present able to do more than assert, as we have, our paramount claims and powers at the head of the Persian Gulf."

Cox's proposal to advance to Baghdad . . . as a matter of fact after consultation with Beauchamp Duff I had arrived at the conclusion that it would be impossible to execute at present . . . ."

This conclusion was come to after the receipt of answers from General Barrett to the Chief of the General Staff's telegrams of 25th and 26th November, which more than confirmed the views held at Indian Army Headquarters that from a military point of view the proposal was unsound. General Barrett had reported that he had only three steamers and four iron lighters, whose capacity was two battalions with a week's supply, available for navigation above Qurna, and that armed vessels of not more than three and a half feet draught would be necessary in case a larger force had to be moved above Qurna ; the local Arabs were generally friendly, but the Muntafik Shaikh Ajaimi who had been helping the Turks had not come in ;* the local supplies and transport were only sufficient for the inhabitants ; a small force of the enemy with two guns was at Qurna and they were also holding Ezra's Tomb and Nasiriya ; and the enemy were well armed with good supplies of ammunition and were living on the country.

On 29th November, General Barrett telegraphed to India the following appreciation of the situation. It is, however, to be noted that this telegram never reached India, and it was not till 18th December that General Barrett realised it had not reached its destination and repeated it.† " It appears desirable, so that our position at Basra may be consolidated, to place at Qurna a fortified post and another five miles north of Zubair at Shaiba. These will be in addition to the Basra garrison. In order to destroy the Turkish gunboat *Marmariss* and any other armed vessels that may be sent to oppose our advance by the Turks, two or more river steamers of light draught carrying four-inch B.L. guns should form the naval force. Upon the decision as to whether you propose advancing to Baghdad or not, and upon the declaration of our permanent occupation of the country or otherwise, must depend the military strength of this garrison. The attitude of the Shaikh of Kuwait has always been satisfactory, and in our immediate neighbourhood the tribes are disposed to be most friendly. When once they are told that we have come to stay it may be

---

* See Sir P. Cox's telegram of 23rd November *ante*. Ajaimi remained on the Turkish side throughout the war.

† A check instituted between the Chief of the General Staff, India and General Barrett to obviate such miscarriage of telegrams did not, owing apparently to a clerical error, have the desired effect in this instance.

assumed with safety that their warm support may be reckoned on. Nothing has yet been heard from Ibn Saud.

"I do not favour an advance on Baghdad by land on account of the scarcity of water at camps and the difficulty of feeding transport animals. More suitable boats than I have now would be required to move sufficient forces by river. It is probable that the advance will be obstructed by boats sunk in the water-way, possibly by guns in position on land and perhaps in boats. I am, therefore, in favour of advancing in bounds. Firstly, to advance a small party, by shallow draught steamers and flats, to establish a fortified post and supply depôt at Qurna. Friendly relations could then be established with the neighbouring tribes round Qurna and our sphere of influence would be enlarged. Our next step up the river would be to Amara. As I make good our position it may be expected that the Arabs will gradually come over to us, seeing that we should be strong enough to beat any Turkish force likely to oppose us or likely to be sent from Baghdad by steamer against us. In this manner we should probably be able to defeat the enemy in detail and pave the way for the final advance to Baghdad. For this purpose the force under my command is, I consider, sufficient, and I therefore intend to occupy Qurna as soon as our stores have been got ashore, and other matters prepared. At present, pending further orders, I am only getting the mules off their ships and am leaving the camels on board."

One of the most noticeable features in the foregoing appreciation and correspondence is the constant repetition of the necessity for Arab co-operation. The British force in Mesopotamia being only of the strength of one division, the Arabs were as important a factor in 1914 as they had been in 1857, when Sir James Outram had taken a British expedition up the Shatt al Arab to operate against the Persians in Mohammerah. Then, as in 1914, the Arab inhabitants of the area consisted of warlike and turbulent predatory tribes, nominally Persian or Turkish subjects, but in reality disaffected to both governments. Then, also, as Outram pointed out, their natural tendencies prevented their remaining idle during the operations, and if he did not invite or accept their friendship he must be prepared to expect their hostility, i.e., his supplies and information would be cut off and his baggage and convoys plundered whenever opportunity offered. It was mainly to secure the Arabs on our side that on 27th November Sir P. Cox telegraphed to the Viceroy asking if he could make a public announcement that our occupation of Basra would be permanent. Without some such assurance it was becoming clear that the Arabs were not likely to commit themselves definitely, for fear of subsequent Turkish reprisals. After full consideration, the Government of India telegraphed on the 7th December to the Secretary of State recommending the proposal strongly. But the British Government were unable to agree, as they held that such a course would be considered by their Allies as a breach of faith. Having regard to the various political complications entailed by our alliances and by our relations with neutral Powers, there is no reason to question the correctness of this decision. Judging, however, by subsequent events, it would appear to afford a good illustration of how military operations are at times rendered more difficult through the exigencies of national policy.

On the 25th November the *Espiègle* and *Odin* reconnoitred to within three miles of Qurna, where they found a force of about five hundred Turks with two guns and the *Marmariss*. The Turkish guns and the *Marmariss* retired on being shelled, and the shallowness of the river, partially blocked about two miles below Qurna by a sunken lighter, prevented for the time being any further advance by our ships. The *Odin* also damaged her rudder in the shallow waters, and this impeded her manœuvring power. On the same day Sir P. Cox reported to India and the Secretary of State that the defeat of the Turks on the 17th had turned out to be much more decisive than was supposed, and that the Arab contingents who had fought there were much disgusted with their treatment by the Turks; also that he had received a report from an Englishman in Baghdad, dated the 12th, saying that the Arab element there was very well disposed towards us, and that there were only two thousand Turkish troops and six guns remaining there.

In the next few days the remainder of the 6th Division, including the 17th Brigade (1st Oxfordshire and Buckinghamshire Light Infantry, 22nd Punjabis, 103rd Mahratta Light Infantry and 119th Infantry), under Brigadier-General W. H. Dobbie, C.B., arrived in the river, giving General Barrett a total fighting force of one cavalry regiment, five batteries of field or mountain artillery, two sapper companies, and thirteen battalions of infantry.* A camp was opened at Maqil for part of the force; the passage past the obstruction near Dabba island was buoyed and regulated by watchmen; improved communications ashore were beginning to take shape; the

---

* For composition of Force " D " at this time, see Appendix III, p. 348.

troops got all their baggage and a great part of their stores ashore; and General Barrett had decided, as stated in his telegram of the 29th, to turn the remnants of the Turkish force from Basra out of Qurna and to hold this place and Shaiba* as the necessary outposts to secure his position at Basra.

On the 30th, orders were issued for a force under Lieutenant-Colonel Frazer, 110th Mahratta Light Infantry, to proceed up the river on 3rd December. The force consisted of two guns of the 82nd Battery R.F.A., half the 17th company Sappers and Miners, one company Norfolks, the 104th Rifles and 110th Mahratta Light Infantry. The navy would co-operate with two warships and two armed launches.† The force was to be transported in four river steamers,‡ towing lighters with supplies; and next day orders were issued for the field artillery to mount two 18-pounder Q.F. field guns on board each of two of the river steamers (*Mejidieh* and *Blosse Lynch*), which were to be placed under the orders of the Senior Naval Officer as soon as they had disembarked the troops they were carrying. General Barrett's information led him to believe that the Turks had about five hundred cavalry and five hundred infantry with four guns at Qurna and that the *Marmariss* was near Ezra's Tomb. His instructions to Lieutenant-Colonel Frazer were to land his force at a point selected by the Senior Naval Officer on the left bank of the river, a few miles below Qurna, and, in concert with the navy, to clear the left bank of the enemy up to and beyond Qurna; after this he had a free hand to cross the Tigris and attack Qurna, or to hold on to the left bank and await reinforcements, as he considered best.

By 5 a.m. on the 4th December the river steamers had joined the warships, which had preceded them up the river, and then disembarked the troops at the spot selected, which was on the northern bank of the Shwaiyib river at its junction with the Shatt al Arab. To cover the landing the *Espiègle* and *Lawrence* steamed a short way up the river, anchoring round the bend in sight of Qurna point;§ while the *Odin*, which— owing to her damaged rudder—could only manœuvre with difficulty, anchored with the armed launches off the landing-place. Two Turkish guns to the south-west of Muzaira'a village and at Qurna opened fire on the *Espiègle* and *Lawrence* to which both they and the *Odin* replied. The disembarkation

* On 4th December a half squadron 33rd Cavalry and a half battalion 20th Punjabis were sent to hold Shaiba " as an outpost to the west."
† Three launches actually took part, i.e., *Miner, Lewis Pelly,* and *Shaitan.*
‡ *Malamir, Mejidieh, Blosse Lynch,* and *Salimi.*
§ See Map 2.

of the troops was carried out quickly and without difficulty, and the whole force was ashore and beginning to advance by 8.30 a.m.

By this time the *Mejidieh* and *Blosse Lynch* had joined the warships and launches and had come into action with their 18-pounder guns, at three thousand yards, against the Turkish guns to the south-west of Muzaira'a. These were soon silenced.

The advance on shore was slow. In the absence of cavalry, reconnaissance had to be carried out by infantry scouts, and the mirage and lack of cover rendered their work difficult. The half battalion 110th, composing the advanced guard, advanced towards the east of Muzaira'a till the scouts reported that it was unoccupied, when they changed direction towards the village. It soon became clear that the enemy were occupying trenches along the plantations between Muzaira'a and the Shatt al Arab, and the advanced guard, reinforced on their left* by the remainder of the 110th, was ordered to attack them.

Muzaira'a proved after all to be held by the enemy ;† and the Norfolk company, and subsequently the half 17th Sapper company, were sent up to support that part of the 110th attacking the village. To these attacking troops Muzaira'a appeared, at first, through the mirage to be a substantial mud-bastioned and loopholed structure ; and it was only when they got close that they could see that the defences consisted of trenches inside the mud and reed huts. The artillery support from the ships and the 82nd Battery section on land was most effective. The guns on shore, without observation ladders,‡ had found observation difficult owing to the level plain and the mirage ; but the ships, who at 10 a.m. had advanced about one thousand yards upstream to get to closer ranges, had found observation easy owing to their higher outlook. By about 11 a.m. the Turks were driven out of Muzaira'a and the trenches to southward, the 110th taking over sixty prisoners and two 9-pounder field guns.

The British force was now covered by the plantations from the Turkish guns at Qurna, but a heavy rifle fire was still maintained by the Turkish infantry in the plantations, where they got excellent cover. A portion of the enemy's force to

---

* A flag was carried on the left of the firing line to indicate its position to the ships. The bearer of this flag, Lance-Naick Apa Bagwe, 110th Mahratta Light Infantry, was specially mentioned for gallantry throughout the attack in carrying this flag in the open under the heavy fire directed against him.

† Information from Turkish sources shows that Muzaira'a was held by about nine hundred infantry. See Appendix VI, p. 352.

‡ At this time artillery were not equipped with these.

the north of Muzaira'a was driven by the Norfolks through the plantations to the open desert to the northward, while the 110th and Sappers inclined to their left and advanced towards Qurna through the date plantations. Covered by their rearguards, most of the Turks appear to have crossed the river and to have established a strong firing line at Qurna.* The Tigris was here about two hundred yards wide, and all the native boats were alongside the right bank under the rifles of the enemy.

About 1 p.m. a company from the 104th, hitherto in reserve, were advanced through the plantations towards Qurna to clear up the situation, and about the same time the Senior Naval Officer, finding the water too shallow† for a further advance by his sloops, sent forward the launches *Miner*, *Shaitan*, and *Lewis Pelly*. The Turks allowed these to get within one thousand yards of Qurna and then opened such a heavy gun and rifle fire on them as to stop their further advance. The launches presented an admirable target, and it was only the indifferent shooting of the Turks that saved them from annihilation. The *Miner*, however, was holed by a shell in the engine-room at the water-line; and it was mainly owing to the gallant way in which the wounded engine-room staff stuck to their posts that the commander was able to save the launch from sinking in deep water in sight of the enemy and to ground her near the *Espiègle*. In the meantime, the remainder of the 104th had been pushed forward to join their advanced company opposite Qurna; and they endeavoured to establish a sufficient fire superiority over the Turkish line on the opposite bank to allow of an attempt at crossing. The 17th Sapper half company were also ordered across to the left flank to give any assistance they could to a crossing. This fire fight continued for about an hour and the Turks were forced by it to evacuate some of their positions; but it became clear that, even if boats were obtained, no crossing could be attempted without further artillery support. This could not be given either by the guns on the ships,‡ or by those on shore, who could not move through the plantations. The whole of the British infantry

---

* The records contain no mention of where this crossing was effected. General Barrett in his report says that owing to the thick plantations touch was lost with the Turks, thus enabling them to cross the river unmolested higher up.

† The deepest channel here for a length of over a mile was seven feet, rising at high tide to about twelve feet.

‡ The *Shaitan* and *Lewis Pelly* were still in action at short range, but they had only one 12-pounder and two 3-pounders between them and were still under a heavy Turkish fire.

were now lining the left bank of the Tigris, the Norfolk company being on the extreme right of the line, with about twenty to thirty Turks opposite them, holding what appeared to be the northern limit of the Turkish position.

Lieutenant-Colonel Frazer decided that he must wait for further reinforcements before attempting to cross, and, having no transport animals to bring up his supplies, etc., he ordered a retirement of the whole force to camp at the Shwaiyib landing point.* The retirement was covered by the fire of the ships, the sloops firing at such portion of Qurna as they could discern, and by the 104th, who had to withdraw under a heavy fire. The land force was all back in camp soon after 5 p.m., having killed many Turks and captured seventy-eight prisoners, including three officers, and two field guns. The British casualties had been one Indian officer and nineteen Indian other ranks killed, one British officer and three British and fifty Indian other ranks wounded. At 4 p.m. the launches—the conduct of whose crews had been gallant in the extreme and who had done very good work—were ordered to retire; and about 6.15 p.m., the other ships having come down-stream, the Turks opened a heavy gun fire on the *Espiègle* and the *Miner*. The shell hole in the *Miner* was plugged by about 6.30 p.m., when, the tide having risen, the *Espiègle*, which had been practically aground, was able once again to manœuvre, and she and the *Miner* reached camp about 7 p.m. The naval casualties had been one officer, one petty officer, one stoker and one native rating wounded.

General Barrett had been kept informed of events by wireless, and when he heard that Lieutenant-Colonel Frazer had decided not to attempt the crossing to Qurna until reinforced, he sent an order to General Fry, commanding 18th Brigade, to be prepared to take up reinforcements consisting of the remainder of the Norfolks, the 7th Rajputs and half the 120th.

The prisoners and wounded reached Basra the next morning. The Senior Naval Officer also went down to Basra and with Lieutenant-Colonel Frazer's staff officer explained the situation to General Barrett. On hearing their report, General Barrett decided to include four guns of the 76th Battery in General Fry's force, and issued instructions to General Fry that he was to reconnoitre the ground thoroughly before renewing the

* In his report on this action, General Barrett said: " I consider that Lieutenant-Colonel Frazer accomplished all that could have been expected of him, having regard to the limited number of troops at his command. The Turks had been reinforced before the action and were in greater strength than had been expected."

ARRIVAL OF REINFORCEMENTS

engagement, and to let General Barrett know if he required more troops.

Early on the 6th, General Fry reached Shwaiyib camp with his reinforcements and learnt that a reconnaissance on the previous day had proved that the Turks had re-occupied Muzaira'a. During the afternoon he held a conference with the Senior Naval Officer, at which Sir P. Cox was also present, on board the *Lawrence*, from whose decks a good view was obtained of the enemy's former position. He was seen to be entrenching at Muzaira'a. In the meantime a reconnaissance was being carried out by one and a half companies of infantry on land and by the *Shaitan* and *Lewis Pelly* up the river. General Fry's intelligence was to the effect that the Turks had been reinforced since the 4th, and that they had now about twelve hundred to fifteen hundred men* at Muzaira'a with six guns and another eight hundred men with four guns at Qurna. General Fry decided that it was essential to make an early attack on Muzaira'a and to clear the left bank of the enemy before they received any further reinforcements. The first day's operations were to be confined to these objectives and to preparing to cross the Tigris above and out of sight of Qurna. To allow of his force remaining in occupation of captured ground, General Fry asked General Barrett to send him a mountain battery and three hundred and twenty transport mules, to carry a minimum quantity of baggage and stores from Shwaiyib landing-place.

Just after 2 p.m., a force of the enemy, about five hundred strong with two guns, were seen advancing across the plain from Muzaira'a. Our outposts were reinforced and the *Espiègle* and *Lawrence* moved upstream; and they and some field artillery guns on shore opened fire, with the result that the enemy retired with some loss in about an hour's time. A further fruitless minor attack on our outposts at dusk preceded a peaceful night.

With the 30th Mountain Battery—which arrived at Shwaiyib about 7 a.m. on the 7th—General Fry's force amounted to a total strength of about three thousand seven hundred with twelve guns, in addition to the guns on the warships and launches and the four field artillery guns on the river steamers. His plan of attack was as follows : the Norfolks and the half battalion 120th were to attack Muzaira'a and the trenches south of it, while the 110th were to carry out a turning movement

---

* It was ascertained subsequently that they had a total on both banks of about three thousand.

against the north of Muzaira'a; the four guns of the 76th Battery were to support the attack on Muzaira'a, and the two guns of the 82nd Battery the attack by the rest of the line, while the 30th Mountain Battery, moving between the two, was to support either attack as required; and the 7th Rajputs and 104th Rifles were to be in reserve. Arrangements were made with the Senior Naval Officer for the close co-operation of the guns under his command.

On the 7th the force assembled north of the creek above the camp, and verbal instructions for the attack were issued to unit commanders about 10 a.m.* The advance across the open and bare sandy plain commenced about an hour later, when Muzaira'a village was just visible in the mirage. At 9.45 the ships had weighed and anchored about a mile up-stream, the *Espiègle* leading with the *Lawrence* astern, the *Odin* and launches to the south-eastward, and the *Mejidieh* and *Blosse Lynch* in positions on the port side of the *Espiègle*. As soon as the ships were seen† from Muzaira'a and Qurna the enemy's guns opened on them and the ships replied with lyddite, also shelling the trenches to aid the land attack.

The Norfolks advanced on the centre of Muzaira'a with the 120th on their left, and the 110th, who were to make the turning movement, echeloned back on their right; and the 7th and 104th were in reserve. About 11.30 the artillery came into action against Muzaira'a and the trenches to the south of it. The enemy had opened fire from their trenches at and near Muzaira'a and from two guns north of that village, but these guns were quickly silenced by the 76th Battery and were subsequently captured intact. The whole of the British artillery, both naval and military, made excellent practice against the enemy's position in spite of the mirage, which was found particularly bad by the guns on shore. The Turks, when they saw the direction of the British attack, tried to make a diversion by reinforcing their right and firing heavily from trenches hitherto silent. This caused several casualties to the 120th and the Norfolks, whose lines they enfiladed. The advance of the 120th was temporarily checked, but General Fry reinforced them with a company of the 7th and directed the 82nd Battery to support them, while asking for a similar

---

* There had been some delay owing to the exceptionally high tide in the creek.

† Although Qurna, except the point of the peninsula, could not be properly seen from the decks of the ships owing to the intervening palm-trees, the masts of the sloops could be seen from Qurna and afforded the Turks good ranging marks.

switch by the naval guns. The ships moved a little further up the stream—the *Espiègle* practically dragging through the mud—and afforded the desired co-operation. Thus supported, the 120th with the company of the 7th advanced and drove the Turks out with the bayonet.

In the meantime the Norfolks and the 110th had been advancing steadily, with their supporting artillery moving up to closer ranges; and just before 1 p.m. Muzaira'a was carried at the point of the bayonet, the enemy not waiting to receive the charge. Owing to the mirage it was only when our artillery had got within sixteen hundred yards of the enemy's position that they were able to see the enemy's trenches clearly.

The Turks had now evacuated the village and the trenches south of it and were retiring through the plantations in a northerly direction; but they were still holding some trenches to the northward of Muzaira'a. The 104th, who had closed up, were ordered to attack these, which were in part enfilading the line of the 110th. Passing through the 110th, who were in and near Muzaira'a, and supported by the 76th and 30th Batteries, they drove the Turks out under the vigorous fire of our artillery. The 104th pushed on in pursuit for about a mile and a half north of Muzaira'a, the 76th Battery well up on their right and the 30th and 82nd Batteries following up on their left rear. The Turks could be seen by these units in general retreat northwards on both banks of the Tigris, and our artillery shelled them vigorously. At this stage the 76th Battery suddenly found itself enfiladed by two Turkish guns some four thousand eight hundred yards to the east-north-east. The 76th and 30th both opened fire on these guns at once and silenced them in a few minutes, their teams being seen to gallop away and abandon the guns. The British, however, had no cavalry, and their main force had pushed on into the plantations facing Qurna. It was too far for the batteries and 104th to advance unsupported and capture these two guns, and they were removed by the enemy after dark.

The 104th were meanwhile reconnoitring the left bank of the Tigris to the north of the plantations, and by 4 p.m. a gun of the 82nd Battery was brought into action here and enfiladed the Turkish line at Qurna.

The Norfolks and 110th, reforming after the capture of Muzaira'a, pushed on into the plantations and reached the river-bank, where they encountered a heavy fire from Qurna. The British firing line on the river-bank now comprised the 120th (half battalion), 7th (one company), Norfolks, and 110th, and their advance in this direction appears to have somewhat diverted the Turkish fire from the ships. For, owing to the fire against them slackening, the ships managed to get a little further upstream, the *Mejidieh* amd *Blosse Lynch** getting to within two thousand yards of Qurna. The Senior Naval Officer was also able to send an officer to locate and sound round the lighter sunk in the channel, and to send forward the *Miner*, *Shaitan* and *Lewis Pelly* to help the left flank of the troops in the plantations. The launches were fired on heavily from Qurna, and the *Shaitan* received a direct hit on the bridge, killing the commander (Lieutenant-Commander Elkes, R.N.R.), wounding the petty officer at the wheel, and stunning the civilian master. The steering gear was smashed, and Petty Officer Vale saved the launch by steering her out of action by her twin-screws. The other two launches remained in action under heavy fire till 3.45, when Captain Hayes-Sadler considered it advisable to recall them. They had done very good work and were both riddled by bullets.

The fighting continued till dusk, when the troops were withdrawn to the camp by Muzaira'a. This was hidden from Qurna by the plantation, and though the enemy fired a few shells at it early in the night no damage was done. The artillery duel between Qurna and the ships was carried on till dark, and when the moon rose the enemy fired a few shells. But the night was generally uneventful. The enemy, whose numbers on the left bank had amounted to about two thousand, had lost some two hundred killed, one hundred and thirty prisoners, several hundred wounded, and three field guns. The British casualties were ten killed and one hundred and eighteen wounded, including five British and three Indian officers: that they were not more was due mainly to the close support and co-operation of the artillery, naval and military.

General Fry had carried out his first day's operations successfully and was prepared to renew the fight next day to effect the crossing of the Tigris. That this might be easier than he had anticipated was indicated by the intelligence that came in during the night. Fifteen hundred of the enemy were said to have retreated northwards in steamers, leaving about eight hundred men and four guns in Qurna.

Early on the 8th, part of the force moved out to reconnoitre and prepare for the crossing. The 104th reconnoitred for

---

* These river steamers could pass the obstruction as they drew less water than the sloops.

ATTACK ON QURNA

some four miles upstream on the left bank to cover that flank from surprise; the 7th and 120th moved into the plantations opposite Qurna to stop any attempt by the enemy at crossing the river; and a sapper officer was sent back to the landing-place at Shwaiyib to bring up the stores required for a flying bridge. At 8.30 a.m. the ships had not been fired on, and Captain Hayes-Sadler ordered the *Lewis Pelly* up towards Qurna to ascertain if the Turks were still in occupation. She was allowed to get within about four hundred yards of Qurna, when a heavy gun and rifle fire was opened on her and she was ordered back. About the same time the camp at Muzaira'a was shelled from Qurna, and soon afterwards the force in camp moved out to take up a position of readiness on the edge of the plantations north-west of Muzaira'a. It had been decided to construct a flying bridge a short distance north of the plantations on the left bank. A gun of the 82nd Battery came into action here against Qurna, in the position it had been in the previous evening, and between 10 and 11 a.m. the half (17th) Sapper Company arrived to construct the bridge.

By this time the fire of the ship's guns had neutralised the Turkish gun fire from Qurna, and a navigating officer from the *Espiègle*, after sounding and buoying the outer side of the lighter sunk in the channel, had reported that there was just room for the *Espiègle* to pass it. She moved upstream, accordingly, about 11 a.m., scraping through the mud, with the *Lewis Pelly* sounding ahead, and anchored within about two thousand yards range of Qurna. All the ships then opened fire on such parts of Qurna as they could discern through the trees, the 7th and 120th Companies also keeping up a fire from the plantations.

In the meantime the 104th reconnoitring upstream had found the usual *débris* of a flight but no enemy, and they induced two *mahailas* to stop and come into the left bank about three miles north and out of sight of Qurna. The officer commanding the 104th sent word to General Fry that he had done so, and suggested that he should take his battalion across the river here and move down the right bank to assist the crossing of the 110th. General Fry approved of this suggestion, and sent up four guns of the 76th Battery and half the Norfolks to take the place of the 104th, and to support their crossing.

About 11.30, at the site selected for the flying bridge, Havildar Ghulam Nabi, Lance-Naick Nur Dad and Sapper Ghulam Haidar, all of the 17th Company, Sappers and

Miners, very gallantly swam across the Tigris with a log line. The river was about one hundred and thirty yards wide with a strong current, but fortunately the Turks did not notice them and they succeeded in reaching the right bank. Lieutenant Campbell and two other men of the same unit followed them, and hauling over a wire cable they fixed the running tackle for a flying bridge, attaching a *mahaila* secured with the assistance of some friendly Arabs. By this time some of the Turks, however, had seen what was happening and had begun to fire on them from some *mahailas* downstream. The first party of the 110th, consisting of about seventy men under Lieutenant-Colonel Frazer, got across about 1.20 p.m., and the rest of the battalion followed in successive trips. In addition to the gun of the 82nd Battery north of the plantations, the 30th Mountain Battery were entrenched in a position a little further north to support the crossing. It was not found necessary, however, to utilise their fire. The Turks in Qurna appeared to be unaware of the significance of the movement upstream, and the sappers and the 110th were only subjected to moderate rifle and shell fire while making the crossing.

The first party of the 104th crossed, it is said, just after Colonel Frazer's party, but the whole battalion were on the right bank, about one and a half miles above the flying bridge, before 2 p.m. They then moved southward, and came into touch with part of the 110th, who were also advancing south. Pushing on together they found themselves opposed by the enemy holding a line of towers and trenches at right angles to the river. Two mountain guns of the 30th Battery, without mules, had meanwhile crossed by the flying bridge; but Lieutenant-Colonel Frazer, meeting with this opposition, decided that it was too late in the day to start an action which seemed likely to entangle his force in the thick plantations and in the lanes of Qurna in the dark.* At 3.30 p.m., he ordered the force under him on the right bank to draw out of the fight and to retire to bivouac near the flying bridge. He was then unaware that Lieutenant-Colonel Britten of the 110th, with a company, had succeeded in getting round the enemy's left and occupying some of their towers. Lieutenant-Colonel Britten subsequently received the order to retire, and, seeing no signs of any reinforcements, withdrew his detachment also to the bivouac.

On the left bank, General Fry, on receiving the report of

---

* Sunset was about 4.55 p.m.

Lieutenant-Colonel Frazer's withdrawal, ordered back his force to the camp near Muzaira'a, leaving the Norfolks on the riverbank by the flying bridge to support the force opposite. At the cost of some twenty-three rank and file wounded, he had established a footing across the river and prepared to make it good and attack Qurna the next morning. Firing continued between Qurna and the ships till dark, when it died down and was not renewed.

At 11.40 p.m. the warships sighted a small steamer coming down the river, and it was found that she had a deputation of three Turkish military officers on board who had come to discuss terms of surrender. These consisted of the chief staff officer to Subhi Bey, *Vali* of Basra, who was commanding at Qurna, and two other Turkish military officers. The Senior Naval Officer received them and endeavoured without success to communicate with General Fry, and at 3.30 a.m. he made provisional arrangements for an unconditional surrender, which after some demur the Turkish officers agreed to. They returned to Qurna with instructions to return to the *Espiègle* at 8.30 a.m., to meet General Fry; and a message was sent to General Fry at Muzaira'a, acquainting him with the arrangement made.

At 8.30 a.m., on the 9th, General Fry met the deputation on board the *Espiègle* and arranged for the surrender; and all movement of troops was stopped. About 10 a.m. the *Espiègle*, taking advantage of the high tide, pushed through the mud, and with the *Lawrence*, river steamers and launches moved slowly up the river. Turning into the Tigris, they anchored off Qurna just before 11 a.m. The close co-operation of the Royal Navy had been invaluable and was acknowledged fully by General Fry in his despatch. The two river steamers belonging to Messrs. Lynch had been particularly useful. They had transported troops, been used as gunboats, and had been frequently under fire. The Admiralty notified the civilian masters of these steamers of their high appreciation and thanks by special letters.

At 1.30 p.m., General Fry with Captain Hayes-Sadler and Sir P. Cox received the *Vali's* surrender on shore. Meanwhile the 104th and 110th had moved on Qurna, surrounding the town with piquets and also the surrendering Turkish force.

The Turkish prisoners numbered 45 officers and 989 men, belonging mainly to the 28th Artillery regiment, the 26th and *Murattab* Infantry regiments and to the Basra gendarmerie, and the captures included two field and two mountain guns.

A British Maxim gun, which had been lost on the 4th, was also recovered. It transpired that the *Marmariss* had been present on the 7th, but had been driven up the river by the fire of the British artillery; also on the same day a Turkish armed motor patrol boat had been sunk off Qurna by the indirect fire from the ships.*

Qurna, according to a popular Mahomedan fiction the site of the Garden of Eden, was a sad disappointment to our men. A collection of filthy lanes and mud and reed hovels, with a few brick houses, barracks, and a custom house, it had been left at far from its best by the Turks. A disgusted soldier was heard to remark that it would have required no angel with a flaming sword to keep him out of Qurna, and subsequently during the British occupation there was much sarcasm expended on its Eden-like qualities. It was, however, a position of considerable strategic importance, and although it may be said that it was rather far from Basra to station a detached post—having regard to the size of General Barrett's force—it was the best advanced position we could have held. It commanded the Turks main line of approach via the Tigris, and a British force there threatened the Turkish communications between the lower Tigris and the district round Nasiriya. The difficulties of navigation of the lower Euphrates, of the Shwaiyib river, and of the various creeks in the neighbourhood were not altogether a disadvantage. The Arabs were the only people who could move about at all freely in their native boats†; and although neither we nor the Turks could rely with any certainty on their friendly co-operation, we were better provided in the way of river steamers than the Turks, who were beginning to experience difficulty in obtaining fuel for their steamers in lower Mesopotamia.

In the spring and till the floods subside, the whole country for some distance to the north of Qurna is under water; and to the east and west lie extensive marshes. Qurna itself was only kept from inundation by protective earthworks, and for some time after its capture much work and effort was expended in rendering it fit for occupation and in securing it from the coming floods. Garrisoned by two squadrons of cavalry, two batteries of artillery, a company of sappers and miners, and an infantry brigade, with a proportion of medical units and

---

* For some remarks by a Turkish writer upon the capture of Qurna, see Appendix VI, p. 352.

† The *mashuf* was the boat in general use in this area—smaller than the *bellum*, it is constructed of thin laths or reeds covered with bitumen. It is heavy and rather unwieldy, especially in a high wind.

QURNA.

mule* transport, its occupation may be said to have closed the first phase of the operations.

This first phase had been attended with gratifying success. The 6th Indian Division, owing much to the cordial co-operation of the Royal Navy, had decisively defeated the local Turkish force and had secured Basra and the Shatt al Arab. Our naval position in the Persian Gulf was rendered secure, and the Arabs on the littoral of the Persian Gulf had been given an example of British power. Much of the success had been due to the rapidity with which the British operations had followed the declaration of hostilities. The Turks had been surprised, and, unable to reinforce their garrisons in Iraq in time or in force, they had been crushed in detail.

Unless the Turks were prepared to acquiesce in the British occupation of the head of the Gulf, they must transfer relatively a larger proportion of troops from a more important theatre of war to restore the position—a lengthy operation requiring considerable effort. The only alternative was to raise the local Arabs against the invaders. To the British, at any rate, there seemed small likelihood of this. Uncertain factor as the Arabs were, all indications seemed to point the other way, namely, to the Arabs, supported by the British, rising against the Turk.

Neutral Persian territory, the Shaikh of Mohammerah and the Arabs appeared to safeguard the oil-tanks and pipe-line. For the time being, therefore, there seemed little chance of the British position being seriously disputed.

---

* General Barrett had already arranged to return to India all but three hundred of the camels brought from there, as he found it difficult to obtain grazing for them, and it appeared improbable that his force would have to make any large movements by land.

CHAPTER VIII.

COMMENCEMENT OF THE TURKISH COUNTER-OFFENSIVE.

THE capture of Qurna achieved two immediate results. In the first place, the neighbouring Arabs became more friendly; during the fighting they had preserved a neutral attitude, but now many of their Shaikhs came forward and expressed their intention of adhering to our side. Secondly, the information gleaned from the captured prisoners cleared up the uncertainty regarding Turkish numbers and dispositions. Timely and adequate intelligence of the Turkish dispositions and numbers had been difficult to obtain. The nature of the country and the lack of aeroplanes limited military reconnaissance; and the news brought in by Arabs could not be deemed altogether reliable.

It was now ascertained that, after their defeat at Muzaira'a, the main Turkish force had retired to Amara; most of the remnants of the 38th Division from Basra were on the Euphrates about Suq ash Shuyukh and Nasiriya; and Ajaimi with some of his Muntafik following were also about Nasiriya. There were only five reserve and gendarmerie battalions of infantry with six hundred cavalry and a few guns at Baghdad; but reinforcements were on their way there. These were said to consist of four infantry battalions and some guns from Constantinople, as well as two infantry battalions, a field battery, and some Kurdish tribesmen from Mosul.

On receipt of this news at the India Office, the Secretary of State asked the Government of India if it was practicable to send a force to eject the Turks and to occupy Nasiriya. Such occupation, Lord Crewe observed, would block the approaches from Baghdad either by the Euphrates or by the Shatt al Hai and would protect the Muntafik Arabs from Turkish interference. He understood that Suq ash Shuyukh could be reached by water from Qurna in two to three days, and he emphasised the advantages of an occupation of the triangle Basra-Qurna-Nasiriya.

In the meantime, General Barrett had been informed that there was as yet no intention of ordering his force to advance on Baghdad. He replied that, if it had been decided definitely that no further advance was to be made, the occupation of Qurna was sufficient for the defence of the delta to this point. If, however, a further advance was a possible contingency, he advocated an early occupation of Amara in order to retain the adherence of the Arabs. He believed that if this advance were to take place soon, the Arabs would desert the Turks; but that if it were delayed and the Turks were thus enabled to re-establish themselves,* our occupation of Amara would be much more difficult. He proposed to advance on Amara by stages, consolidating as he went, and giving the local Arabs time to declare their attitude.

This proposal appeared to the Commander-in-Chief in India to have much to recommend it. But the India Office telegram had crossed the one from General Barrett, who was therefore asked to weigh the two proposals and to telegraph his opinion. At the same time, Sir Beauchamp Duff pointed out to General Barrett that no more troops could be sent to Mesopotamia. General Barrett's reply of 18th December admitted the advantages of an occupation of Nasiriya. In this connection, he said, the chief factor to be considered was the attitude of the Muntafik. If care were taken not to alarm them by premature action, there was some hope of obtaining Muntafik concurrence in the location of a British post at Nasiriya. General Barrett inferred, however, that it would require the occupation by us of Baghdad to ensure them against Turkish interference†; and their belief in our power and willingness to effect this would be the predominant factor in determining their attitude towards us. For this reason he considered it more politic to advance first to Amara.

He had soon, however, reason to change his opinion. On the 23rd, news reached him from the G.O.C. Egypt that the IVth Turkish Army Corps was reported to be moving from Syria either on Aqaba (Red Sea) or on Basra. Consisting of 36,000 men and a considerable number of guns, this force was said to be accompanied by many German officers and to be specially equipped with boats in sections and motor transport. This equipment was quite compatible with a movement down

---

* A few days earlier, a telegram from G.O.C. Egypt stated that Turkish troops from Damascus were reported as probably moving towards Baghdad.
† The area occupied by the Muntafik extended for some distance to the north and north-west of Nasiriya.

the Euphrates; and this idea seemed to be further confirmed by the report that the force was bringing with it many rifles and much ammunition, as these would be required to arm the Arabs.* General Barrett at once telegraphed to India that a move to Amara might lock up troops required to meet a Turkish advance down the Euphrates. He therefore, now recommended that an advance to Suq ash Shuyukh and Nasiriya should be undertaken first. Although the attitude of Ajaimi was uncertain, another of the Muntafik notables had assured Sir P. Cox that the tribe would be friendly to us if we would protect them permanently from the Turks. The occupation of Nasiriya would go some way towards accomplishing this. General Barrett also believed that Ibn Saud was moving north in the direction of Nasiriya, and it was hoped to arrange for his co-operation. By holding Qurna and Nasiriya we should be favourably situated to meet the Turks either on the Tigris or on the Euphrates.

In the next few days, the news that reinforcements were on their way to Baghdad from Constantinople was confirmed. It was also reported from several sources that the XIIth (Mosul) Army Corps had left Aleppo for Baghdad. This consisted of the 35th and 36th Divisions, composed mainly of Arabs and Kurds, with a nominal strength of 25,000, with seventy-two old-pattern guns. Large numbers, however, had deserted, and it was said that the corps had been found unfit to fight in Syria.

The Government of India came to the conclusion that the situation was still too indefinite to allow of a decision. They wished to hear more of Ibn Saud and of conditions on the Euphrates. Lord Crewe agreed that it was necessary to await developments, and General Barrett was told on the 4th January not to advance on Amara or Nasiriya without previous reference to India.

Towards the end of December the Turkish force from Amara under Djavid Pasha moved south to Ezra's Tomb, twenty-two miles from Qurna, near which place the Arabs were daily becoming more aggressive. The British garrison of Qurna had

---

* It was subsequently ascertained that the IVth Turkish Army Corps was not moving on Basra. But this report exemplifies one of our greatest difficulties. Forces in Asia Minor and Syria were constantly reported on the move to Mesopotamia. But transportation was slow, and there were many possible points of diversion to other theatres of operations. News took time to come through and was often unreliable. Consequently, further news of any given force was frequently not received for weeks. In the meantime a force commander could only hope that the first confirmation of reported reinforcements would not be their arrival opposite our troops in the field.

been reduced soon after its capture to a brigade of infantry, two squadrons of cavalry, two batteries of artillery, and a company of sappers ; but to meet the possibility of a Turkish attack, General Barrett now reinforced it by half a pioneer and two infantry battalions.

On the 1st January, a small force under General Dobbie moved up the right bank of the Tigris to attack a Turkish force reported to be at Muzaibila,* with the *Espiègle* and the *Blosse Lynch*, on board which two field artillery 18-pounders were mounted, co-operating on their right. After some slight opposition from Arabs, the advanced guard reached Muzaibila, whence a Turkish camp at Sakrikiya, three to four miles to the north, could be seen. From the size of the camp, the Turkish force was estimated as about 1,200 strong.

On observing the British at Muzaibila, the Turks moved out and occupied a line of trenches on both banks of the Tigris about four thousand yards off. Two unfordable creeks intervened ; and an obstruction in the fairway of the Tigris (caused by two lighters sunk by the Turks just below Ruta) prevented the British steamers advancing to within gun range of the Turkish position. To the west there were extensive marshes, and for some days the water in these had been rising steadily and had encroached considerably towards the Tigris. In consequence, after a personal reconnaissance, General Dobbie decided that so long as the obstruction in the river stopped the steamers no attack was practicable ; and as he thought no useful purpose could be effected by his force remaining in observation of the Turks he ordered a retirement to Qurna. This the enemy made no attempt to interfere with.

About this period, some alterations in the composition of the British forces in Mesopotamia had occurred or had been arranged for. On the 13th December, Captain Hayes-Sadler, R.N., had left for Egypt in H.M.S. *Ocean* and had handed over the duties of Senior Naval Officer to Commander W. Nunn, R.N., of H.M.S. *Espiègle* ; H.M.S. *Odin* had left for Bombay to have her rudder repaired ; General Barrett had been obliged to send back to India all but three hundred of his transport camels owing to the difficulty of obtaining grazing for them ; a company of Sirmur sappers and miners (Imperial Service troops), a survey section, and a searchlight section (manned by Calcutta Volunteer Engineers) had joined the force ; and the 104th Heavy Battery R.G.A. (four bullock-drawn 4-inch guns) were under orders to leave India for Basra in the middle of January.

* See Map 2.

General Barrett had asked for seven additional river steamers and four gunboats,* all of light draught, to meet the possible contingency of an advance on Amara or Nasiriya. The Indian authorities were arranging to get the river steamers in India and had asked the India Office to apply to the Admiralty for the gunboats. On 9th January, General Barrett felt compelled to apply again for aeroplanes. The continued rising of the water round Qurna, the obstruction in the Tigris near Ruta, and the difficulties of navigating the Hammar lake limited his powers of reconnaissance to a dangerous extent; while the increasing hostility of the Arabs rendered it at the same time more difficult and more necessary to obtain adequate news of the Turkish reinforcements now so constantly being reported. India, however, had sent her few aviators and machines to Egypt at the request of the War Office, and the War Office were unable to spare any for Force " D."

Early in January it became known that the Turkish force at Ezra's Tomb had been reinforced. The reinforcements, consisting of several battalions and guns, were under the command of Sulaiman Askari Bey, a highly educated and keen soldier; and his guns were reported to be handled by German officers. At the same time it was reported that Ajaimi was collecting tribesmen at Nasiriya, where a prominent Muntafik *Sayad* was preaching *Jahad*. It was said that a combined Turco-Arab force would advance from Nasiriya and attack Basra.

Reconnaissances from Qurna on the 5th and 6th January showed that there was little danger of the Turks being able to outflank the Qurna position by water. The channel of the Shwaiyib river for ten miles from its mouth was reconnoitred and found to be too narrow for navigation by even small steamers; and on the other flank it was found that, as had been reported, the Hammar lake was impassable by steamers drawing over three feet of water.

On the 6th, owing to reports of a hostile gathering at Allawi, twenty-five miles west of Shaiba, a small force was despatched to disperse it. In this they were completely successful; they met with little opposition and encountered no signs of an advance by a large force.

---

* The river steamers were to allow for the advance of a force consisting of one squadron of cavalry, one battery of artillery, one company of sappers and one brigade of infantry, with five hundred mules. The draught of the river steamers was to be not more than four and a half feet and the Admiralty were asked to provide gunboats of a draught not exceeding four feet.

The difficulties of organising any really formidable Arab force and of advancing with it across the desert were obviously considerable. Consequently, General Barrett came to the conclusion that an attack on Basra from the west was a less immediate danger than an advance by Sulaiman Askari against Qurna. Accordingly, on the 10th January, he issued orders for the force at Qurna to be reinforced. It was now to be made up to two squadrons of cavalry, four batteries of field and mountain artillery, two companies of sappers and miners, and two brigades of infantry, with half a battalion of pioneers. In the meantime, the waters had risen and were still rising, and the ground to the north of Qurna on the right bank of the Tigris was becoming unfit for military operations. On the left bank, to the north of Muzaira'a, the water had not encroached to the same extent; and it was consequently decided to construct a defensive position on this bank to be held in addition to Qurna. The rain and inundations, besides causing much additional work, entailed great discomfort to the troops, whose tents were frequently flooded.

At this period, news was received of the decisive defeat of the Turks by the Russian army in the Caucasus. The effect of this in Mesopotamia was likely to be considerable, as it seemed probable that some of the Turkish reinforcements recently reported as *en route* to Mesopotamia would now be diverted to Armenia or Kurdistan. On the other hand, a Turco-Kurdish force was advancing through Persian territory on Tabriz, which the Russians evacuated. This re-acted on the situation in Persia where, since the middle of November, the Persian Government had been protesting to the Russian Legation and the Turkish Embassy against their respective troops' violation of Persian neutrality. For some time previous to the war, it had been obvious that the positions on the Persian frontier occupied by Russian and Turkish troops would lead to some such violation in the event of hostilities. But Persia was powerless to prevent it. Germany exploited the situation and utilised the overt hatred of Russia in Persia to the disadvantage of the British. If a second large independent Moslem State could be brought into the war on the side of Germany, the effect in Afghanistan and India would be considerable. By the end of December our Minister in Tehran reported that the country was becoming restless under the untiring hostile propaganda; and by the end of January, news was received from the same source that Swedish officers of the Persian gendarmerie were participating in the intrigues against us.

The general indications of an augmentation of the Turkish army in Mesopotamia, which would expose General Barrett's force to attack by superior numbers, led to the question of reinforcing Force " D." On the 5th January, Sir Beauchamp Duff, in a private telegram to Lord Kitchener, expressed his inability to send to France three more Indian battalions which had been asked for. He said, " As there are signs of possible attack on both Basra and Aden in force, I am becoming anxious about them, and if a necessity to support them arises, I do not know from where to take extra troops." He pointed out at the same time how the call for drafts to replace casualties in France had exceeded greatly anything that had been thought of in India before.* The Indian reservists were turning out disappointing, Sir Beauchamp Duff said, and the organisation in India was unequal to the demands made on it.

India had at this period many anxieties. On the North-West Frontier, two big raids, based on the idea that there were no troops left in India, had taken place, and efforts were being made to start a *Jahad*. Although the attitude of the Amir of Afghanistan was reassuring, it was felt that he might be unable to restrain the extremists, who regretted openly his refusal to comply with the Turkish request for assistance. The trans-frontier Pathans in the Indian army were showing reluctance to fight the Turks, and their attitude towards a *Jahad* was doubtful. Internally there were serious symptoms of unrest, especially in the Punjab—our main recruiting area; and military precautions had to be taken. All Indian units in India were 25 per cent. below their establishment in British officers, and suitable candidates were displaying a disconcerting preference for service with their own race in Europe. The recently arrived Territorials had to be re-armed and partially re-clothed and re-equipped, while their training was still backward.

Thus it was felt very undesirable either to weaken the frontier or to make further reductions in the internal garrison. A way, however, was found. The Nepal Durbar offered a contingent of Gurkhas for service in India, and this was accepted gratefully. Even though they would require several months training and complete re-armament and re-equipment, they provided a valuable reserve.† Further, the situation in the Pacific

---

* He quoted three cases where the drafts sent so far, i.e., after two months fighting, had amounted to 62, 74 and 110 per cent. of the field service strength of the battalions.

† Subsequently they proved their fighting worth on several occasions on the North-West Frontier.

appeared to allow of a reduction of the Indian garrison in Hong Kong, and it was decided to ask the War Office to let any troops that could be spared return to India.* In consequence of these potential reserves, the Viceroy agreed, on the 15th January, to a brigade of infantry being mobilized in readiness to proceed to Basra. In a letter to Sir T. Holderness at the India Office of the 20th January, Lord Hardinge stated how unwillingly he had done this in view of the situation in India, on the frontier, and in Persia. If Persia joined the Turks in the *Jahad* it would be very difficult, the Viceroy said, for the Amir to keep the Afghans quiet.

On the 15th January, Sir Percy Cox telegraphed that the political situation in Mesopotamia had taken an unsatisfactory turn. This he attributed to our standing fast at Qurna instead of advancing to Nasiriya and Amara as expected and desired by the local Shaikhs. In consequence some of them, abandoning their overtures to us, had joined the Turks, who were thus able to utilise the factor of *Jahad* with more effect. At Basra, Amara, and in Arabistan this factor was producing some results and the Shaikh of Mohammerah was becoming perturbed. Sir P. Cox gathered that H.M. Government contemplated Qurna as the final limit of our advance. He urged strongly, on political, administrative and commercial grounds, a reconsideration of any such idea in favour of an advance to Nasiriya and Amara. Our occupation of these two places would not in any way oblige us, he said, to advance farther.

The Government of India gave this telegram careful consideration. Sir Beauchamp Duff considered that Force " D " was too weak and lacked sufficient river craft to carry out an advance to Nasiriya or Amara and to hold the line of communication. Sir Percy Cox was, therefore, informed by the Government of India that our policy for the time being was to consolidate our positions at Basra and Qurna and to await developments; that it had not been finally determined that Qurna should be the limit of our advance; but that any further advance was not yet desirable. These instructions received the approval of the Secretary of State.

On the 16th, Sir P. Cox received a letter from Major Shakespear, dated the 4th, reporting his arrival at the headquarters of Ibn Saud† and describing the situation there. Ibn Saud had some time previously assured Sir P. Cox that he was

---
* In this way a mountain battery and two Indian infantry battalions were added to the strength in India two months later.
† Amir Abdul Aziz ibn Abdur Rahman ibn Faisal (ibn Saud).

entirely on the side of the British and that one of his chief desires was the liberation of Basra and its severance from Turkey. There was no reason to doubt this assurance, which was further confirmed by Major Shakespear's report. He wrote that there had been unaffected rejoicing in Central Arabia at our capture of Basra and Qurna; and our proclamation regarding the immunity of the Moslem Holy Places had been much appreciated. The *Jahad* was receiving no support in Southern Nejd.

Ibn Saud had explained the original Turkish plan for utilizing against us the tribes of Arabia; i.e., a reconciliation was to be effected between the two rival Emirs, Ibn Saud and Ibn Rashid; Ibn Saud was then to defend Basra and oppose a British advance; Ibn Rashid and the Anaiza* were to join the western tribes in an advance on the Sinai Peninsula and Egypt; and the Sharif of Mecca, the Imam Yahya and Sayad Idrisi were to defend the Yemen, the Hejaz, and the Holy Places. According to Ibn Saud, his intervention had caused this plan to miscarry. The Sharif of Mecca, the Anaiza and Ibn Saud had decided to hold together, and the Anaiza had promised to co-operate with Ibn Saud against Ibn Rashid. Ibn Saud explained, however, that he had been obliged to temporise with the Turks. He had expressed to them his inability to be reconciled with Ibn Rashid and the consequent necessity of his remaining to protect Nejd until Ibn Rashid had advanced against Egypt. Major Shakespear said that at the time he wrote, Ibn Saud was on his way to attack Ibn Rashid, whom he hoped to defeat by the end of January. Ibn Saud asked for a definite treaty with Great Britain, as his present indefinite position was embarrassing. Unless such a treaty could be arranged, there was always the danger that force of circumstances might oblige him to take action apparently favourable to Turkey. This report was satisfactory so far as it went; but, having regard to the distances and forces involved, it showed that we could not expect any help from Ibn Saud in the region of the Euphrates for some time to come.

By the 18th January, when General Barrett visited Qurna, the Turkish and Arab activity in that vicinity had much increased. The Turkish outposts were occupying a line of sand-hills about two miles south of Ruta creek† and they were making night

---

* The Anaiza form what is probably the largest group of Arab tribes. Occupying the desert between the Euphrates and Syria, they are at feud with the Shammar, the dominant Arab group in Upper Mesopotamia.

† See Map 2.

reconnaissances right up to our trenches ; and large numbers of Arabs were engaged in sniping and raiding by night and in guerilla hostilities by day. For some time most of our troops had been restricted to a defensive rôle ; and although our cavalry reconnoitred the sand-hills daily (the limit of the dry ground), part of the garrison appeared to General Barrett to be getting rather stale from their inactivity in the monotonous surroundings.

Our cavalry had been unable to penetrate the marshes between the sand-hills and the Ruta creek, where the Turks appeared to hold a strong position. Their numbers and dispositions could only be guessed at, and it appeared possible that the marshes might prove passable for infantry. A Turkish attack did not, however, appear probable in the near future, as their activity indicated rather an intention of gradually pushing their trenches and gun positions farther south. But should heavy guns (reported as coming to them) arrive, a slow methodical Turkish advance was likely to limit the sphere of utility of our naval sloops, since any such advance southward would probably synchronise with the placing of further obstructions in the Tigris. Ultimately, moreover, such an advance would bring Qurna within range of their guns, when we should be obliged to attack them. Rather than lose the initiative in such a way, General Barrett considered it better to attempt to stop their progress at once, and at a safe distance from Qurna ; since, later on, if reports were true, the floods would render such a Turkish advance difficult, if not impossible. On the other hand, General Barrett had insufficient forces to hold Ruta in addition to Qurna. So that, whatever action might be determined on, an ultimate retirement to Qurna would be necessary.

General Barrett came to the conclusion that a strong demonstration should give satisfactory results. It would show the Turks and Arabs that we were willing and able to adopt offensive tactics when we felt inclined to do so ; it would revivify our own troops ; and it would clear up the doubts regarding the Turkish position and the nature of the country beyond the sand-hills. General Barrett arranged accordingly for an attack on the sand-hills to be undertaken on the 20th. The force employed consisted of two squadrons 33rd Cavalry, 63rd Battery R.F.A., two sections 76th R.F.A. and 30th Mountain Batteries, 17th Company of Sappers and Miners, 17th Infantry Brigade, the Norfolks, and half 7th Rajputs. The *Espiègle, Miner* and *Mejidieh* (two R.F.A. 18-pounders) were to co-operate from the Tigris.

The advanced guard left Muzaira'a at 6 a.m. and about an hour later came under fire from the enemy's outposts on the sand-hills, when the cavalry withdrew to the flanks. The leading line of infantry (1st Oxfordshire and Buckinghamshire Light Infantry and 103rd Mahrattas) occupied the sand-hills with but little opposition and came under fire from six Turkish guns on the north of Ruta creek and from trenches on its banks. The *Espiègle* and *Mejidieh* came into action against the Turkish guns and had practically silenced them by 10.45 a.m. The *Miner* anchored off Abu Aran village, and throughout the fight successfully engaged parties of Arabs and cavalry on the right bank of the Tigris. In the meantime, the Oxfords and the 103rd had been ordered to advance from the sand-hills. They were to test the practicability of the marshes, to locate the enemy's trenches, and to ascertain their dispositions. As, however, General Barrett had previously informed the force that he had no intention of crossing the creek and had made no arrangements for doing so, these units were instructed not to get involved too far. They advanced to between eight hundred and a thousand yards of the creek, sinking over their knees in the marsh and coming under an enfilade fire from trenches on the right bank of the Tigris.

At this stage, some confusion was observed among the enemy and a portion of them appeared to be retiring, while the fire of their guns had almost ceased. General Barrett felt much inclined to order a general advance on Ruta village, to destroy the Turkish camp and possibly to capture his guns. But the force was not prepared for crossing the creek; and the advance through the marsh—where the depth of water and the two-feet high grass detracted from the effectiveness of our infantry fire—would probably have entailed considerable casualties. About 9.30 a.m., therefore, General Barrett issued orders for the leading troops to stand fast, preparatory to withdrawing. The second line of troops on the sand-hills and the ships on the river covered this withdrawal, which was carried out successfully. The 103rd, however, experiencing some difficulty in extricating themselves, suffered most of their casualties at this stage. The Turks, who were themselves preparing to retire, made no attempt to interfere with the further British withdrawal; and the British force was all back in Muzaira'a by 2 p.m., having lost seven killed and fifty-one wounded.

The enemy's strength was estimated at five thousand. They were reported to have been much demoralised by the

DISPOSITIONS

attack and to have lost two to three hundred killed and many wounded, including their commander Sulaiman Askari Bey, who was taken back to Baghdad with severe injuries. Their artillery fire had been better directed than at Sahil, but a large proportion of their shell were blind or burst on graze; and consequently their effect had been slight. Our retirement is said to have been regarded by the Arabs as a defeat, but whether the Turks themselves so regarded it seems doubtful. For the time being their progress was checked; and, as it turned out, our attack stopped any idea they may have held of a further advance south in force before the rising of the waters. Another result was to reduce the nightly sniping and raiding by the neighbouring Arabs.

On the 19th, the War Office had telegraphed that, excluding 2,500 men, said to have reached Baghdad, the XIIth Turkish Army Corps was reported to have been diverted to the Caucasus, where the presence of the 37th Division was also reported. This news was to some extent confirmed by local intelligence in Mesopotamia, which gave the Turkish force in Lower Mesopotamia at twenty battalions of about six hundred men each. Of these, six were said to consist of Turks who had come with Sulaiman Askari, five belonged to the XIIth Army Corps (35th Division), and nine were the remnants of the 38th Division, gendarmerie or units which had fought at Sahil and Qurna. These units were in three separate bodies—one at Amara, another about Ezra's Tomb, and the third was intended to cross the lower Euphrates and advance by land on Basra.

On the 22nd, General Barrett reported that there was no urgent necessity for reinforcing him, as the enemy seemed to be adopting a defensive rather than an offensive policy. He himself could not advance and assume the offensive, however, without reinforcements. On the 23rd, Lord Crewe asked the Government of India if, in view of the Turkish numbers and dispositions, they could reinforce Force " D." They replied that they were holding the 12th Infantry Brigade ready to go if General Barrett required it, though its despatch would weaken the North-West Frontier. They might with difficulty spare a cavalry regiment also; but its necessity would be less if a flight of aeroplanes, which General Barrett had again asked for as an urgent requirement, could be spared. They were sending two armoured motor cars and two light motor lorries to test their utility on the desert to the west of Basra.

By the 26th, however, developments in the situation obliged General Barrett to ask for reinforcements to protect Basra and Mohammerah. A Turkish cavalry regiment and a battalion of infantry with Shaikh Ghazban of the Bani Lam* and a large number of Arabs were moving eastward from Amara to Bisaitin. The Bani Turuf† had joined them in response to the call of *Jahad*, and their primary objective was probably a raid on Ahwaz or the oil-fields. At the same time, it was reported that two thousand Turkish troops with five guns, accompanied by Ajaimi and fifteen thousand Arabs, intended to advance at once across the desert and attack Basra from the west. Ghazban was, it was also reported, to attack Basra simultaneously from the east. The Turkish force about Ezra's Tomb, now reported as increased to thirteen battalions and eleven guns, would presumably co-operate with these flank attacks by an advance on Qurna. The Government of India at once made arrangements for the 12th Infantry Brigade (2nd Queen's Own Royal West Kent Regiment, 4th Rajputs, 44th Merwara Infantry, and 90th Punjabis), under Major-General K. Davison, C.B., to leave India for Basra by the 1st February.

The Shaikh of Mohammerah required a few days to mobilize his tribes to deal with the threat towards Ahwaz. In the meantime, General Barrett decided to send the *Comet* with a small British infantry detachment on board to prevent the raiders crossing the river; and, for the reassurance of the Shaikh and people, to send half a battalion of infantry to Mohammerah. The possibility of a Turkish attack on Qurna rendered it undesirable to reduce its garrison; but General Barrett took the precaution of holding a field battery and two infantry battalions there in readiness to reinforce Basra, in case it should be attacked before the arrival of the 12th Infantry Brigade from India.

As a matter of fact, the only attack made on Qurna was a very minor affair, carried out by two to three hundred Turks on the night of the 29th-30th, against the Muzaira'a lines. It had been expected and was beaten off without difficulty, with a loss to the enemy of forty-six prisoners, besides a few killed and wounded. The only apparent reason for such an attack was to satisfy the Arabs, who had urged the Turks to attack us, being tired of their own ineffective activities.

At this period the rising of the waters made it necessary to improvise some method of penetrating the numerous minor

---

* Semi-nomads on the left bank of the Tigris between Amara and Kut al Amara and also in Arabistan. Mostly Shiahs.

† Semi-nomads between the Karun and the Tigris—noted as turbulent robbers. Shiahs.

SITUATION AT AHWAZ

waterways for purposes of reconnaissance and of better control over Arab activities during the flood season. In consequence, orders were issued for the organisation of a *bellum* squadron. Every infantry battalion was to have four *bellums*, for each of which they were to train crews of eight men. Each *bellum* was to be a self-contained unit carrying the necessary kit, rations and ammunition supply for its crew. In this way, our means of reconnaissance and inter-communication would be improved; the organisation would also provide a method of dealing with minor hostile enterprises, as well as a mobile bridge train for crossing small waterways.

The news from Ahwaz grew more disquieting. A large section of the population was believed to be ready to join in the *Jahad* and the Shaikh of Mohammerah acknowledged that he had lost control of them. In consequence he could not guarantee the lives of the Europeans there. The Persian Foreign Minister in Tehran promised immediate attention to the matter of protecting British subjects and property, but it was clear that the Persian Government was afraid, for fear of public disapproval, of taking any action likely to lead to war with Turkey. The Bakhtiaris assured our Minister in Tehran of their intention to oppose any Turkish advance into Arabistan, but here also it was evident that Turco-German intrigue and private rivalries would probably do much to nullify this assurance. On the other hand, however, the leading *mullahs* in Tehran had informed our Minister that they anticipated with pleasure a British control of the Shiah Holy Places in Mesopotamia; and in Azerbaijan a Russian landing at Astara had forced the Turks to retire from Tabriz.

On the 29th January, Lord Crewe asked the Government of India if it were possible to despatch a small force forthwith by river to Ahwaz. The 12th Infantry Brigade seemed unlikely to arrive in time for the protection of the pipe-line and the oilfields; and unless some force was despatched, Arabs and Bakhtiaris might lose confidence in our ability to assist them. The Secretary of State went on to say that he was pressing the War Office to send some second-line troops to India to enable the authorities there to bring General Barrett's strength up to two divisions, as Lord Crewe understood that India could not do this without getting reinforcements. After some telegraphic correspondence with the Viceroy, who had started to pay a visit to the Persian Gulf and Mesopotamia*, the Government

---
*In the beginning of January, Lord Crewe had agreed to this visit, which Lord Hardinge considered would do good by encouraging the loyal Arab Shaikhs.

of India replied on the 30th. They protested against protection of the oil-fields and pipe-line being regarded as one of the principal objects of Force " D " ; it was much more necessary, they considered, to crush any attacks on Qurna or Basra ; for a reverse at either of these places would also involve the destruction of the oil-fields and pipe-line. General Barrett should not, in their opinion, detach any troops to Ahwaz, unless he was confident that he could spare them, and this they doubted. They were, however, repeating the correspondence to General Barrett and leaving the decision to him. They would welcome reinforcements, without which they could only send General Barrett three squadrons of cavalry and possibly a Territorial battery of artillery.

Lord Hardinge himself emphasised these views very strongly in a private telegram to Lord Crewe the next day, from Kuwait, where he had met and discussed the situation with Sir Percy Cox. He observed that to detach troops to Ahwaz was to fall in with the desires of the Turks and he minimised the threat to Ahwaz. He agreed as to the necessity of increasing Force " D " to a strength of two divisions ; this would allow of an occupation of Amara and Nasiriya should the military authorities find this desirable ; from a political point of view Sir Percy Cox considered it very necessary.

In the meantime, the *Comet*, after two breakdowns, had started on the 29th for Ahwaz. On her way there she met a steamer bringing all Europeans away, as it had been decided that the risk of their remaining was too great.* On the 30th, the G.O.C. Qurna reported that the Turks showed signs of advancing south from Ruta ; but on the same day a small force from Qurna destroyed some Arab villages north of the Barbukh creek without meeting with serious opposition. To the west of Basra, on the same day, small detachments of Turkish troops were encountered seven miles westward of Shaiba, and Arabs in large numbers were reported to have left Nasiriya on their way to attack Basra. Nevertheless, General Barrett decided to send an Indian infantry battalion (7th Rajputs) from Qurna to Ahwaz, but reported that he could not afford to send more.†
As it was, it would leave Basra and Shaiba with a garrison of only four and a quarter infantry battalions, two cavalry squadrons, and two batteries of artillery.

---

* It was significant that the only European who decided to remain was a German employé of Wonckhaus. His subsequent arrest by us was fully justified by the correspondence found in his possession.

† General Barrett agreed with the India Office view that the moral effect of a Turkish occupation of Ahwaz and a raid on the oil-fields would have been serious.

TROOPS SENT TO AHWAZ

One result of the despatch of this small force to Ahwaz was to bring at once into prominence the shortage in river craft; and the Government of India at once arranged to requisition in India the seven river steamers that General Barrett had asked for. It would, however, take a month to procure them and fit them for their voyage to Basra and their work in Mesopotamia. At the same time the Admiralty were trying to arrange for the loan of three Egyptian river gunboats; but it was not till the end of the month that arrangements were made to convert at Cairo two Nile stern-wheelers into gunboats and to despatch the sloop *Clio** to Basra.

Meanwhile Shaikh Ghazban had continued his advance towards Ahwaz and was expected to arrive within twenty miles of that place on the 1st February. By this date the *Comet* and *Shaitan*, with thirty of the Dorsets on board, had arrived at Ahwaz, and the 7th Rajputs were on their way up the Karun river. The Shaikh of Mohammerah had also a thousand to fifteen hundred of his following on the spot, but one of his tribes, the Bawi, who inhabit the country on the east of the Karun river, had declined to obey his summons. The Persian Government lodged a vigorous protest at Constantinople against the Turkish aggression; they raised no objection to the despatch of British troops to Ahwaz; but beyond instructing the Bakhtiaris to defend the oil-fields, they were unable apparently to take further preventive action. Moreover, it was soon established that little reliance could be placed on the tribes in the neighbourhood nominally under the Shaikh of Mohammerah.

Lord Crewe had acknowledged that the security of Qurna and Basra must be our main object. But he suggested that prompt support of the Shaikh of Mohammerah on the Karun river might be prudent if troops could be spared; for it might obviate any bad political effects of a Turkish success there as well as larger military efforts thereafter.

News of large Turkish reinforcements on their way to Baghdad still continued to come in from many sources, but the information concerning them was indefinite and inconclusive. The General Staff in India were carefully watching this situation, and on the 1st February the persistent reports induced them to warn General Barrett that it was possible, from the intelligence received, that as many as six Turkish divisions, in addition to the 35th, might be on their way to Baghdad. The reports received show that they were justified in this warning, but subsequent events proved this estimate

---

* Six 4-inch and four 3-pounder guns.

to be excessive. The instance is quoted as showing the uncertainty that prevailed at the time.

On the 4th February, when Lord Hardinge arrived at Basra, the position appeared as follows. The Turks had five thousand troops with seventeen guns opposite Qurna—Muzaira'a, two thousand about Nasiriya,* and seven hundred with two guns moving towards Ahwaz; this estimate left about four thousand unaccounted for, who were probably at Amara or moving towards the Euphrates; and further reinforcements were reported to be on their way both to the Euphrates and the Tigris forces. On each front our troops were engaged constantly in minor hostilities with Arabs, of whom large numbers were with each Turkish force. The *Jahad* was having apparently increasing effect in the region of the lower Euphrates, in Arabistan, and even in Basra itself. There was perpetual intercourse between Basra and the areas in Turkish occupation, and Turkish agents were busy in Basra threatening reprisals and causing a general feeling of unrest. Lord Hardinge told the Mesopotamia Commission that he came away from his visit realising fully that, to maintain the security of Basra, it would be necessary sooner or later to push the enemy back somewhere. General Barrett had, roughly speaking, two-thirds of his division at Qurna and Muzaira'a and the other third at Basra, with detachments at Shaiba and Ahwaz. The 12th Infantry Brigade and the 16th Cavalry were on their way from India to Basra; "S" Battery R.H.A.† and the 7th Lancers

---

* Information from Turkish sources shows that at the end of January the Turkish troops (excluding Arab tribal auxiliaries) at Nasiriya actually comprised:—

Two Arab battalions of about four hundred men each; } Remnants of
One squadron of cavalry; } 38th Division.
Six field and two mountain guns. }
Two battalions Fire Brigade regiment, each about } Just arrived from
one thousand strong. } Constantinople.

The Fire Brigade battalions, under Ali Bey, left Constantinople on the 3rd and 4th December 1914. Moving first to Alexandretta they then went—partly by march and partly by rail—to Jerablus, on the Euphrates. Thence they moved by water down the Euphrates, transported by a fleet of about eighty *shakhturs*, each capable of carrying thirty-two men. They reached Nasiriya on the 27th January 1915, their journey from Constantinople thus taking fifty-four days.

Ali Bey was appointed to the command of the Turkish right wing at Nasiriya. Other reinforcements *en route*, or under orders for Nasiriya, included the Osmanjik battalion and the remnants of the 1/26th Regiment from the Tigris, also the bulk of the 35th Division from Syria.

As to the Arab auxiliaries with the Turkish right wing, in addition to Ajaimi and his Muntafik followers, certain *sayads* threw in their lot with the Turks on account of the proclamation of a *Jahad*. Also, some of the Kurdish tribes from the Sulaimaniya and Kirkuk districts had sent down mounted contingents; the numbers sent were exaggerated by the tribal leaders in their reports to Constantinople.

† This battery had embarked at Bombay to proceed to England, when the Government of India decided to send it to Basra.

were under orders to leave India for Basra; and another infantry brigade was being made up in India to meet possible eventualities.

Sir Percy Cox had just received letters, dated 19th January, from Ibn Saud and Major Shakespear. A messenger from the Sharif of Mecca and his son Abdulla had reached Ibn Saud on the 17th. This messenger said that the Turks were pressing the Sharif to proclaim a *Jahad* and to mobilize his tribesmen. But before doing so, the Sharif was anxious to ascertain the views and attitude of Ibn Saud. After consultation with Shakespear, Ibn Saud was said to have urged the Sharif to avoid compliance and to have explained to the messenger how he himself had temporised with the Turks. At the time Sir P. Cox received this letter, one of those rumours, common to the East and difficult to investigate or explain, was current in Kuwait, to the effect that Ibn Saud's force had been checked by tribesmen under Ibn Rashid. In any case, the news received confirmed the opinion that for the time being Ibn Saud was unable to intervene effectively in the Arab situation on the Euphrates.

In his reply to an address by a deputation from the British community of Basra, Lord Hardinge said that he had come to see for himself the local conditions, so that he could deal adequately and promptly with the problems regarding our administration of the area. While it was impossible, he said, to lay down plans for the future, without a full exchange of views with the other great Powers who were our Allies, he felt confident that a more benign administration would restore to Iraq the prosperity which was her due. Lord Hardinge thanked the British community for the unremitting and cordial assistance they had rendered to Force " D "; and he assured them that, in the post-war settlement, steps would be taken to protect them and their interests, as well as those of all well-disposed inhabitants of Basra and the country around.*

---

* On the 3rd March, Lord Hardinge sent Lord Crewe a memorandum enbodying his views on the future status and administration of Basra. For administrative reasons and to give security to our oil interests in Persian Arabistan, Lord Hardinge advocated the occupation by our troops of Amara and Nasiriya as embracing the *vilayet* of Basra. From a military point of view the operation appeared, he said, to offer little difficulty, provided it was undertaken at the most seasonable time of year and with a sufficiency of troops and river transport.

He did not raise any question of an advance to Baghdad, though he showed that, if we were to redeem the assurances given to certain Arab chiefs, in return for their support, that Basra would never again be subject to Turkish authority, a continuance in the future of Turkish authority in Baghdad would be most detrimental to the prosperity and security of Basra.

The memorandum was intended to induce a discussion which would prepare H.M. Government for the inevitable post-war decision, and it did so. We are not concerned here with this discussion beyond the fact that it shows that Lord Crewe and the India Office regarded the occupation by us of Basra *vilayet* as inevitable sooner or later.

On the 5th, 6th and 7th February, Lord Hardinge visited the defences at Shaiba, Qurna, and Muzaira'a. Although on the days previous there had been hostile demonstrations by large bodies of Arabs at Qurna and Shaiba, nothing of the sort happened during his visit to interfere with his inspection of the lines of defences. Before his departure on the 8th, to return to India, Lord Hardinge sent General Barrett a letter for publication in Force Orders, expressing the favourable impressions he had formed from what he had seen of the troops. This letter informed all ranks of his appreciation and of that of the Government of India of the gallantry and skill displayed, which, under General Barrett's leadership, had contributed to make the expedition such a complete success. During his visit, Lord Hardinge visited the hospitals and found conditions good and the men happy and comfortable. The efficiency of the medical arrangements at that time were further confirmed by the fact that there had been only twenty-five deaths in the whole force from disease during the two and three-quarter months they had been in the country.

Lord Hardinge took the opportunity during this visit to discuss the military situation with General Barrett and the Senior Naval Officer. Among the points discussed were the desirability of driving the Turks back from Ruta before they could be reinforced further; the possibility of an occupation of Amara and Nasiriya, as advocated by Sir P. Cox; and whether General Barrett felt confident that he could hold on to Basra with the force he then had. In regard to the latter point, the Viceroy impressed on General Barrett that it would be almost impossible to send any more troops to Mesopotamia, and Lord Hardinge gave him to understand that, in view of this, the Government were not contemplating any considerable advance. The question of a possible future advance to Baghdad was not mentioned at all. General Barrett gave Lord Hardinge a written memorandum on the situation which the Viceroy brought back to India. In this, General Barrett, after discussing the disadvantages of an attack on Ruta, proposed to concentrate three brigades of infantry to render the position Qurna–Muzaira'a–Shwaiyib secure against any possible attack. There would remain a brigade of infantry at Basra, with a cavalry brigade at Shaiba; this would afford a strong movable column for offensive operations across the desert to the west and north-west of Shaiba. General Barrett also said that if the situation at Ahwaz obliged him to reinforce the battalion already there, he would certainly require more infantry from India; otherwise he had a sufficient force for the time being. It would, he continued, be to our advantage if the Turks were to attack us in the Qurna-Muzaira'a position; for their probable defeat with heavy loss would clear the way for our future advance, and by that time we might have the extra river transport which was so badly needed. It is to be noted, in regard to the above memorandum, that local opinion at that time placed the floods at Qurna as due about the 15th-25th March, and that no one then foresaw that owing to the exceptional weather these would occur a month earlier.

Shortly after Lord Hardinge's departure the whole situation assumed a different and more critical aspect. This was unfortunate, as it rendered the impressions Lord Hardinge had gathered from his visit of less value. These impressions appear, at any rate, to have led him to the conclusion that there was no immediate necessity to send further reinforcements from India; for Sir Beauchamp Duff, on the 8th February, issued orders that in consequence of a private telegram he had received from the Viceroy, all action regarding the preparation of another infantry brigade for Mesopotamia was to be held in abeyance; and on the 16th, after Lord Hardinge's return to Delhi, he issued definite orders that this brigade was not to be sent, though the 7th Lancers and another heavy battery should go.

On the 5th February the Bakhtiari Khans reached the oil-fields. So long as they remained loyal to their undertakings the oil-fields were no longer in danger. But reliable information was received that the *Vali* of Pusht-i-Kuh* had agreed to join the Turks; and the Bawi rose, in spite of the Shaikh of Mohammerah's orders, and proceeded to loot the oil-stores and to breach the pipe-line. The Shaikh of Mohammerah pressed urgently for reinforcements, without which, he said, most of his tribes would probably join the Turks. Sir Percy Cox also considered that reinforcements should be sent. General Barrett formed the definite conclusion that little or no reliance could be placed on assistance from the Shaikh of Mohammerah; and he had to reconsider the whole situation, as it was being forced upon him on every side that he could no longer expect any effective Arab co-operation. The 12th Infantry Brigade had arrived at Basra, but instead of sending them all to Qurna as he had intended, he was obliged to retain a portion to reinforce Ahwaz if necessary. He realised, moreover, that if it was considered essential to ensure the supply of oil, he would

---

* The mountain region to the north-west of the oil-fields.

have to send up some of the cavalry coming from India. Fortunately the rising of the waters had caused extensive floods near Qurna and to the west of Basra, and these lessened the chances of an immediate Turkish advance on either of these flanks. The authorities in India were, however, opposed to any further dispersion of troops, and they pointed out to Lord Crewe, who had asked if they meant to reinforce Ahwaz, that it was impossible with the force available to protect one hundred and thirty miles of pipe-line against such an elusive enemy as the Arab.

By the 10th February, seven hundred Turkish troops with two guns, and accompanied by about a thousand Arabs, had reached the Karkha river, about twenty-four miles to the north-west of Ahwaz ; and they were reported to be collecting boats to cross the river. The Bawi had made no further raids and were said to be wavering in their attitude ; but the unrest had spread to the Cha'ab tribe (of Fallahiya district) and some of them had joined the Bawi insurgents. On the 11th, on receipt of news that 2,500 Turkish troops had left Muzaibila for Amara on their way to Ahwaz, General Barrett decided to send reinforcements up the Karun. He quite realised that the defence of the pipe-line was a secondary consideration. But local political opinion was that, unless the Turkish advance on Ahwaz was checked, all the Arabs to the east of the Tigris and the Shatt al Arab would probably join actively in the *Jahad*. This would, of course, constitute a serious menace to his line of communications. Orders were accordingly issued for Brigadier-General C. T. Robinson (C.R.A. of the Division) to take up reinforcements and defend Ahwaz. The force sent brought the total force at Ahwaz up to thirty sabres 33rd Cavalry, one section 23rd Mountain Battery, thirty rifles 2nd Dorsetshire, the 4th and 7th Rajputs, and one section 22nd Company Sappers and Miners. A section of the 76th Battery R.F.A., without horses, also went in the *Blosse Lynch* ; and his artillery brigade-major and orderly officer accompanied General Robinson as his staff officers. This force was considered sufficient to check the Turkish advance but not to protect the pipe-line.

At Qurna the waters were steadily rising, and Fort Snipe had been flooded out immediately after Lord Hardinge's departure. A few days later the Turks were seen to be shifting their camp at Ruta, evidently owing to the floods. On the 10th February, General Davison arrived with two battalions of his brigade (12th), and received reports that the Turks were holding a conference at Ruta to decide whether to attack Qurna or merely to leave a "holding" detachment opposite it; and two days later their decision could be inferred from the fact that three Turkish battalions were said to have left, leaving only five Arab and Kurdish battalions. On the 14th, a widely extended force of some hundreds of Arabs advanced from the north-west of Qurna, but would not face the fire of our guns.

At this time also, a Turkish motor patrol boat was reported to have entered the Hammar lake and to be threatening Arabs, who had been friendly to us, with reprisals. On the 15th, therefore, Generals Davison and Fry made a reconnaissance up the Euphrates to select a position which would afford us a closer control of the various water-ways; but they came to the conclusion that the extent of the marshes and flood, passable everywhere by the Arab *mashuf*, prohibited any such idea.

On the 17th the issue became clear. The controlling banks of the Tigris just above Muzaira'a were broken* in several places and the water from the Shwaiyib river extended westward to north of Muzaira'a. The whole area round Muzaira'a became a sheet of water or a sea of mud, and the area could evidently not be held for much longer. All the troops and several hundred Arab coolies were put on to combat the inundations, but they had little effect; and General Barrett reported to India on the 17th that he intended to withdraw troops gradually from Qurna and Muzaira'a to Basra. Till the end of February the troops and Arabs laboured at keeping the water within bounds, but then any idea of holding Muzaira'a was abandoned. A pontoon bridge, connecting Qurna with the left bank of the Tigris, constructed by a bridging train sent from India, was completed by the 26th February, and it was decided only to leave a detachment on the left bank to guard the bridge-head. Troops had been withdrawing daily and a new post was established at Kurmat Ali, consisting of three heavy guns and a battalion of infantry, to watch the "new channel" of the Euphrates.

The floods were also affecting the situation to the west of Basra, the desert between there and Shaiba being under water, in places to a depth of three feet. Camels could not travel through these floods with their sticky, muddy bottom, and at times even carts could not proceed. This made it very difficult

---

* It is not certain whether this was done by hostile agency or caused by the rough weather, but it was probably the latter.

to keep up a proper supply at Shaiba at the very time that its importance was becoming more pronounced; for Ajaimi's force was slowly materialising at Qurainat, eighteen miles north-west of Shaiba. On the 9th February our cavalry were engaged with Ajaimi's men near Nukhaila; and by the 17th he was reported to have fifteen hundred Turkish troops with six guns, in addition to about three thousand Arab tribesmen. Two days later this force was reported within fifteen miles of Shaiba, and General Delamain was despatched with the Basra movable column (five squadrons of cavalry,* four field and four mountain guns, three and a quarter battalions of infantry and half a battalion of pioneers) to attack them.

General Delamain had intended to march from Basra to Shwaibda the first day, but the floods prevented this. The first five miles after leaving Basra was through thick mud over the men's ankles or water up to their knees, and although the last three or four miles to Shaiba was over sand or gravel, the force had to face a strong gale of wind; this carried much sand and grit with it, and by the end of the march the men were considerably distressed. The field artillery teams had all been increased to eight horses, but even then the draught work was exceedingly heavy. To add further to their difficulties the flood rose higher in the afternoon and the water then spread the whole way to Shaiba. Here the force bivouacked in great discomfort owing to the heavy rain, and marched the next morning to Shwaibda.

The going in the desert country to the west of Shaiba was not affected by the rain, but its sand proved heavy going for the guns, wheeled vehicles and transport animals. No fodder or fuel was procurable locally, and all that the force required had to be carried on pack mules. In consequence, the number of these was abnormal and their protection was difficult to arrange for.

At Shwaibda, General Delamain received information from Force Headquarters that the hostile force near Nukhaila had been reinforced. They were now said to comprise 2,500 regular troops with twelve field and two mountain guns, including quick-firers, in addition to a force of some thousands of Arabs; and General Barrett could send no reinforcements to General Delamain. The enemy were said to be holding an entrenched position to the south-east of Nukhaila, extending from the river to the At Tuba mounds, and

---

* The 16th Cavalry (three squadrons strong) had disembarked at Basra from India on the 14th.

SITUATION IN INDIA

General Delamain came to the conclusion that, in all the circumstances, it would be too risky to advance farther. Indeed, he considered it probable that the enemy with their superior numbers would attack him. They did not do so, however, and after another comfortless night of heavy rain at Shwaibda the force returned to Shaiba, and thence to Basra.

On the 5th and 12th February the Secretary of State for India had telegraphed to India regarding the necessity for sending more troops to General Barrett's force, which he considered should be made up to a strength of two divisions. The War Office were unable to spare any men from England or Egypt, and prompt action seemed essential. In a long telegram of the 16th, the Viceroy placed the views of the Government of India before H.M. Government. Lord Hardinge pointed out that India had been depleted of troops to an extent never contemplated; that the Territorials sent out were not yet fit to take the field; and that the limit of risk which could be imposed on the Indian public had been reached. The Government of India were anxious about the situation in Mesopotamia, which had been complicated by the diversion of troops to Ahwaz and which, in their opinion, required the despatch to Basra of another division; but they urged strongly that the War Office should reconsider their refusal to send reinforcements.

It is to be noted that at the time this telegram was sent the Government of India were considerably perturbed regarding the position in Aden and their own internal situation. Efforts had been made to tamper with the Indian troops in all cantonments in the Punjab, where an extensive conspiracy had just been discovered. The revolutionary elements had arranged for a general rising on the 21st February, with organised attacks on most of the arsenals and many of the chief magazines and treasuries; and it was uncertain if all the ramifications of the plot had yet been discerned. On the other hand, from the information they possessed, it appeared to the Government of India that the War Office might be able to return some of the Indian troops from Egypt. An attack on the Suez Canal by the Turks had just been defeated with considerable loss to the Turks, who were reported as having retreated well to the east; Lord Kitchener had told Sir Beauchamp Duff that on the 15th the navy would start a serious bombardment of the Dardanelles with a view to forcing a passage; and, including the Australian and New Zealand Divisions, there was now a considerable force in Egypt.

On the 16th Sir Percy Cox reported that he had heard from Ibn Saud of the death of Major Shakespear. This was a great misfortune, as his knowledge of the Arabs and his personal influence with them was an asset to us of considerable value at this time. It transpired that while a spectator he had been killed by a chance bullet in a battle between the forces of Ibn Saud and Ibn Rashid. In this action Ibn Saud claimed to have defeated Ibn Rashid; but independent reports said that both sides had lost heavily and both had retired to their respective headquarters. Accounts, however, all agreed that neither side was likely to indulge in further hostilities for some time to come, and this proved to be correct. The last chance of effective timely co-operation by Ibn Saud thus passed away.

During the latter half of February there was great uncertainty regarding the Turkish numbers and dispositions in Mesopotamia. The Turkish screen, extending from Nukhaila on their right to the Karkha river (north-west of Ahwaz) on their left, was composed of units of the 35th Division, or of gendarmerie, and it was found impossible to discover what was behind them. Although it was practically certain that the 36th and 37th Turkish Divisions were on the Caucasus front, the information from Egypt still pointed to there being as many as seven divisions either in or on their way to Mesopotamia. At Nasiriya and Nukhaila the Turkish regulars were said to amount to one thousand cavalry, eight infantry battalions and fourteen guns; and there were persistent reports that the Turks were taking advantage of the exceptionally high water to send troops down the Shatt al Hai by steamer to Shatrat Al Muntafik* (twenty-seven miles north of Nasiriya). Near Shaiba the Arab and Kurdish cavalry were becoming more enterprising, and on several occasions infantry and guns had to move out from Shaiba to support our reconnoitring cavalry. The situation here was so uncertain that, on the 24th, General Barrett ordered the reinforcement of Shaiba. General Delamain was to take the 16th Infantry Brigade (less the 117th Mahrattas at Kurmat Ali), and they were to be followed by the 76th R.F.A. Battery and the 6th Cavalry Brigade.†

---

* Below this the Shatt al Hai spread into the Hammar marshes and was not passable for steamers.

† Orders to organise this brigade were sent from India on the 21st. It was to consist of " S " Battery R.H.A., 7th Lancers (to leave India on the 28th for Basra), 16th Cavalry and 33rd Cavalry, under command of Brigadier-General H. Kennedy. The 7th Lancers and 16th Cavalry had only three squadrons each, so General Barrett took the fourth squadron of the 33rd Cavalry to act as divisional squadron.

During this period, the garrison of Qurna and Muzaira'a was being reduced as quickly as the few available steamers would permit. The Turks had shown little activity here beyond laying mines in the Tigris below the obstruction near Ruta, and their garrison in this neighbourhood had apparently been reduced to two battalions of infantry and six guns.

At Ahwaz the reinforcements under General Robinson had at first had a reassuring effect. The insurgent Bawi had been defeated by the Shaikh of Mohammerah's loyal levies, and there were signs that they and the other tribes in the neighbourhood were wavering in regard to the attitude they should adopt. But on the 20th, Wassmuss and other German agents arrived at Shushtar on their way to Shiraz (in Fars) and Hawiza, and the effect of the German propaganda in Arabistan at once became more apparent. Arab cavalry were being encountered daily within ten miles to the north-west of Ahwaz, but our own cavalry were too few in number to be able to cope with them effectually.

The Turkish Minister at Tehran had informed the Bakhtiari Khans that the Turkish force only intended to get behind the British at Basra and not to invade Bakhtiari territory; and that they had some such intention was confirmed by the news on the 27th, that four thousand Turkish troops with fourteen guns and fifteen thousand Arabs were in camps on the Karkha river. On the 24th the *Espiègle* had visited Mashur on the Hor Musa (east of the Shatt al Arab), to show the flag and to exhort the Cha'ab Shaikhs to remain loyal to Mohammerah; and on the 26th the same ship reconnoitred for some distance up the Karun river. The attitude of the tribes east of the Karun and the Shatt al Arab was now so threatening that small garrisons were placed at Abadan and at Marid on the Karun river.

On the 25th the General Staff in India, in appreciating the situation, came to the conclusion that the position in Mesopotamia might become critical at any moment, while that on the North-West Frontier was not so critical though it might become so in a few months time; and the arrest of the chief conspirators in the Punjab had so eased the internal situation that the Territorials and Volunteers should be able to deal with its difficulties. The Chief of the General Staff, however, telegraphed on the 27th to the Chief of the Imperial General Staff that owing to the news from Egypt and from other sources beyond the control of India being so conflicting, he would like to receive an authoritative appreciation of the Turkish intentions and dispositions; and he also asked if it was intended to create a diversion by landing a force at any point in Turkish territory. On the 1st March the War Office sent their reply. They estimated that a division of the Ist Army Corps (a new formation of twelve battalions lately arrived in Baghdad), the 35th and the 38th Divisions formed the Turkish force in Mesopotamia ; the attack on the Dardanelles, which was progressing favourably, would, in their opinion, relieve the pressure on General Barrett ; and they did not anticipate that any further Turkish reinforcements would be sent to Mesopotamia, either from the Caucasus front or from elsewhere.

While this appreciation put the situation in Mesopotamia in a better light, Army Headquarters in India were much concerned at the lack of mobility on land of General Barrett's force. In reply to a query as to how he stood in this respect, General Barrett had replied on the 28th that his land transport amounted to 300 camels, 440 mule carts and 3,000 pack mules. These were only just sufficient to supply Shaiba and did not admit of any movement in force by land. This lack of transport had not hitherto been important, as all main movements had been by river. General Barrett's efforts to obtain camels locally had failed owing to lack of grazing and to the floods, and he now considered that, for an advance on Nasiriya, the best solution lay in a light railway for part or all of the way. General Barrett was at once asked for any suggestions he might have for improving the mobility of his force and for a definite plan for a light railway.* He was also asked whether he considered that the state of the country prevented any Turkish advance in force on Basra, as it appeared to the Chief of the General Staff in India that Force " D " seemed to be rather unduly dispersed to meet such an attack.

On the 3rd March, General Barrett replied that this dispersion of his force had been only a temporary makeshift and that it was now possible to reduce the Qurna garrison still further. At the same time, he was obliged to retain posts on the Karun in view of the persistent reports of the Turkish intention to advance by that flank. The Turkish main strength, however, was on the Euphrates, where they must be confronted with great supply and transport difficulties, and where orders were

---

* The idea of such a light railway was not seriously considered at this stage as a possible immediate project. The floods would make it impossible to construct for some months to come. Force " D " could not advance till reinforced considerably. There seemed small probability of this for some time, and it might then prove better to use the Euphrates river route and to construct a good road to Zubair or Shaiba.

RECONNAISSANCE FROM SHAIBA

said to have been received that, pending the arrival of more reinforcements, no attack was to be made on Basra. Since it was unlikely that the Turks possessed much land transport, they might decide to move on Qurna or Kurmat Ali by water. Consequently, General Barrett must establish a reserve at Basra to be able to reinforce Qurna, Kurmat Ali or Shaiba. He then had six battalions and ten guns at Basra, as well as the base depôt, which provided the equivalent of another battalion ; and he intended to send another infantry battalion to Shaiba, where his strong cavalry force would give him timely warning of any hostile advance.

For some days before this the Turks had been reported to be sending supplies to Nukhaila by *mahailas*, and on the 2nd March orders were issued for a steamer to attack them next day, taking infantry and guns for the purpose from Kurmat Ali. At the same time, General Delamain was instructed to divert Turkish attention from this attack by sending a cavalry force from Shaiba to reconnoitre towards Nukhaila. In accordance with these instructions, two sections of " S " Battery R.H.A. and the 16th and 33rd Cavalry (totalling five hundred sabres), under Lieutenant-Colonel Wogan Browne, 33rd Cavalry, left Shaiba* at 7 a.m. on the 3rd. They were followed at 9 a.m. by a supporting detachment of half a battalion of the Dorsets and a section of the 76th Field Battery, under command of Lieutenant-Colonel Rosher, of the Dorsets. As arranged at a conference with the cavalry commander the previous evening, Lieutenant-Colonel Rosher took up a position about four miles west of Shaiba.

The 33rd Cavalry, who were leading the cavalry force, arrived, practically unopposed, within three or four miles of the enemy's position south-east of Nukhaila. A few bodies of hostile cavalry had been seen in the distance, and a few shells had been fired at the 33rd advanced squadron. The 33rd remained till about 2 p.m. in observation of the enemy's position, and during this period there were indications that hostile mounted bodies were moving round towards the left flank of the British force at a considerable distance off. At 2 p.m. the retirement commenced. The enemy immediately began to close in and follow up the retirement, their numbers rapidly increasing to between fifteen hundred and two thousand. Lightly equipped and widely extended, they made constant efforts to envelop the flanks of the retiring force. But they

* See Map 3.

were always checked by fire or fell back before counter-charges, only to come on again as the retirement proceeded. The heavy sand impeded the movement of the guns in spite of their eight-horse teams, and in consequence retarded the pace of the retirement. Near Shwaibda, however, after an unsuccessful effort to cut in on the line of the British retirement, the hostile pursuit slackened off and the engagement appeared to be nearly over.

The ground now necessitated a half-turn to the left, and in making this movement the cavalry on the wings—in the cloud of dust caused by the horses and guns—closed in rather far, masking the guns, whose horses were at the time temporarily in difficulties in the heavy sand. At this moment, a fresh body of hostile cavalry emerged from Barjisiya woods and charged in to close quarters; and at once the remainder of the pursuers turned back from their retirement and also charged in. There was more dust, the sun was getting low and was in the faces of the Indian cavalry as they faced round; and some of the 16th Cavalry were driven right across the British front, carrying disorder into the ranks of the 33rd. Lieutenant-Colonel Stack, of the 33rd, at the head of one of his squadrons, charged into the enemy who had penetrated into the force, but he was himself severely wounded, and the success gained was merely temporary. In the confusion some dozen Arabs had got into the battery, whose officers and N.C.O.s were obliged to use their revolvers freely on Arabs shooting from their saddles and cutting at the horses and harness. Some of the team horses of a gun and a wagon were shot and both teams came down.

For a few minutes the situation was distinctly critical. But, although unknown to most of the cavalry, they were now within a hundred yards of the supporting force under Lieutenant-Colonel Rosher.* This force had been unable to see clearly what was happening owing to the sun in their eyes, the dust, and the mirage. All they could discern was a widely spread mass of mounted men in a cloud of dust bearing straight down on them. It was impossible to distinguish friend from foe, and not until the horses came right through them could they open fire with their rifles, guns and machine guns. Their steadiness in the emergency had an immediate effect. The enemy, surprised and panic-stricken, turned and fled, making

---

* Although Lieutenant-Colonel Rosher had sent word of the approximate situation of the position he was holding to Lieutenant-Colonel Wogan Browne, a cavalry officer sent back during the retirement to ascertain it exactly had only just rejoined the cavalry when the final charge took place.

no attempt to stand. It was now just after 4 p.m. After reforming, the cavalry searched the country for some way back; the gun and wagon were re-horsed; and the whole force withdrew unmolested to Shaiba. There had been many acts of individual gallantry among the British force, and the guns had manœuvred and been handled with traditional steadiness. The losses of the British totalled twenty-five, but they included four British and one Indian officer killed and two British officers wounded; and a machine gun had been lost. The enemy's casualties are unknown, but they were believed to be considerable.

On the same day the British force at Ahwaz had also been engaged. General Robinson, who was encamped with his force on the right bank of the Karun river opposite Bandar Nasiri, had information that two separate bodies of the enemy in the neighbourhood were about to effect a junction in order to attack him. The Turkish force with some of their Arab allies were in camp at Ghadir—which lies among low hills about ten miles to the north-west of Ahwaz—and Ghazban of the Bani Lam, together with the Bani Turuf, were said to be on their way to the same spot. General Robinson decided to strike a blow at the Ghadir camp before the junction could be effected. He appears to have been convinced that if he could get his guns within effective range of the hostile camp without alarming them, he would do so much damage with his quick-firing artillery that the enemy would retire or disperse. On the 2nd he held a conference of commanding officers and told them of his intentions; but, although all arrangements for the advance were then made, no definite plan seems to have been formulated in regard to a possible forced retirement. At 2 a.m., on the 3rd, the force concerned moved out of camp. It consisted of two troops 33rd Cavalry, one section 82nd Battery, R.F.A., one section 23rd Mountain Battery, twenty rifles of the Dorsets and three companies of each of the 4th and 7th Rajputs. The advance was along a low feature to the north-west, averaging about a mile in width and containing a central depression or trough, running through a series of long narrow eminences on either side.

Just an hour before sunrise the force reached the point previously selected. This was about six thousand yards from the hostile camp, whose fires could be discerned, and as soon as there was sufficient light the British guns opened fire. At once large bodies of Arabs poured out of the camp, moving towards the British right, and, at about four thousand yards distance, along the British left. The right flank guard, composed of two companies of the 7th Rajputs, became so heavily engaged that it became necessary to support them with the mountain battery section and the third company of the 7th. About 7.15 General Robinson decided to order a retirement as the enemy were threatening to outflank him. The 7th began retiring in good order from their left, but almost at once an order reached their right and their supports to retire at once. How this mistake arose is not explained, but it resulted in isolating the centre of the 7th, who were also obliged to retire by the outflanking advance of the Arabs. This simultaneous retirement of the whole of the infantry nearest to the enemy resulted naturally in some confusion, and at this period, to add to the confusion, Lieutenant-Colonel Parr, commanding the 7th, was severely wounded. The accounts of what followed are not at all clear. Apparently the 4th Rajputs were not as yet ready to cover the retirement; certainly they were thrown into confusion. The regularity of the movement was completely broken, and individual officers had to do the best they could by collecting the men nearest them to oppose the Arabs, who were now all round the force. The horses of one of the field guns and the mules of a mountain gun were shot, with the result that the field gun and part of a mountain gun had to be abandoned. The fighting was continuous and close, the enemy following up within five hundred yards and closing in from the flanks to shoot within fifty yards, in spite of the endeavours of the guns and cavalry to keep them at a distance.

The situation was critical in the extreme, and General Robinson reported that if it had not been for the great resolution and courage displayed by parts of the force—he specially commended the cavalry, the gunners, and the Dorsets—a disaster would have occurred. When about five miles from camp, the enemy were found on the last remaining intervening ridge and were taking up positions there in rapidly increasing numbers. The only thing to do was to attack them at once. The cavalry dashed round to the south of this ridge, and the advanced British troops, headed by some of the Dorsets, attacked and drove the Arabs out at the point of the bayonet. From this point onwards the hostile attacks decreased in strength, and General Robinson was able to signal to the British camp to send out troops to cover the rest of the retirement. At this stage the enemy opened fire for the first time with three guns, which were evidently directed by trained gunners and which caused us some loss.

AFFAIR NEAR AHWAZ

The British losses were considerable. They amounted to sixty-two killed, including five British and one Indian officer, and to one hundred and twenty-seven wounded, including three British and four Indian officers. It transpired that the Bani Lam, led by Ghazban, and the Bani Turuf had reached Ghadir the previous evening and it was their attack on the British right flank that had given most trouble. The enemy had, however, suffered very severe losses. They admitted to having lost between two and three hundred killed, including many leaders, and about six hundred wounded. Owing to this they made no attempt at a further advance or attack, but remained at Ghadir.

In considering these and other engagements with the Arabs it is necessary to bear in mind their extraordinary mobility. When mounted they could always outpace our cavalry and even when dismounted their fleetness of foot more than enabled them to hold their own with our horses. The experience of an Indian cavalry officer affords a good illustration of this. After being cut off in an action in the desert, and although he was mounted on a polo pony which had been a reserve mount for the International polo match with America, he found that the Arabs on foot could go faster than he could ; and it was only the intervention of some British artillery that enabled him to make good his escape.

In reporting on this engagement, General Barrett pointed out the very difficult situation with which General Robinson had been faced. In addition to the numerically superior force of Turks and Arabs to the north-west, he was threatened by a rising of the tribes to the east. In these circumstances, General Barrett considered that General Robinson had been justified in trying to break up one portion of the enemy's force before it could be joined by the other. General Robinson's conduct of the retirement and the excellent behaviour of the British and certain of the Indian troops were to be commended. General Barrett immediately ordered a section of the 82nd Battery R.F.A. and half the 90th Punjabis from Marid to reinforce him.

In the meantime, the question of increasing the strength of Force "D" was still under discussion. The 86th Heavy Battery R.G.A. (four bullock-drawn 5-inch guns) were under orders to leave India for Basra on the 2nd March, but no other troops were definitely under orders to go, as it was still hoped that the War Office would be able to spare men from Egypt or East Africa. On the 17th February, Lord Crewe wrote in a private letter to Lord Hardinge : " It seems to me, however, that sooner or later we must advance to Nasiriya and Amara." On the 23rd, the Secretary of State telegraphed officially that the Mesopotamian situation was causing him anxiety, and he suggested that another infantry brigade, a cavalry regiment, and a Territorial field battery should be sent from India. In view of the great issues in Europe, the War Office were unable to assist. This was followed by a private telegram on the 26th, in which Lord Crewe expressed the wish that we could strike at the Turkish force on the Euphrates before more troops could be massed there, and he asked for General Barrett's views and for Lord Hardinge's opinion on them.

In a private telegram of the 28th replying to this, Lord Hardinge summarised the situation at Qurna and on the lower Euphrates as it had altered since his visit to Mesopotamia. He concluded : " The forces at Barrett's disposal seem to me strong enough to cope with any forces at present opposed to him, but in view of constant rumours of troops being on the march to Baghdad from Syria and elsewhere, I would like to see his command made up to two divisions. . . . . An advance to Nasiriya and Amara seems to me absolutely necessary if quiet is to prevail at Basra, but Barrett told me that his great difficulty is shortness of river transport."

On the 2nd March, the Government of India sent an official reply to Lord Crewe's telegram of the 23rd. After summarising the situation in Mesopotamia, the Indian authorities came to the conclusion that the enemy on the Euphrates would probably advance on a wide front with their right in the desert outflanking Barrett, who had only 14,400 men and 40 guns at Basra, including the detachment at Ahwaz. Turning to available resources in India, they could only send—in addition to the cavalry regiment and the heavy battery then on their way— two battalions of Indian infantry (being replaced from China), a Territorial battery, and possibly an Imperial Service Indian infantry battalion. They emphasised their heavy responsibilities to the Indian and European population of India. The internal situation was again getting worse, and they had to make provision for the trouble which seemed probable on the North-West Frontier in the spring. Most of the frontier tribes were showing signs of unrest and many agents were preaching *Jahad* among them ; and from several different sources German officers had been reported as on their way to Afghanistan. In addition, the attitude of some of the Mahomedan troops seemed uncertain, as they were averse to

REINFORCEMENTS FROM INDIA

fighting against the Turks; there had been and were still considerable desertions among trans-frontier Pathan soldiers; and it was difficult to say what the attitude of Mahomedan troops generally might be in case of a *Jahad* on the frontier. This factor rendered it impossible to spare Hindu troops.

Before he had received this telegram Lord Crewe wired on the 3rd saying definitely that any force for Aden or Mesopotamia must be found from India, and he suggested that a brigade of two Territorial and two Indian battalions should be sent. On the 4th, the news of the fighting near Shaiba and Ahwaz on the 3rd was received at the India Office. The situation was considered at a Cabinet Council that afternoon and on the same day the Cabinet's decision was telegraphed to India. The Government of India was to despatch a brigade of Territorials to Mesopotamia as soon as possible, the numerical deficiency thus caused in India being replaced at an early date from Egypt or East Africa in accordance with the military situation. Lord Crewe concluded the telegram by saying: "I hope the Dardanelles operations will shortly relieve the political tension and enable us to give greater consideration to India."

The India Office had received on the same day a telegraphic report dated the 4th on the general situation from Sir Percy Cox. Intelligence reports, he said, confirmed by the recommencement of overtures to him by Shaikhs between Qurna and Amara, indicated that for the present our position in that direction was secure. An attack on Basra from the west might be expected at any time, but there was no likelihood of surprise, as we could watch the hostile movements there from day to day. Sir Percy Cox, however, expressed considerable anxiety regarding the situation at Ahwaz. General Barrett had done what he could, but Sir P. Cox was afraid that the grave possibilities of the rapidly deteriorating situation resulting from Turkish intrusion into Arabistan were not yet fully appreciated. All but one of his tribes (the Muhaisin) had deserted the Shaikh of Mohammerah, and this tribe threatened to abandon Ahwaz unless reinforced. Ramuz* had risen and rebels there had overrun the district south-east of Ahwaz. Although the British detachment near Ahwaz might be strong enough to defend itself against any present Turkish attack, it was insufficient to protect Ahwaz from the Arabs to the east. Sir Percy Cox regretted having to appear as an alarmist,

---
* Ram Hormuz, fifty-five miles east of Ahwaz; largely under the Bakhtiari Khans, it possessed a predominantly Persian population.

but the loss of Ahwaz would provide the enemy, he said, with an excellent and well-supplied base from which to threaten our flank; it would mean the loss of the oil supply; and would greatly stimulate and extend the scope of the native rising in Arabistan. Pressure on Turkey elsewhere would not affect the situation in Arabistan in sufficient time, and he strongly urged that adequate military measures should be taken to give us control of the situation while this was still possible.

On the 5th, Lord Crewe, mainly on the advice of General Barrow, sent a telegram to India in modification of his telegram of the 3rd. The Government of India were told that it was considered better on general grounds that they should send a mixed brigade rather than four Territorial battalions, and they were informed that the General commanding in Egypt had been pressed to return, at any rate, a brigade to India. The Viceroy was informed that H.M. Government definitely ordered the strengthening of General Barrett's force at once, and that both he and the Commander-in-Chief in India were thereby relieved of responsibility for the consequences in India.

Reports from Sir Percy Cox received at the India Office on the 6th and 7th showed that the effects on the situation in Arabistan of General Robinson's action of the 3rd had been misinterpreted. Owing to their heavy losses the demeanour of the enemy was becoming more of a defensive nature. Realizing this, the Shaikh of Mohammerah and his adherents had plucked up their courage and were adopting a stiffer attitude.

On the 7th, the Viceroy informed Lord Crewe that he was sending the 33rd Infantry Brigade (1/4th Hampshire Regiment, 11th Rajputs, 66th and 67th Punjabis), under command of Major-General Gorringe, and the 1/5th Hampshire Howitzer Battery to Mesopotamia at once. It was also at this period that the War Office finally agreed to send two aeroplanes to Mesopotamia, but they could not spare aviators, and these the Government of India had to borrow from Australia and New Zealand. Neither men nor machines, however, could reach Mesopotamia for several weeks.

CHAPTER IX.

DEVELOPMENT AND DEFEAT OF THE TURKISH COUNTER-OFFENSIVE.

DURING the end of February and the beginning of March changes in the Turkish dispositions had necessitated some redistribution of the British forces in Mesopotamia. On the 7th March they were disposed as follows :—

Locality.	Cavalry Squadrons.	Artillery (Guns)				Infantry Battalions.	Pioneer Battalions.	Sappers and Miners Companies.
		R.H.A.	R.F.A.	Heavy.	Mountain.			
Qurna	–	–	–	2	6*	3	½	1½
Kurmat Ali ..	–	–	–	3†	–	1	–	–
Shaiba	6	6	6	–	4	4	¼	¼
Basra	3½	–	8	4	–	4¾	¼	1
Fao and Abadan	–	–	–	–	–	¼	–.	–
Ahwaz	½	–	4	–	2	3	–	–
Total ..	10	6	18	9	12	16	1	3

* Under orders to Basra.
† Including one spare gun, mounted.

On the 10th, Lord Crewe telegraphed that the 30th Infantry Brigade (composed of four Indian battalions*) would shortly sail from Egypt to reinforce Force " D." This would bring the force in Mesopotamia to a strength of two divisions in infantry, but it would still be deficient in artillery, sappers and pioneers, and India was asked if she could make these deficiencies good. Lord Hardinge replied that they could spare the necessary company of sappers, but could not provide pioneers or artillery. He pointed out that many of the guns brought out to India by the Territorial artillery were not yet fit to use as they still required considerable repairs.

---

* One of these battalions included a considerable proportion of trans-frontier Pathans, whom for religious reasons it was subsequently decided not to send to Mesopotamia, and they were sent to Aden and Muscat. The 30th Brigade, therefore, arrived at Basra only three battalions strong.

Of active operations till the end of March there is little to relate. The information received showed that the Turks were gradually increasing the strength of both their wings while decreasing the force in their centre (on the Tigris). Their right wing between Nasiriya and Nukhaila grew to an estimated strength of some 12,000 troops with about twenty-four guns and some thousands of Arab tribesmen.* Sulaiman Askari, though still incapacitated by his wounds, had reassumed the command here in person, and had arranged with Ajaimi for a combined Turco-Arab advance against Shaiba as soon as the Turkish concentration was complete.† This had been interfered with seriously, as will be subsequently explained, by the British Euphrates Blockade force. In the meantime, there were constant skirmishes in the country west of Shaiba, mainly between the mounted forces of both sides.

The Turkish left wing was still at Ghadir, and although their troops there had increased to about a cavalry regiment, nine infantry battalions and eight guns (in addition to the Arabs), they displayed little activity. In consequence, the enthusiasm of the local Arabs for the *Jahad* had decreased considerably.

Qurna was now practically an island. The desert to the north on both banks of the Tigris was under water, with the exception of a few low sandhills ; to the west a vast lake had taken the place of the reedy marshes ; and to the south, again, was more water, the sole exception being a narrow strip of palm-groves and fields on the south bank of the Euphrates. The existence of the British garrison at Qurna was monotonous and trying in the extreme. The days were becoming unpleasantly hot ; flies and mosquitoes—bred in the sheets of water both within and without the defensible enclosure—were a constant torment ; and the garrison's main occupation was a continual struggle in the mud to keep the waters at bay. The Turks were holding most or all of the sandhill islands to the north and on some of them were mounting guns. On the 19th March their artillery opened fire from Gun Hill,‡ and the gunboat *Marmariss* was seen to be under way near Peardrop Bend. H.M.S. *Odin* at once moved up the river to engage her, but the *Marmariss* did not come down below the

---

* Information from Turkish sources indicates that on the 28th March, the actual total strength of the Turkish right wing was about 7,600 men (including non-combatants) with 21 guns, and that at that time the contingent of Arab auxiliaries totalled over 18,000 men.

† For further information regarding Sulaiman Askari, see Appendix VI, p. 352.

‡ See Map 2.

Ruta obstruction. The Turkish action was so suspicious that the *Odin* advanced with caution, until a large observation mine exploding just ahead of her showed clearly that the *Marmariss* was only trying to draw the *Odin* over a minefield.* A few days later it appeared that the Turks had still further reduced the force opposite Qurna.

It thus became evident† that the Turkish right wing, i.e., their main force, meant to advance against Shaiba. This would probably coincide with a demonstration against Qurna and with an attack by the Turkish left wing on Ahwaz.

The operation of the detachment from Kurmat Ali against the Turkish supply *mahailas* about Nukhaila on the 3rd March and subsequent reconnaissances had shown the vulnerability of this point on the Turkish line of communication, and steps were at once taken to exploit the advantage. A naval and military force was organised and despatched from Kurmat Ali on the 11th March. This became known as the Euphrates Blockade force. The vessels employed were the two old sternwheeler river steamers *Shushan* and *Muzaffari*, the tug *Sumana*, a motor-boat and a barge. Two 4-inch guns of the 104th Heavy Battery were mounted in the barge, and there was also a 3-pounder naval gun in the *Shushan*. The combatant personnel consisted of six naval ratings under Lieut.-Com. A. G. Seymour, R.N., forty men of the 104th Heavy Battery, and fifty of the 2nd Norfolk with a maxim machine gun, the whole being under command of Major Farmar, R.G.A. On the 28th this personnel was relieved and, as a result of the experience already gained, its composition was slightly altered. The *Salimi*, in which was mounted an 18-pounder quick-firing field gun, was added to the flotilla ; a second 3-pounder naval gun was mounted in the *Shushan* ; a 5-inch gun mounted in a 200-ton barge replaced the 4-inch guns ; gun detachments from the 63rd Field and the 86th Heavy Batteries took the place of the men of the 104th Battery ; the British infantry detachment was relieved by a similar detachment of the 1/4th Hampshire Regiment ; and Indian infantry (66th Punjabis) detachment of twenty-five men with a maxim and a detachment of sappers were added ; and Lieutenant-Colonel Molesworth, R.G.A., as commander, and Lieutenant Hallett, R.I.M., as Senior Naval Officer succeeded Major Farmar and Lieutenant-Commander Seymour.

---

* The log of the *Marmariss*, subsequently captured, confirmed this.
† See Appendix VI, p. 352.

This force fulfilled its object with considerable success. On the 12th March it shelled the Turkish camp at Nukhaila and the supply *mahailas* there. The next day the process was repeated at Allawi, ten miles upstream ; and further reconnaissance above this showed that the narrowing of the channel would allow of a complete blockade. On the 20th the flotilla returned to Nukhaila and subjected it to a further bombardment. The result of these operations was that the supply *mahailas* stopped at Ghabishiya, about twenty miles above Allawi. To this place the flotilla then proceeded and there established an effective blockade, which was only interrupted by the necessity for returning to Kurmat Ali to replenish ammunition and supplies. The material and moral effects of this blockade added considerably to the Turkish disabilities by intensifying their transport difficulties and by disheartening the Arabs, on whom they were largely dependent.

The situation in Southern Persia was by this time causing considerable anxiety to the Indian authorities. The Germans, backed up by Swedish officers of the Persian gendarmerie and by the Persian Governor-General of Fars, were actively engaged in stirring up the local tribes to attack the British consulates at Bushire and Shiraz The actively hostile conduct of the German Consul of Bushire had forced us in self-defence to arrest and deport him, and we also arrested Wassmuss and his German companions while on their way from Arabistan to Shiraz. Wassmuss, who had formerly been German Consul at Bushire and Baghdad, unfortunately escaped again.* He had at the time no recognised status in Persia and was acting solely as an anti-British agent. On the 12th March, the Persian Government protested to our Minister at Tehran against the arrest of these Germans. But the Persian ministers practically admitted that they themselves were powerless to restrain these and the many other German agents who, posing as consuls, were arranging for active hostilities against the British in Persia. Proof of the German breaches of neutrality were met with in many places, including papers† found in Wassmuss' baggage, which showed that the Germans were scheming to raise Persia and Afghanistan against the British, with India as their ultimate objective.

---

* He remained at large in South Persia throughout the war and was the cause of constant embarrassment to us.

† Among them were many pamphlets in various Indian dialects intended to corrupt Indian troops.

THE TURKISH COUNTER-OFFENSIVE

H.M.S. *Clio* had been despatched to Bushire in consequence of a request from the British Consul there for military support; and on the 13th March General Barrett reported that he had authorised the British Resident at Bushire to stop—if the necessity arose and after consultation with the senior military officer on the spot—one of the transports conveying troops to Mesopotamia and to disembark any troops required.

Between the 17th and the 25th March the greater part* of the 33rd Infantry Brigade, the 1/5th Hampshire Howitzer Battery and the 12th Company of Sappers and Miners reached Basra. The 30th Infantry Brigade were on their way from Egypt, but it was questionable if they would arrive in time for the Turkish attack. On the 31st March General Barrett received information that the Turkish main force had left Nasiriya for a forward concentration; hostile cavalry and infantry in considerable numbers reconnoitred to within two miles of Shaiba on the 1st April; and on the 3rd the enemy were reported in some strength south of Zubair. From the news received by the next day General Barrett expected that the Turkish advance on Shaiba would take place within the next ten days —an estimate which was confirmed by the report on the 6th that the Turkish concentration near Nukhaila was complete. Their strength in this area was estimated at twelve thousand regulars with twenty-four to thirty guns and some eight to ten thousand Arab tribesmen.

On the Ahwaz line the weak British cavalry outposts had been forced by Turks to retire on the 31st March and again on the 6th April; and on the 3rd the *Espiègle* had been engaged by Turkish field guns to the north of Qurna, and in reply had inflicted some loss on the enemy, her own casualties only amounting to three wounded. Everywhere the indications pointed to the imminence of a Turkish offensive.

With the augmentation of the strength of Force "D" there arose the question of a senior commander and additional staff to cope with the increased duties of command and maintenance. The Government of India decided on the 18th March to organise the force as an army corps of one cavalry brigade and two infantry divisions under the command of General Sir John Nixon, who was then commanding the Northern Army in India.†

---
* 1/4th Hampshire, 66th and 67th Punjabis, under the command of Major-General G. F. Gorringe. The 11th Rajputs, the fourth battalion, did not arrive till the 9th April.

† See Appendix IV., p. 350.

Sir John Nixon arrived at Basra on the 9th April. He had been summoned to Army Headquarters (India), where he was given his instructions on the 24th March. The portion of his written instructions* in regard to military policy was as follows :—

"Your force is intended to retain complete control of the lower portion of Mesopotamia, comprising the Basra *Vilayet* and including all outlets to the sea and such portions of the neighbouring territories as may affect your operations.

"2. So far as you may find feasible without prejudicing your main operations you should endeavour to secure the safety of the oil-fields, pipe-line and refineries of the Anglo-Persian Oil Company.

"3. After acquainting yourself on the spot with the present situation you will submit :—

(i) a plan for the effective occupation of the Basra *Vilayet ;*

(ii) a plan for a subsequent advance on Baghdad.

"4. In all operations you will respect the neutrality of Persia, so far as military and political exigencies permit."

In addition to the above, General Nixon was given on 30th March the following written orders :—

"The following points are to be specially reported upon by you, after examination of the conditions in Mesopotamia :—

"1. The advisability of reinforcing the 6th Cavalry Brigade by one regiment of Imperial Service cavalry, which could be utilised for guarding the oil pipe-line.

"2. The quantity and description of animal transport required for Force " D " in the operations contemplated.

"3. The employment of a light railway, of which 137 miles of track, 20 locomotives, 240 trucks, 22 brake-vans and two traction engines are reported available and in good condition.

"4. The employment of armoured motors and mechanical transport.

"5. Aircraft.

"6. The adequacy and suitability of the river gunboats and transport now *en route*, namely :—

Two Nile gunboats, armament not yet known ;

---

* A copy was forwarded on the 7th April by post to the India Office.

Seven paddlers from the Irrawaddy Flotilla Company, with two flats from the Eastern Bengal State Railway;

Two motor-boats;

Four tugs;

Four steam launches and two steam cutters and two horse-boats understood to be coming from Egypt."

Further, on the 31st March, the Chief of the General Staff, India, telegraphed to General Nixon (who had then left Army Headquarters) an appreciation of the situation in Mesopotamia, as it presented itself to the General Staff that day :—

"The dispositions of the Turkish troops consist of two wings which are greatly separated, and a central body.

"The left wing, which is west of Ahwaz at Ghadir, comprises one division, strength about 8,000 men. Muhammad Daghistani commands this wing.

"The centre, which is on the Tigris at Ruta, consists of a detachment principally composed of gendarmerie.

"The right wing, which is on the Euphrates downstream from Khamisiya, consists of one cavalry brigade and two divisions. This force, which has a strength of about 18,000 men, is commanded by Sulaiman Askari.

"In addition, another division may possibly be in the Euphrates valley in reserve.

"In every case the Turkish forces are supplemented by local tribesmen.

"The Turks had planned to attack Basra from the west and simultaneously to advance to the Karun. This latter move was intended to exert pressure on Persia to throw in her lot with them, and to mete out punishment on Mohammerah for having thrown in his lot with us.

"Up to the present this plan has not matured, probably and chiefly by reason of the incapacitation of Sulaiman Askari by wounds. Moreover, it appears that Muhammad Daghistani is an old man, and he is said to be antipathetic to the young Turks, with whom Sulaiman Askari is in sympathy. Further, the question of supply must also be causing great difficulties.

"Be that as it may, reports state that owing to their inactivity, the loyalty of the local Arab tribesmen is affected and they are deserting.

"Once your light draught steamers reach Basra, it is hoped that your river transport will enable you to assume the offensive against these separated Turkish forces.

If there is no change in Turkish numbers and dispositions, it is thought that an opportunity should present itself of concentrating your forces in such a way that you will be able to defeat them piecemeal."

The Mesopotamia Commission took the evidence of Generals Sir Beauchamp Duff and Sir John Nixon with reference to the exact intention and interpretation of these orders. The "occupation of the Basra *Vilayet*" meant the occupation of Nasiriya and Amara, and General Nixon was so informed while at Army Headquarters. The occupation of Nasiriya had been suggested by the India Office in December, and the authorities in India and Mesopotamia had inferred from the correspondence exchanged that it was the intention of H.M. Government that both Amara and Nasiriya should be occupied sooner or later. By asking General Nixon to submit plans for their occupation and for a subsequent advance to Baghdad, Sir Beauchamp Duff stated that he was only doing what seemed prudent in view of possible eventualities. These plans were only meant for execution should H.M. Government issue orders to that effect, and until they did so telegraphic orders could easily restrict the scope of operations to the required extent. Sir John Nixon, however, informed the Commission that he took the instructions as meaning that he was to take the offensive rather than remain on the defensive; in fact, that he looked on them as indicating a change of policy.

On the 5th April, General Nixon arrived at Bushire on his way to Basra. The situation in Fars and at Bushire was disquieting owing to the anti-British activities of Turco-German agents. But the Government of India impressed on General Nixon the importance of avoiding any action in Bushire beyond what was necessary to safeguard the life and property of British subjects. On the 9th April, he arrived at Basra, and took over command of Force " D." General Barrett, whose health had been failing, proceeded to India three days later. He had thus to hand over his task at the very moment that a decisive action appeared to be imminent.

The 30th Infantry Brigade, consisting of the 24th and 76th Punjabis and the 2/7 Gurkhas, under command of Major-General C. J. Melliss, had reached Basra on the 6th April; and the fourth battalion of the 33rd Brigade (the 11th Rajputs) on the 9th April. During the preceding month the British dispositions had undergone some adjustment in order to meet the changes in the situation. Qurna garrison had been reduced, the size of the force at Ahwaz had

BRITISH DISPOSITIONS

been increased slightly, and the bulk of Force "D" was concentrated in the Basra–Shaiba area. The details of the dispositions on the 11th April were as follows :—

At Qurna, under command of Brigadier-General Dobbie, were three battalions of his own (17th) Brigade* (1st Oxfordshire and Buckinghamshire Light Infantry, 22nd Punjabis, 103rd Mahrattas), four heavy guns (two of the 86th and two of the 104th Batteries), the Sirmur Sapper and Miner Company, the Bridging Train, and a section of the 34th Divisional Signal Company.

At Ahwaz, under command of Major-General Davison, were a half squadron 33rd Cavalry, the 82nd Battery R.F.A., the 12th Infantry Brigade, the 67th Punjabis (of the 33rd Infantry Brigade), a section of the 22nd Company of Sappers, a pack set Wireless Troop and a section of the 12th Divisional Signal Company.

At Shaiba, under command of Major-General Fry, were the 6th Cavalry Brigade, the 10th R.F.A. Brigade less the 82nd Battery and one gun of the 63rd Battery,† the 23rd Mountain Battery, the 16th Infantry Brigade, the 18th Infantry Brigade less one battalion (7th Rajputs), the 48th Pioneers, the 17th and 22nd Companies of Sappers less one section, the 34th Divisional Signal Company less one section, and the Wireless Troop less two pack sets.

At Basra, under command of Major-General Gorringe, were half a squadron 33rd Cavalry, the 30th Mountain Battery, one gun of the 86th Heavy Battery (one gun being with the Euphrates Blockade force), the 1/5th Hants Howitzer Battery, the 30th Infantry Brigade, two battalions (1/4th Hampshire‡ and 11th Rajputs) of the 33rd Infantry Brigade, the 7th Rajputs (18th Brigade) and the 20th Punjabis.

The 66th Punjabis (33rd Infantry Brigade) were distributed between Kurmat Ali, Fao and Abadan and furnished a detachment for the Euphrates Blockade force; and two guns of the 104th Heavy Battery were at Kurmat Ali.

The organisation of the force into an army corps, as laid down in Appendix IV, had not yet been carried into full effect.

---

* The 119th Infantry had been posted to the 16th Infantry Brigade in place of the 20th Punjabis, who had been allotted for garrison duties at Basra.
† With the Euphrates Blockade force.
‡ Less a detachment with the Euphrates Blockade force.

The state of the country all round Basra, owing to the floods, rendered military operations singularly difficult. The Tigris had overflowed and the country between Basra city and the settlement along the banks of the Tigris was practically under water at every tide. Beyond Basra the Euphrates water, extending to Zubair and Shaiba, complicated the question of supplying the force at Shaiba. For though the depth of the water varied with the wind—the north wind made it deeper though the south wind blew it back a bit—there was a creek or water-cut across the most direct route that was always unfordable. The transport mules moved along a southerly route to the ruins of Old Basra* where the water, though somewhat shallower, generally came up to the mules' bellies, and convoys of *bellums* had been organised to carry men and supplies direct to Shaiba; but both these methods of transport had to be employed continuously to provide the necessary amount of stores. It was, however, a military necessity to hold a position at or near Shaiba, both to retain the power of initiative in operations and to prevent the Turks spreading down the Shatt al Arab between Basra and the sea.

General Barrett's intention had been to send out to Shaiba every man that he could spare from the local defence of Basra. But the floods might render the supply situation there serious at any moment, and General Nixon—who was on his way from India—might take a different view of the position and the detachment of so many troops to Shaiba might not prove to be in conformity with his plans. General Barrett himself felt no anxiety regarding a Turkish attack on Shaiba, whose garrison were more than capable of holding their own, and from his previous experience of them, he expected that the Turks would in the first instance take up a position near Shaiba. In this case, the British would have to move out and attack them, when every man that could be sent out would be required to make victory as decisive as possible. In the meantime, therefore, General Barrett thought it best to utilise all available transport to increase the stock of supplies at Shaiba before sending out more troops.

Up to General Nixon's arrival, the staff of the 6th Division had carried out the work of the Force headquarters staff at Basra, but this was now handed over to the staff of the army corps which had accompanied General Nixon from India. The command of the 6th Division, rendered vacant by General

---

* See Map 3.

Barrett's departure, devolved temporarily on the senior brigade commander in the division, Major-General Fry, who was in command at Shaiba. Major-General Melliss, commanding the 30th Infantry Brigade, was, however, senior to Major-General Fry, and as General Nixon decided on the 11th to send the 30th Infantry Brigade and the 30th Mountain Battery to Shaiba next day, General Melliss would naturally assume command. The 6th Divisional staff was at the same time to proceed to Shaiba, and was placed at the disposal of General Melliss. General Nixon also arranged to proceed himself to Shaiba on the morning of the 12th. He had come to the conclusion that, as it did not cover its communications with Basra, the position at Shaiba was unsatisfactory, as a Turkish advance in strength might cut the Shaiba garrison off and force them to adopt a passive defence.* In such an event it would be difficult to reinforce and supply Shaiba, for the direct water route, unfordable by men and animals, was still too shallow for anything but *bellums*, and even they could not always cross. General Nixon had landed imbude with the opinion that it would be best to take offensive action against the Turks whenever they came within reach and before they could concentrate in strength. But, as matters stood, he agreed with General Barrett that reinforcements should not be sent to Shaiba till the latest possible moment on account of the supply difficulty. This, he was informed, would be lessened shortly, as the inundation would become passable by sailing boats. He determined, therefore, to go to Shaiba and see the local conditions for himself.

On the morning of the 11th, General Fry reported the advance towards Shaiba of what appeared to him to be the advanced guard of the main Turco-Arab force, and he considered that this indicated the probability of serious hostilities within the next day or two. Our cavalry had located hostile mounted troops in, and to the west of, Barjisiya wood; a column of some four thousand Turkish infantry were advancing from the direction of Nukhaila on Shwaibda; and a considerable number of Arabs could be seen to the north-west of Shwaibda. During the same afternoon our cavalry reconnoitring patrols were forced to withdraw by superior numbers of hostile cavalry; but these fell back into Barjisiya

---

* This position, it should be noted, had been occupied long before the floods set in; and it had been reported that no position existed which covered the crossing of the inundation and where drinking water was to be found. After the battle of Shaiba such a position was found.

wood when the British reinforced their reconnoitring patrols. Before nightfall, General Fry received information that the enemy intended to attack during the night with a force consisting of twelve thousand Turkish troops, with twelve field guns and ten thousand Arab tribesmen. It was said that the Arabs would attack the Shaiba entrenchment from the north and south, while the Turks would direct their attack against Shaiba Fort from the south-west. In consequence of this information, the British force manned the Shaiba trenches throughout the night.

The British entrenched camp at Shaiba—over three and a half miles in circumference—was situated with its rear face on the edge of the flood area and its western face on a slight elevation, on about the centre of which stood the walled *serai* known as Shaiba Fort. The defensive perimeter consisted of an irregular line of trenches behind wire entanglements, and its northern and southern faces were bent back to the flooded ground. The main features in the position besides the fort were a brick kiln sixty feet high, known as Kiln Post, and a salient just south of the fort called South salient.

The ground to the north-west of the camp was slightly undulating, open and treeless, except for a grove of small palm-trees and three houses with walled gardens a few hundred yards from the British trenches; while beyond these, at about nine hundred yards distance from the perimeter, was a small hillock known as North mound.

Westward and south-westward, the ground—treeless but covered in places with stunted bushes—sloped very gently in scarcely perceptible undulating folds upwards for some two miles. Here a ridge, which was roughly parallel to and only about ten feet higher than the western face of the Shaiba entrenchment, was marked at its southern extremity by the Watch Tower of Zubair—a prominent landmark some four miles distant from Shaiba Fort. The only other outstanding feature was a hillock known as South mound, about half-way between Shaiba and the Watch Tower. Westward from the ridge, the ground sloped downward, still in slightly undulating folds, to the Barjisiya wood. The wood lay in a slight depression, and beyond it the ground rose gradually in a featureless plain.

To the south and south-east, between Shaiba and Zubair, there was a slight depression and the ground was broken by a number of small hillocks and several small groves of tamarisk trees. The ruins of Old Basra—the city of Sinbad the Sailor—

lay east of Zubair on the edge of the flooded area. Both Zubair and Old Basra were distant about three miles from Shaiba Fort.

During the night of the 11th–12th, the British were disposed in the following manner along the Shaiba position. The trench line on the extreme right, facing north, was occupied by half the 117th Mahrattas. Next to the 117th, and at the corner where the trenches swung round to face west, were the 104th Rifles. On their left the 119th Infantry carried on the line almost to Shaiba Fort. The remainder of the 16th Infantry Brigade, namely the Dorsets and half the 117th Mahrattas, were in local reserve near the extreme right of the position, where also was the 22nd Company of Sappers and Miners.

To the left of the 119th Infantry the 18th Infantry Brigade carried on the front line, the 48th Pioneers (temporarily attached to the 18th Brigade) being in trenches in front of Shaiba Fort, with half of the 2nd Norfolk Regiment and half the 110th Mahrattas in local reserve in rear of the fort. Next to the 48th Pioneers the 17th Company Sappers and Miners occupied the South salient, with the Norfolks' machine gun section and a searchlight section. The 120th Infantry carried on the line to the left in trenches facing south, and echeloned back on their left again were half the 110th Mahrattas facing south-east with their outer flank almost on the water-line.

Half the 2nd Norfolk Regiment was stationed as a general reserve in rear of the centre of the position and for this were also available the 6th Cavalry Brigade, who were camped close to the edge of the water-line and well in rear of the trenches. The 63rd Battery R.F.A. (five guns) was in rear of the British right, the 23rd Mountain Battery (six guns) behind the centre, and the 76th Battery R.F.A. (six guns) in rear of the left. The whole front of the position was covered by a line of piquets a few hundred yards in advance of the trenches.

The anticipated Turkish attack materialised at about 5 a.m. on the 12th. Heavy rifle fire was opened against the Fort section of the defences from the west and south-west just as it was getting light, and the British piquets in this direction, having fulfilled their purpose, withdrew into the position without loss. About 5.45 a.m.—the approximate hour of sunrise—two Turkish guns opened fire from the westward, and gradually all the ten remaining Turkish guns*

---

* The Turkish guns employed were two mountain guns, eight field guns (8·5 c.m.), and two heavy guns (12·5 c.m.).

came into action. They were disposed in an arc extending from the west to the south of Shaiba. All of them were quickly located by the British artillery, who silenced completely the greater part of the Turkish field guns within about fifteen minutes of their coming into action. These field guns were mostly in position on the forward slopes near South mound and as they were without shields their gun detachments suffered severe loss. They were withdrawn during the middle of the day, their movement being unseen owing to the mirage, and some of them subsequently came into action to the southward of Shaiba. The two Turkish heavy guns kept up an accurate fire, though they never managed to locate the British batteries, from whose fire their longer range rendered them immune. On the whole, the Turkish artillery did little harm to the British throughout the day.

The Turkish infantry attack was mainly directed against South salient, though their attacking line extended on both sides of this—on the north as far as Kiln Post and on the south to cover the portion of the defences held by the 120th Infantry. This attack was definitely repulsed without much difficulty by 8 a.m., when the enemy retired, leaving small parties in observation. Some of these dug themselves in to the west and south-west, about seventeen hundred yards from the British trenches, and considerable numbers of the enemy collected in the tamarisk groves to the south. " S " Battery R.H.A. had, in the meanwhile, taken up a position in rear of the British left, where it remained all day.

At this time the British right had not yet been seriously engaged, but about 9 a.m. a large body of Arabs with six standards occupied North mound. From here, throughout the day and the subsequent night, they made several halfhearted attempts to advance, but these were easily broken up by rifle and machine-gun fire.

About 1.30 p.m., some thirty hostile *mahailas* made an unsuccessful attempt to sail into the area between Shaiba and Basra, but except for this there was a definite lull in the fighting till 2 p.m. Shortly after this hour the Turkish infantry renewed their attack against South salient and the British left, assisted to some extent by Arab tribesmen. The right of their line on this occasion extended almost to the water-line, but the Arabs here displayed no great vigour. Their snipers, however, were troublesome, especially to the British artillery observation post on the extreme British left, and Major Wheeler of the 7th Lancers volunteered to move out with

FAILURE OF TURKISH ATTACK

his squadron and clear them away. Permission was granted, and the manœuvre was carried out effectively.* Supported by the fire of " S " Battery, Major Wheeler took his squadron out at a gallop and drove off the snipers, now and then getting home with the lance, and withdrew to the camp again, having had only one man and three horses wounded, an attempted counter-attack by hostile cavalry having been checked by " S " battery and the British machine guns. By 3 p.m., the enemy's attack had again withered away. Though pressed with some vigour towards South salient by the Turkish infantry, the Arabs on their right—advancing from Old Basra—had shown little inclination to come to close quarters and had been easily kept in check by the fire of " S " Battery. As the attack developed, General Fry had reinforced his southern front with half of the 2nd Norfolk Regiment from the reserve, but the result had never really been in doubt.

From 3 p.m. a desultory and ineffective fire was maintained by the enemy for about three hours, interrupted only by a distinct rearward movement of many Arabs from North mound about 5 p.m. At dusk† a vigorous attack was again delivered from the south, supported by heavy rifle and machine-gun fire against South salient and the line on either side of it. The British searchlight in the salient was placed *hors de combat* by rifle fire within fifteen minutes of its lighting up, and one of the British machine guns there was put out of action for two hours. But the attack failed and gradually died away to desultory firing. This continued for many hours, occasionally breaking out into heavy bursts of fire made to cover bold attempts to cut the wire entanglement. But they were all unsuccessful. After a final effort about 3.30 a.m. the Turks finally relinquished the attack and all became quiet. The brunt of the fighting had fallen on the 48th Pioneers and the 17th Company of Sappers and Miners, who had withstood the onslaught with conspicuous steadiness, assisted by the particularly good work of the Norfolks' machine gun section. The total British casualties during the 12th and the night of the 12th–13th only amounted to five killed and sixty-six wounded—a slight price to pay for the results obtained.

As already mentioned, General Nixon had intended to proceed himself to Shaiba, with General Melliss and some reinforcements, on the morning of the 12th. On arrival at

---

* The exact hour of this operation is uncertain. The official records give several different hours between 2.30 and 4 p.m.

† Sunset was approximately 6.30 p.m.

the Zubair Gate of Basra, however, at about 7.30 a.m., it was found that all the local boatmen had disappeared. This was owing to the attack on Shaiba, whence the sound of heavy artillery fire had been heard since daylight and where incidents of the fighting could be seen through field glasses. General Nixon, therefore, established his Force Headquarters for the time at Zubair Gate.*

In consequence of messages from General Fry that he was being attacked in force from the south, and that the enemy were in occupation of Old Basra, General Melliss was ordered about 8.15 a.m. to advance on Old Basra with the 30th Mountain Battery and the 30th Infantry Brigade; and General Fry was asked to co-operate in the movement. This force moved off about 9 a.m., by which time the artillery fire at Shaiba had almost ceased; some two hours later General Nixon received a message from General Fry recommending that it should withdraw to Basra. General Fry said that he could only spare two battalions to co-operate with General Melliss, whose attempt to land at Old Basra would, he considered, be very risky.

On receipt of this message, General Nixon sent an aide-de-camp to General Melliss to acquaint him with General Fry's report of the situation and to ascertain if it were possible for his force to move by a more direct route on Shaiba, so as to facilitate co-operation from there. General Melliss sent the aide-de-camp back with a message that the depth of water prevented his taking a more direct route. General Nixon thereupon decided that General Melliss' troops should remain where they were, as although they could not proceed they would oblige the enemy to retain a force in opposition to prevent a landing. By this time General Melliss' advanced guard was about a third of the way across the water† which came over the men's knees. An hour or so later General Fry reported that he was confident of being able to resist all enemy attacks. General Nixon, therefore, decided to withdraw General Melliss' force to Basra and to send as many

---

* A British civil official at Basra describes the crowd of Basra inhabitants collected round the Zubair Gate and watching what they could see of the operations. Nearly all, he says, were ready and prepared with offerings, etc., to acclaim the Turks on their entry into Basra; for, from the accounts they had received of the Turco-Arab numbers and preparations, they were convinced that the British would be driven out of Basra. It was curious, he says, to watch the typically imperturable attitude towards this crowd of the few British soldiers whose duty took them through it towards Shaiba.

† The force had halted on a dry mound where General Melliss collected his troops.

GENERAL MELLISS REACHES SHAIBA

of them as possible direct to Shaiba by *bellum*. They began to withdraw about 12.45 p.m. and were all back in Basra by 3 p.m.

Steps were now taken to impress all available *bellums*. By about 4 p.m. some eighty had been collected, but the boatmen absolutely refused to man them. The difficulty was, however, surmounted by utilising volunteers from the 20th Punjabis to propel the *bellums*. They moved off, conveying General Melliss, the 6th Divisional Staff and about three-quarters of the 24th Punjabis, about 4.30 p.m. For the first three hours progress was comparatively easy, but after that the shallowness of the water forced officers and men into the water to push the boats for the remainder of the journey. The leading boats with General Melliss and his staff reached Shaiba about 8.30 p.m., but the last of them did not arrive till about midnight. Though most of the boats came under enemy fire as they neared Shaiba, no real opposition was encountered. On the return journey the *bellums* were attacked by hostile boats in some force and incurred twenty-two Indian casualties, mostly killed. On the 13th, a convoy of *bellums* with gun ammunition attempted to cross from Basra to Shaiba, but was compelled by hostile boats to withdraw to Basra.

When General Melliss arrived at Shaiba, fighting was still in progress; it was dark and he was necessarily not fully acquainted with the local situation; and consequently he did not take over command from General Fry till daylight on the 13th. Then, having made a personal inspection of the defences, he established his headquarters at Kiln Post, whence an excellent view was obtainable, especially of the ground to the north-west and west.

At 7 a.m. on the 13th, the cavalry brigade moved out towards North mound to clear that area of Arabs who had been engaged in hostilities with the British right since daybreak, and to ascertain the enemy's strength and dispositions. The orders for this movement had been given by General Fry the previous evening and General Melliss let them stand, though he gave General Kennedy, the cavalry brigadier, instructions not to commit his brigade if he encountered serious opposition. The brigade moved out with eight squadrons of cavalry and two horse artillery guns and was supported by the 104th Rifles, who were placed under General Kennedy's orders.

The cavalry trotted out from camp along the edge of the flooded area, while the 104th advanced direct upon North mound from their position at the north-west corner of the perimeter. Three houses with walled gardens were in the direct line of advance of the 104th, while, to their right and between them and an open strip along the water's edge, was a plantation of small palm-trees. After passing the first house the 104th were temporarily checked by heavy fire from North mound, from the second house and from the palm-grove to their right front. In the meantime the 7th Lancers, forming the cavalry advanced guard, had come under heavy fire from the palm-grove, but, pushing past it, they charged North mound. Reaching its vicinity, they found that they could not hold it owing to heavy fire from the trenches in its rear and from the adjacent two houses. They consequently withdrew. General Melliss' report of this combat specially brings to notice the great gallantry of Major Wheeler and Jemadar Sudham Singh, both of the 7th Lancers, who charged the mound ahead of their squadron and were killed there while attempting to capture an Arab standard. When the 7th Lancers rejoined the main body of the cavalry, General Kennedy decided that, in view of the enemy's strength, his instructions did not justify a further advance and he withdrew to camp. In this small affair the 7th Lancers had twenty-one men and eighty-one horses killed and wounded and the 104th lost six killed and twenty-two wounded.

From his point of vantage at Kiln Post, General Melliss now observed large hostile bodies advancing near North mound and to the east of it, and at 8.30 a.m. he issued orders for a fresh attack. General Delamain was to attack North mound with three battalions (2nd Dorsetshire, 104th Rifles and 24th Punjabis*) of his 16th Brigade, his advance being supported by the concentrated fire of the whole of the British field and mountain artillery.

This advance commenced at about 10.30 a.m. Well supported by artillery fire, the infantry moved forward without a check and North mound was in their possession by 11 a.m. with the enemy garrison in full retreat. Many of the Arabs had held on with great tenacity, and ninety dead were found on the mound itself; but the cavalry brigade† were not up to take advantage of the opportunity presented by the fleeing remainder of the Arabs. A section of " S " Battery, however, was present and did considerable execution.

In the meantime, the enemy to the west, south-west and south of Shaiba had been carrying on desultory hostilities, which culminated now and then in half-hearted attacks. The

---

* Temporarily attached to 16th Brigade.   † They were watering their horses.

BRITISH COUNTER-ATTACK

result of these was that a few Turks managed to get in to close quarters, where they found themselves unsupported and isolated, and eventually seven Turkish officers and one hundred and twelve other ranks came into the British lines and surrendered to the 18th Infantry Brigade.

About noon, General Delamain signalled to General Melliss asking whether he was to withdraw his force from North mound towards camp. As, however, a considerable number of the enemy had now become visible to the westward, General Melliss decided to continue the clearing movement with the troops under General Delamain, and incidentally to capture two hostile mountain guns, which had been apparently abandoned by the Turks owing to the accurate British shell-fire. With this object, General Delamain was to swing round to the westward, holding North mound to protect his right rear, and to advance roughly in a south-westerly direction. The cavalry brigade was also put under General Delamain's orders for the protection of his right flank, and General Melliss reinforced General Delamain's force with half the 119th Infantry and, a little later, with the 2nd Norfolk Regiment and half the 48th Pioneers.

Leaving the Dorsets to hold North mound, General Delamain commenced his advance to the south-west shortly after noon, with the cavalry brigade operating wide on his right. The 104th Rifles led the infantry advance, half battalions of the 24th Punjabis and of the 119th Infantry being echeloned back on the right and left rear respectively. The remainder of the 24th Punjabis* followed in rear in reserve. A little later, the 2nd Norfolk and half the 48th Pioneers arrived and prolonged the left.

Although the abandoned guns could be seen clearly from Kiln Post, they were invisible to General Delamain's force, who were uncertain of their exact direction and were further handicapped by the mirage, which was then at its worst.† An advance generally in the right direction was, however, steadily maintained, and met at first with little opposition. Soon, however, the 104th came upon a strong body of Turks, in successive lines of trenches, who offered a stiff resistance. Well supported by accurate fire from the British artillery at Shaiba, the 104th cleared these lines at the point of the bayonet and, successfully beating off a Turkish counter-attack,

---

* There were still only three-quarters of the battalion at Shaiba.
† Usually the atmosphere was clear of mirage till 10 a.m., after which hour it continued till dusk.

captured a hundred and fifty prisoners. In the meantime, the 24th Punjabis on the right, experiencing little opposition, had come upon the abandoned guns and captured them and their gun detachments who were sheltering close by. The cavalry brigade charged a number of the retreating enemy, inflicting considerable loss and capturing a number of exhausted stragglers.

By 2.30 p.m., General Delamain had cleared the western vicinity of the Shaiba position of the enemy; but there were still considerable numbers of them in the direction of South mound, then some three miles distant. Turks and Arabs appeared to be concentrating there, and their guns were still firing intermittently on Shaiba. General Delamain proposed to General Melliss that he should advance on South mound, though his troops were somewhat exhausted and the infantry had used up most of the ammunition they had with them. The men had been under arms continuously since the previous afternoon and a fresh attack on South mound might involve them in fighting after dark. General Melliss decided, therefore, that it was inadvisable to carry out the project and at 3 p.m. he issued orders for the troops to withdraw to camp. This they did without further fighting and the ensuing night was quiet and undisturbed.*

The enemy's casualties were estimated at a thousand, and over four hundred prisoners, two mountain guns and a standard had fallen into British hands. During the day, the total British casualties only amounted to one hundred and thirty-two including those incurred in the first unsuccessful attack by the cavalry brigade on North mound. Forty-eight of these casualties had occurred in the 104th Rifles, whose behaviour was specially commended by General Delamain.† He also mentions the fine spirit of the 24th Punjabis, who—having arrived at Shaiba by *bellum* during the night—had been without food for twenty-four hours when they started upon the operations of the 13th. At 6.15 p.m. on the 13th, General Melliss estimated the enemy opposite him at ten

---

* Though Sulaiman Askari was in chief command of the Turkish force, Ali Bey was in virtual executive command throughout the fighting at Shaiba. Information derived from Turkish sources indicates that Ali Bey intended, if the night attack of the 12th–13th proved unsuccessful, to retire to the Barjisiya wood before daylight, entrench there and await a British counter-attack, thus forcing the enemy to come out into the open. The night attack was unsuccessful, but Sulaiman Askari insisted upon renewing the attack next morning.

† In his report, General Delamain refers to " the remarkably good work done by the 104th Rifles on every occasion it has been engaged."

thousand men with six guns, but he believed that there was still in the vicinity of Old Basra a large enemy force which had not yet been engaged; and a large hostile concentration had just been reported as advancing from beyond South mound.

At dawn on the 14th April, personal observation disclosed to General Melliss that, although the immediate vicinity of Shaiba was clear of the enemy, considerable hostile bodies remained in the neighbourhood of South mound; and, although the exact whereabouts of the enemy's main force was uncertain, hostile bodies were still believed to be in the Old Basra area. It seemed evident, however, that the enemy had been considerably shaken by his unsuccessful attacks and by our counter-strokes, and reports had been received of enemy withdrawals to the north-west from Barjisiya wood. If this was true, it was obviously desirable to follow the enemy up and if possible inflict a crushing blow upon him before he could get away; and it might prejudice General Melliss' chances of effecting this if he waited for the arrival of the rest of the 30th Brigade from Basra, as they would probably be delayed should Old Basra be still in possession of the enemy.

General Melliss decided that he would move out to attack the enemy with the greater part of his force, leaving only two battalions (48th Pioneers and 104th Rifles) with three field and two horse artillery guns to hold the camp. The infantry took with them two hundred rounds of rifle ammunition on the man and one hundred rounds per rifle on pack mules. His first objective was to be South mound. After this, it seems to have been in General Melliss' mind that he might have to clear Zubair and Old Basra of any enemy still remaining there, but this, of course, would depend on how the situation developed.

At 9.30 a.m. the force moved off, the 16th Infantry Brigade directing the advance with its centre on a point just to the west of South mound. The diagram below shows approximately the positions of the units of the advancing troops.

The main reason for this special formation was the possibility of an attack from the direction of Old Basra or Zubair. Advanced cavalry patrols covered the front of the infantry, and half a squadron was detached to watch the extreme left flank.

The cavalry established contact with the enemy at a point about a mile to the north-west of South mound, whence enemy infantry were seen advancing from the direction of

Barjisiya wood, and hostile cavalry were observed on South mound. "S" Battery, with the cavalry brigade, opened on both these enemy bodies and the hostile cavalry immediately left South mound. The enemy infantry, under fire from

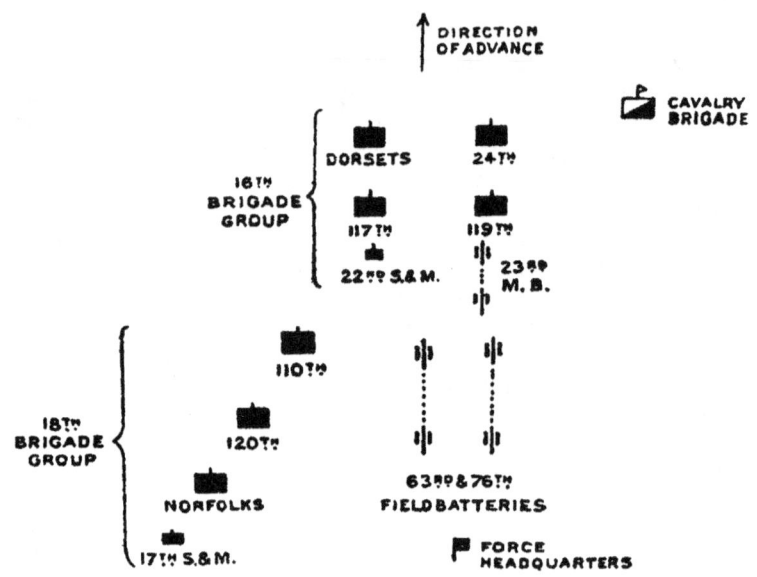

the horse artillery guns and from dismounted cavalry, lay down, either in trenches ready made or dug themselves in. A portion of the British cavalry followed up the hostile cavalry retiring from South mound and reached a position about half-way between South mound and the Watch Tower, in which vicinity there was a large body of enemy cavalry. From this second position of the British cavalry some hundreds of infantry were seen advancing from the south end of Barjisiya wood. Two British horse artillery guns now advanced to this second position and opened fire on the hostile cavalry near the Watch Tower and on the infantry advancing from Barjisiya wood. The enemy cavalry at once retired and the infantry also soon disappeared from view below an intervening fold in the ground. They also apparently dug themselves in or took up positions in ready-made trenches. In any case the enemy made no attempts to advance farther eastward, though some Arabs to the northward endeavoured at one time to encircle the right of the British cavalry. General Melliss' infantry were thus able to occupy South mound without

GENERAL MELLISS' DISPOSITIONS

difficulty ; and here General Melliss established his headquarters while his infantry dug a few trenches along the ridge.

It now seemed evident to General Melliss that the Turkish main body was in position near Barjisiya wood and that Zubair and Old Basra were not being held in any strength. He thereupon issued orders for the 16th Brigade to prepare to advance with their left directed on a point to the north of the Watch Tower, and for two battalions of the 18th Brigade—Norfolks and 120th Infantry—to move across to the right rear of the 16th Brigade ; while the third battalion of the 18th Brigade—110th Mahrattas—were to remain echeloned on the left rear of the 16th Brigade.

While this redistribution was taking place, General Melliss rode out to the cavalry position to make a personal reconnaissance. He found, however, that owing to the mirage and the shape of the ground he could make out little of the enemy's dispositions. He convinced himself that the Turkish right lay to the west of the Watch Tower, but he was unable to fix the position of their left. That the Turks meant to stay and fight in their position seemed clear.

Heavy masses of Arabs hung round the Turkish flanks. Although their dispositions were also somewhat obscured by the mirage, it was clear that their position secured the Turkish flanks against surprise and would add to the risks of a turning movement by the small British force round the wide Turkish front. This decided General Melliss not to attempt such a turning movement.

On his return to South mound, General Melliss ordered the left of the advance of the 16th Brigade to be directed on the Watch Tower and the 110th Mahrattas to pass over to the right rear of the 18th Brigade. His plan was to engage what appeared to be the enemy's right and centre with the 16th Brigade, and to attack the hostile left with the 18th Brigade, in co-operation with the cavalry brigade, whose commander was given a free hand to seize any opportunity for vigorous action which might offer. He thus hoped to strike at the enemy's line of retirement to Nukhaila.

Before the advance began, however, General Melliss discovered definitely that the enemy's line covered over three miles, extending from west of the Watch Tower to the north end of Barjisiya wood. As this meant that it was more extended than he had at first supposed, he ordered the two leading battalions of the 18th Brigade—2nd Norfolk and 120th—up into line with the 16th Brigade.

The advance began between 11.30 a.m. and noon, the disposition of the units being as follows* :—

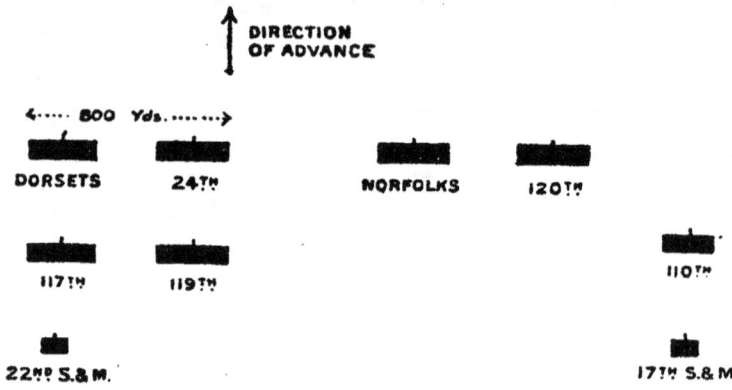

The eight field and six mountain guns were in position near South mound.

The general advance of the infantry proceeded for about a mile without incident, except that a body of mounted Arabs showed up in some force on the left flank and half the 117th Infantry were pushed out as a left flank guard. Just before the infantry came up to the position occupied by the cavalry, the cavalry brigade moved off to a position about one and a half miles to the north-east of the northern end of Barjisiya wood. Here they were checked by rifle fire from a hostile trench which could not be located.

As the troops were moving forward, General Melliss considered it advisable, in view of the uncertainty regarding the position of the Turkish left, to issue instructions that the leading battalions should not become closely engaged without definite orders. But before this warning could reach them the foremost lines of the Dorsets and the 24th Punjabis had topped the ridge, where they came suddenly under heavy rifle and machine-gun fire at effective ranges. Soon afterwards the Norfolks and the 120th Infantry became hotly engaged. This was about 12.20 p.m. The enemy were in position about nine hundred yards to the front of the Dorsets, about six hundred yards from the 24th Punjabis, and some four hundred yards

---

* This diagram taken from official sources, shows the Norfolks and 120th in line with the 16th Brigade. From a private account, written by General Delamain two days after the fight, it appears that they did not come into line until the 16th Brigade had been engaged with the enemy for a short time; and other accounts confirm this. When they came into line there was a larger gap between the two brigades than is shown here.

from the Norfolks and 120th*. The Turkish trenches were at an angle to the British line of advance and to save themselves from enfilade fire some of the British troops on the right now brought up their left shoulders.

The British were at a further disadvantage. The Turkish first-line trenches faced upwards on a *glacis*-like slope leading down past them to Barjisiya wood and they opened a heavy fire as soon as the British appeared on the skyline. This checked the British firing line before they had reached the edge of the slope, with the consequence that for a time they could only see to fire by sitting, kneeling or, in some cases, by standing; and for the same reason the British artillery, already hampered sufficiently by the mirage, could not fire effectively on the Turkish trenches.

There was also a second line of Turkish trenches some five or six hundred yards farther back, which were particularly well sited and concealed from view among small shrubs and with a favourable background. To these, owing to the shape of the ground, the British firing line presented a very good target, and the battalions of the 16th Brigade suffered somewhat severely at this stage. On the other hand, the Turkish first and second lines were not connected by communication trenches with each other or with their reserves, so that reinforcement would be difficult; and the Turkish artillery, being badly served, was having little effect.

By about 1 p.m., the Norfolks and 120th, on the right, had managed to push slightly forward, but were kept from a further advance by the well-maintained Turkish rifle and machine-gun fire. The Dorsets and the 24th had also managed by creeping forward to make a slight advance and could fire on the enemy from a lying-down position. But there was still a large gap between the 16th and 18th Brigades; and General Melliss ordered General Delamain to fill this gap. As his men were closely engaged, however, he considered this impossible, and ordered half the 117th,† half the 119th and the 22nd Company of Sappers to move to the right to close this interval and to get into touch with the Norfolks. The 119th half battalion, however, missed its direction, and, instead of moving into the gap, reinforced

---

* At this time there was a gap of some twelve hundred yards between the 16th and 18th Brigades.

† During the afternoon, a company of the 117th, withdrawn from the left flank guard, reinforced the left of the Dorsets firing line. The exact time is not given in the records.

the Dorsets and the 24th. The 16th Brigade thus used up almost the whole of its reserve.

In the meantime General Fry had prolonged the right of his 18th Brigade with half the 110th; and the 63rd Field and 23rd Mountain Batteries had moved up in closer support in rear of the 18th Brigade.

The fight soon became practically stationary. The firing line of the 16th Brigade, after its reinforcement by half the 119th, had managed to advance a little, getting to within four hundred yards of the Turkish line. But the British right was still overlapped by the Turks. The cavalry brigade was still held up by hostile rifle fire, and though the remainder of the 110th had reinforced the leading half battalion, the Turkish enfilading fire stopped all further progress in that quarter.

At 2.30 p.m., General Melliss called upon the cavalry brigade for vigorous action on his extreme right, so as to assist the infantry advance, and he sent the 23rd Mountain Battery to support the 110th. After making a wide *détour*, the cavalry brigade found that the Turks were holding positions right up to the mud on the edge of the flood area; they, therefore, returned to their original position, and about 3 p.m. opened fire from there.

The fight now resolved itself into an intense fire-fight all along the line. In a few places the British infantry gained a little ground, but the heat of the day was extreme* and the British were enduring heavy casualties. The British artillery were working their hardest. Ignoring altogether the hostile artillery, they turned every gun on to the Turkish trenches, but the configuration of the ground, the mirage, and the clever concealment of the Turkish trenches all combined to hamper their efforts in spite of a large expenditure of ammunition; and there was still little evident progress.

At 3.30 p.m., General Melliss decided that the time had come for a fresh effort, for if the attack was to be successful there was not much time before darkness set in. He informed his brigadiers that they must call on their men for a fresh effort; a general advance must be made and the enemy's

---

* The commanding officer of one of the Indian battalions describes the exhaustion of his men at this stage: " A peculiar manifestation revealed itself during the long period the firing line was held up; officers and men who had never been under fire previously were overcome by sleep for periods of ten to fifteen minutes. The general condition was that of alternate men sleeping, while their next door neighbours fired with slow deliberate aim: there was a complete absence of rapid fire."

position taken; and the whole of the artillery must work in the closest possible support. The troops responded gallantly. The 76th Field Battery pushed on and came into action close to the Watch Tower, and General Delamain sent in all his reserves except a half company of the 119th. In this way a little ground was gained. On the right, the commander of the 63rd Field Battery sent a *liaison* officer right into the firing line of the Norfolks, and was thus able to render this battalion more effective assistance. By 4 p.m., however decisive progress was still lacking, and General Melliss, as a precautionary measure, issued orders for the 48th Pioneers to move out to South mound with all available transport carts for the carriage of the wounded and to cover a retirement, if it became necessary.*

As a matter of fact, however, the tide was just about to turn in favour of the British. About 4 p.m.† the Turkish guns ceased to fire and it soon seemed as if the Turkish resistance was beginning to weaken. The British line had by this time got within about two hundred yards of the Turkish front line, and part of the firing line, realising the situation, dashed forward with the utmost gallantry at the Turkish trenches about 4.15 p.m.‡ The remainder at once followed their example and the front trenches opposite the whole line were won. All along this first line a considerable number of prisoners—all Turks—were captured and the enemy had entirely abandoned it by 5 p.m.

There still remained the second line of enemy trenches. The British were preparing to attack these, when their Turk and Arab garrisons put up the white flag. Following this incident almost immediately, a mass of fugitives were seen to leave Barjisiya wood, and the Turks and Arabs from the second line at once followed in a disordered mass. These offered a fine target to the British artillery, of which, however, they were unable to take full advantage owing to shortage of ammunition.

Pursuit by the British infantry would have been difficult in the extreme, for the strain of the attack and the great heat, coming at the end of their three days' fighting, had thoroughly

---

* A warning order that they might be required had been sent about half an hour earlier.

† The accuracy of this timing and of that of the subsequent successful assault is doubtful.

‡ Both brigades claim that they were the first into the Turkish trenches, but they were so far apart and so widely extended that senior officers on the spot regard it as impossible to prove which brigade was actually the first to move and to reach the trenches.

exhausted them and they had used up nearly all their ammunition; and the cavalry were not in a position to follow up the fleeing enemy. General Melliss had issued instructions to his brigadiers that unless the Turkish position could be carried by 5.30 p.m. he would have to fall back, for he had no intention of risking a retirement after dark with the heavy masses of Arabs, whose movements were still obscured by the mirage, threatening his flanks. To cover this retirement, the cavalry brigade were to take up positions on both flanks of the infantry, and when the flight of Turks and Arabs commenced from Barjisiya wood about half the cavalry were already moving across to the British left and the remainder had just broken off their fire action on the right.

When the Turkish advanced trenches had been taken, General Melliss did not realise that the battle was really won and that the Turks were on the point of flight. He anticipated that they would hold their main entrenched position close to Barjisiya wood, against which—in view of the exhaustion of his own troops and the lateness of the hour—it was out of the question to launch a fresh attack.

Although the opportunity of inflicting heavier casualties was thus lost by the British, it is questionable whether they could have done the fleeing Turks more damage than did the Arabs. For no sooner was the issue no longer in doubt than these treacherous people turned on their erstwhile allies and harassed their retreat in the most merciless manner.

General Melliss considered it essential to withdraw his troops to Shaiba for the night. Their retirement commenced at 6 p.m. and was entirely unmolested, and by 8.30 p.m. the troops with all their wounded were back in camp. The total British casualties* for the day amounted to 1,062, of whom 161 were killed. On the morning of the 14th, the strength of the British force engaged that day amounted to 733 sabres and 4,595 rifles. The cavalry casualties had been comparatively slight, totalling 22; but the infantry had lost about 20 per cent. of their numbers, the heaviest casualties being in the 120th, who had lost 29 per cent., in the 24th who had lost 27 per cent., and in the Dorsets who had lost 23 per cent.

The conduct of British and Indian troops had been excellent; and, among the many acts of gallantry performed,

---

* Killed: 11 British officers and 53 British other ranks; 6 Indian officers and 91 Indian other ranks. Wounded: 42 British officers and 220 British other ranks; 17 Indian officers, 620 Indian other ranks and 2 followers.

TURKISH STRENGTH AND CASUALTIES

General Delamain selected the conduct of the Indian mule-drivers, who took ammunition to the firing line of the Dorsets and 24th Punjabis, as worthy of special commendation. He cited an instance of a mule-driver, wounded himself, holding on to his struggling and wounded mules under very heavy rifle fire, as one of the most courageous acts that had come under his notice.

Although the first estimate of the enemy's casualties was considerably lower, it was later calculated that in the three days' fighting the hostile losses in killed and wounded totalled some six thousand,* including two thousand Arab tribesmen. In addition, the British had taken prisoner 18 officers and 724 other ranks. The enemy strength at the commencement of the fighting had been estimated† at one regular cavalry

---

* Information from Turkish sources places the effective strength of the Turkish regular troops at under 7,000 and their casualties at under 3,000, excluding Arab tribesmen.

† The Turkish " Order of Battle " was :—

As given in General Melliss' report.			As derived from Turkish sources.	
	31st Cavalry Regiment.		Headquarters of the Right Wing command.	
			Headquarters, 35th Division.	
			Three cavalry squadrons.	
32 guns	Seven batteries of field artillery (35th and 37th Regiments) each armed with four 8·7 c.m. guns. Two mountain guns, 38th Regiment. Two heavy guns (12·5 c.m.).		35th Division artillery regiment of two batteries field artillery, each of six guns. Murattab field battery of five guns. Two mountain guns. Two howitzers (10·5 c.m.).	21 guns.
	Engineer Company (from Aleppo).		Engineer Company (35th Division).	
35th Division under Raza Bey (killed)	Two battalions, 103rd Infantry Regiment. Two battalions, 104th Infantry Regiment. Two battalions, 105th Infantry Regiment.		Two battalions, 104th Regiment. Two battalions, 105th Regiment.	35th Division.
38th Division under Ali Bey	Two battalions, Fire Brigade Regiment. One battalion, Osmanjik Volunteers. One battalion, Baghdad gendarmerie. Two battalions, remnants of original 38th Division.		Two battalions, Fire Brigade Regiment. One Murattab battalion (amalgamation of Osmanjik battalion and 1/26th Regiment). Two Arab battalions, Murattab Iraq Regiment.	
(Note.—Each infantry battalion had been made up to 1,000 strong by the addition of Kurdish irregulars.)			(Note.—Ali Bey, the commander of the Fire Brigade Regiment, was in executive command of the whole force under the direction of Sulaiman Askari.)	
Two Red Crescent companies. 3,000 Arabs under *Sayad* Yezdi, 9,000 under Ajaimi, 2,000 in boats.			Field Hospital. Over 18,000 Arab tribesmen, including 3,700 horsemen, under Ajaimi and other leaders.	

regiment, 12,000 regular Turco-Arab infantry and 32 guns, assisted by 11,000 Arab Tribesmen, of whom 2,000 were in country boats in the adjacent waters. General Melliss calculated the hostile strength engaged on the 14th as 15,000 in all, including six regular battalions and six guns. The Turks had fought excellently; it was they alone who had held the line of trenches so gallantly on the 14th. The Arabs had given on the whole but feeble assistance.

It seems clear from accounts of the fight derived from Turkish soldiers that the Turks had formed no definite plan of action for the 14th.* The trenches they dug were shallow and hurriedly constructed, and many of their orders appear to have been marked by indecision. This no doubt is largely accounted for by the failure of the Arabs to co-operate. Early in the afternoon, Horse Artillery officers with the cavalry brigade saw an enemy column of troops and transport, stretching as far as the eye could see, retiring to the north-west from Barjisiya wood, but unfortunately this information did not reach General Melliss.

Whatever may have been the Turkish intentions they have every reason to be proud of the fight in which, in spite of their inferior artillery and the failure of their Arab allies, they nearly succeeded in beating off the British attack. General Melliss described it as a " Soldiers' Battle," which we may interpret by saying that superiority in manœuvre had little to do with gaining the victory, which was almost entirely attributable to the splendid fighting of the British and Indian regimental officers and men.

The siting of the Turkish trenches, facilitating concealment from hostile gunfire and offering an excellent field of rifle fire, had the disadvantage of making reinforcement very difficult and of rendering very costly in lives any withdrawal or retirement.

The Turks retreated to the north-west in wild confusion, harassed and robbed by the Arabs, and scarcely halted till they reached Khamisiya, about ninety miles distant from Shaiba. Their commander, Sulaiman Askari, insisted, it was said, on having the bed from which he could not move kept in Barjisiya wood throughout the fighting. After the day was lost, he assembled his officers and, denouncing the faithlessness

---

* There is nothing whatever in our own records, nor in the Turkish accounts of the battle, to suggest that there is any truth in a statement, sometimes published, that the final flight of the Turks was induced by the sight, on the sky-line, of what they took for fresh reinforcements, but which was in reality the line of transport carts escorted by the 48th Pioneers.

of the Arabs, shot himself rather than live to see the ruin of his project.

The decisive nature of the British victory was not at first fully realised. On the 15th, the cavalry brigade moved out to reconnoitre, and that night General Melliss reported that Old Basra, Zubair and Barjisiya were clear of the enemy, who had all retreated to Nukhaila and beyond it to the north-west.

General Nixon had been unable to despatch any reinforcements to Shaiba from Basra till the 14th. That morning a special convoy guard, organised with mountain guns on rafts, reached Shaiba without meeting serious opposition, carrying the remainder of the 24th Punjabis and ammunition. The boats returned to Basra that evening carrying wounded and Turkish prisoners.

The Euphrates Blockade flotilla had been too far off the scene of the fighting to afford any assistance on the 14th, but next morning they proceeded towards Nukhaila. Here finding many of the enemy escaping in boats, they pursued as far as Ratawi, destroying eight and capturing four large *mahailas*. On the 16th, a heavy gale prevented further pursuit, but next day, reinforced by two naval 4·7-inch guns* mounted in horse-boats, the flotilla pushed on to Ghabishiya, which was found to be deserted, and scattered enemy groups were observed retiring across the desert but offered no target. The flotilla, however, picked up much abandoned ammunition and stores.

At Qurna the Turks had carried out an ineffective bombardment of the British position from the 11th to the 13th, and on the 12th, a Turkish floating mine damaged seriously the British bridge of boats. But the results were entirely negligible, owing largely to the material assistance rendered by the *Espiègle, Odin, Miner* and *Lewis Pelly*.

Similarly, at Ahwaz there had been only a show of enemy activity. On the 11th, the *Comet* was hit and slightly damaged by several shells fired by an enemy gun near the banks of the Karun. On the 12th, the Turks shelled the British camp near Ahwaz and bodies of hostile cavalry and infantry were seen to the south and west of it, but the attack did not materialise and next day all was quiet.

In order to concentrate a striking force at Basra, General Nixon arranged, on the 17th, to withdraw a great part of the troops from Shaiba. The cavalry brigade less the 33rd Cavalry,

---

* Four of these guns had recently arrived from England; also four horse-boats from Suez in which to mount them.

the 18th Infantry Brigade and the 48th Pioneers were, however, to remain in a camp near Zubair, under the command of General Fry. On the same date, General Nixon asked India to expedite the despatch to Mesopotamia of the seven light draught steamers which had been procured at the request of General Barrett, as he pointed out that the presence of ample light draught river craft was essential for operations in the direction of Nasiriya. He also reported that he had sent orders to the Euphrates flotilla to blockade the main channel of the Euphrates at Suq ash Shuyukh; to operate against the Turkish columns there and at Khamisiya; and to report as to the feasibility of further operations. With these objects, this force was being reinforced from Qurna by one company each from the Oxfordshire and Buckinghamshire Light Infantry and the 103rd Mahrattas. On the 18th, the British cavalry, reconnoitring to Nukhaila, got into touch with the Blockade force and found that the enemy were reported to be between Khamisiya and Nasiriya, where it was said that they were being harassed and attacked by Arabs. The inland route taken by the Turks rendered them immune from attack by the Blockade force, which was now ordered to reconnoitre the water approaches of the Hammar lake and to Suq ash Shuyukh.

The Mesopotamia Commission Report says: " The occupation of Qurna . . . . and the victory at Barjisiya . . . . had realised the plan of the British Government in sending the expedition, save that something still remained to be done to complete the protection of the supply of oil." In view, however, of the decided opinion expressed by Lord Hardinge and others on the spot, and acquiesced in by the India Office, that Basra could not be considered as secure without the occupation of Nasiriya and Amara, this statement appears open to question.

The battle of Shaiba had several decisive results. It cleared the western approaches to Basra of a dangerous menace; it restored the power of initiative to the British; and it dissipated for the time being any chance of effective action by the Turks. Moreover, it gave General Nixon time and opportunity to consider the situation and to decide on the action he would take.

There were several alternatives before him. He could push on towards Nasiriya and, taking advantage of the Turks' disorganisation and the enmity now being displayed towards them by the Arabs, might even be able to occupy Nasiriya, one of his main objectives. It appears that General Nixon would have liked to follow this plan. But he lacked the necessary transport to move a sufficient force either across the desert or by water. Moreover, he had very little definite information regarding the country and the difficult water routes of this area; and it would take some little time to obtain what was necessary in this respect.

An advance might be made up the Tigris towards Amara from Qurna. Such an operation, besides threatening the line of retreat of the Turkish forces near Ahwaz, would probably make the Turks apprehensive of a movement on Baghdad. It would also probably have a settling effect on the Arab tribes near the Tigris and, if it caused the Turks to evacuate Arabistan, should react favourably on the Arab situation there. But here again the lack of river transport rendered such an operation out of the question for the time being.

Another alternative was to concentrate a British force at Ahwaz to operate against the Turks and Arabs in Arabistan. Such operations, if successful, would free General Nixon's eastern flank, would secure the position of the Shaikh of Mohammerah, and would restore the supply of oil, which had been interrupted. The chief difficulties to be encountered in this area, without considering the lack of land and river transport, were likely to lie in the desert nature of the country and in the daily increasing heat. The reports General Nixon received at this time of the local situation round Ahwaz conveyed to him the impression that immediate action there was very desirable, owing to the threatening attitude of the Turco-Arab forces, who were said to be in considerable strength, and also owing to the difficulty of obtaining supplies.

General Nixon decided to commence with operations in the Ahwaz direction. Here, the Bawi tribesmen—whose attitude had been rather uncertain—were said to have joined hands east of Ahwaz with the Cha'ab Arabs on the 15th April; the same day the Mohammerah levies, supported by the British armed launch *Shaitan*, successfully engaged a Bawi gathering on the east bank of the Karun below Ahwaz; while early that morning the Turks shelled the British camp and made a half-hearted demonstration against it. On the night of the 18th–19th, there was some sniping into the British camp, and General Davison, commanding at Ahwaz, reported that the Turco-Arab force was still at Ghadir and a Cha'ab-Bawi concentration about twelve miles to the east of Ahwaz.

On the 21st, General Nixon reported to India that he had begun to transfer troops to the left bank of the Shatt al Arab near Basra with the object of concentrating in the direction of Ahwaz. He was probably strengthened in his decision to undertake the offensive in Arabistan by a telegram of the 19th from the Secretary of State to the Viceroy. This telegram was repeated from India on the 21st to General Nixon, who was directed to use his discretion in the matter. Lord Crewe's telegram ran as follows :—

" . . . . Admiralty most anxious for early repair pipe-line as oil question becoming serious. Recent victory having averted danger from west, Government would welcome immediate move against enemy on Karun side if supply and transport render operation feasible. Moral effect of Shaiba followed up by successful attack from Ahwaz would probably terminate Arab disaffection and ensure future security of pipe-line. Early expulsion of Turks from Persian Arabistan very desirable. Such service to Persian Government may enable us to negotiate for summer quarters in Bakhtiari Hills.* I assume Nixon can concentrate ten thousand men near Ahwaz by end April for these operations."

On the 19th, General Nixon had wired to India asking for the reinforcement of his command by another cavalry brigade and a battalion of pioneers, saying that the cavalry then in Mesopotamia could not meet the demands that would shortly be made on that arm, and that more pioneers were required in view of the heavy labour that would be caused by obstructions in the rivers and by other works. On the 22nd, India replied that they could spare no more cavalry or pioneers. Their decision, which was approved by Lord Crewe, was influenced by their own anxieties regarding the internal situation in India and on the North-West Frontier. There was trouble with the Mohmands, and a great part of the Peshawar Division had been engaged in a fight with about four thousand Mohmands on the 18th.

Preparations continued for the operations in Arabistan, where, on the 23rd, Brigadier-General Lean (commanding 12th Infantry Brigade) took over command of Ahwaz from Major-General Davison, who had been appointed Inspector-General of Communications.

---

* This suggestion emanating from the India Office did not commend itself to General Nixon, who did not understand it and considered that it conflicted with the spirit of the instructions he had received in India.

In the meanwhile, the Euphrates flotilla were reconnoitring the waterways westward of the Hammar lake, and before the end of the month ascertained that none of those leading to Suq ash Shuyukh were navigable by British river steamers. This debarred an advance on Nasiriya by water for the time being.

The position at Qurna was unaltered, and when Major-General Townshend arrived at Basra on the 22nd to take over command of the 6th Division he was at once sent to report upon the situation at Qurna and the possibility of taking the offensive up the Tigris. Imbued with the necessity for striking before the Turks could reorganise, and undeterred by the physical difficulties before him, General Nixon was preparing with energy to carry out his instructions.

At the end of April, General Nixon calculated that the Turco-Arab forces in Mesopotamia were still disposed in three groups. There were six to seven thousand regular Turco-Kurdish troops with twenty guns between Nasiriya and Khamisiya, but still much disorganised. North of Qurna on the Tigris, there were four battalions with eight guns and two to three thousand Arabs. The *Marmariss* was on the Tigris in this neighbourhood; some thirty to sixty Germans were said to be with the Turkish forces here; and there was possibly a Turkish battalion at Amara. In Arabistan, at Illa,* there were two cavalry regiments, eight infantry battalions and seven guns, with three to five thousand Arabs.

On the 25th April, the British force was disposed as below :—

Locality.	Cavalry Squadrons.	Artillery (Guns and Howitzers).				Naval 4·7″ Guns.	Infantry Battalions.	Pioneer Battalions.	Sapper and Miner Coys.
		R.H.A.	R.F.A.	Mountain.	Heavy.				
Ahwaz	¾	—	6	—	—	—	5	—	¾
En route to Ahwaz*	6¼	6	11	—	—	—	6	¼	1
Qurna	—	—	—	—	4	—	3	—	1†
Basra	—	—	4	6	3	2‡	5½	—	½
Fao and Abadan	—	—	—	—	—	—	‡	—	—
Kurmat Ali	—	—	—	—	—	—	‡	—	—
Euphrates Blockade	—	—	1	—	1	2	Detachments.	—	—
Camp near Zubair	3	—	—	6	—	—	3	¼	—
Total	10	6	22	12	8	4	23	1	3

* Under command of General Gorringe, commanding the 12th Division.
† Also the bridging train.
‡ Being mounted in horse-boats.

* See Map 4.

CHAPTER X.

OPERATIONS IN ARABISTAN AND THE CAPTURE OF AMARA.

AS indicated in the previous chapter, General Nixon had decided to undertake operations in Persian Arabistan, and he entrusted their conduct to General Gorringe, the commander of the 12th Division. The primary object of these operations was the early expulsion of the Turks from Arabistan. Having accomplished this, General Gorringe was to take such military measures as might be necessary to allow of the oil pipe-line being repaired.

Neither the Turco-Arab force at Ghadir—consisting of some eight regular infantry battalions with eight guns and about seven thousand tribesmen—nor the three thousand Cha'ab and Bawi Arabs gathered to the eastward of Ahwaz had made any serious attempt to attack the British camp near Ahwaz.* The British force here comprised two troops 33rd Cavalry, the 82nd Field Battery, the 12th Infantry Brigade (2nd Queen's Own Royal West Kent Regiment, 4th Rajputs, 44th Merwara Infantry, 90th Punjabis) and the 67th Punjabis (33rd Infantry Brigade), the whole being under the command of Brigadier-General Lean, the commander of the 12th Infantry Brigade.

As has been already mentioned, the Government of India had been unable to complete the force in Mesopotamia up to the full authorised complement of two division. The main deficiencies were in field artillery, pioneers, field ambulances, signalling units, and transport. To meet local requirements, therefore, certain temporary or improvised units had to be organised. The available field artillery and pioneers were attached to either of the divisions as the operations required; combined field ambulances were organised to include sections for British and Indian troops; and a divisional signal unit for the 12th Division was formed by transfers of personnel and equipment from regimental units.

The column to move from Basra, which (in addition to the force mentioned above at Ahwaz) was to come under

---

* See Map 4.

AHWAZ.

ADVANCE UP THE KARUN

General Gorringe's orders for operations in Arabistan, was composed of two cavalry regiments, a horse artillery battery, two field artillery batteries (eleven guns), a Maxim battery (organised locally with six Maxim machine guns), a sapper and miner company, and six infantry battalions, together with the necessary administrative and transport units. The transport itself consisted of about 2,600 mules and 400 ponies. The whole force was organised as the 6th Cavalry Brigade, the 12th and 30th Infantry Brigades and Divisional Troops. As the 33rd Infantry Brigade had been broken up temporarily, two of its battalions were included among the Divisional Troops.*

The force from Basra effected its concentration on the Karun river partly by land and partly by river. Troops and transport began to cross to the left bank of the Shatt al Arab opposite Basra on the 21st April, whence they marched some thirty miles to the right bank of the Karun river. Here, at a point about fourteen miles above Mohammerah, they were joined by General Gorringe and his staff with a part of the troops that were to come from Basra by river. The combined force then marched up the right bank of the Karun to Saba, a distance of about twenty-five miles, where they were joined by the remainder of the troops coming by river from Basra. The whole movement had been considerably delayed by heavy rains.

On the 24th, General Gorringe received information that there was no lack of supplies at Ahwaz and that there were no signs of the enemy on the Karun, south of Ahwaz; though the Turco-Arab force was still between the Karun and the Karkha rivers. On the 27th, General Lean came from Ahwaz to see General Gorringe, who then learnt that the enemy had left Ghadir for Illa, but were believed to be still on the left, or near, bank of the Karkha river. As this river was reported to be in flood, every effort was now made to expedite the British advance in order to bring the enemy to action before they could cross it. General Lean at once returned to Ahwaz accompanied by the Divisional Engineer Commander to hasten on the arrangements for transporting overland from Ahwaz an improvised bridging train which General Gorringe had brought from Basra; and the column continued its advance up the Karun to Braika. The Arabs were now also adopting a different attitude; the Bawi were offering to guarantee the safety of the caravan routes through their country; and the Bani Turuf wished to negotiate.

---

* The full order of battle of this force is given in Appendix V.

On the 29th, a cavalry reconnaissance was sent out from Braika to ascertain whether, as reported by the Arabs, there was a sufficient water supply in the old bed of the Karkha river.* Major Anderson, 33rd Cavalry, was in command and had under him one squadron of his own regiment and one of the 7th Lancers. Reaching the old Karkha river-bed near Ali Ibn Husain, he encountered a body of Arabs, who professed to be entirely friendly and showed him where water was obtainable. Taking military precautions, the horses were watered by detachments; but by the time they had finished, the number of Arabs had increased and began to close in towards the British in an ominous manner. Thereupon Major Anderson called up the Arab Shaikh, while he gave orders that the main body should mount and retire. Major Anderson himself remained behind to speak to the Shaikh, who displayed some excitement and exclaimed: "The troops must go." On this, Major Anderson sent two British officers to withdraw the flank patrols and to call back the advanced guard respectively; and he sent a third British officer, who was with him, to join the main body.

Almost immediately, however, the Arabs on the flanks—who were about fifteen hundred strong—opened fire and began closing in on the retiring main body. They also attacked the advanced guard and the flanking patrols as they withdrew; and both the British officers who had been sent to order this withdrawal and Major Anderson himself were killed before they could rejoin the main body, thus falling victims to Arab treachery. The British force succeeded, however, in getting clear, and—keeping the Arabs at bay—carried out a steady retirement, in which they suffered twelve casualties in addition to the three British officers. They had, however, achieved their purpose; for they could report that the ground between Braika and the old bed of the Karkha offered no obstacle to the movement of guns and wheeled transport and that the water supply was probably sufficient.

On the 1st May, General Melliss, the commander of the 30th Infantry Brigade, took out from Braika another reconnoitring force—composed of the 6th Cavalry Brigade, the 63rd Field Battery, the 30th Infantry Brigade and a company of the 48th Pioneers—to select a suitable position for an advanced depôt on the old Karkha river. Owing to

---

* The maps of Arabistan were inaccurate and misleading, and before all the operations there, at this period, preliminary ground reconnaissance was a necessity.

PREPARATIONS FOR FURTHER ADVANCE 227

the desert nature of the country, any force operating away from the Karun river had to carry with it all the fuel and fodder it required, besides other supplies; and General Gorringe's transport could only carry sufficient for two days. To give him the necessary freedom of manœuvre to cope with the opposition that might be expected, General Gorringe was, therefore, obliged to adopt the system of sending a portion of his force ahead to form an advanced depôt; which depôt he had to fill up with sufficient supplies for any projected operations before he could bring up to it the remainder of his force. General Melliss having reported that he had found a suitable position with an ample water supply near Ali Ibn Husain, General Gorringe decided to form his first advanced depôt there.

In spite of adverse weather—a strong dust-storm blew all day on the 2nd, causing great discomfort to the men, and heavy rain at other times impeded the transport—supplies for ten days were collected at Ali Ibn Husain by the evening of the 3rd May. Next day the whole force was concentrated there, except the 4th Rajputs, left to garrison the camp near Ahwaz and the bridging train, which, in spite of strenuous exertions on the part of the engineers, did not arrive from Ahwaz till the night of the 5th–6th. In the meantime, reconnaissance had shown that the Turkish force about Illa had all crossed over to the right bank of the Karkha, which was reported to be in flood and at least two hundred yards wide.

General Gorringe decided to push on to Illa in the hope of bringing the Turks to action and thus assisting the operations projected by General Nixon from Qurna. The cavalry were therefore despatched to Illa to reconnoitre and discover a place for crossing the Karkha. This was found near Illa, and although the actual width to be spanned there was two hundred and fifty yards, it was decided on as the best place to cross both from a tactical and a technical point of view. An advance was therefore made on Illa during the night 6th–7th by the cavalry, the field artillery and the 30th Infantry Brigade; and by 6 a.m. on the 7th a sufficient number of the canvas boats* with the bridging train had been assembled to commence a flying bridge. Although the crossing was unopposed, the construction of a bridge proved very difficult. The river, two hundred and fifty yards wide, with steep clay banks, was in full flood with a strong current. A gale of wind was blowing and the material for the flying bridge—designed

---

* These boats were improvised of planks enclosed in service tarpaulins.

for a maximum width of one hundred and fifty yards—had to be adapted to cover the increased span. While the bridge was in course of construction, troops were ferried across the river in canvas boats and in a motor-boat which had been brought from Ahwaz. But it was a tedious and difficult operation; and by dusk only three-quarters of the 76th Punjabis and half the 2/7th Gurkhas had been got across, and had entrenched themselves on the further, or right bank.*

During the day, the Cavalry Brigade had made a demonstration downstream to divert attention from the crossing. They encountered some hostile Arabs who dispersed on being shelled, and about five miles to the northward—in the low hills and broken ground—enemy patrols could be seen observing the British movements.

On the morning of the 8th, the rest of General Gorringe's force reached Illa, but the flying bridge was not in working order till late on the 9th. Even then the crossing remained difficult, as the canvas boats of which this bridge was mainly composed afforded a somewhat unstable structure. The heavy gale which prevailed also hindered the crossing and the swimming across of the horses and mules;† and it was not till the 13th that the Cavalry Brigade, the 30th Infantry Brigade and the 82nd Field Battery managed to get across. Supplies for ten days had now reached Illa and the 44th Merwara Infantry were sent back to Ghadir to form a post there on the line of communication with Ahwaz.

In the meantime the Turks were reported to have retired beyond Khafajiya; and on the afternoon of the 13th, part of the British force commenced an advance in pursuit to the north-west. They moved in two columns with the intention of ascertaining whether the Turks were at Bisaitin and also of punishing, at Khafajiya, the Bani Turuf Arabs, who had mutilated our wounded in the action of the 3rd March.

The first column, under the personal command of General Gorringe, moved along the northern, or right, bank of the Karkha. It consisted of the 6th Cavalry Brigade,‡ the Maxim Battery, the 30th Infantry Brigade (less 1/4th Hampshire and 24th Punjabis), and the 82nd Field Battery.

---

* The Karkha river (as shown in Map 4) flows southward and then westward, finally wasting itself into marshes.

† General Gorringe brought specially to notice the excellent work of men of the 66th and 76 Punjabis in manning the boats and in helping to swim the animals across.

‡ Only one section of the R.H.A. Battery accompanied the brigade.

The second column, under General Lean, comprised the West Kents, the 67th Punjabis, half the 12th Sapper and Miner Company with canvas boats and bridging material, and a company of the 48th Pioneers. This column moved along the left bank of the Karkha.

The remainder of the troops remained at Illa to protect the crossing and to assist in bringing up more supplies. A second flying bridge was erected here by them and more canvas boats were put together.

Before daylight on the 14th, the infantry and field battery of General Gorringe's column under General Melliss occupied a concealed position in the hills east of Khafajiya, while General Gorringe with the Cavalry Brigade and the Maxim Battery reconnoitred as far as Bisaitin. Here no signs of the enemy were found and it was subsequently ascertained that they had retired from there towards Amara one or two days earlier.

General Lean's column, which had in the meanwhile been advancing in readiness to co-operate if necessary with the cavalry retirement, was now ordered to move on Khafajiya, as the cavalry were experiencing no opposition. At 4 p.m., General Gorringe instructed General Melliss to move down to the Karkha and try to seize some boats for operations next day against Khafajiya in co-operation with General Lean. But General Melliss had already commenced an advance towards Khafajiya in response to a request from General Lean for artillery support in case of opposition. The advance of General Melliss' force was strongly opposed by the Arabs; but, well supported by the fire of the 82nd Field Battery, his two battalions (76th Punjabis and 2/7th Gurkhas) pushed their way through the intervening marsh to the right bank of the river opposite the Shaikh's fort at Khafajiya. This place, which was held by the Arabs, consisted of a collection of straggling villages composed of mud houses and stretched for about four miles along the left bank of the Karkha. By 5 p.m., the cavalry had returned, and although many of the men were suffering from the effects of the intense heat, the horse artillery and maxim batteries came into action to support General Melliss' advance.

The progress of General Lean's column had, however, been very slow on account of the physical difficulties it had encountered. The great heat had affected the troops considerably, and the ground to be traversed was intersected by numerous creeks and marshes. Many men fell out affected by the heat and these had to be placed on the bridging rafts and boats, which were being towed downstream.

The Arabs opposing General Melliss suffered considerable losses; an attempt by them to work round the British right flank had been easily frustrated by the horse artillery guns; and many of the Arab houses had been set on fire by the British shells. But the day was waning and General Gorringe ordered the troops to withdraw northward to their bivouac. This withdrawal—which was almost unmolested—was covered by the 66th Punjabis, who had been sent for from Illa by General Melliss when he started his advance. General Lean's column bivouacked in the evening about five miles short of Khafajiya.

On the 15th, General Gorringe sent back the horse artillery and the 33rd Cavalry to Illa, as he was finding it difficult to get up sufficient supplies and also the ground was unsuitable for mounted operations. At 8 a.m., General Melliss was instructed to resume operations against Khafajiya. General Lean's column was now in sight, but its advance was being much delayed by having to cross various canals; and General Melliss' infantry moved forward to the river-bank under cover of its own field artillery fire. A crossing of the river was now effected by a party of volunteers from the 76th Punjabis of his force. These, led with great gallantry by Subadar-Major Ajab Khan, swam across and captured a boat on the opposite bank, the operation being covered by the fire of the 82nd Field Battery and of the remainder of the infantry. This boat was now used to ferry other men over, carrying about twenty at a time. There were about a thousand Arabs opposing the crossing and a similar number were seen to be retiring before General Lean's column. But the accurate artillery and rifle covering fire of the British drove the enemy back from the vicinity of the river and set on fire several huts near the bank; and a company of the 76th Punjabis, under Major C. L. Perrin, successfully made good their footing on the further bank. Owing to the excellence of the covering fire they had sustained but few casualties.

The enemy could now be seen retiring everywhere and only a few remained firing from various houses. In one of the largest of these, whose walls were double and could therefore withstand artillery fire, there were about fifty Arabs who asked for an officer to come forward and accept their surrender, only, however, to shoot at him and at the political officer when they advanced for this purpose. But they soon paid for

CAPTURE OF KHAFAJIFA

their treachery. It was decided to set fire to the roof to save undue loss of life; and after this had been done, the enclosure was assaulted and captured by the 76th company, who killed thirty-three Arabs in the operation and took prisoner eleven more. After this, opposition gradually slackened and, as the day had been very hot and trying for the troops, General Gorringe broke off operations at 4 p.m. By this time, another company of the 76th Punjabis had been ferried across and joined the first company whose action had been so admirable. This half battalion then bivouacked for the night on the left bank of the river.

Meanwhile the advance of General Lean's column had continued to be very slow. Although the Arabs offered the column a certain amount of opposition, the delay was mainly due to the various water-ways that had to be bridged. By nightfall the column was still short of Khafajiya and their rear-guard did not get into bivouac till 11 p.m. The total British casualties during the day, from enemy action, only amounted to fifteen, of whom thirteen were among the 76th Punjabis.

At 8 a.m. on the 16th, General Lean's column joined hands with the 76th Punjabis; and punitive measures against the Arabs in Khafajiya were continued. Their casualties are unknown, but a hundred dead bodies were counted. Large quantities of their grain were destroyed and about a thousand sheep and cattle were captured. They thus learnt their mistake in relying on the Turks to protect them and received a salutary lesson for their inhumanity and treachery in action.

General Gorringe had now effected his task of driving the Turks out of Arabistan and thus enabled General Nixon to reduce the British forces there; orders being sent for the withdrawal to Basra of the 63rd Field Battery and of the 30th Infantry Brigade. General Gorringe was, however, instructed to carry out demonstrations towards Amara until the 26th, in order to prevent the Turks withdrawing troops from Amara to reinforce their detachment in front of Qurna. Leaving General Lean for this purpose in camp near Khafajiya with the 7th Lancers, 82nd Field Battery, the West Kents and the 67th Punjabis, General Gorringe himself moved back with the rest of the force to Illa.

On receiving instructions from General Nixon that the demonstrations towards Amara were to be continued until the 29th, General Gorringe decided to reconnoitre personally as far as Umm Chir. Taking with him two horse artillery guns, the 33rd Cavalry, the Maxim Battery and the 90th Punjabis, General Gorringe moved to Khafajiya on the 26th. From there he moved out with his whole force (except the 90th Punjabis) on the night of the 27th–28th as far as Bisaitin, while he pushed the cavalry on to Umm Chir, but without finding any signs of the enemy. He ascertained, however, that the Turkish force which had retired to Amara had moved with their guns along a direct route, which he had hitherto been led to believe was impassable for a force of all three arms. This being so, there was no reason why the British should not also send a force by this route, if it became necessary. His force now remained at Bisaitin for some days.

By this time the extreme heat and the trying conditions of this desert area had had a considerably adverse effect on the health of the British troops. Exposure to the sun, lack of fresh vegetables and the indifferent nature of the drinking water had caused much sickness, and many of the force were suffering from diarrhœa or dysentery. This applied specially to the cavalry, who had become practically incapable of any severe or long-continued work; for most of the officers and men—though not actually on the sick list—were in bad health and thoroughly run down. The 7th Lancers and 33rd Cavalry, though nominally each comprising three squadrons, could on the night of the 27th–28th only turn out between them a total of ten British officers and four hundred and thirty-three Indian ranks. The medical personnel were also feeling the strain and the hospitals were overworked and overcrowded. India had been unable to send sufficient medical units with the last two brigades and could not always replace the casualties now beginning to occur among the medical personnel. This particularly applied to the Indian sub-assistant surgeon class.*

On the 29th, General Lean had to be placed on the sick list, and next day General Gorringe moved back with the 33rd Cavalry from Bisaitin to Illa. General Kennedy, the cavalry commander, was left in command at Bisaitin with instructions to make arrangements for an advance on Amara. For this purpose he was to organise the collection of local supplies and local transport.

On the 3rd June, however, Amara had fallen to General Townshend, and two days later General Gorringe received

---

* A separate history is being compiled of the medical arrangements in the different theatres of the world-war and in consequence the subject is not being entered into here in any detail. It may, however, be said that up till May, 1915, the medical arrangements gave little cause for complaint.

instructions to send a cavalry regiment and a field battery for garrison duty there; three battalions of the 12th Infantry Brigade were to accompany them and subsequently to proceed thence by river to Basra. In accordance with these orders, the 7th Lancers, the 82nd Field Battery, three-quarters of the West Kents and the 67th and 90th Punjabis left Bisaitin on the 9th June, reaching Amara on the 14th without opposition. This was fortunate, as the intense heat and the brackish or salt marshes made the march sufficiently trying for men and animals, already enervated by their seven weeks' campaigning in Arabistan.*

Meanwhile General Gorringe had obtained information that the Ayahshah section of the Bani Tamin tribe—who had been responsible for the treacherous attack on Major Anderson's cavalry on the 29th April—were collecting their crops and were camped in the neighbourhood of Ali Ibn Husain. As soon as arrangements had been made for the despatch of the force mentioned above to Amara, General Gorringe moved out of Illa on the night 8th-9th June to surprise all the three encampments in which these Arabs had been located. The British column consisted of the 33rd Cavalry, two guns of the 76th Field Battery, the Maxim Battery, the 11th Rajputs, 44th Infantry and 66th Punjabis, with some signal and medical units. Marching by night, these troops reached a point of assembly about one and a half miles equidistant from all three Arab encampments, against each of which a portion of the force advanced at 4 a.m. The surprise was nearly entirely successful, but as the troops approached some men and dogs gave the alarm and most of the Arabs escaped. They had no time, however, to remove their ammunition, household effects or grain, which fell into our hands. The 66th Punjabis and 11th Rajputs returned in the evening to Illa and Ghadir respectively, while the rest of the force marched to Ahwaz. The heat during the day had again been intense and four of our men succumbed to its effects.

This ended the operations in Arabistan, which had been completely successful. The oil pipe-line had been repaired by the Anglo-Persian Oil Company under an escort of Bawi tribesmen and by the 13th June oil was once again reaching the refinery at Abadan. General Gorringe himself left Ahwaz for Basra on the 15th and further evacuation of troops was carried out as quickly as possible.

---

* Candler in his " Long Road to Baghdad " (p. 244) cites the vivid details of this march given him by an officer who took part in it.

Although the force had suffered few casualties in action, the effect of the local conditions on them had been serious. On the 24th April the total strength of the force had amounted to 12,556, and, though this number was considerably reduced by withdrawal of units from the 17th May onwards, there had been, up to the 12th June, 2,773 admissions to hospital on account of sickness. It was therefore with much relief that officers and men left Arabistan, even though it might be for the sodden heat of Basra. The lack of trees, bushes or grass in the burning desert of Arabistan gave a tiring monotony, which was usually only broken by hot sand-storms; and these only aggravated the general discomfort by filling the atmosphere with a hot, suffocating grit or sand. The only time of moderate comfort was after sunset, when usually the wonderful cool silent nights—only to be appreciated fully in a desert country like this—came as a perfect godsend after the days of scorching and blinding heat.

In these operations the work of the auxiliary services had been in some cases even more arduous than those of the combatant units. The medical and transport personnel in particular had been labouring continuously under most trying conditions, and the corps they represented have every reason to be proud of their work here.

By the 20th June, the force remaining at Ahwaz consisted of the Cavalry Brigade (23rd* and 33rd Cavalry and " S " Battery R.H.A.), 76th Field Battery, a section of the 12th Sapper and Miner Company, the 33rd Infantry Brigade (now composed of the 4th and 11th Rajputs and the 66th Punjabis) and a pack wireless set; the whole being under command of Major-General R. Wapshare, who had recently arrived from East Africa to command the 33rd Brigade.

In the meantime, there had been a certain amount of telegraphic correspondence between the India Office, India, and General Nixon in regard to the operations proposed by the latter in pursuance of his instructions. It will be recalled that General Nixon had been ordered to prepare plans for the effective occupation of the Basra *vilayet*, i.e., of Amara and Nasiriya; and that a copy of his instructions had been sent to the India Office by post on the 7th April. A study of the evidence taken by the Mesopotamia Commission and of the records shows that the tenor of these instructions, which had reached the India Office by the 2nd May, had not been thoroughly appreciated there.

---

* The 23rd Cavalry had arrived at Ahwaz from India on the 10th June.

In agreeing with the decision of the Government of India in refusing General Nixon's request for an additional cavalry brigade, as mentioned in the last chapter, Lord Crewe had wired on the 24th April as follows :—

"... with reference to Nixon's request for a cavalry brigade, I concur in your decision, as, apart from impossibility of complying, the approach of hot season renders despatch of more troops, especially British, inadvisable. Nixon's demand implies intention on his part of important offensive movement. I presume he clearly understands that Government will not sanction at this moment any advance beyond present theatre of operations. We must confine ourselves during summer to defence of Basra *vilayet* and oil interests in Arabistan. If, after smashing enemy in Karun direction, it is possible to advance to Amara with view to establishing an outpost which will control tribesmen between there and Karun and so contribute to security of pipe-line, I should be prepared to accept such a proposal provided it is supported by you, but I deprecate any plan involving undue extension and possible demands for reinforcements. Strategically our present position is a sound one, and at present we cannot afford to take risks by unduly extending it. We must play a safe game in Mesopotamia."

This telegram was repeated by India next day to General Nixon. In regard to this and subsequent telegrams, Lord Crewe told the Mesopotamia Commission that he personally regarded the proposal to advance to Amara at that time with no enthusiasm. Although he certainly had in his mind that in due course the whole of the Basra *vilayet* would be occupied and administered, there appeared to him to be certain drawbacks to doing it then, i.e., the approach of the hot weather, the necessary extension of the line of communication which would put a further strain on the transport and medical arrangements, and the fact that the War Office could give no help. He also had in his mind that General Nixon appeared to be inclined towards a too ambitious extension of operations and might not realise that India could send him no more troops. In justice to General Nixon, it must be said that his main reason for deprecating any unnecessary delay was to allow the Turks no time to reinforce or reorganise their defences.

On the 17th May, General Nixon telegraphed to India a brief appreciation of the situation in Mesopotamia. Most of the Turkish regular troops which had been engaged at Shaiba had left Nasiriya for Kut al Amara and were thought to have gone thence to Baghdad to reorganise, and to have no intention of joining in any anticipated fighting near Amara; about three battalions had remained at Nasiriya, where Ajaimi with a force of Arabs and some guns was believed to be in no condition to initiate an offensive movement; Arabistan had been cleared of the Turks by General Gorringe who was also dealing effectively with the hostile Arabs there; and at Ruta on the Tigris, the Turks had about four battalions and six guns with a party of Germans assisting them by the construction and lodgment of floating mines. General Nixon stated that the lack of shallow-draught steamers* necessitated postponement for the time being of any advance towards Nasiriya, but he was arranging to attack the Turkish positions near Ruta, so that the 6th Division might be able, with the help of the Royal Navy, to advance to Amara. He was withdrawing from Ahwaz to Basra all the troops that the small amount of dry ground at Basra enabled him to encamp there.

Thereupon, General Nixon was asked by India for an assurance that he would not require reinforcements for the contemplated advance to Amara, as the Secretary of State would probably ask for this before sanctioning the operation. General Nixon replied on the 21st giving the necessary assurance; and on the 23rd May the Viceroy sent the following telegram to Lord Crewe:—

"Your telegram of 24th ultimo . . . Nixon proposes to take offensive from Qurna up Tigris on 24th and does not consider any reinforcement will be required. We consider this move desirable in order to extend our control over Tigris valley, thereby securing the pipe-line and protecting the Basra *vilayet* in accordance with his orders, and do not propose to interfere with his intention. He will not of course proceed beyond Amara without your sanction."

As mentioned above, Lord Crewe, while admitting that the possession of Amara might secure Ahwaz from raids, was not in favour of the operation, as he considered that there was a risk in holding so advanced a post during the summer months and before there were available† sufficient light-draught gun-

---

* Five of the steamers and four launches of those asked for from India had arrived by this time and two more steamers and four tugs arrived two days later. But they all required much overhauling after their oversea voyage before they were fit to use.

† The two river gunboats sent by the Admiralty from Egypt had sunk in their passage through the Red Sea in April; and on the 6th May Lord Crewe telegraphed to India that the Admiralty had arranged for twelve river gunboats for Mesopotamia, of which four would be ready for use in October.

AMARA ADVANCE SANCTIONED

boats to secure the line of communication ; he also considered that by this advance we were giving up an impregnable position for one of dissemination of forces. It is of interest to note, in regard to this opinion, that General Barrow, Lord Crewe's principal military adviser, informed the Mesopotamia Commission that he had since come to the conclusion, in the light of subsequent events, that the Government of India were justified in recommending this movement. His reason for this conclusion was that the Turkish operations towards Ahwaz showed the necessity of holding Amara in order to ensure the security of the oil-fields and pipe-line.

Lord Crewe on the same day sent a " clear the line " telegram sanctioning the proposed movement on the clear understanding that General Nixon was satisfied that he could concentrate a sufficient garrison at Amara to withstand any attack during the summer from Baghdad, as it might be difficult during that period to move up reinforcements, and General Nixon must understand clearly that no more troops could be sent to Mesopotamia. Lord Crewe went on to say that he should have been consulted regarding this movement before the last moment, for, as he said, " Questions jointly involving civil and military policy should under present circumstances only be decided by the Cabinet."

The Viceroy's telegram of the 23rd and Lord Crewe's reply were repeated from India on the 24th to General Nixon for his information and guidance. On the same day Lord Crewe telegraphed to the Viceroy asking him to impress on General Nixon the necessity of protecting the pipe-line throughout, as the Admiralty attached great importance to the uninterrupted maintenance of oil supply at Abadan and regarded it as a matter of extreme urgency.

On the 25th May, General Nixon wired to India at some length. He requested definite orders as to whether the occupation of Amara and Nasiriya was to be carried out in order to obtain control of the Basra *vilayet* or not. It seemed to him that the policy laid down in the written orders given to him on the 24th March at Army Headquarters in India and that laid down in the Secretary of State's telegram of the 23rd May were at variance. He did not think it probable that the Turks would be able to collect very superior forces at Baghdad, but no guarantee could be given that they would not. He took exception to Lord Crewe's apparent umbrage at having been informed of the intended advance on Amara only at the eleventh hour, pointing out that the possibility of an offensive movement from Qurna had been referred to in a telegram of his (i.e., Nixon's) to India on the 24th April; and that he had, on the 27th April in another telegram to India, stated that he was attending to the organisation and preparations for operations on the Tigris line. He stated that the enemy had recently been strengthening their position on the Tigris about Ruta, and that it was necessary to attack them there whether the advance was continued beyond that spot or not.

General Nixon went on to say that unless we were prepared to occupy Nasiriya and gain control of the powerful Arab tribes of the western portion of the Basra *vilayet*, our attitude at Basra could only be a defensive one—and he instanced the battle of Shaiba as the result of such an attitude. In his opinion, our safest policy was to take up a position at Nasiriya or Suq ash Shuyukh with a line of communication by water; and he asked for definite sanction to an advance on Nasiriya as soon as water transport was available from the Tigris. He pointed out that if this advance were delayed until after the middle of July, the lack of water in the Hammar lake would prevent our bringing up guns to force an opposed landing and would, therefore, entail a march across one hundred and ten miles of desert.

General Nixon concluded by saying that he did not contemplate any advance beyond Amara and Nasiriya and that the force at his disposal could effect the occupation of these two places. He pointed out that another Turkish advance on Ahwaz could not be prevented without the occupation of Amara; but that with Amara in British hands our troops could eventually be withdrawn from Ahwaz and be set free for work on either the Tigris or the Euphrates.

These several telegrams were not repeated to the India Office at the time, but in replying on the 27th May to General Nixon's wire of the 25th May the Chief of the General Staff, India, pointed out that the India Office must have received a copy* of General Nixon's instructions before Lord Crewe sent his telegram of the 23rd May, which was not regarded in India as conflicting with the general directions given General Nixon on the 24th March, but rather as conveying instructions that no reinforcements would be sent to Mesopotamia. As regards Lord Crewe's complaint of only being informed of the proposed advance on Amara at the last moment, the Government of

---

* This copy, sent by mail but delayed in transit, did not come to the notice of either Lord Crewe or General Barrow when the telegrams in question were sent.

India were well aware of General Nixon's intentions and were responsible if any delay occurred in informing the Secretary of State. The Commander-in-Chief in India agreed with General Nixon's views in regard to the reasons for and importance of occupying Amara and Nasiriya, and considered that it ought to be his first object to expel the Turks from the river Tigris below Amara.

The telegram then went on to repeat Lord Crewe's telegram of the 24th May regarding the importance of protecting the pipe-line and pointed out that this object would be achieved by General Nixon's movement on Amara ; which would also enable General Nixon both to form a better opinion as to whether the Turks were receiving reinforcements or not and to judge the best time for an advance on Nasiriya, should he consider this desirable later on.

On the 26th, General Nixon in his daily progress report, which was as usual repeated to the India Office, stated that General Townshend reported that by the 31st his arrangements for an offensive movement from Qurna against Ruta would be complete ; and General Nixon hoped that by the time General Townshend had reorganised his river transport, after this offensive movement, clear orders would have reached him regarding the policy to be followed in the matter of an advance towards Amara. This telegram reached the India Office on the 27th May, the day that Mr. Austen Chamberlain succeeded Lord Crewe as Secretary of State for India ; and on the next day Mr. Chamberlain sent the following telegram to the Viceroy :—

" . . . Please see my predecessor's telegram of the 24th April.* I cannot give further instructions till I know with what force he (Nixon) is advancing and immediate objects contemplated. Our policy must depend partly on local factors, forces locally available and resistance expected, and partly on situation elsewhere. If you contemplate occupation of Amara I should like to know what force Nixon considers necessary for its garrison during summer and how generally he proposes to distribute his troops during summer months."

The Viceroy replied on the 1st June :—

" . . . General Nixon was instructed on the 27th May that his first object is to expel Turks from lower Tigris below Amara, thereby securing the safety of Basra and

---

* This was the telegram given above saying that we must play a safe game in Mesopotamia.

Qurna from attack from the north and at the same time guarding the oil supply as directed in your telegram of 24th May. He (i.e., Nixon) reports that this operation will begin on 31st May

"Its progress should give him data which will enable him to give us better the information you now request. We feel however that while military operations are actually in progress and in present quite uncertain military situation in Lower Mesopotamia it would be undesirable and even dangerous to tie him down with precise orders which might not fit in with the local situation which confronts him. He may possibly find himself opposed by superior military forces on the Tigris which may impose on him a defensive attitude or he may find himself strong enough to dominate situation. But neither he nor we can yet say.

"We therefore think it desirable for the present not to alter our original instructions to him which were sent you by post on 7th April, except in so far as they have been modified by your subsequently received directions and in particular those which directed safeguarding of pipe-line, i.e., your telegram of 24th May. Under the original instructions, he will, as soon as he is in a position to do so, submit a plan for the occupation of the Basra *vilayet* which includes Amara. This he will do with a far more complete knowledge of the local situation than is now available and we will then report to you for further orders. We should not propose to authorise any advance beyond Amara, for which his force is not adequate."

In addition to the chance that we might have to face further risings of Arabs instead of looking for effective co-operation from them, there were other reasons which at this stage influenced the India Office in adopting a cautious policy in Mesopotamia. Persian affairs were in a critical state; the German Minister was almost complete master of the situation at Tehran; and the attitude of the Bakhtiaris was giving some anxiety. Such a state of affairs was very likely to react on the situation in Afghanistan,* and also in India where, though the position was rather more reassuring owing to the precautionary measures that had been taken, there were still many causes for anxiety. The Turks were also now threatening Aden. But most important of all, perhaps, was the question

---

* During May reports reached H.M. Government from various sources that parties of Turkish and German officers were well on their way to Afghanistan.

SITUATION ON THE EUPHRATES

of the Dardanelles operations. These were being watched with particular interest by Moslems, especially in Afghanistan and India, and the results might, therefore, be expected to have considerable effect in the East. But the force under Sir Ian Hamilton had, for the time being, been brought to a complete standstill; and H.M. Government were as yet uncertain whether, with the resources at their disposal, they could make the necessary effort in Gallipoli and at the same time meet the demands of the Western front.

To turn again to the operations westward and northward of Basra. By the end of May, the British detachment near Zubair had been gradually reduced till it consisted of the 16th Cavalry, 23rd Mountain Battery, 7th Rajputs and 110th Mahrattas, under command of General Fry. It was now located in a new post called Fort George, near Old Basra, and owing to the high floods had to be supplied entirely by water. By the middle of May the duties of the Euphrates blockade force had been taken over by the navy, who carried out the work with armed launches. In addition to patrolling, these launches reconnoitred and examined the channels leading into the western end of the Hammar lake, where on several occasions they encountered and exchanged fire with two Turkish "Thornycroft" launches and at times with hostile riflemen. It had been ascertained that the Akaika channel* was blocked by a dam, and the Turkish launches, firing from behind this, were safe from close attack and could retire unmolested out of range whenever the British fire became too dangerous. It was also reported that the Turks had placed artillery in position above the dam, that they had mined the Akaika channel, and had placed an obstruction in the fairway of the Euphrates between Suq ash Shuyukh and Nasiriya. These precautions showed that the Turks were still nervous of a British advance in this direction, though by this time the intelligence reports were all to the effect that practically all the Turkish regular troops from Nasiriya had retired up the Shatt al Hai.

On the 24th April, General Townshend arrived at Qurna to report, as indicated in the last chapter, on the possibility of taking the offensive from there. The garrison at Qurna then consisted of four heavy guns (two 5-inch and two 4-inch), the Sirmur sapper and miner company, three infantry battalions of the 17th Brigade, a bridging train and a searchlight section,

---

* Leading to above Suq ash Shuyukh from the Hammar lake.

all under command of General Dobbie; and three days later the 1/5th Hants Howitzer Battery R.F.A. (four 5-inch howitzers) joined the garrison.

The defensive perimeter at Qurna included the Arab town; an inconvenient arrangement, rendering the defensive line unduly extensive for the size of the garrison and, owing to the Arab traffic, making enemy espionage easy. There was a bridge of boats connecting Qurna with the left bank of the Tigris, the bridge-head on the left bank being held by the 22nd Punjabis. To protect this bridge and the British ships from floating mines, a boom had been placed across the river close to and under the fire of Fort Snipe, the British advanced post two thousand yards to the north of the Qurna defences on the right bank of the Tigris, which was held by a company of infantry. This boom was not altogether satisfactory, being rather far away, and a second boom was now constructed only three hundred yards above the bridge.

A prominent feature in the British position was the observation tower ninety feet high, which had been constructed by the sappers with platforms at intervals. From here, far above the tops of the highest palm-trees, an extensive view was obtainable of the surrounding country. The garrison were accommodated in reed huts constructed among the palm-trees by the sappers, and two pumps (worked by oil engines) had been installed to keep the water within reasonable limits. But unceasing work on the raised roads and the protective *bunds* was nevertheless necessary to keep the water from breaking through, while nothing could prevent considerable quantities percolating through the soil. The heat was intense and moist and the effect on the men of this uncomfortable existence, combined with their enforced military inactivity, was depressing and enervating in the extreme. Bad as the conditions were in Arabistan and near Basra, there were few at Qurna who would not have welcomed an exchange of duties; and the constant cheeriness of the garrison under conditions that can only be realised properly by those who experienced them is worthy of our highest admiration. At this, as in later stages of the Mesopotamian operations, congratulations from people at home to officers and men belonging to Force " D " on their absence from the water-logged trenches in Flanders were a source of considerable amusement.

From the observation tower as far as the eye could see the view consisted of a vast expanse of water westward, northward and eastward. The only variations were partially submerged palm-trees in the neighbourhood of Qurna, some miles of reeds* and the sandhill islands held by the Turks.† Between these islands and Qurna the depth of water averaged one to three feet, but channels of varying breadth and depth ran in every direction and were quite undistinguishable among the general flood. These rendered it out of the question to advance by wading ; while the shallowness of the greater part of the area, the concealment of the deeper channels and the presence of Turkish mines limited the extent to which the ordinary river craft could be utilised.

The Turkish main position was astride the Tigris about Abu Aran, Muzaibila and Ruta ; while they held advanced positions on the sandhills in front of Ruta, on One Tree Hill, and on the hillocks to the north and south of Barbukh creek.† The enemy's strength was estimated at five or six infantry battalions with eight guns and two thousand Arabs.

Before leaving Basra for Qurna General Townshend had an interview with General Nixon, to whom he suggested that the Turks should be driven north of Amara by a combined movement from Qurna and Ahwaz. His reason for this was that the flooded nature of the country in the region of the Tigris rendered all manœuvre impossible. He reached Qurna on the 24th April, and after inspecting there, proceeded in the *Odin*, first for four or five miles up the Tigris and then along the Euphrates to reconnoitre the Al Huwair creek. General Dobbie advised him that a turning movement to the east of the Tigris up the Shwaiyib river was not feasible, owing to the narrowness of the Shwaiyib channel and the probability that it had been mined. After instructing General Dobbie to sent out reconnaissances to see if a practicable fordable route could be found north-eastward of Muzaira'a towards the sandhills and the Ruta creek, General Townshend returned on the 26th to Basra. Next day he made his report to General Nixon. He had satisfied himself that the Turkish positions north of Qurna could not be turned tactically and he again suggested a turning movement from Ahwaz.

Such a plan did not then commend itself to General Nixon. General Gorringe's force had only just commenced its operations in Arabistan and General Nixon was not sure how far H.M. Government would approve of operations in Persian

---

* These reeds were practically everywhere except in the immediate neighbourhood of the banks of the Tigris and of the various creeks. They grew to heights varying from three to six feet.

† See Map 2.

territory beyond what was necessary to expel the Turks. Moreover, the Turkish force from Shaiba was at that time still in the Nasiriya area and General Nixon informed General Townshend that he might have to go there to clear up the situation before advancing from Qurna. In the course of the discussion, General Nixon told General Townshend that the force in Mesopotamia was intended to make good the old province of Basra, i.e., the triangle contained by Basra-Nasiriya-Amara, but that the Government considered that this was as much as could be achieved by the available troops.

On the same day, General Nixon reported to India that there was for the time being no urgency for operations against the enemy on the Tigris, for which careful preparation and organisation were necessary. He said that he was taking measures to this end, but that he must await the result of General Gorringe's operations before making further definite plans.

General Nixon appears to have come to the conclusion soon after the battle of Shaiba that *bellums* would afford the necessary means for an attack on the Turkish positions north of Qurna. It will be recollected that some time before this a *bellum* squadron had been organised in the force and that battalions had been training men to propel or paddle these boats. On the 18th April, each battalion at Qurna received orders to increase the numbers of men so trained up to two hundred and on the 27th, at General Nixon's request, General Townshend went into the question of utilising *bellums*. It was decided to provide some eighty of these for each battalion of the attacking line and, of them, thirty-two were to be armoured by fixing machine-gun shields across their bows. Arrangements to obtain and prepare the additional *bellums* required and to mount guns and machine guns on rafts, etc., as well as to provide floating hospital accommodation, would all take time and careful organisation. At this time, however, and for the greater part of May, the operations in Arabistan required the services of most of the available river craft up the Karun river, so that delay was in any case inevitable.

During May the Turks on the Tigris, though continuously engaged in strengthening their positions, displayed little offensive activity. They were, of course, in no great strength here and the floods must have been as troublesome to them as they were to us. Periodically a few of their guns would fire a few rounds ; and there was a certain amount of sniping, notably by Arabs in boats in the neighbourhood of Qurna. On the 5th May, an attack by a friendly Arab Shaikh on a hostile

Arab village to the south-west of Qurna was supported successfully by a British detachment from Qurna in co-operation with the *Odin* and *Espiègle*. On the 8th, another successful raid was carried out against one of a series of hostile Arab villages on the right bank of the Euphrates which had been responsible for much of the sniping. The force from Qurna consisted of the *Espiègle, Clio*, three hundred infantry in river steamers, and twenty-four *bellums* containing eight men each, furnished by the three battalions of the Qurna garrison. The Arabs did not await the attack, but many of their *mahailas* and live-stock were captured, and the tribe concerned at once asked for terms. In addition to this satisfactory result, the operation afforded the *bellum* squadron a practical test, in which it acquitted itself well, and gave the men confidence in their newly acquired craft.

By the 7th May, a new artillery position at Nuhairat, four hundred yards south of Fort Snipe, had been occupied by the 1/5th Hants Howitzer Battery so as to afford effective artillery fire against the Turkish positions as far north as One Tower Hill: three days later the British howitzers made particularly good practice from here against One Tree and Tower Hills.

On the 9th, a reconnaissance of the Al Huwair creek was undertaken in the river steamer *Shushan*, in which were two naval 3-pounders, three maxims, and a detachment of thirty of the Oxfordshire and Buckinghamshire Light Infantry. Considerable opposition was encountered from Arabs, who obtained good cover from the six-feet high reeds surrounding the creek and thus were able to maintain a heavy rifle fire on the steamer on all sides from close range. Three soldiers were wounded and also Lieutenant-Commander Cookson, R.N., who was in command. Realising that the reeds rendered this route impracticable for an advance and that further reconnaissance was useless and dangerous, Lieutenant-Commander Cookson, though severely wounded, held on to his command and brought the steamer out into the Euphrates without further loss.

On the 11th May, the progress of General Gorringe's operations against the retiring Turks in Arabistan enabled General Nixon to issue definite orders for the offensive up the Tigris. These instructions stated that: " The object of the advance from Qurna is not only to drive the enemy from his present positions between the Pear Drop Bend and Qurna and capture his guns, but also to push him up river and occupy Amara, the operation to be continuous." The instructions also gave the details of the troops and ships that could be placed at General Townshend's disposal for the operations, indicated certain positions where obstructions in the river were to be removed and where posts should be located for the future line of communication control, asked that the operation orders should be framed in accordance with the instructions in the " Field Service Regulations," and requested General Townshend to submit a report as to the measures he proposed for carrying out General Nixon's instructions.

Next day, General Townshend submitted a memorandum to General Nixon giving his views on the situation. There appeared to him to be three alternative methods of attacking the Turkish position. The first, involving a turning movement to the west of the Tigris, was, he considered, undesirable and almost impossible, owing to the flooded marshes with their high reeds and the depth of the creeks that would have to be crossed. The second, involving a similar turning movement, but to the east of the Tigris, he also dismissed, as it would mean crossing the Ruta creek and the Tigris and did not menace the Turkish line of retreat. The third, which was the method he proposed to adopt, was a frontal attack in strength, assisted by an enveloping movement by a detachment along the eastern bank of the Tigris. This attack was to be undertaken methodically in successive phases, and would depend for its success on the intimate co-operation of the land force and the ships and on the effect of the heavy gunfire being what was expected.

General Nixon gave his general approval to General Townshend's plan; but in view of his own responsibility for pressing on General Townshend the attack in *bellums* and realising that its success would, in a great measure, be dependent on details, General Nixon spent much of his time during the next two or three weeks in discussing with him the various arrangements for the operations. This, while it may have had the disadvantage of apparent interference with his subordinate's initiative, enabled General Nixon, as the supreme commander, to intervene effectively and without delay to put right any difficulties which might arise.

From this time onwards, preparations for the advance were carried out energetically. At Basra, the sappers were kept very busy preparing water craft, including the shielded *bellums*, rafts for mountain and machine guns, barges for heavy guns, and *mahailas* for hospital purposes and for engineering and other stores. Every requirement of the attacking force had to be thought out and arranged for beforehand and most detailed instructions had to be issued for the information and guidance of those who were to take part in the attack, including lists of the gear, stores, ammunition and rations to be carried in each of the various vessels.

The fourth battalion of the 17th Brigade (119th Infantry) were moved up to Qurna from Basra on the 11th May, and next day General Nixon visited Qurna himself in company with General Townshend. The brigade commanders and chief staff officers of the force that was to be employed had by this time heard from General Townshend of the action that was to be taken ; and on the 13th General Nixon at Qurna announced to the troops his intention of advancing on Amara. Four days later, he telegraphed to India the appreciation of the situation which has already been referred to, in which he mentioned his intended action on the Tigris.

General Townshend in his book " My Campaign in Mesopotamia " describes his misgivings and those of the commander of the 17th Brigade and his officers at this projected frontal attack in boats; for they were all impressed by the strength of the Turkish position. From the brigade and regimental officers' point of view the proposal appeared to have many disadvantages ; these officers had at this time no great confidence in their men's ability to attain sufficient skill in manœuvring the hundreds of *bellums* in suitable formations, and this they felt, would aggravate the loss of control by officers over the men during the fighting which the dispersion in boats must in any case entail ; it would, they considered, be impossible to develop and direct a sufficient volume of fire from the infantry boats ; and there did not appear to be much chance of attending to or removing the wounded. They could not help recalling that the Turks had been preparing their defensive positions for the last four months and it seemed to them that, unless it was considered necessary for political reasons to advance at once, it would be better to wait till July when the floods would subside and the attack could be carried out over dry land. General Townshend says that the mines reported to be strewn in the river caused him and the Senior Naval Officer some uncertainty as to whether the warships would be able to develop sufficient gunfire to enable the infantry to assault ; and he regarded the possibility of the naval ships being sunk by the field guns in the Turkish redoubts as a real danger, as the mined and obstructed channel of the Tigris—sufficiently difficult of navigation without these—must limit considerably the manœuvring power of the ships.

So impressed was he by these considerations and by the idea that the attack might fail and result in serious consequences that he decided to put this point of view to General Nixon in the possibility that the situation might allow of a postponement of the attack till it could be carried out over dry ground. General Nixon, however, decided that the attack was to take place as proposed. As will be seen, his decision was justified fully by subsequent events.

General Townshend maintained his headquarters at Basra while superintending the preparations for the attack, though he made frequent visits to Qurna. This action on his part, as well as the decision not to concentrate the attacking force at Qurna till the last few days, was intended to leave the Turks in doubt as to whether the coming attack was to be made up the Tigris or the Euphrates. A further reason was that until the latter part of May the operations in Arabistan still called for the use of most of the river steamers on the Karun.

On the 19th May, the enemy displayed considerable activity on the sandhills northward of Qurna ; they were evidently placing guns in positions there and during the next week there was a great increase in the sniping by night. Reports were also received that the Turks had placed a gun in position west of the Al Huwair creek to cover the approaches to their right flank. It was evident they were anticipating an attack.

On the 21st, General Dobbie, commanding the 17th Brigade, was invalided and Colonel Climo, 24th Punjabis, was appointed temporarily to take his place. At this period General Townshend was rather anxious to have some additional troops placed at his disposal for the coming attack ; and, although General Nixon had some idea of sending him the 30th Infantry Brigade just back from Ahwaz, he finally decided not to do so. By the 26th, the greater part of the *bellums,* stores, etc., for the advance had reached Qurna, and General Townshend with his Divisional Headquarters, the 30th Mountain Battery and the 117th Mahrattas had also arrived at Qurna. The 117th were to garrison Qurna when the advance commenced. He had informed General Nixon a day or two before that he did not think his preparations would allow of an advance before the 1st June, but on it being pointed out to him that General Gorringe's demonstration towards Amara would have lost its effect by then, General Townshend said on the 26th that he would attack on the 31st. This was approved.

A memorandum was issued by General Townshend on the 26th, which gave detailed instructions for units which were to take part in the operations. After warning the troops of the danger of land and floating mines, the allotment of *bellums* was given. The total of these was 372, of which 296 were allotted to carry 2,560 officers and men of the 17th Infantry Brigade; and of these, 96 were "shielded." The rest were allotted, in varying proportion, to the 30th Mountain Battery, the Sirmur Sappers, to two sections of the Divisional Signal Company, and to No. 1 Field Ambulance. Each *bellum* was to carry ten men, including one non-commissioned officer, and carried a reserve of 125 rounds of ammunition per rifle, a day's ration, a waterproof sheet and two sandbags per man, in addition to certain boat stores. A small number of *bellums* were told off to bring up supplies and cooking pots to units as opportunity offered, and the arrangements for refilling points were indicated.

In addition, there were rafts for the machine guns—the 17th Brigade being allotted four additional machine guns for the operations—the mountain guns and the field ambulance; and five heavy and field guns—two 5-inch, two 4-inch and a spare 18-pounder Q.F.—were mounted in barges.

On the 28th, the *bellum* arrangements were tested by a parade of the force which was to attack in them along the right bank of the Tigris. Moving out from the perimeter at Qurna in three columns, the *bellums* and rafts deployed into two lines at the rendezvous west of Fort Snipe whence the attack was to start on the 31st. The movement was successfully carried out and gave the troops confidence in their ability to manœuvre with some measure of precision. As a result of this parade an adjustment of the machine-gun shields on the *bellums* was carried out next day to permit of easier movement.

The weather at this time was intensely hot, the temperature rising well above 100°, and there were many cases of heatstroke—for instance, on the 29th, one hundred and seventeen men went sick from the effects of the heat—and the heat was even greater in the ships on the river than on the land. By the night of the 29th–30th the whole of the force intended for the operation had been concentrated at Qurna; and on the 30th, General Nixon had also arrived there. Although he informed General Townshend that he had no intention of interfering with the conduct of the operations, he had announced his intention of being present while they were carried out. In view of the unusual nature of the operations, of the fact that he was himself controlling the demonstrations on either flank, and of a feeling existing, as has been already explained, that more troops should have been detailed for the attack, General Nixon felt that his presence on the spot might be helpful. If it became clear that more troops would be required, he could expedite their despatch.

On the 28th, General Townshend issued the following operation order for the attack :—

1. (a) No pronounced change in the enemy's dispositions astride of the Tigris north of Qurna. His main positions are briefly the localities of Abu Aran, Ruta, Muzaibila, Sakrikiya; advanced posts to the Ruta position on the sandhills and to the Abu Aran position at Norfolk Hill, One Tree Hill, One Tower Hill, Gun Hill;

    (b) The advanced posts One Tower Hill, Gun Hill, One Tree Hill, are supported at under 5,000 yards range from Abu Aran (One Tree Hill at under 6,000 yards).

    The Abu Aran position is supported by artillery fire from Ruta and Muzaibila; and Sakrikiya is 4,500 yards from Muzaibila.

    (c) It is probable that mines are placed in the Tigris channel north of the boom at Fort Snipe.

    (d) According to our intelligence reports the Turkish force comprises some 5 battalions, 10 guns and about 600 *Mujahidin*,* the *Marmariss* river steamer† and some 1,200 Arab riflemen with one of the guns mentioned above in the marshes on the west flank of Norfolk Hill and Gun Hill, possibly to counter-attack our infantry advance along the west side of the Tigris.

    The positions of the guns are reported to be as follows :—

        One gun at Rumla (in marshes to west).
        Two guns on Gun Hill.
        One gun on One Tower Hill.
        One gun at Abu Aran (at Eastern Tower).
        One gun at Ruta.
        Four guns, newly arrived and not yet located, but thought to be one at Ruta and three at Abu Aran.

    (e) The flooded state of the country renders the above a position of strength, and demands an operation methodically undertaken in successive phases as in siege warfare, every effort being made to obtain concentric fire action by the force on the west side of the Tigris, the naval flotilla and the force on the east side of the river.

2. The enemy will be attacked on May 31st by combined frontal and turning attacks :—

    (i) *Frontal Attack*. A frontal decisive attack, supported by the artillery and the naval flotilla, will move against the enemy's position on the west side of the Tigris, assisted by a turning attack on the east side of the Tigris.

---

* Volunteer irregulars fighting under the influence of *Jahad*.
† The Turkish gunboat.

OPERATION ORDERS 251

(ii) *Demonstrations on East and West.*—In order to engage the attention of the Arabs on both flanks of the Turkish positions, demonstrations up the Shwaiyib and Al Huwair creeks by friendly Arabs supported by gunboats are being arranged by Army Headquarters.*

3. *Distribution of Troops for the First Phase.*

(a) *Advanced Guard Group.*

Frontal Attack.
Lt.-Col. Climo.
RED FLAGS.
- 17th Infantry Brigade (less 22nd Punjabis) with Brigade Signal Section.
- Half Sirmur Sappers and Miners.
- 30th Mountain Battery (less one section).
- One section British Field Ambulance.
- One section Indian Field Ambulance.

Turning Attack.
Lt.-Col. Blois-Johnson.
RED FLAGS.
(b) 22nd Punjabis.
- Half Sirmur Sappers and Miners.
- One section 30th Mountain Battery.
- One section Indian Field Ambulance.

No. 3 Group.
C.R.A.
BLUE FLAGS.
(c) *No. 3 Group. Artillery.*
- Land Section.†
- River Section.‡
- Half 22nd Company Sappers and Miners.
- Bridging train.

No. 1 Group.
G.O.C. 16th Brigade.
GREEN FLAGS.
(d) *16th Infantry Brigade Group* (in ships).
- 2nd Dorsetshire.
- 104th Rifles.
- 48th Pioneers.
- Brigade Signal Section.
- 63rd Battery R.F.A.
- Half 22nd Company Sappers and Miners.
- One section British and two sections Indian Field Ambulances.

General Reserve.
Lt.-Col. Peebles.
YELLOW FLAGS.
(e) *No. 2 Group* (in ships).
- 2nd Norfolk.
- One section British and one section Indian Field Ambulances.

4. *Orders for the Attack, First Phase.*

Objective—the line of the Barbukh Creek.

(a) At 5 a.m. on May 31st, the artillery (land section) will commence a bombardment of the enemy's positions, their fire being distributed on Norfolk Hill, One Tree Hill, One Tower Hill, Gun Hill, in accordance with detailed instructions issued by the C.R.A.

The Naval Flotilla§ will co-operate against Norfolk Hill and Gun Hill.

The River Section¶ will be in readiness to move up when ordered from their rendezvous position at Qurna. Two tugs are allotted for this purpose.

(b) The frontal attack will advance from its position of assembly west of Fort Snipe at 6 a.m. Objectives—Norfolk Hill, One Tower Hill and Gun Hill.

---

* i.e., by General Nixon.

† 1/5th Hants Howitzer Battery (four guns) at Nuhairat, 104th Heavy Battery (two guns) and 86th Heavy Battery (two guns) at Qurna.

‡ In barges: 104th Heavy Battery (two guns), 86th Heavy Battery (two guns) and a spare 18-pounder field gun.

§ This consisted of *Espiègle, Odin, Clio, Lawrence, Shaitan, Sumana* and *Miner*, also three naval 4·7-inch guns mounted in horse-boats. The *Comet* and one 4·7-inch gun in horse-boat were detached to proceed up the Shwaiyib river and the *Shushan* two (3-pounders) up the Al Huwair Creek.

¶ i.e., the five heavy and field guns in barges.

The O.C. will ensure the protection of his left flank during this advance.

(c) The turning attack will start from its rendezvous at 1 a.m. Objective—One Tree Hill. The O.C. will time his movement so as to conform with the artillery bombardment.

(d) The O.C. turning attack will detail a party to look for and explode by rifle fire any mines found along the river-bank.

(e) Mine-sweeping operations by the naval flotilla will be conducted under orders of the S.N.O. during the artillery bombardment. The subsequent forward movement of the warships and river section barges will be regulated by the progress of the mine-sweepers.

5. No. 1 (16th Brigade) Group and No. 2 (General Reserve) Group in transports will be brought up the Tigris when ordered as follows :—
Mejidieh, Blosse Lynch, P.1, P.3.

Medical.

6. The Ordnance Barge, Hospital Ship,* R.E. Park (Group 4) and the Divisional Supply Column (Group 5) will remain at Qurna till ordered up.

7. The Dressing Station of the force will be on Norfolk Hill. This will be provided by the Field Ambulance attached to the General Reserve.

Reports.

8. Reports to Divisional Headquarters on board H.M.S. *Espiègle* from 6 p.m. on May 30th.

From the above, it will be seen that the attack on the Turkish advanced positions was to be made by the 17th Infantry Brigade, 30th Mountain Battery and Sirmur Sappers, advancing in *bellums*, preceded and supported by a bombardment by the eight howitzers and heavy guns in position at and near Qurna ; and further supported by the naval guns and the heavy and field guns in barges as soon as the mine-sweeping operations allowed of their advance. The remainder of the force, organised in groups and consisting of a field battery, four infantry battalions and a company of sappers and miners, with units of the various auxiliary services, were to follow in ships and to be used as circumstances dictated.

Before dawn† on the 31st May, the *Espiègle* and *Clio* were close to the bridge of boats at Qurna ready to advance up the Tigris ; the *Odin* was in the Shatt al Arab, about a mile below Qurna, in a position to enfilade the enemy's gun positions on One Tower Hill ; and the *Lawrence* and *Miner,* with three of the 4·7-inch guns in horse-boats, were in the Euphrates just west of Qurna.

---

* Steamer *P.4*. The "P" steamers were the seven river steamers requisitioned in Burma by the Indian Government and recently arrived in Mesopotamia.
† Sunrise was about 5 a.m.

SECOND ACTION OF QURNA

Soon after 1 a.m. the "Turning Attack" under Lieutenant-Colonel Blois-Johnson, consisting of a section of the 30th Mountain Battery, 22nd Punjabis, some Sirmur Sappers and a field ambulance section, pushed forward in their *bellums* towards One Tree Hill. The *bellum* for mine destroying, manned by Sirmur Sappers, in accordance with its instructions, had proceeded to search along the left bank of the Tigris till opposite Fort Snipe, where it was due by 6 a.m. After going a short distance, the 22nd Punjabis and the mountain battery section found the water so shallow they had to get out of the boats and rafts and push them. It was very hard work to get along, and the mountain battery section, finding progress impossible, had to return to Qurna. The 22nd Punjabis managed to continue and before 5 a.m. had deployed at the pre-arranged point and had advanced to about fifteen hundred yards east-south-east of One Tree Hill. Here they awaited the commencement of the artillery bombardment.

At 5 a.m., the warships and the howitzers and heavy guns at Qurna commenced their bombardment of Norfolk, Gun, One Tower, and One Tree Hills. The enemy guns did not reply for some twenty minutes, when they opened fire on the Fort Snipe area; directed apparently against our war-ships and artillery. The *Espiègle* and *Clio* had now passed through the boat bridge and, taking up position near Fort Snipe, engaged the Turkish guns on Gun Hill.

Meanwhile the advanced guard group under Lieutenant-Colonel Climo had formed up west of Fort Snipe, unmolested by the Turkish artillery, and had started their advance before 6 a.m. The boats and rafts advanced in the following formation:—

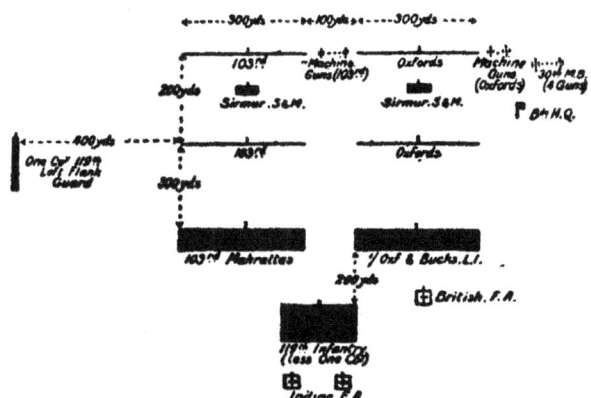

The right half of the force (Oxfords and Sirmur Sappers) were to capture first Norfolk Hill and then One Tower Hill, while the left half (103rd and Sirmur Sappers) were to take Gun Hill. The machine guns of the Oxfords were to direct the whole advance and to regulate its pace; and each unit was instructed to move on a point westward of their respective objectives in order not to mask the supporting gunfire till the last moment. Their right flanks having reached a point about four hundred yards to the south-west of the hill to be attacked, each unit was to change direction towards the right and assault the enemy's flanks.

Before 5.30 a.m., the 30th Mountain Battery had opened fire upon Norfolk Hill at a range of 2,700 yards, apparently with good effect; and about 6 a.m., Colonel Climo pushed forward a section of the mountain battery, advancing with them himself, and from this time onwards this battery pushed forward by alternate sections in close support of the infantry. These were advancing without a check, steadily and methodically.

From his headquarters on board the *Espiègle*, General Townshend could see the 22nd Punjabis making good progress in their attack against One Tree Hill, which they captured at 6.30 a.m. The opposition they encountered was easily overcome, as the hill was only held by twenty of the enemy, three of whom were killed and the remainder captured. The 22nd now entrenched themselves here and opened with their machine guns on One Tower Hill, suffering seven casualties from the Turkish guns at Abu Aran in the operation. About 7 a.m., the mine-destroying *bellum* rejoined them, having destroyed a number of mine connections *en route*.

Just before 6.30 a.m., the 4-inch and 5-inch guns of the river section were pushed a little distance up the Tigris to engage the enemy guns on One Tower Hill; and soon after this General Townshend ordered the ships containing Nos. 1 and 2 Groups (i.e., 16th Brigade Group and the Norfolks) to advance through the boat bridge at Qurna.

Less than half an hour later, the machine guns of the Oxfords and of the 119th* came into action against Norfolk Hill. The enemy replied with rifle fire, which was quickly suppressed, except on the extreme west flank, by the 30th Battery mountain guns firing at 1,750 yards range. Under cover of the machine and mountain gun fire, the Oxfords rapidly covered six hundred

---

* The 119th machine guns had been sent forward to join those of the Oxfords a short time before.

of the remaining seven hundred yards of water, and, leaping from their boats at a hundred yards distance from it, their leading company captured Norfolk Hill by a fine assault about 7.30 a.m. Of the enemy garrison—which with the exception of one Turkish officer were all Arab soldiers—seventy-five had been killed, twenty-six were wounded and thirty-four taken prisoner. Although Norfolk Hill was honeycombed with trenches, these had afforded evidently but indifferent protection against the British guns. The British casualties in this part of the operations only amounted to one officer killed and five men wounded.

About this time a British aeroplane was seen flying over the *Espiègle*. Two had arrived at Basra on the 14th May, but lack of dry ground delayed their use and it was not until the 27th that the first machine made a flight. By the strenuous exertions of the Air Force, both machines were in the air by dawn of the 31st, and rendered most useful service from then onwards.

Norfolk Hill having been captured, the main effort was now concentrated on One Tower Hill. The Oxfords re-embarked, transferring their shielded *bellums** to the third line and, supported by the 30th Mountain Battery (who came into action at about two thousand yards range), and the howitzers and guns at Qurna, advanced against One Tower Hill. Preceded by the mine-sweeping armed launches† *Shaitan* and *Sumana*, the *Espiègle* and *Clio* now moved up and anchored off Norfolk Hill to join in the bombardment of One Tower Hill; and the *Odin*, *Lawrence* and *Miner* also moved up in support. These warships still continued to be the main target for the Turkish guns and both the *Espiègle* and *Odin* were hit by shells, without, however, sustaining much damage or loss. The enemy opened a heavy rifle fire from One Tower Hill on the advancing Oxfordshire Light Infantry, but it was not very effective, and by 9 a.m., when the infantry machine guns came into action, had been almost completely suppressed by the British gunfire. The 119th Infantry had by this time been ordered forward to support the Oxfordshire assault. This was again directed against the enemy's western flank, and by 9.30 a.m., with the loss of only two wounded, had met with complete success. The enemy's losses on this hill amounted

---

* These had delayed the advance up to this point and the protection they afforded was not so essential as to compensate for this delay.

† The launches *Bahrein* and *Lewis Pelly* were kept in reserve as spare mine-sweepers.

to four Arab soldiers wounded and a Turkish officer and eighty-six Arab soldiers taken prisoner. A 16-pounder field gun fell into our hands, and a switchboard for electrically firing twenty-four mines in the Tigris was also found here. The Turkish officer in charge of this and of the mines in the locality was taken prisoner at the same time and was subsequently induced to point out where the mines were, but not before several had been exploded or disconnected by our own engineers.

In the meantime, the 103rd Mahrattas had been pushing steadily forward, much hampered by the reeds, which were especially thick on their line of advance, and by 9.30 a.m. they were about a mile south of Shrapnel Hill. For about an hour the guns of the river section had been firing on Gun Hill* and now most of the naval guns, the 30th Mountain Battery, and all the machine guns of the advanced guard group, as well as the rifle fire of the Oxfords from One Tower Hill, were all concentrated against this position. The 103rd, though their punt poles disclosed their position to the enemy, could themselves neither see nor fire at their objective owing to the reeds, but could only push steadily forward. The volume of the British gun and supporting fire gradually asserted its superiority and soon after 11 a.m. the Turkish guns on Gun Hill ceased fire, the enemy rifle fire grew less and, as the 103rd approached, the Turkish garrison surrendered. Gun Hill was thus occupied soon after 11.30 a.m. The 103rd had very small casualties—only two wounded—and they captured on the hill two 16-pounder guns, one Turkish officer and one hundred and thirty-two Arab soldiers, of whom five were wounded.

During the morning's fighting, the left flank guard of the 119th Infantry had been continuously engaged with numerous Arabs among the thick reeds to the westward and had successfully protected the left flank of the advance. The Arab fire had been heavy but, owing to the reeds and the enemy's bad marksmanship, the 119th only sustained seven casualties.

The first phase of the operation had thus met with complete and unexpectedly easy success. After the capture of Norfolk Hill there had been little resistance, due mainly to the overwhelming superiority of the British artillery, to whom the different islands afforded a target easy to range on. Other contributory causes were the cover afforded to the *bellums* by the reeds, and the lack of effect obtained by the Turkish

---

* This hill was out of range of the 1/5th Hants howitzers.

COMPLETION OF DAY'S OPERATIONS

guns* and mines. The Turkish advanced positions were difficult to reinforce or withdraw from and their defensive arrangements had proved inadequate. But the Turkish main position was still intact and here a vigorous resistance was expected.

All firing had now ceased and General Townshend decided to cease operations for the day. The heat was extreme, the glare of the sun off the water very trying, and the "Advanced guard" and "Turning attack" groups had been through a hard and tiring time in getting their *bellums* along. The 17th Infantry Brigade groups occupied the positions they had won and the ships containing Nos. 1 and 2 groups moved up the Tigris and anchored just below the war vessels, a boom being placed up-stream of all the vessels to keep off mines.

While these main operations were taking place, demonstrations had been carried out on either flank. The *Comet* with a naval 4·7-inch gun in a horse-boat, and with an infantry detachment in a river steamer in support, had moved at daylight up the Shwaiyib river and had bombarded the enemy positions at Ruta and on the sandhills. On the other flank, the river steamers *Shushan* and *Muzaffari*, having on board two naval 3-pounders and some infantry detachments, had moved up the Al Huwair creek, acting in co-operation with some friendly Arabs. Though they diverted the attention of some of the marsh Arabs from the main attack, the difficulties of navigation were too great for them to make much progress and they rejoined the main force in the course of the afternoon.

At 4 p.m. General Townshend issued operation orders for the next day's attack. Abu Aran was to be the first objective and the 6th Division order ran as follows :—

" 1. . . . .
   2. A frontal attack will be carried out by the Royal Naval flotilla and artillery ; bombardment and mine-sweeping to commence at 5 a.m. under detailed instructions issued by the Senior Naval Officer and C.R.A. respectively.
   3. 17th Brigade will make an enveloping attack well to the west of Abu Aran ridge, starting from its position of assembly near Gun Hill at 5.45 a.m.
   4. 16th Brigade will be landed when ordered at Abu Aran under cover of the bombardment and the support of the 17th Brigade.
   5. 16th Brigade will then undertake a frontal attack along Abu Aran ridge towards Muzaibila while the 17th Brigade continues its enveloping movement on the same objective."

The night passed quietly, many hours of it being spent by the troops of the 17th Brigade in removing the shields from their *bellums*, with a view to speeding up their pace next day.

---
* Many of the Turkish guns had been so sited that they could only fire at long ranges.

The next morning (1st June) the British guns opened fire on Abu Aran about 5.30, but without drawing a reply. About an hour later, the naval ships preceded by their mine-sweepers steamed up the river. On board one of the mine-sweepers went the captured Turkish engineer officer ; and his information assisted much in the discovery and destruction of the leads of many mines. Meanwhile the 17th Infantry Brigade were advancing in their *bellums*, but owing to the thickness of the reeds their progress was extremely slow. There was still no opposition and General Townshend describes in his book the astonished silence with which the British force continued to approach Abu Aran. This was only explained when one of the British aeroplanes dropped a message for the *Espiègle* saying that Abu Aran, Ruta and Muzaibila had all been evacuated by the enemy, who were fleeing northward in every available craft.

General Townshend at once issued orders for his whole force to assemble at Abu Aran, where the leading half company of the 17th Brigade arrived in time to fire on the last boatload of retreating Turks. Before 11 a.m. the naval flotilla had anchored off Abu Aran, then in occupation of the 17th Brigade ; and General Townshend, leaving his senior general staff officer to assemble the troops and transport at Abu Aran, proceeded in a launch with the Senior Naval Officer to ascertain whether the obstruction in the Tigris near Ruta really closed the channel. Fortunately it was found that it did not and, after discovering and cutting the leads of three large observation mines, a practicable channel was found and marked with buoys. Through this channel the armed mine-sweeping launches *Shaitan* and *Sumana* were at once sent, with orders to chase up river after the enemy shipping, whose smoke could be seen in the distance.

At 2.30 p.m. after an interview with General Nixon at Abu Aran, in which General Townshend expressed the hope that he might be able to enter Amara with the Turkish fugitives, he issued orders expressing his intention to push on to Ezra's Tomb. He ordered the 16th Brigade to disembark and stay at Abu Aran with the 30th Mountain Battery and the barge containing the 18-pounder. The 17th Brigade* were to embark in the ships vacated by the

---

* General Townshend wished the 17th Brigade to have the honour of leading the advance. They had undergone a trying time at Qurna and had seen less fighting than any of the other brigades. There was no reason to anticipate that a direct and unopposed advance to Amara would be possible, so that the few hours' delay entailed by the transhipment seemed to him unobjectionable.

16th Brigade and were to proceed up-stream, together with the 63rd Field Battery, the Norfolks, the " river section " of the heavy artillery and the hospital steamer.

Soon after 3 p.m., the *Espiègle*, with General Townshend and the Senior Naval Officer on board, followed by the *Clio* and *Odin*, passed the obstruction—to remove which a naval party had already been set to work—and started in pursuit up the river. But only a rough chart was available and navigation was extremely difficult, owing to the bends and twists of the river channel, whose banks were not easily discernible in the floods. The Turkish gunboat *Marmariss* and other river craft were soon sighted ; and before 6 p.m. the *Shaitan*, which was leading, was able to open fire with her 12-pounder, doing considerable damage. In less than an hour, the *Espiègle, Clio* and *Odin* opened fire in turn—as they came within range—with their 4-inch guns on the river steamer *Mosul* and then on the *Marmariss*. This fire evidently had some effect, for the Turkish steamers, in their efforts to escape, began casting off the lighters and *mahailas* they were towing ; and at 7.30 p.m. many of these, full of troops and warlike stores, were found at Ezra's Tomb. Here the *Odin* was left behind to capture them and to prevent their being looted by Arabs ; and in the *Odin* General Townshend left his senior general staff officer to unite his troops there and to send them forward by *echelon* of brigades as soon as possible.

The chase continued in the gathering darkness* and a short way farther on the *Shaitan* took possession of a *mahaila* full of Turkish troops. But soon the enemy could no longer be distinguished to fire at, and as the navigation was becoming increasingly intricate and difficult,† Captain Nunn, the Senior Naval Officer, decided to anchor and await the rising of the moon. The ships anchored just after 8 p.m., close to some more Turkish lighters full of troops and stores ; and our searchlights disclosed the steamer *Bulbul*, submerged in the river just ahead, having been sunk by a shell from the *Shaitan*.

During the day's pursuit up the river, some two hundred Turkish soldiers, three field guns and a large quantity of stores, explosives and mines had been captured without loss to ourselves. Moreover, there had been no casualties from the heat, either on that or the previous day, though the usual high temperature had prevailed.

---

* Sunset was about 6.55 p.m.
† The stretch of river between Ezra's Tomb and Qala Salih, comprising the " Narrows," is one of the most difficult parts of the Tigris to navigate.

At 2 a.m. on the 2nd, after the moon had risen, the *Espiègle*, *Clio, Comet,** *Miner, Shaitan* and *Sumana* again took up the pursuit. But the navigation difficulties increased and in about two hours the *Espiègle* went aground and she and the *Clio* could go no farther. By this time, however, they had overhauled the *Marmariss*, who was now aground and had been abandoned. She was on fire from a British shell and showed many shell hits; and near her was a lighter from which thirty Turks were taken prisoner. In the next reach the steamer *Mosul*, with another lighter and seven *mahailas*, surrendered. Altogether about one hundred and forty prisoners, two 15-pounder field guns and large quantities of rifles and ammunition were captured here.

It was evident that the Turkish retirement had become a demoralised rout; and consequently, after consultation with General Townshend, Captain Nunn decided to push on with the light-draught vessels to keep the Turks on the run and to try to ascertain the condition of affairs at Amara. They both transferred to the *Comet* and proceeded up the river, followed by the *Sumana, Shaitan, Lewis Pelly* and three horse-boats each containing a 4·7-inch gun. Sir Percy Cox also accompanied them. About 7 p.m., they anchored for the night about six miles above Qala Salih.† The marsh area had now been left behind. An apparently endless plain covered with low scrub appeared on either bank, with occasional Arab villages; and much relief was experienced from the drier air.

Early on the 3rd the flotilla again pushed forward. All the villages on either bank were flying white flags and the Arab inhabitants everywhere gave signs of their friendliness. Twelve miles from Amara General Townshend called a halt. He considered it advisable to await the arrival of his leading brigade, as he anticipated that the Turks would defend Amara and he felt that it would be ridiculous to attempt to take the place with the few small vessels he had with him. Captain Nunn was anxious that they should go on, but General Townshend declined at first to do so. An hour later, however, he told Captain Nunn that he " would go on and chance it."‡

---

* The *Comet* had rejoined the flotilla from the Shwaiyib river on the 31st May and had followed up the Tigris on the 1st June.

† The Shaikh from here came on board the *Comet* and, with a view to his spreading the news, General Townshend ordered him to collect supplies for 15,000 men who would arrive very shortly.

‡ " My Campaign in Mesopotamia," p. 70.

THE DARING *SHAITAN*

At about 9.45 a.m. the advance again commenced, the *Shaitan* and a small launch being sent to scout well ahead. About this time General Townshend received a wireless message* from General Nixon saying that three Turkish river steamers were fleeing ahead of the naval flotilla, that east of Amara there were three weak battalions of Daghistani's force retiring from Arabistan, but that the remainder of this force had either passed through Amara or were actually at that place. This information had been obtained by the aeroplanes.

No enemy troops were sighted by the *Shaitan* until the straight reach of the river below Amara was entered—within three miles of the town—when enemy troops were seen crossing the bridge of boats and entering a barge attached to a steamer lying alongside the right bank of the river. The bridge of boats was then opened and the steamer tried to get through; but on a shot being fired by the *Shaitan's* 12-pounder the troops hurriedly abandoned the barge and fled up the right bank. Just above the bridge the river takes an abrupt bend to the westward and a few minutes later a body of some fifteen hundred troops were seen here retiring westward along the river-bank. The *Shaitan* still pushed on and passed through the bridge. Amara town on the left bank was full of troops, who fled back from the bank in confusion on seeing the launch; north of the town more troops were seen, about a thousand on the left bank—some of them making westward and northward—and, about five hundred yards away, the fifteen hundred already mentioned moving westward on the right bank.

None of them fired a shot and the *Shaitan*, also without firing, steamed on for about another half-mile. Then she tied up to the bank and accepted the surrender of six officers and about a hundred soldiers, all fully armed. The officers, rifles and ammunition were taken on board and the men were ordered to march downstream again, keeping alongside the *Shaitan* which now moved back towards Amara. A few hundred yards downstream about a hundred and fifty more Turkish soldiers emerged from the trees and surrendered, throwing down their arms. Here the same process as before was carried out and the *Shaitan* proceeded back to Amara, the prisoners walking unattended along the bank till they reached the bridge of boats, where they sat by a coffee-shop on the right bank until time could be found to take them into custody. At this time the *Comet* was still nearly a mile away.

---
* The *Comet* could receive, though she could not send, wireless messages.

Greater daring than that of the *Shaitan* can hardly be imagined. The total crew of this launch consisted of eight sailors under the command of Lieutenant Mark Singleton, R.N., and a very little resolution on the enemy's side would have disposed of them easily at point-blank range. For his gallantry, which caused the flight of over two thousand Turkish troops—besides the actual capture of eleven officers and two hundred and fifty men—and contributed so greatly to the unopposed capture of Amara, Lieutenant Singleton was awarded the Distinguished Service Order and two of his small crew the Distinguished Service medal. These rewards can seldom have been better deserved.

On the arrival of the *Comet* and the rest of the flotilla between 1.30 and 2.15 p.m., General Townshend, Captain Nunn and other officers landed at the Custom House, and here the civil governor of Amara, the commandant and a number of Turkish officers came and surrendered. To the civil governor General Townshend gave orders to arrange at once for the collection of supplies for fifteen thousand men who would arrive very shortly; and, after hoisting the Union Jack, arrangements were made to secure the town with the very small force available. This, excluding the few officers, amounted to a total of only forty-one men, made up as follows:—

Comet—Three sailors, two marines and twelve soldiers.
Shaitan—Eight sailors.
Sumana—Eight sailors.
Lewis Pelly—Four sailors, one marine.
Launch *L-2*—Two sailors, one marine.

Lieutenant Palmer, R.N., of the *Comet*, was posted on shore to keep order on the town front with all the men that could be spared off the vessels, i.e., two sailors, one marine and twelve soldiers of the West Kents and the 1/4th Hampshire. A battalion of the Constantinople Fire Brigade Regiment sent down word that they were ready to surrender at the barracks in the town; and Lieutenant Palmer was sent there with a seaman, a marine and an interpreter to accept the surrender. Lieutenant Palmer found this battalion of about four hundred Turkish soldiers there with their officers, all fully armed, and marched them down to the quay and on to a big lighter, which when filled with about eight hundred prisoners was anchored in mid-stream under the guns of the flotilla. A little later, a formed body of fifty Turkish soldiers marched up to the Turkish naval barracks and surrendering their arms were taken into custody by three British soldiers who had been posted there.

During the course of the afternoon, some two thousand Turkish troops had been seen approaching Amara from the north-east, evidently part of the Turkish force retiring from Arabistan. The *Shaitan*, however, proceeding to the northern end of the town, fired a few shells at them and making prisoners of the advanced guard, consisting of about fifty Turkish soldiers, dispersed the remainder of the force who fled in confusion to the north-west. The Turkish troops were apparently quite demoralised by the unexpected rapidity of the British advance and, fearing to fall into the hands of the Arabs, numbers kept coming in and surrendering. But the British military and naval commanders and their tiny force had an anxious time, as it was evident that their weakness could not be concealed from the enemy for very long. Early in the afternoon messages had been sent down the river for troops to come up as quickly as possible; and in the evening the searchlight rays of a river steamer coming up could be seen in the distance, but she came no closer and was evidently halted.

Meanwhile all possible precautions had been taken for the night. Four British seamen held the Turkish military barracks, two soldiers and one sailor the naval barracks, and the vessels took positions along the river facing the town and kept a careful watch. A proclamation was also issued warning the inhabitants that, under penalty of being shot, all must remain indoors after dark.

Fortunately the night passed quietly; but early on the 4th, the Arabs, beginning to realise the British weakness, commenced to loot, and to make an attack from the west. In the nick of time, about 6.30 a.m., the 2nd Norfolks arrived in the *P.3*, rapidly disembarked and soon restored order. More troops arrived during the afternoon and the situation became quite secure; and in the evening General Nixon himself reached Amara.

We must now turn back to the progress of the troops up the Tigris from Abu Aran. The disembarkation here of the 16th Infantry Brigade and the embarkation in their place of the 17th Infantry Brigade necessarily took some time; and it was not till early on the 2nd that the ships started upstream from Abu Aran, accompanied by General Nixon and some of his staff in their launches. On arrival at Ezra's Tomb, where they arrived about noon—and where, as mentioned before, General Townshend had left his senior general staff officer to unite his troops and push them on by brigades—the

17th Brigade disembarked in accordance with General Townshend's instructions; and their ships were then sent back to Abu Aran to bring up the 16th Brigade. General Nixon pushed on in his launch for about six miles farther and spent the night near the *Espiègle* and *Clio*.

At 2.30 p.m.* on the 2nd, the Norfolks in the *P.3* at Ezra's Tomb received orders to push on to Qala Salih, but owing to the congestion of traffic in the river they did not get away till 5.30 p.m. and had to anchor for the night at 7.20 p.m. They then received orders not to halt at Qala Salih, but to push on as early as possible the next day to join the *Comet*. Starting at 4.30 a.m. on the 3rd they passed Qala Salih about noon and some five and a half hours later met a naval pinnace bringing orders from General Townshend that the regiment was to push on and join him at Amara. Darkness and the weakness of their searchlight, however, obliged them to stop for the night some eight miles short of Amara.

Meanwhile at dawn on the 3rd, the steamers sent back from Ezra's Tomb began arriving at Abu Aran; and at 8.15 a.m. General Delamain received orders for his, the 16th, brigade, to go in them to Qala Salih. Starting shortly after 11 a.m., General Delamain had an interview with General Nixon at Ezra's Tomb and received instructions that, failing receipt of any orders from General Townshend, he was to push on with his brigade until he obtained touch with General Townshend on board the *Comet*. The 17th Infantry Brigade, who had been designed by General Townshend to lead the advance, were much mortified at seeing the 16th Brigade pass them; but by that time the necessity for speed in pushing up reinforcements overrode every other consideration, and General Nixon, who knew that Daghistani's force from Arabistan was near Amara, intervened to add vigour to the reinforcing arrangements, which in view of the few river steamers available were naturally causing him anxiety. Pushing on in the darkness, the 16th Brigade reached Qala Salih about 1 a.m. on the 4th, and some five hours later received orders from General Townshend to push on to Amara.

Amara, whose occupation was now complete, was a comparatively new town of pleasing appearance and some commercial importance. Composed of ten to twelve thousand inhabitants, it was located at the Tigris end of a main trade route

---

* This was some two and a half hours after General Townshend and Captain Nunn had gone on in the *Comet*, after the *Espiègle* and *Clio* had been forced to stop.

CAPTURE OF AMARA

to Persia and provided passably good quarters for the force except in the hottest weather. Being drier and healthier than Basra it also afforded a much-needed location for military hospitals.

The combined naval and military operations of the four days 31st May to 3rd June had been a brilliant success. General Nixon attributed much of this success in his report " to a careful study of detail in the initial stages of the organisation, to the skilful manner in which these details were worked out and to the loyal co-operation of all concerned in putting the whole machine in motion."

Though the operations had been carried out during a period of intense heat, the British casualties had been surprisingly small whilst the spirit, dash and vigour of the sailors and soldiers were worthy of the highest traditions of our Imperial Forces. The British casualties totalled only 4 killed and 21 wounded. The enemy, between the 31st May and 4th June, sustained about 120 casualties in killed and wounded and had 1,773 men taken prisoner. The British also captured twelve field guns, five naval guns and a large quantity of arms and ammunition; and of the Turkish river craft, the gunboat *Marmariss*, one paddle steamer and a steam tug were sunk, while one steamer, two steam tugs, two motor-boats and a number of barges and *mahailas* were captured. The loss to the Turks of the steamers was especially serious as they could not be replaced.

In his report General Nixon praised General Townshend for the manner in which he carried out the operations and especially for his prompt action in following up the enemy and for the dash and enterprise he displayed in occupying Amara. The close co-operation between the Navy and the Army was, General Nixon pointed out, a marked feature of the operations and he felt that he could not speak too highly of the part played by the officers and men of the Royal Navy under the command of Captain Nunn.

From the 4th, the next few days were spent in reconnaissance and exploration of the vicinity of Amara, in taking over the administration of the town and in organising the line of communication on the Tigris. The bulk of the military force with which General Townshend had left Qurna was gradually concentrated at Amara, leaving detachments to hold Ezra's Tomb and Qala Salih as posts on the line of communication. This, extending up to but exclusive of Amara, was to be under the charge of the Inspector-General of Communications and was divided into two sections: Basra—Ezra's Tomb (exclusive) and Ezra's Tomb—Amara (exclusive).

The *Comet* and *Shaitan* were left at Amara, but the rest of the naval flotilla withdrew down the stream; and on the 8th General Nixon also left for Basra.

CHAPTER XI.

OPERATIONS ON THE EUPHRATES AND THE OCCUPATION OF NASIRIYA.

AFTER the capture of Amara, the British forces in Mesopotamia were disposed in four main groups, i.e., about Amara, Qurna, Ahwaz and Basra.

At Amara on the 13th June were a cavalry regiment, ten guns, nine infantry battalions, half a battalion of pioneers, two sapper companies and the bridging train; at Qurna four infantry battalions and fourteen guns, with a battalion and a field battery on the line of communication between Qurna and Amara;* at Ahwaz two cavalry regiments, twelve guns, four infantry battalions, a company of pioneers and a sapper company; and at Basra and Fort George were a cavalry regiment, six guns, five infantry battalions, a company of pioneers and a sapper company. Force Headquarters were at Basra, while those of the 6th and 12th Divisions were at Amara and Ahwaz respectively. Owing, however, to the way in which the operations had developed, the divisional organisation had been temporarily broken up, the three brigades of the 12th Division being at Ahwaz, Amara and Qurna, while the 6th Division had detachments from the Basra area to Amara.

During May, a good deal had been done to improve the organisation of the force and a few additions to it had been made. Amongst other arrangements, separate organisation of the lines of communication under an Inspector General (Major-General Davison) had been carried out and the Adjutant-General's branch at the base had been placed on a proper footing; a brigade headquarters was formed for the heavy artillery; and the nucleus of a mechanical transport service was started. Owing to the Begum of Bhopal having placed an Imperial Service cavalry regiment at their disposal,

---

* At Ezra's Tomb and Qala Salih. An attempt to hold Abu Aran, the only dry ground within many miles of Qurna, had been given up, owing to the intense heat there.

the Government of India had been able to despatch the 23rd Cavalry to Mesopotamia ; and they also arranged to send to General Nixon, at his request, twelve 15-pounder field guns for use in defensive posts.

Of the naval force, the *Clio* had to be sent for repairs to Bombay ; the *Lawrence* had already gone to Bushire ; therefore, the only naval sloops now remaining were the *Espiègle* and the *Odin* ; and the first of the new river gunboats were, as stated in the last chapter, not expected till the autumn.

The river steamers and tugs now amounted to a total of twenty-one* and included those which General Barrett had asked for in December 1914. Since then the force had increased and its sphere of operations had been considerably extended. General Nixon had been instructed in March to report as to the adequacy of the river craft ; and on the 27th May he telegraphed pointing out that shortly the conditions of the rivers would prevent many of his steamers and tugs moving up the Karun, above Qurna on the Tigris and Kubaish on the Euphrates, and he asked for six powerful tugs to be sent to him as soon as possible, with a draught not exceeding three feet and each capable of towing two large flats ; he also asked for twelve 10–12-knot motor launches. The Indian authorities searched everywhere in India for tugs of the type demanded but failed to find any, and on the 20th June informed General Nixon of this and that they were asking the India Office to try and obtain them in England. General Nixon replied on the 25th urging the provision of these tugs as soon as possible as he anticipated much difficulty between the 15th July and the 15th October, when the rivers would be at their lowest.

It seems necessary to offer at this stage a few general remarks with regard to the supply of river transport during the first eighteen months of the operations. On several occasions, the shortage of river transport made all the difference between decisive success and complete or comparative failure of the operations. These occasions have been and will be alluded to as they occur ; and while it is easy to point out the shortage, it is not so easy to indicate how the mistakes and omissions occurred which led to this shortage. The provision of river-craft, either for combatant, or for maintenance and transport, purposes was not an easy matter. The type of vessel required scarcely existed elsewhere and consequently would have to be specially constructed. But usually time did not admit of this and the most

---

* Four " Tigris " steamers, seven " P " steamers, three " Lynch " tugs, four Indian tugs, and three small stern-wheelers.

SHORTAGE OF RIVER TRANSPORT

suitable available craft had to be requisitioned. Such vessels were seldom satisfactory and many of them sunk or were badly damaged on the overseas voyage. The evidence given before the Mesopotamia Commission shows many of the difficulties and the mistakes made; but whether the Commission were correct in their allocation of the blame for the shortage is another matter.* The whole question is very involved and technical; many individuals and several different authorities were concerned; and all the relevant facts do not appear to have been brought to light, and are still somewhat obscure. In these circumstances, to enter into great, but unavoidably incomplete, detail in this narrative might lead the reader to draw inaccurate conclusions.

On the 12th June, General Nixon asked for more aeroplanes. The Viceroy telegraphed the gist of his report to the India Office a few days later and strongly recommended the provision of more and better aircraft; and by the end of the month he received a reply that the War Office had agreed to detail two flights of the Royal Flying Corps from Egypt for service in Mesopotamia.

By the middle of June the heat everywhere in Mesopotamia had become so great as to affect seriously the health of the troops; and this was further aggravated by the difficulty of convalescence in this trying climate.† Owing to the amount of sickness and the numbers of the medical corps who had been invalided, General Nixon was obliged on the 18th to make a special application for more medical personnel; and these the Government of India proceeded to arrange for. As an instance of the amount of sickness, General Nixon reported on the 24th that the 1/4th Hampshire Regiment could only muster 16 officers and 289 other ranks medically fit for service; but nevertheless, he had to utilise this battalion in the impending operations up the Euphrates.

A few days after the capture of Amara, General Nixon estimated the situation of the Turkish troops as follows: at Baghdad, four battalions; at Kut al Amara, ten battalions and twelve guns; at Nasiriya, five to seven battalions with a few guns; and retiring up the Tigris from Amara, the remnants of twelve battalions, a cavalry regiment and nine guns.

---

* The speech of the Attorney-General on the 12th July, 1917, in the House of Commons, during the debate on the Commission's report, gives reasons why some of their conclusions may be open to doubt.

† Old residents at Basra stated that they could recollect no instance when the heat had been so oppressive.

At this period, the Turks were fully occupied in Armenia and the region of Lake Van, where the Russians had just gained some considerable success. In Persia, the German activities were becoming so pronounced that there seemed every chance that Persia might come into the war on the German side; in Aden, the small British force could only take up a purely defensive attitude before a Turco-Arab advance within our administrative frontier; at Gallipoli, the British force was only holding its own and unable to progress; and in India, trouble was again threatening the North-West Frontier, this time from the Mohmand country.

On the 10th June, the Chief of the General Staff, India, telegraphed to General Nixon asking for his plan for the effective occupation of the Basra *vilayet*, to which the Government of India desired to obtain the sanction of H.M. Government. In reply, next day, General Nixon stated that he was making preparations for an advance on Nasiriya, the occupation of which place—with that of Amara—would, he considered, achieve the required purpose. He considered that to occupy Kut al Amara would render our position still more effective, as we should thus hold both ends of the Shatt al Hai. He would, however, first occupy Nasiriya and open relations with the Arab tribes in that neighbourhood. If, after this, he still considered it possible to advance from Amara to Kut, he would then determine the force advisable for the operation and the extra reinforcements he would require. He was at once told from India that he must not expect any reinforcements.

On the 13th, the Viceroy wired to Mr. Chamberlain:

" Nixon wires that he proposes that two brigades should now move on Nasiriya in order to secure Euphrates portion of Basra *vilayet*. We concur in this operation, which should have a good effect on the Euphrates tribes, and propose to instruct him to proceed as soon as his preparations are complete. His present force should be quite sufficient for the success of operation and the maintenance of new position."

To this telegram the Viceroy received no reply; assuming that H.M. Government had agreed, sanction to advance was sent from India to General Nixon on the 22nd; and Mr. Chamberlain was informed on the 27th that General Nixon was commencing his advance on Nasiriya.

This advance to Nasiriya had to a great extent been advocated and agreed to on political grounds; for Nasiriya was the headquarters of the powerful Muntafik tribes. But General

Nixon held that there were also good military reasons for this operation. He considered that a Turkish garrison at Nasiriya would be a permanent menace to his line of communications, as the slightest reverse or check up the Tigris might again bring Ajaimi and thousands of Arabs, acting under Turkish instigation and supported possibly by Turkish troops, against the Lower Tigris and the Shatt al Arab. The Commander-in-Chief in India accepted General Nixon's view rather than that of his own General Staff, who did not consider the advance on Nasiriya as altogether desirable from a purely military point of view, having specially in mind that, were an advance to Baghdad to be ordered later on, a detachment at Nasiriya would weaken the force available for such an operation.

As regards the proposal to advance to Kut al Amara, the Viceroy* and the Commander-in-Chief in India were at first averse to the proposal, as was also Mr. Chamberlain, advised by General Barrow. The subsequent decision to make this advance was so fateful that it is well to state clearly the reasons which led to it, as they arose. General Nixon's reason given on the 11th June was that it would enable us to hold both ends of the Shatt al Hai. The Turks had used this waterway during the previous four months or so for the despatch of troops both to and from Nasiriya, and it was generally believed that it extended as a navigable route for steamers for the whole distance between Nasiriya and Kut. It was not then known that steamers could only use it for the five months or so of high water and then only from Kut to Shatrat al Muntafik, whence troops had to march by land for the last thirty miles† to Nasiriya, or had to proceed by boat down the Baidha channel to the Hammar lake. On the 13th June, General Nixon gave as a further reason for occupying Kut that it would improve our position greatly in regard to the tribes on the Tigris line, whose attitude after the capture of Amara appeared to be satisfactory for the time being. These tribes, it may be noted, subsequently gave us considerable trouble owing to their predatory and treacherous habits; and even during June the movement of Turkish detachments southward of Kut was causing unrest among them.

In the meantime, the General Staff in India, in one of their periodical appreciations of the situation, had been considering

---

* Lord Hardinge, however, wrote to Mr. Chamberlain on the 17th June, pointing out that from the point of view of irrigation and water control the occupation of Kut would have advantages.

† Though a road of sorts existed it was difficult to traverse owing to the numerous canals or creeks to be crossed.

the question of an advance to Baghdad. They were aware that many of the political authorities at Home and in India advocated its occupation, mainly owing to the great moral—and therefore settling—effect it would have not only on the Arabs in Mesopotamia, but also in Persia, Afghanistan and India.* The fact that the leading Russians to the south of Lake Van were now less than thirty marches off Baghdad indicated that its occupation might soon be brought up as an operation to be seriously considered. The intentions of the Russians were not known, but, as they were as much concerned as we were to preserve the neutrality of Persia, it appeared possible that they might be contemplating an advance on Mosul or Baghdad, in order to block the way to Persia, and that we might be asked to co-operate.† In their appreciation, the General Staff came to the conclusion that were General Nixon to be sent certain reinforcements—which they placed at one cavalry brigade, two infantry brigades and twenty-four guns, which they considered India could spare‡—the occupation of Baghdad in the early future was a feasible operation. The main reasons which led to this conclusion were: the position of the Russian forces about Lake Van; the demoralisation of the Turkish troops after their recent defeats by the British and Russians; and the Turkish preoccupation with the Dardanelles operations which would detract from their ability to reinforce Baghdad. It is interesting to note that the Turkish General Staff admit that at this period they would have had great difficulty in stopping a determined British advance up the Tigris.

In regard to Kut, the General Staff considered that it afforded an advantageous position on which to base a further advance on Baghdad; and that in any case a British force there was well placed strategically to protect Basra *vilayet* from any Turkish advance from Baghdad and to restrict Turkish traffic by river between Baghdad and Nasiriya to the Euphrates. This opinion was also based, it should be noted, on the idea that the Shatt al Hai was a navigable route between Kut and

---

* In December 1914, it had been noted at the India Office that from a political point of view the occupation of Baghdad was so desirable as to be practically essential; the Foreign Office would also have welcomed its occupation; and on the 12th February 1915, in a telegram to Lord Crewe, Lord Hardinge had indicated Baghdad as our probable ultimate objective.

† On the 25th June the War Office learnt that the Russians intended to advance on Bitlis from Van, and not till the 20th July did they find out that the Russians were really manœuvring to turn the Turkish right south of Erzerum.

‡ This opinion was not shared by the Viceroy, nor apparently by the Commander-in-Chief in India.

Nasiriya. On the 14th June the total Turkish strength in Mesopotamia was estimated at fifteen thousand regulars with thirty-four guns; they were reported to be faced with serious disorder at Baghdad and Najaf; and were said to be withdrawing troops from their Caucasus force to defend the Dardanelles and Constantinople. Against a move to Kut, the main questions to be considered were the adequacy of General Nixon's force and the efficiency of the available river transport for its maintenance.

To what extent the above opinion influenced Sir Beauchamp Duff is uncertain, but on the 19th he ordered his Chief of the General Staff to telegraph to General Nixon asking for a thorough appreciation, in regard to the advisability of occupying Kut, to be sent to India by post. At the same time, General Nixon was warned that in this appreciation he must show clearly whether he was convinced of his ability not only to hold Kut with the troops then at his disposal, but also to feed and maintain them there under all conditions of the river. To this, General Nixon replied on the 24th in a lengthy memorandum, which will be dealt with later.

Lord Hardinge does not seem to have been aware of this discussion, for on the 24th he wrote in a private letter to Mr. Chamberlain that General Nixon had asked for reinforcements to enable him to advance to Kut and had been told at once that he could have no more troops; since when they had heard nothing more from him on the subject. Mr. Chamberlain himself was at this period rather anxious about General Nixon's intentions. In a private letter of the 25th to Lord Hardinge, he wrote: " I hope that Nixon fully realises how short you are of troops and the extreme difficulty there would be in reinforcing him. It is difficult from a distance to say when a forward movement increases our responsibilities and when it is in fact the best measure of defence. Provided he understands clearly the governing circumstances of the situation and does not embark on new operations in the belief that he can call for more troops whenever he wishes, I shall be satisfied to rely in the main on his judgment. But it would be dangerous to allow him to suppose that there are large resources on which he could draw."

During June the situation in Persia had grown worse; and on the 24th General Nixon was informed by India that he might be called upon to reinforce Bushire at short notice, as Wassmuss, the German agent, was doing his best to induce the local tribes to attack the British Residency there. On the 28th the Government of India made General Nixon responsible for the defence of Bushire, and informed him that the British attitude there should be strictly defensive. He accordingly reinforced the British garrison* at Bushire with two captured 13-pounder Turkish guns with four artillery gunlayers and instructors. At the same time he lodged an objection to this extension of his responsibilities to a place two hundred miles in his rear. But the Government of India were very anxious to avoid anything like a diversion of force to Bushire; and as General Nixon was much nearer to the scene of action than they were, and could, therefore, act more rapidly than they, the Government of India thought it better to place him in control than to appoint an independent commander who might develop ambitious tendencies.

Owing to a Russian force having landed recently at Enzeli on the Caspian, the German activities were now largely transferred from Tehran to Isfahan and South Persia. The German Consul at Isfahan was said to have raised a body of two hundred armed retainers, and Wassmuss was intriguing to raise South Persia against the British, being aided to some extent by some of the Swedish officers of the Persian Gendarmerie. With regard to the action of these officers, Mr. (now Sir Charles) Marling, H.M. Minister at Tehran, reported that most of them had been led unwittingly by their anti-Russian sentiments, their ignorance of Persian ways and by German propaganda, into unneutral action, whose dangers had now been explained to them; and he believed that their attitude for the future would be better.†

In other directions also, there was extended anti-British action. Parties of Germans—accompanied by locally recruited and armed men, and strengthened by Austrian prisoners of war who had escaped in some numbers from Transcaspia—were moving towards Afghanistan via Meshed, Birjand and Kerman. To try and prevent these entering Afghanistan, the Russians moved Cossacks to Meshed and the Indian authorities moved troops to Robat on the Baluchistan frontier, thus beginning what was subsequently known as the " East Persia Cordon."

Immediately after the capture of Amara, General Nixon commenced his arrangements for an advance on Nasiriya; and, on his arrival at Basra from Ahwaz on the 16th June,

---

* Consisting of the 96th Infantry.

† In order to keep any order in Persia it was necessary to retain these Swedish officers, who were not under the Swedish, but under the Persian Government.

General Gorringe was entrusted with the conduct of these operations. For these, the force placed at his disposal at first consisted of an infantry brigade with certain divisional troops; and a naval flotilla under Captain Nunn was to co-operate with him. General Nixon had decided that the advance should be made by water across the Hammar lake and up the Euphrates, as he considered that to move by the desert route at that time of year would be a very hazardous operation, requiring much preparation and a large amount of transport. As, therefore, it was anticipated that all movement would be by water, no animal transport* was arranged for. In addition to the naval guns, field guns would be mounted in river steamers, mountain guns and machine guns would be put on rafts, and as many *bellums* as it was possible to tow would be taken.

The instructions given by General Nixon on the 23rd June to General Gorringe were to the effect that he was to open the waterway from the Hammar lake to the Euphrates and to secure effective occupation of Suq ash Shuyukh and Nasiriya.

Just above Suq ash Shuyukh, the water of the Euphrates dispersed into a maze of channels on its way to the Hammar lake.† Only two of these channels, the Akaika or Kurma Safha and the Mazliq, were navigable by steamers; and in 1915, the Mazliq channel was closed by a bar to vessels larger than an ordinary *mahaila*. The other channels could only be traversed by *mashufs* or at the best by light *bellums*. The ground along and near the banks of these various channels was often comparatively high and capable of cultivation, while in between them were generally reed-grown swampy depressions or inundations, according to the time of year. While, in June 1915, the British force knew little of the area to the west of the Hammar lake, they had ascertained by reconnaissance that the best water route to Nasiriya lay along the old channel of the Euphrates via Qurna, across the Hammar lake and up the Akaika channel. This channel was known to be blocked by a solid looking dam about half a mile from its entrance to the Hammar lake.

General Nixon had endeavoured to increase his knowledge of the area from local and native sources and by areoplane reconnaissance; but the two Maurice Farman aeroplanes were of old pattern, unsuitable for flying in the extreme heat,

---

* In any case, with the shipping available it would have been impossible to send transport animals.
† See Map 5.

and, being hampered by lack of a landing ground amidst the floods, could make little progress.

Up to Kubaish, the water route presented little difficulty; but beyond this steamers had to move along a tortuous channel through the shallow Hammar lake. At the end of June this channel was five feet deep; by the middle of July the depth had sunk to three feet; and by the end of July *bellums* using it had to be dragged through a mixture of mud and water. It is doubtful if so rapid a fall was anticipated by General Nixon, but in any case there was considerable reason for an early movement.

General Nixon's information led him to believe that, as the bulk of the Turkish troops from Nasiriya had withdrawn to Kut, no great opposition was likely to be encountered by General Gorringe's force. This was concentrated by the 26th June at Qurna and consisted of: Headquarters 12th Division, 30th Infantry Brigade (1/4th Hampshire Regiment, 2/7th Gurkhas, 24th and 76th Punjabis) under command of General Melliss, the 63rd Field and 30th Mountain Batteries, two-thirds of the 12th Sapper and Miner Company, half the 48th Pioneers, one section Divisional Signal Company, a wireless section, one field ambulance and certain supply units. Owing to sickness, the 30th Infantry Brigade only mustered a total of 1,994 rifles, of which the Hampshire Battalion (from the 33rd Brigade) contributed only 297.

The naval flotilla, assembled at Qurna under Captain Nunn, consisted of the sloops *Espiègle* and *Odin*, the armed launches *Miner* and *Sumana*, the stern-wheeler river steamers *Shushan*, *Mahsoudi* and *Muzaffari* and two horse-boats with a 4·7-inch gun in each. As, however, the *Espiègle*, *Odin* and *Miner* could not go beyond Kubaish, the *Sumana*, the 4·7-inch horse boats and the three stern-wheelers were the only naval vessels really available for the operations. These stern-wheelers—which had been specially prepared, armed, and provided with naval crews for these operations—were very old, the *Shushan* having been built originally for the relief of General Gordon at Khartoum. The *Shushan* was armed with a 12-pounder,* a 3-pounder and a Maxim, the *Mahsoudi*

---

* Conrad Cato in " The Navy in Mesopotamia " describes the troubles of the gun's crew of this temporarily mounted 12-pounder. " After every round, they examined the deck carefully, to see how much of it had carried away : and when they found that on the port side the deck could stand the strain no more, they shifted the gun over to the starboard side and went on gaily firing until a violent recoil very nearly sent the gun, the mounting and the remainder of the deck through the bulkhead of the cabin."

with a 3-pounder and a Maxim and the *Muzaffari* with a Maxim. The Senior Naval Officer was on board the *Shushan*.

The troops were accommodated in the river steamers *Blosse Lynch*, *Mejidieh* and *Malamir*, on each of whose foredecks were mounted two of the 63rd Battery's 18-pounders. The tugs *Shuhrur*, *Shirin*, *T1*. and *T4*. and three launches also accompanied the force, and they and the river steamers towed six mountain and two machine gun rafts, several *mahailas* and lighters full of ammunition or stores and 175 *bellums*.

The naval flotilla, the *Blosse Lynch* (carrying General Gorringe and his staff) and three tugs concentrated near Kubaish on the evening of the 26th. The information then available to General Gorringe, whilst somewhat contradictory, indicated only slight opposition in the Akaika channel—where there were two Turkish " Thornycroft " launches near the dam—but the presence of three pairs of guns, each with small detachments of troops, posted on the banks of the Euphrates to command the western portion of the Akaika channel; while it was also estimated that, owing to the return of some of the enemy's troops from the direction of Kut, there might be as many as fourteen hundred regular Turkish infantry at Nasiriya.

Early on the 27th, the naval flotilla, followed by the *Blosse Lynch* and three tugs, moved across the Hammar lake. At the same time the remainder of the vessels conveying the force left Qurna and following the leading vessels joined them the same evening.

At about 1.30 p.m., as the British gunboats approached the mouth of the Akaika channel, they came under fire from two Turkish launches on the further side of the dam, but these quickly retired before the British fire. Preceded by minesweepers, General Gorringe accompanied the Senior Naval Officer in the *Shushan* up the channel and reached the dam. No mines had been found and the naval flotilla anchored at 4 p.m. just below the dam. This was a solid erection rising some feet above the water and about thirty feet thick at the top.

Troops were at once landed to occupy the adjacent villages, and the sappers and pioneers began to prepare the dam for demolition by explosives. The work continued throughout the night, and the next morning (28th) the northern end of the dam was blown away, clearing a channel about thirty feet wide and seven feet deep. During the day this channel was extended to a width of about one hundred and fifty feet with an average depth of four to five feet. This clearance revealed the presence of four *mahailas* which had been sunk to form the base of the dam when it had been constructed two years before, i.e., in 1913, for irrigation purposes. There was now a great rush of water pouring through the newly opened channel and this made not only the demolition of the base of the dam a very difficult matter, but also proved too strong for the unwieldy old stern-wheelers to steam their way through.

The difficulty was overcome by attaching wire hawsers to each vessel and, by dint of much effort on the part of the troops, combined with the ships' engines working at full pressure, the *Shushan* and *Mahsoudi* were coaxed through the opening before dark.* But attempts to pass the 4·7-inch horse-boats through during the night were unsuccessful and it was not till the next day that they were laboriously hauled through.

On the 30th Captain Nunn, with the *Shushan, Mahsoudi* and the 4·7-inch horse-boats, and accompanied by one of General Gorringe's staff officers and the Commandant of the 76th Punjabis, proceeded to reconnoitre up the channel and to examine the enemy's position, reported to be on the right bank of the Euphrates opposite the western entrance to the Akaika channel. Useful results were obtained; the enemy's guns and the approximate position of the enemy's mines were located; and the general lie and nature of the country was ascertained, the best positions for British artillery observation being noted; but detailed observations were rendered impossible by the hostility of Arabs.

During the 30th a strong gale prevented the passage of any more steamers through the obstruction; but on the 1st July two were passed through and the channel was finally cleared. On the 2nd, another reconnaissance was carried out by the naval flotilla accompanied by two hundred infantry; and further useful information was acquired, though the number of hostile Arabs opposing us appeared to have increased.

The Akaika channel was at that time a tortuous stream, about seven miles long and fifty yards broad. The country on either bank as far as the vicinity of a mud tower, about four miles above the dam, was open and chiefly marsh. This tower, located in a cluster of mud and reed huts, was known as " Ati's House." Westward of this, as far as the junction with the Euphrates, both banks were dry for some distance inland

---

* Three hawsers, each manned by about a hundred men, were made fast to each vessel.

and were covered with date plantations and much intersected by irrigation channels and mud walls. From Ati's House a good view was obtainable to the north, but little could be seen from it of the Akaika channel and the view to the westward was greatly restricted by the date palms and by willow trees which grew in some numbers along the banks of the channel.

From Ati's House, a path led along a causeway across the marshes to some Arab villages to the north and north-west, about two thousand five hundred yards distant, lying on the Mishashiya creek. This creek joined the Euphrates about two miles above the Akaika junction. About two thousand yards south-west of Ati's House, the Shatra creek—very deep with a strong current and in places over one hundred yards wide—flowed out of the Akaika. The junction of the Shatra and the Akaika was commanded by two Turkish guns, entrenched and concealed by willow trees on the right bank of the Euphrates opposite the Akaika entrance; and in the intervening stretch of the Akaika the Turks were reported to have laid a mine-field.

By the evening of the 3rd, all the river craft had passed the obstruction in the channel and orders were issued for a forward movement next day. Starting at 4 a.m. on the 4th, the gunboats with the 76th Punjabis, two mountain guns and a company of the 48th Pioneers occupied a position at Ati's House and on the channel bank to the south of it. The poineers then cut a passage for the *bellums* from the Akaika to the inundation northwards of Ati's House, and a reconnoitring party were sent along the path to the Mishashiya creek. It was found that by utilising this route the Turkish position opposite the Akaika channel could be turned, but the idea of using it was discarded, as the opposition encountered from the Arabs showed that the operation would require a force of at least two battalions.

In the meantime the remainder of the force had moved up to the vicinity of Ati's House and about 4 p.m. the 2/7th Gurkhas landed on the south bank opposite, with orders to move up to the Shatra creek. They were to secure a position at the junction of the Shatra and the Akaika which afforded a good point of observation of the Turkish guns, and to make good the crossings over the Shatra. It was hoped to effect these crossings by means of *bellums* which were to be towed by hand after dark along the Akaika.

The advance of the Gurkhas was opposed by Arabs and was much impeded by the thick and intersected date plantations, which made it difficult to maintain touch and direction. By

7 p.m., however, they had established themselves on the near bank of the Shatra, to find that the enemy was holding the further bank. This rendered it impracticable to bring up the *bellums* for crossing. The Gurkhas remained in their position for the night under considerable hostile fire, which, however, was ill-directed and caused but few casualties. During the night the 1/4th Hampshire Regiment was sent to reinforce them and by 5 a.m. on the 5th had come into line on their right.

General Gorringe's intentions for the 5th were to advance his force along both banks of the Akaika and to attack the enemy on the left bank of the Euphrates, preparatory to crossing that river and seizing the Turkish gun position opposite the Akaika entrance. The 1/4th Hampshire and the 2/7th Gurkhas were to cross the Shatra, advance along the south bank of the Akaika, locating as they went the exact position of enemy mines in the channel, and then cross the Akaika again to the left bank of the Euphrates. General Melliss, with the 30th Mountain Battery and the 24th and 76th Punjabis, was to move along the north bank of the Akaika and establish himself on the left bank of the Euphrates well upstream of the Turkish gun position. He should then be able, it was hoped, to cross the Euphrates well above the enemy's position and might possibly succeed in cutting off the two Turkish launches and a steamer reported to have arrived at their gun position. The British artillery, naval and military, excluding the mountain guns, were to be held in readiness to concentrate their fire on the Turkish gun position; General Gorringe's central signalling station and his own report centre were established at Ati's House; and he kept the sapper company and half the battalion 48th Pioneers in hand in reserve.

General Melliss' column commenced its advance at 4.45 a.m., on the 5th. The 76th Punjabis, moving along the narrow strip of date plantations—about six hundred yards wide—between the Akaika and the inundation to the north, reached a point nearly opposite the Shatra entrance without difficulty. Here they came under such heavy fire from the south bank of the Akaika and from mud walls to their right front across the inundation that their advance was checked.

Meanwhile *bellums* and gun rafts had moved through the water cut made the previous day into the inundation north-west of Ati's House; and in these the 24th Punjabis and a section of the 30th Mountain Battery pushed forward about 6.15 a.m. towards the right of the 76th Punjabis, being supported by the fire of two sections of the 30th Battery on rafts near Ati's House. Though subjected to some enemy gun fire their

CLEARING THE AKAIKA CHANNEL

advance progressed steadily till about 7.30 a.m. Arriving then some three hundred yards in rear of the right flank of the 76th Punjabis, and about eight hundred yards from the long line of mud walls sheltering the enemy on their right front, they came under heavy rifle fire. This at once caused them some loss and the *bellums* had to turn broadside on to the enemy to allow the fire to be returned. As a further advance by the *bellums* would obviously entail heavy casualties, General Melliss ordered the 24th Punjabis to disembark and to carry on the attack by land on the right of the 76th Punjabis.

By this time the *Sumana* and *Shushan* had moved up the Akaika to the support of the 76th, coming under heavy gun and rifle fire. The *Sumana* was hit twice by shell and thereby put out of action. The fire of the British artillery at this time was handicapped by the date palms, and the lack of elevation of their guns, which could, therefore, only fire indirectly with the co-operation of forward observing officers ; and some difficulty was experienced in consequence in getting the correct line of fire and range.

Having disembarked, the 24th Punjabis commenced to move forward about 10 a.m. Supported by the British guns and by the rifle fire of the 76th, they reached the left bank of the Euphrates just before noon by a skilful and gallant advance. Here they came under heavy rifle and machine-gun fire from the Turkish position on the right bank of the Euphrates and under " pom-pom " fire from the Turkish launches, now retiring up the Euphrates.

About half an hour later the 76th began to come up into line with the 24th on the river bank, and their combined fire with that of the British guns gradually obtained the mastery over the Turkish fire. At about 1.20 p.m. white flags were hoisted in the Turkish battery and trenches, and firing ceased. *Bellums* were brought up at once and carried by hand across the sixty yards of dry land between the inundation and the Euphrates—no easy task, as each *bellum* required about sixty men to lift it—and at 2 p.m., General Melliss and Colonel Climo (commanding 24th Punjabis) with a few men crossed the Euphrates and took possession of the enemy prisoners and guns. Half the 24th Punjabis soon followed and put out outposts on the right bank of the Euphrates.

In the meantime, the 1/4th Hampshire and the 2/7th Gurkhas had been completely checked at the Shatra creek by the enemy's resistance there ; and General Gorringe had sent a company of the 48th Pioneers to reconnoitre for a possible crossing further up this creek. It was ascertained that the enemy's position on the further bank only extended for about a mile up the creek; and about 11.30 a.m., when the 24th were seen to be progressing successfully, the remaining company of the 48th was sent across the Akaika, and the whole half battalion was ordered to secure a crossing over the Shatra above the enemy's right flank. The 2/7th Gurkhas were left to occupy the enemy's attention in front; the 1/4th Hampshire were withdrawn and concentrated in rear of the Gurkhas; and the fire of the British guns was directed on to the south bank of the Akaika beyond the Shatra creek.

By 2 p.m., the 48th Pioneers had effected an unopposed crossing and were followed by the Hampshire. The Turks retiring before their advance towards the Euphrates found their main position in British hands and surrendered; and their Arab allies fled to the southward.

At 4 p.m., the *Shushan* and *Mahsoudi* moved up the Akaika sweeping for mines; and an hour later the remaining steamers followed, embarking their troops and picking up wounded as they went. By 9 p.m., the Akaika had been cleared of mines and all the ships anchored at the junction.

The enemy's strength that day was estimated at three hundred Turkish troops, two thousand Arabs, two guns and two launches, each armed with a " pom-pom." During the action they had been reinforced by two guns and seven hundred troops brought down by river from Nasiriya. Their casualties could not be estimated, but the British took ninety-one prisoners, two guns and large quantities of ammunition and stores.

The British effective strength had amounted to 1,719 rifles and they had suffered 109 casualties, of whom 25 were killed. Half of these casualties had been incurred by the 76th Punjabis, who had lost 16 killed and 38 wounded out of a total strength of 329.

The Euphrates, in the twenty-five mile stretch extending from the Akaika junction to Nasiriya, had an average width of about two hundred yards and passed through some of the richest country in Mesopotamia. On either bank lay cultivated land, interspersed with gardens, strong towers and villages within walled enclosures. The cultivation being mainly rice, was, in July 1915, almost completely under water. On the left bank, belts of date plantations with an occasional fringe of willow trees were almost continuous, but on the right bank the country was much more open. This difference was especially noticeable in the stretch between Asani* and the Majinina creek,

---
* See Map 6.

ADVANCE UP THE EUPHRATES

i.e., some six to nine miles below Nasiriya. Here almost the only prominent feature on the right bank was a collection of low mounds about a mile west of the mouth of the Majinina creek. On both banks, traffic along the dry belts was much impeded by the numerous irrigation channels which ran in from the river and were of varying width and depth.

Early on the 6th July, Captain Nunn, accompanied by Sir Percy Cox, proceeded down the Euphrates with the *Shushan* and *Mahsoudi* to Suq ash Shuyukh. White flags were flying over the town which was an important centre of Arab trade with a floating population of about twelve thousand. Landing a naval guard and hoisting the Union Jack over the Custom House, the British gave over charge of the town to its Shaikh, who undertook to protect it; and Captain Nunn with his gunboats rejoined General Gorringe at about 10 a.m.

The naval flotilla then proceeded to reconnoitre up the Euphrates, followed by the troops in their river steamers. By about 4 p.m., when General Gorringe reached the Asani bend, the naval ships had located enemy positions near the Majinina creek, and an obstruction in the river some two thousand yards below this creek. The Turks had sunk two steamers here,* but as it turned out had not carried out the work completely as the obstruction did not block the fairway. Further reconnaissance disclosed numbers of the enemy working on entrenchments, and a Thornycroft launch was observed near the enemy's position at a bend of the river which was christened " Thornycroft Point."† The British boats opened fire on this launch and the enemy replied with their " pom-pom " and from a field gun on shore. General Gorringe now decided to halt in the Asani bend and to carry out further reconnaissance before continuing the advance. Arab information indicated that two thousand Turkish troops, with four field and two mountain guns, two Thornycroft launches and large numbers of Arabs were in position about Majinina creek and Thornycroft Point; and it was necessary to proceed with proper precautions.

A careful reconnaissance of the enemy's position was made the next day (7th). The enemy was found to have thrown up strong entrenchments on both banks with their outer flanks resting on the marshes. On the right bank, the trenches lay behind the deep and broad Majinina creek, the approach to which up the right bank was open and devoid of cover. The enemy had four guns here and their position and those

---
* *Frat* and *Risafa*. † See Map 6.

of the advanced trenches were located. On the left bank, the narrow belt of date plantation allowed of a closer approach, but it was not found possible to locate the exact sites of their advanced trenches or guns in this part of their position. The enemy continued to work hard at strengthening their defensive works and their launches made several ineffective attempts to sink *mahailas* at the obstruction in the river.

As a result of the reconnaissance, General Gorringe sent the 24th Punjabis and half the 48th Pioneers, on the night of the 7th/8th, to occupy an advanced position along the near bank of the Umm as Sabiyan creek, in order to prevent further attempts to block the river and to cover artillery positions which had been selected for the British guns. This operation was carried out successfully with but little opposition from the enemy. By this time all the troops except the 63rd Field Battery had disembarked from their steamers and encamped on the south bank of the Euphrates in the Asani bend.*

On the 8th, the British artillery opened on the enemy's position; but owing to the difficulty of observation its fire seemed to have little effect. The enemy paid little attention to it, continuing their work on the trenches, and their guns did not reply.

General Gorringe's effective strength was only nineteen hundred rifles, and owing to the heat many of these were only fit for light duty. The enemy's position was a strong one and was held, it was estimated, by two thousand troops with eight guns besides a large number of Arabs. General Gorringe decided, therefore, that he must send back for reinforcements. The opposition he had encountered had been an unpleasant surprise, but there was no time to be wasted. All the available British light draught steamers were with his force and it would be necessary to send them back to bring up any reinforcements. The water in the Hammar lake was falling very quickly and, unless the operations could be brought soon to a successful conclusion, the water line of communication might become so low as to prove impassable by the requisite steamers. Also, General Nixon was very anxious to have the use of these steamers to complete the withdrawal of troops from Ahwaz, to meet what appeared to be the commencement of the Turkish move down the Tigris from Kut al Amara, which was having a most unsettling effect on the Arabs round Amara.

The *Sumana*, owing to the damage received in action on the 5th, had also to be sent back to Basra for repairs and she and

---
* Owing to the great heat, tents had been sent with the force.

CHECK ON THE EUPHRATES.

the river steamers had a good deal of trouble in getting back across the Hammar lake, owing to the low state of the channel.

Meanwhile General Gorringe continued to advance the positions of his troops on the Euphrates. On the night of the 8th/9th, the 2/7th Gurkhas, supported by the 76th Punjabis, moved up the left bank of the Euphrates to a position about twelve hundred yards south of Thornycroft Point; and on the right bank, a section of the 30th Mountain Battery took up an entrenched position on the right of the 24th Punjabis on the banks of the Umm as Sabiyan, while the 24th Punjabis established an advanced night piquet on the Euphrates bank about eight hundred yards south of the Majinina at a point known as "Sixteen Palms." During the 9th, General Melliss drew the enemy's fire by pretending to attack and thus obtained a good indication of the position of their trenches.*

On the night of the 9th/10th, the 2/7th Gurkhas on the left bank made a further advance and after some opposition established themselves on the south bank of the Atabiya creek. An attempt here, on the morning of the 10th, to relieve the Gurkha outposts drew a heavy fire from four Turkish guns and the enemy trenches on the left bank. The enemy had evidently been reinforced here and he opened fire down the river with six guns. They were answered by the 63rd Battery in barges and by the 4·7-inch in horse-boats from the neighbourhood of Asani. The enemy gunfire, which was chiefly directed against the two British mountain guns on the Umm as Sabiyan, put one of them temporarily out of action and mortally wounded the officer commanding the battery.

On the night of the 10th/11th, another section of mountain guns was moved into a position near the British front line on the left bank of the Euphrates. Here, next morning, the enemy, evidently mistaking a relief movement among the Gurkhas for the commencement of an attack, opened a heavy fire on the 2/7th trenches.

During these four days the British troops had been carrying out continual reconnaissances of the enemy positions and the approaches thereto.

Their lack of land transport hampered them somewhat, for all supplies, ammunition, etc., had to be brought up to the advanced positions by water. This had to be done by tugs, barges and *mahailas* during the hours of darkness, and

---

* Most of the enemy were using black powder and its smoke clearly showed their positions.

at first—until they had learned by experience to work in complete silence and under cover of the banks as far as possible—under heavy enemy fire.

On the 11th, the *Blosse Lynch* arrived with the first of the reinforcements, i.e., the Headquarters 12th Infantry Brigade, 67th Punjabis and a section of the 1/5th Hampshire Howitzer Battery.

On the night of the 11th/12th, the 67th Punjabis relieved the 2/7th Gurkhas, drawing, in the operation, a heavy but ineffective fire from the enemy. The two Hampshire howitzers were placed in position near the Asani camp; and the 63rd Field Battery was brought ashore, as it was considered better to sacrifice the mobility they gained in barges to the greater accuracy they could obtain by firing on land.

On the 12th, the *Mejidieh* arrived with half the 2nd Queen's Own Royal West Kent Regiment and half the 90th Punjabis, both belonging to the 12th Infantry Brigade.* This brigade now took over the advanced positions on the left bank, the 2/7th Gurkhas being retained there as a support, and the 76th Punjabis moving down to safeguard the Asani anchorage. During the night of the 12th/13th, the enemy made three separate attacks against the British front line on the left bank, but they were all beaten off without difficulty by the 67th and 90th Punjabis, who suffered but few casualties.

On the 13th, the *Malamir* arrived with the remaining half of the 90th Punjabis and the 44th Merwara Infantry. The latter battalion took over the duty of protecting the Asani anchorage and camp, thus enabling the 76th Punjabis to join the 30th Brigade on the right bank. The previous night, an officer's patrol in a *bellum* had ascertained that the " sandhills " (i.e., the collection of low mounds west of the Majinina mouth) could be reached by *bellum*. General Gorringe at once determined to seize them and Shukhair village by night, as it appeared likely that the enemy's position on the right bank could be enfiladed from the sandhills.

General Gorringe's plan was, briefly, as follows :—On the right bank to advance the British positions to a line running from Shukhair to " Sixteen Palms " and to establish at the " Sandhills " a force which would then attack the enemy's communications and rear ; while on the left bank a simultaneous attack was made on the enemy's trenches. General Melliss was given charge of the operations on the right bank,

---

* 2nd Queen's Own Royal West Kent, 67th Punjabis, 90th Punjabis, 44th Merwara Infantry.

three battalions (1/4th Hampshire, 24th and 76th Punjabis) of his own (30th) brigade and four mountain guns being placed at his disposal for the purpose, and the half battalion 48th Pioneers was also to be under his orders till the line Shukhair-Sixteen Palms had been established. Lieutenant-Colonel Dunlop, temporarily in command of the 12th Brigade, was instructed to be ready to attack on the left bank, when ordered, with the two mountain guns and the 67th and 90th Punjabis. General Gorringe retained in reserve, at his own disposal, the half battalion West Kents, 2/7th Gurkhas, 44th Merwaras and the sapper company. As soon as the line Shukhair-Sixteen Palms had been established, the half battalion 48th Pioneers was also to join this reserve.

At 12.30 a.m., on the 14th, the 76th Punjabis and the half battalion 48th Pioneers advanced and seized the line Shukhair-Sixteen Palms. The operation was skilfully carried out and met with little real opposition, the British casualties being slight.

Early on the same night, the 1/4th Hampshire took over the trenches along the Umm as Sabiyan from the 24th Punjabis, who started with four mountain guns from the western end of this creek at 12.45 a.m. for their enterprise against the sandhills. This operation, which was to be carried out in *bellums*, was in charge of Lieutenant-Colonel Climo of the 24th Punjabis. Moving in single file, the *bellums* advanced north-westwards along a channel clear of reeds, at a pace regulated by the mountain gun rafts and, therefore, necessarily slow. About 3 a.m. the column was fired on by an enemy piquet and inclined to its left to obtain the shelter of the reeds, where, however, they found progress very slow and exhausting, as it became necessary to man-handle the *bellums* for a great part of the way. About 3.45 a.m. a heavy but inaccurate fire was opened on the column from the north-east, but by 4.30 a.m. a position was reached about a mile to the west of the sandhills. Here Colonel Climo called a brief halt to ascertain his position. About 5 a.m., when it had become sufficiently light to discern his objective, Colonel Climo, leaving his guns with an escort of a company, pushed on with the rest of his *bellums* to within one thousand yards of the sandhills, and there awaited the bombardment of his guns. He considered it necessary to obtain a rapid decision before the enemy garrison could be reinforced or the marsh Arabs could collect to attack him. After a brief bombardment by his guns, therefore, Colonel Climo ordered the attack to proceed.

The advance was carried out with dash and rapidity, the men wading the last stages through water varying from eighteen inches to four feet in depth, over a muddy bottom pitted with deep holes. Open spaces at intervals had to be crossed under heavy fire, but the Punjabis pushed on gallantly and got to within two hundred and fifty yards of the position. From here, however, all attempts at assault proved unsuccessful. The enemy were well entrenched and with heavy fire kept back the British line. Arabs from the marshes had by now begun to attack the left flank and rear of the 24th and the battalion reserve became fully occupied in holding them off. Further, to add to the difficulty of the situation, Turkish guns to the north began to fire, enfilading the attacking lines.

Colonel Climo, realising that success was no longer possible and that delay was hazardous, ordered his men to withdraw to the mountain gun position. But this was no easy matter. His men were exhausted and, much hampered by the wounded, whose fate would be death if abandoned to the Arabs, their progress could only be very slow. Moreover the Arabs, encouraged by the retirement, closed in on them persistently; the Turkish garrison of the sandhills also followed them up; and it was only the cool skill of their commander, the steadfastness of officers and men of the 24th, and the steady and valuable covering fire of the 30th Mountain guns and their infantry escort, that finally effected the desired concentration near the guns.

Here Colonel Climo reorganised the remnants of his small force for their final retirement. He divided his *bellum* flotilla into three parties, two of which consisted each of a section of guns with an infantry escort, and a third, to act as rearguard, of infantry only with their machine guns. In the meantime, the Turkish detachment from the sandhills had advanced to within seven hundred yards and brought a heavy fire to bear on the guns and the infantry *bellums*. The Arabs were still trying to close in and the Turkish gun fire increased in intensity and accuracy. But the training and discipline of the British force prevailed and the retirement was carried out steadily and in good order; though, owing to the continual grounding of the gun-rafts and *bellums*, the pace was very slow. By about 10 a.m., however, the column had reached cover at the point from which it had started some $9\frac{1}{2}$ hours earlier.

That they had failed was no fault of officers or men. They had met with unexpected opposition, and General Gorringe in his report paid special tribute to Colonel Climo's skill and gallantry in a difficult situation. The 24th Punjabis had suffered heavy casualties, the greater part of which had been incurred in the final stages of their unsuccessful assault. Out of a strength of 8 British officers and 428 Indian ranks, they had lost 56 killed and 91 wounded; and, as is usually the case in such circumstances, their losses had been proportionately greatest in British officers, of whom all but two had been killed.

Owing to the failure to capture the sandhills, General Gorringe decided to postpone the attack he had contemplated on the left bank. The Turks, however, had taken alarm at the threat to their right flank and withdrew troops from the left bank and their reserve to strengthen this part of their line; and General Gorringe attributed much of his subsequent success to this fact.

On the 14th, the Turkish troops were estimated to be five to six thousand strong with ten guns, and it seemed clear that they were still being reinforced. General Gorringe's strength in rifles had fallen to three thousand four hundred, owing chiefly to sickness caused by the climate; and all ranks were feeling the effect of the continuous hard work in the excessive heat. He, therefore decided to ask for further reinforcements, especially aeroplanes* and heavy guns. Meanwhile he would postpone further attack, but would push forward his advanced trenches to give the assaulting troops a covered position of assembly nearer to the enemy. The next few days were occupied in this way and in minor fighting of a persistent and harassing nature, in which, however, the British riflemen, much assisted by the fire of the 63rd Battery now in position near the mouth of the Umm as Sabiyan, gradually established fire superiority over the Turks.

On the 19th and 20th July, reinforcements arrived, consisting of the 18th Infantry Brigade (2nd Norfolk, 110th Mahrattas and 120th Infantry) the remaining half battalion West Kents, the 17th Sapper Company, the Maxim gun battery, two 5-inch guns of the 86th Heavy Battery, the remaining section of the 1/5th Hampshire Howitzer Battery, a battery of four 15-pounders manned by Madras Artillery Volunteers (recently arrived from India) and some details. An aeroplane also arrived on the 19th and was followed by a second—which had had to make a forced landing *en route*—three days later.†

---

* The great heat had effected the aeroplanes, and both the British aeroplanes had in consequence been out of action for some time previous to this.
† Two " Caudron " aeroplanes had reached Basra on the 14th July, making a total of four aeroplanes in the country.

In the meantime the enemy, who had been very active in strengthening his defensive works, especially on the right bank, appeared to have been further reinforced ; and had evidently withdrawn his guns to new concealed positions, which could not be located. On the 21st, an aeroplane reconnaissance gave General Gorringe for the first time a comprehensive idea of the enemy's dispositions and the local topography ; and subsequent reconnaissances by both aeroplanes shed further light on the situation, though the hostile guns could still not be located.

Between the 6th and 23rd July, the British force had incurred three hundred and two casualties from enemy action, including those of the 24th Punjabis on the 14th ; of the remainder, forty-seven were in the 67th, thirty in the 90th, and twenty-seven in the 76th Punjabis battalions ; as the British infantry had done no duty in the front trenches their losses had been very small.

The successive batches of reinforcements had experienced very great difficulty in crossing Hammar lake and the dam in the Akaika channel. Constant transhipments and relays of tugs and steamers had been necessary ; and much man-handling and toil was required before all the barges and boats had been punted, dragged, or pushed through the mud and water of the main channel. This work was rendered more trying by the intense moist heat and the virulence of the myriads of mosquitoes. Fortunately, however, the Arabs gave practically no trouble and the gunboat patrols had been able in consequence to ensure the security of the line of communication without much difficulty.

On the evening of the 23rd General Gorringe's force was disposed as follows :—

On the right bank, with their advanced troops entrenched on the line Shukhair-Sixteen Palms, were the 30th Infantry Brigade,* the 17th Sapper Company and a company 48th Pioneers on the Umm as Sabiyan. In position near them were fourteen field guns (six 18-pounders of the 63rd Battery, four Hampshire howitzers and four 15-pounders), while further back near the Asani bend were two 5-inch heavy guns of the 86th Battery on land and two 4·7-inch naval guns in barges on the river.

On the left bank, with their advanced trenches three hundred yards north of the Atabiya creek, were three battalions† of the

---

* The 2/7th Gurkhas were to rejoin the brigade from the left bank that night.
† The fourth battalion (44th Merwaras) was guarding Asani Camp.

12th Infantry Brigade (West Kents, 67th and 90th Punjabis), the 12th Sapper Company and a company of the 48th Pioneers. Close up in position on their right rear were the six guns of the 30th Mountain Battery.

Three battalions of the 18th Infantry Brigade (Norfolks, 110th and 120th) formed the general reserve near the Asani anchorage, two battalions being on the left, and one on the right, bank of the river.

The Maxim battery was on board the *Muzaffari*; and three hundred and fifty soldiers, sick but able to bear arms, were organised as a reserve on board the *Mejidieh* and the *T.4*. A barge had been armoured and, loaded with bridging material, was held in readiness for crossing the Majinina creek; and boats and material for bridging the Maiyadiya were also ready in the Atabiya creek.

The maintenance of telephonic communication had been rendered difficult by the cables being constantly cut by enemy fire and river traffic, but by this time the arrangements were as complete as was possible.

The *Sumana* had rejoined the naval flotilla from Basra and with the *Shushan* and *Mahsoudi* were held in readiness at the western end of the Asani bend to co-operate.

In his order issued on the 23rd for operations next day, General Gorringe announced his intention of capturing the enemy's advanced trenches on both banks.

After a concentrated artillery bombardment, the troops on the left bank were, at 5.30 a.m., to attack the enemy's trenches opposite them and to make good the south bank of the Maiyadiya creek. This attack was to be supported by the covering fire of the troops on the right bank and of the 63rd Battery.

At the same time the fire of the heavy guns and the howitzers was to be concentrated on the eastern faces of the enemy's works on the right bank beyond the mouth of the Majinina creek. By 6 a.m., the troops on the right bank were to be prepared to move forward (when the artillery bombardment had sufficiently broken down the enemy's resistance), cross the Majinina creek, and attack the enemy's trenches opposite. The *Sumana* would be in readiness near the Atabiya creek to tow the armoured barge with bridging material across and run her aground in the Majinina creek to provide a passage for the infantry.

Of the general reserve, the 18th Brigade headquarters with the Norfolks and 110th Mahrattas were to assemble by 5 a.m.

close to, and south of, the Atabiya creek; while the 120th Infantry were at the same time to be in position near the Umm as Sabiyan creek.

Two hundred rounds per rifle and four sandbags per man were to be carried by the troops, who were also to be provided with yellow flags to indicate their position to the artillery.

General Gorringe's headquarters were to be established in a tower on the left bank near the obstruction in the river.

The morning of the 24th dawned with a comparatively cool breeze, which was a perfect godsend for the troops. At 5 a.m. the British artillery opened the engagement, the four 15-pounders firing on the sandhills, the heavy 5-inch guns and the howitzers searching the enemy's trenches near Thornycroft Point and the 4·7-inch guns bombarding the eastern flank of the Majinina trenches.

At 5.30 a.m., the 12th Brigade advanced to the attack on the left bank, supported by the fire of the 30th Mountain and 63rd Field Batteries and by the rifle and machine gun fire of the 24th Punjabis from Sixteen Palms; while the 5-inch heavies and the howitzers switched on to the Majinina position. The West Kents, advancing on a two hundred yards frontage with their left on the Euphrates, led the attack, supported by the rifle fire of half the 90th Punjabis on their right and by the massed fire of the six brigade machine guns still further on their right. The other half of the 90th Punjabis followed the West Kents in close support and the brigade commander (Lieutenant Colonel Dunlop) held the 67th Punjabis in local reserve.

The attack was carried out with great dash and gallantry over two hundred yards of open and cleared ground, and in spite of the enemy's stout resistance the British infantry had carried the trenches near Thornycroft Point by 6.40 a.m., shooting many of the enemy at close quarters and bayoneting others in their trenches. In this affair the West Kents displayed marked gallantry, for which they received high praise in General Gorringe's report.

Having secured their footing, the 12th Brigade, supported by the close fire of the 30th Mountain Battery, proceeded to clear the remainder of the enemy trenches south of the Maiyadiya creek. In this they met with stout opposition, and at 8.40 a.m.—when Colonel Dunlop put his last man into the fight—stubborn resistance was still being encountered. The 110th Mahrattas from the general reserve were, therefore, sent up to reinforce the 12th Brigade, but before they had reached the fighting line (about 10 a.m.), renewed efforts by the 12th

FIGHTING ON THE RIGHT BANK 293

Brigade had succeeded in clearing the enemy out of all their positions south of the Maiyadiya creek. The creek itself was crossed by the enemy's boat bridge and the Maiyadiya position, including six guns, fell into our hands. The 12th Brigade was then reorganised by its commander and shortly after noon resumed the advance northward, the 67th Punjabis leading, with the West Kents and 90th Punjabis following in support.

Meanwhile, on the right bank, at 6.40 a.m. (when it was seen that the force on the left bank had established themselves in the Thornycroft Point trenches), the 30th Brigade under General Mellis was ordered to advance. At the same time, the *Sumana* started to tow the armoured barge across the river to the Majinina creek, and the *Shushan*, *Mahsoudi* and *Muzaffari* (Maxim battery) moved up-stream to co-operate by close range fire. On board the *Sumana*, commanded by Lieutenant Harris, R.N., were the 17th Sapper Company under Captain Loring, R.E., and fifty men of the 48th Pioneers, under Captain Hewett; and in the armoured bridging barge was a covering party of the 1/4th Hampshire Regiment, under Captain Parsons. The barge was to be run aground both to afford a means of crossing the creek and to bring to the spot material for the erection of two trestle bridges.

The operation was carried out most gallantly, under heavy artillery and rifle fire, with great coolness and skill. The enemy's position had to be approached very closely and both the *Sumana* and the barge were swept with bullets, and the barge was holed by enemy shell. The *Sumana* was badly damaged, but managed to withdraw pitted with bullet marks, after successfully grounding the barge in the required position, about 8.15 a.m. The British casualties on board these two vessels had been considerable, especially in the Hampshire and the 17th Sapper Company, which had suffered twenty casualties each out of the detachments numbering thirty-five* and fifty-five respectively.

While this was being effected, the enemy's position was being heavily bombarded by the British guns; and the assaulting line of the 30th Brigade—composed of the 1/4th Hampshire and 2/7th Gurkhas—were advancing on the Majinina creek. They were met by heavy fire and the ground they had to cross was devoid of cover except for grass about two feet high. But this high grass rendered it almost impossible for men to fire when lying down. By 7.30 a.m., however, the line had established itself close to the south bank of the creek about

---

* This was the total effective strength of No. 3 Company on this date.

three hundred yards from the enemy's trenches; and here, under heavy fire, the line waited for the barge and bridges to be placed in position. By 8.15 a.m. they were reinforced on their left by a part of the 76th Punjabis, who had followed the two leading battalions in close support.

As soon as the barge had grounded, the remnant of the Hampshire covering party landed on the north bank of the creek, and the sappers and pioneers started to construct the two trestle bridges west of the barge. They were under the close range fire of the enemy, but fortunately obtained good cover from the steep bank on the enemy's side of the creek.

After about an hour's work had been carried out on the bridges, the 30th Brigade delivered their assault. This was most gallantly carried out, the Hampshire Regiment and a Gurkha company leading, followed by the remainder of the Gurkhas and the 76th Punjabis. The barge and the bridges proved too difficult to use, but fortunately the barge had acted as a sort of dam and in consequence had lessened the depth of water in the creek. Assisted by the sappers and pioneers, the infantry waded waist-deep across here and made good their footing on the further bank, to find themselves confronted by another water channel—about three feet deep—running along the front of the enemy's trenches, which were about sixty to seventy yards off. These trenches, which had been considerably damaged by the British Artillery fire, were strongly constructed with loopholes and overhead cover, barbed wire on the flanks and connected with the rear by communication trenches. But the enemy fled from them before the British onset, abandoning five field guns, many rifles and much ammunition. Before 10 a.m., the whole of the Majinina position and about a hundred prisoners were in British hands.

Part of the 2/7th Gurkhas at once took up the pursuit of the retiring enemy along the river bank; steps were taken to consolidate the Majinina position, and, joined by the 120th Infantry who had been pushed up from the reserve, the remainder of the 2/7th Gurkhas and the 76th Punjabis also joined in the pursuit. The 1/4th Hampshire were retained in the position, where they were joined by the 24th Punjabis from Sixteen Palms.

Meanwhile the *Shushan* and *Muzaffari* had been moving up the river, and under heavy rifle and gun fire, in which the *Muzaffari* was holed by a shell, the Maxim battery was skilfully landed at the Majinina position. Although the enemy were retreating they still offered considerable opposition, and for some time the ships continued to be engaged heavily.

The close nature of the country, the great heat,* and the lack of land transport all combined to hamper an effective pursuit.

At 10 a.m., two sections of the 63rd Field Battery began to embark in the *Mejidieh* and in a gun barge. They were all on board by noon, when the Norfolks from the general reserve were also embarked in the *Mejidieh*, which then received orders to proceed upstream. General Gorringe intended to concentrate the 18th Infantry Brigade on the left bank of the river, preparatory to an attack on the enemy's rearward position on the Sadanawiya creek. At 1 p.m.,† he himself proceeded upstream to interview brigade commanders personally and to complete arrangements for the further advance.

At this hour, the general situation was as follows :—

On the right bank, the leading lines of the 30th Brigade were about two thousand yards north of the Majinina creek. To their left, but well out of reach, were some five hundred of the enemy who had garrisoned the sandhills and were now retiring on Nasiriya. To their front appeared an enemy entrenched position, whose river approach was commanded by two guns at the mouth of the Sadanawiya creek.

On the left bank, the 12th Brigade were some nineteen hundred yards north of the Maiyadiya creek—slightly in advance of the 30th Brigade on the opposite bank—and were engaging the enemy in the Sadanawiya trenches.

The *Shushan* and *Sumana* were almost abreast of the 30th Brigade ; and the *Mahsoudi*, with the 4·7-inch guns, and the *Mejidieh* were near Thornycroft Point on their way upstream. Here the Norfolks received orders to disembark on the right bank of the river.

For the next two hours or so, the battle became stationary while the 12th Brigade were carrying out reconnaissances of the Turkish left, and General Gorringe proceeded upstream and reviewed the situation after personal discussion with his subordinate commanders. Between 3 and 4 p.m. he received information from the 12th Brigade that the enemy along the Sadanawiya creek showed signs of retiring, evidently owing to the effect of the fire of the *Shushan* and the naval 4·7-inch guns.

---

* The temperature was well over 110° Fahrenheit in the shade.

† By this time telephonic communication between General Gorringe's headquarters and the brigades had been completely interrupted.

General Gorringe at once issued orders for the forces on both banks to advance ; and the naval boats pushed upstream. The Norfolks, with Colonel Frazer, temporarily in command of the 18th Brigade, were ordered to re-embark in the *Mejidieh*, which was then to proceed upstream, picking up General Gorringe and his headquarters as they went. This having been done, she steamed on abreast of the brigades on either bank, who were now advancing slowly but steadily. Captain Nunn now moved in quite close to the Sadanawiya position with the *Shushan* and brought every gun he had to bear on the defenders at point-blank range, being well supported by the 18-pounders in the *Mejidieh* firing at about one thousand yards range. The result was decisive. The enemy offered little further resistance and fled northwards across the marshes in disorder.

The Norfolks were landed and, with the 12th Brigade, halted for the night in the Sadanawiya position, the 30th Brigade occupying a position opposite them on the right bank of the Euphrates.

It was now 6 p.m., and Captain Nunn in the *Shushan*, accompanied by the *Sumana* and the *Mahsoudi*, pushed on to reconnoitre towards Nasiriya. As he approached the town, a Turkish " Thornycroft " launch fled upstream at full speed, opening a rapid fire from her " pom-pom " and Maxim. By this time the 12-pounder in the *Shushan* was in a very insecure state and it was doubtful if the gun-mounting and the deck would stand any more firing. However, Lieutenant-Commander Seymour, in charge, decided to take the risk and, laying the gun himself, got a direct hit at the third shot. This set the launch* on fire and her crew ran her ashore and fled. Seeing white flags displayed over Nasiriya, the naval flotilla approached the town ; but Turkish troops from a housetop opened a heavy fire, wounding Lieutenant-Commander Seymour and a stoker in the *Shushan*. As the light was failing, Captain Nunn decided to withdraw and anchor below Nasiriya for the night.

About 6 a.m. the next morning (25th) a deputation of leading Arab citizens came alongside the *Shushan* and invited the British to occupy Nasiriya, which they said had been evacuated by the Turks during the night. Captain Nunn at once communicated with General Melliss, commanding the 30th Brigade, who was encamped not far away ; and he with a hundred Gurkhas in the *Shushan*, *Sumana* and *Mahsoudi* proceeded to take over

---

* The second Thornycroft launch is said to have been scuttled by the Turks about four miles upstream of Nasiriya.

Nasiriya. The 12th and 30th Brigades marched in during the day, while the 18th Brigade cleared up the battlefield and held the line of communication with Asani.

In the action of the 24th, the enemy force under command of Ahmed Bey was, after the fight, estimated to have consisted of about 4,200 Turkish troops with 15 guns* and a large number of Arab tribesmen. Of these some 1,500 troops with 5 guns were understood to have been defending the right bank of the river, 1,700 with 6 guns were on the left bank, and about 1,000 with 4 guns on the Sadanawiya position. The British captured all the 15 guns, 5 machine guns, a large quantity of arms, ammunition and stores and 3 motor boats. The Turkish casualties were roughly estimated at 2,000 killed and wounded; and in addition the British captured 450 prisoners on the 24th, a number which had increased by the 29th to 951. The Turks had fought stubbornly and their gun fire had been unusually accurate and efficient.

The effective strength of the British troops on the 24th July was about 4,600 rifles with 26 naval and military guns (excluding the naval 3-pounders). The infantry battalions were all much below establishment, varying in numbers from 140 in the 1/4th Hampshire Regiment to 620 in the 120th Infantry. The battle casualties on that day amounted to 104 killed and 429 wounded, of which 44 killed and 110 wounded had been in the West Kents, who had gone into action under 500 strong; and the 1/4th Hampshire had incurred 45 casualties out of their total of 140. Of the 12th Divisional Signal Company more than half had been disabled by sickness and casualties in action in the course of the heavy and continuous work they had to carry out during these operations.

During the operations on the Euphrates the naval casualties in action had been two officers and three men wounded.

General Nixon in his despatch reporting these operations, which had been such a complete and brilliant success, says :—

"I cannot praise too highly the skill and determination with which General Gorringe conducted the task assigned to him—nor the gallant and devoted manner in which the troops under his command responded to the strenuous calls which were made upon them.

"Seldom, if ever, have our troops been called upon to campaign in more trying heat than they have experienced this summer in the marshy plains of Mesopotamia.

"Many indeed succumbed† to the effects of the sun when

---

* One 4-inch heavy gun, twelve field guns and two mountain guns.

† 373 fighting ranks were transferred sick to Basra from the Euphrates between 26th June and 23rd July, and on the 24th July there were 316 sick in hospital at Asani.

trenches had to be manned without a vestige of shade; and others were worn out by illness and by restless nights, spent in digging and carrying stores from the ships, or disturbed by the attacks and fire of the enemy.

"Yet in spite of diminished numbers, the spirit of the troops never flagged and in the assault of the entrenchments, which the Turks thought impregnable, British and Indian soldiers vied with each other and displayed a gallantry and devotion to duty worthy of the highest traditions of the service.

"I would also place on record my high opinion of the excellent work performed by the officers and men of the Royal Flying Corps, whose valuable reconnaissances so materially assisted in clearing up the situation before the battle of the 24th July.

"Nor can I fail to express my deep appreciation of the valuable and whole-hearted co-operation of the officers and men of the Royal Navy under the command of Captain W. Nunn, D.S.O., Senior Naval Officer. It was in a great measure due to the excellent work performed by the Royal Navy that these amphibious operations were brought to so successful a conclusion . . . ."

All the ranks of General Gorringe's force were much gratified at hearing the following message which His Majesty the King sent General Nixon on the 28th July:—

"The splendid achievement of General Gorringe's column in spite of many hardships and intense heat fills me with admiration."

Nasiriya, which had thus come into British occupation, was a comparatively modern town of some ten thousand inhabitants, which had been founded on the left bank of the Euphrates by Nasir Pasha, chief of the Muntafik Arabs. A centre of considerable trade, its importance was mainly due to its being the Turkish headquarters in the Muntafik country; and the Muntafik were the most powerful and warlike of the Arabs in Lower Mesopotamia. The town was laid out in wide parallel streets and possessed some good buildings, but the greater part consisted of native houses whose dirty and insanitary conditions precluded their use by the British force. This was unfortunate, as the field ambulances with the force were overcrowded and the health of officers and men was causing General Gorringe some anxiety. At the time of our occupation Nasiriya was, owing to the floods, practically an island.

NASIRIYA.

CHAPTER XII.

THE BATTLE OF KUT AND OCCUPATION OF AZIZIYA.

TOWARDS the end of June the Turks at Kut had begun pushing detachments down the Tigris, with, as it seemed, the triple object of covering their concentration at Kut, of creating a diversion to assist their force at Nasiriya, and of encouraging the local Arabs to rise against the British.

Below and above Amara the Tigris passes through the territory of the Albu Muhammad and Bani Lam Arabs. Both these tribes—and particularly the Bani Lam—had, in centuries of piratical independence, acquired habits which were difficult to eradicate and which necessitated constant military precautions by all our detachments. The Shaikhs of these tribes possessed no great authority over them, and the dominating factor in the Arab mind was personal profit, preferably at the expense of the losing side, but generally regardless of any but local and temporary considerations. The behaviour of the most famous Shaikh of the Bani Lam—Ghazban—is a typical example. Induced by Turkish bribes and by his hatred of the Shaikh of Mohammerah to join the Turks in their raid into Arabistan, no sooner did he see that they were cut off from Amara by General Townshend's occupation than he turned against them. Attacking the Turkish force as they approached Amara, he had taken from them much plunder and two guns; and these he had sent in to us saying that he had been presented with them by the Turks ! Not long after this he offered us his formal submission and expressed his willingness to co-operate with us in our advance on Kut; but he soon accepted another heavy Turkish bribe and rejoined forces with them.

General Townshend fell sick a few days after he had captured Amara, and, soon after, he proceeded on sick leave to India. In order to counter the Turkish activities, General Delamain, who had temporarily succeeded to the command of the 6th Division, established on the 3rd July an advanced post at Kumait, about twenty-eight miles above Amara. But the withdrawal of British troops from the Tigris to reinforce General Gorringe, the shortage of river transport, the defection of the Bani Lam, and the continued advance down the river of Turkish troops rendered it advisable to substitute for the Kumait post a " River column " to support the naval flotilla, and Kumait was evacuated on the 20th.* The new column consisted of the *Shaitan* and *Comet*, a detachment of Sappers and the 22nd Punjabis carried in two river steamers, and a launch.

The Turks then occupied Kumait, but only for a few days, as the news of the capture of Nasiriya caused a general Turkish retirement on the Tigris towards Kut. At the same time General Nixon decided to push forward his troops on the Tigris and get into touch with the Turks; if, as seemed likely, they were to retire, the British might be able to prevent the removal of any Turkish guns which had been pushed down the river. Orders were accordingly issued to General Fry, now in command at Amara, to send detachments to reinforce the river column and push gradually forward to get into touch with the Turks. For the time being, this advance was not to proceed beyond Ali Gharbi, some fifty miles by land or eighty by water above Amara.

Owing, however, to the shortage of river transport, arrangements could not be made for this movement to take place before the 30th. On that day General Delamain advanced from Amara with a small column in steamers; next day he joined forces with the river column and, preceded by the *Shaitah* and *Comet*, occupied Ali Gharbi without opposition. From here, General Delamain's river steamers had to return to Amara to bring up the remainder of his force; but the naval flotilla continued to reconnoitre upstream for some fifteen miles, meeting with no opposition. The nearest Turkish detachment, reported to be about three hundred strong with two guns, was said to be at Shaikh Sa'ad.

At the end of July the dispositions of the British force were :—At Nasiriya, under General Gorringe, the 63rd Field, 30th Mountain, Volunteer 15-pounder and Maxim Batteries, the 12th Sapper Company and the 12th and 30th Infantry Brigades (eight battalions). *En route*, or under orders to move, from Nasiriya to Amara, were the 1/5th Hants Howitzer and a section of the 86th Heavy Batteries, the 17th Sapper Company, 48th Pioneers and the 18th Infantry Brigade (Norfolks, 110th and 120th).

---

* General Nixon had temporarily to give up any idea of taking the offensive against the Turks up the Tigris.

DISPOSITIONS OF THE COMBATANTS

At Ali Gharbi, on the Tigris, under General Delamain were one troop 7th Lancers, the 82nd Field and a section of the 104th Heavy Batteries, half the 22nd Sapper Company, the 16th Infantry Brigade (Dorsets, 104th and 117th) and the 22nd Punjabis. Here also were the *Comet, Shaitan* and two 4·7-inch guns in horse-boats.

At Amara were the headquarters of the 6th Division, 7th Lancers, the 76th Field Battery and one section each of the 86th and 104th Heavy Batteries, four 15-pounders, a spare 18-pounder in a barge, half the 22nd Sapper Company, the 17th Infantry Brigade (Oxfords, 103rd and 119th) and the bridging train.

On the Tigris line of communication were the 20th Punjabis at Qala Salih and half the 66th Punjabis at Qurna.

At Ahwaz were the 6th Cavalry Brigade ("S" Battery R.H.A., 23rd and 33rd Cavalry); and at Basra were two squadrons 16th Cavalry, 23rd Mountain Battery, Sirmur Sappers and the 33rd Infantry Brigade (4th Rajputs and half 66th Punjabis). The 11th Rajputs were about to leave Basra for Bushire, where the British garrison consisted of a squadron 16th Cavalry, five captured Turkish guns (recently sent from Basra) and the 96th Infantry.

The Turkish numbers and dispositions were estimated as follows :—At and near Kut, the reformed 38th Division with a strength of about 5,000 rifles and 19 guns; retiring on Kut from Nasiriya the remnants* of the 35th Division, consisting of about 2,000 rifles; and at or near Baghdad, the 37th Reserve Division totalling about 2,700 rifles with two guns.

General Nixon's memorandum of the 24th June dealing with the question of an advance to Kut, which was mentioned in the last chapter, was received at Army Headquarters in India on the 6th July. General Nixon considered that the occupation of Kut would consolidate our military position and would have considerable advantages. By concentrating at Kut, the Turks threatened both Amara and Nasiriya, and this forced us to divide our striking force so as to garrison both places strongly and to hold a large reserve in a central position, such as Qurna. If we ourselves occupied Kut and concentrated our striking force there, we should cover Nasiriya† to a considerable extent

---

* The actual numbers and movements of these were uncertain. After the action of the 24th July they had escaped detection by our aeroplanes. The Turkish troops were said to have stripped off their uniforms and to be making their way north in disorganised bodies without arms.

† It is to be noted that by this time General Nixon had learned that steamers could only move down the Shatt al Hai as far as Shatrat al Muntafik.

and permit of its being held by a reduced garrison, sufficient to watch the local tribes and the Euphrates valley. A Turkish advance on Nasiriya by this valley was unlikely owing to the physical difficulties and, if made while we were at Kut, would expose Baghdad to a British counter-stroke from there. In short, General Nixon considered that our occupation of Kut, while depriving the enemy of two alternative lines of operation, would enable us to concentrate our main forces on a single line of advance.

He then went on to point out the political advantage of interposing a military force between the Turks and the important Bani Lam tribe, which inhabited a large portion of the northern part of the Basra *vilayet*. Until the whole of that tribe became amenable to our authority, it could not be said that we were in secure occupation of the entire Basra *vilayet*, which, as a matter of fact, extended to within four miles of Kut.

Another argument in favour of an early occupation of Kut was that it would enable us to obtain from the Shatt al Hai district large quantities of cereals which would otherwise be taken by the Turks.

The disadvantage of an advance to Kut was, according to General Nixon, that it would extend our line of communication by 153 miles, necessitating more troops to guard our communications and rendering supply, etc., a more lengthy operation. Against this, General Nixon put the possible reduction of the Nasiriya garrison and the comparatively easy navigation of the Tigris between Amara and Kut.

In order to occupy Kut it would be necessary to defeat the Turkish force covering that place, under the command of Nur-ud-Din, the recently appointed commander of the Turkish forces in Mesopotamia. It was estimated (this was on the 24th June) that Nur-ud-Din's force might total 8,500 infantry with 23 guns, exclusive of Arab tribesmen. But many of the troops were of doubtful quality and had already suffered severe defeat, and the Turks had no fresh forces in Mesopotamia to bring into the field.

Ten battalions of the British 6th Division and at least thirty guns could be made available for operations above Amara, as soon as the Nasiriya operations had been concluded, and General Nixon estimated that such a strength should be sufficient to defeat Nur-ud-Din's force.

Finally, General Nixon said :—

"As regards the maintenance of a division or more at Kut, this force can be maintained in all conditions of

ADVANCE ON KUT RECOMMENDED

river. Supplies will be accumulated at Amara and beyond, sufficient to tide over difficulties at the worst period of low river, which mainly affect the reach between Qurna and Amara."

On the 12th July Mr. Chamberlain telegraphed to India :—

" . . . . Reference protection of Anglo-Persian oil interests. The Admiralty are most anxious that there should be no further interruption of supply, and urge effective military protection irrespective of tribal guarantees. They are informed that military are proposing to withdraw troops from Ahwaz and pressing oil company to subsidise the Bawi tribe. Probably two thousand cavalry, infantry and guns will suffice for this duty, but you in communication with Nixon can advise on this point. Nixon must be warned that the present situation in Persia and Aden renders it more than ever advisable not to rely entirely on Arab or Bakhtiari guarantees. I understand that, as no further reinforcements for Persian Gulf are possible, you will not sanction further advance, but will be content for the time to hold the Basra *vilayet* and the pipe-line."

On the 27th July, two days after the capture of Nasiriya, the Viceroy sent the following telegram to the India Office :—

" . . . . Now that Nasiriya has been occupied, the occupation of Kut al Amara is considered by us to be a strategic necessity. Kut al Amara is only four miles beyond limit of Basra *vilayet*; it commands the lower reaches of the Tigris and also the Euphrates by way of Shatt al Hai, and its occupation will facilitate the reinforcement of our position on either river and also enable us to control the powerful Bani Lam tribe and effectively safeguard the oil-fields against aggression from the Tigris. Once securely in possession, we could probably reduce materially our garrisons at Nasiriya and Amara and thus economise our troops.

Nixon has, owing to sick, found it necessary to demand reinforcements. He is also being directed to despatch an Indian battalion to Bushire. In order to strengthen Nixon for the purpose of securing Kut al Amara, we consider 28th Brigade should be moved from Aden to Force ' D ' when this brigade can be spared from Aden. . . . It will . . . be possible to spare 28th Brigade from Aden shortly in order to assist Nixon in the capture of Kut al Amara, after which the brigade could again return to Aden. We request your sanction to our authorising Nixon to capture Kut al Amara and to employ 28th Brigade in the operation, which we calculate would begin not later than early in September and should be completed in time for the 28th Brigade to be back in Aden by November."

In the meantime Lord Hardinge, in his weekly private letters to Mr. Chamberlain and in his private telegrams, had also alluded to the military operations. On the 23rd July he wrote that the situation on the North-West Frontier was satisfactory for the moment, and that the attitude of the Amir of Afghanistan was all that could be desired; but that the Amir was losing influence owing to his determination to maintain an attitude of neutrality and his refusal to proclaim a *Jahad*. It was always possible, Lord Hardinge said, that in that turbulent country the Amir might be murdered or that he might be swept off his legs by the rising of some powerful tribe. Lord Hardinge said that he wanted aeroplanes badly for the frontier, but could not get them from the War Office; and he had come to the conclusion that we could not stop the Germans getting into Afghanistan; in consequence of which he had asked the Amir to intern them. On the 26th he had wired in the sense of his official telegram of the 27th (given above) and had expressed his opinion that the capture and occupation of Kut was very necessary in order to ensure future tranquillity both at Amara and Nasiriya. He had told Mr. Chamberlain that there were then two cavalry regiments, six guns and some infantry at and near Ahwaz for the protection of the oil-pipe line; but that this force appeared excessive, as there were no Turks in Arabistan, and without Turkish encouragement the local tribes were not likely to interfere. He suggested, however, that before reducing the force we should await developments in Persia. In his letter of the 30th July he told Mr. Chamberlain that at first both he and the Commander-in-Chief had opposed the occupation of Kut al Amara, but that they did so no longer, as it had been made clear to them that it would enable us thoroughly to consolidate our position in Mesopotamia.

The 28th Infantry Brigade alluded to in the Viceroy's telegrams of the 26th and 27th had been sent from Egypt to prevent the Turks from overrunning Aden and was under the command of Major-General G. Younghusband. On the 27th, Mr. Chamberlain sent a private telegram to Lord Hardinge informing him that Lord Kitchener wanted Younghusband's brigade back in Egypt, when it was no longer required in Aden, and was counting on it to carry out his engagements elsewhere ; and that consequently it would not be practicable to send it to Mesopotamia. This was followed on the 30th by the following official reply to the Viceroy's official telegram of the 27th:—

". . . . Mesopotamian operations ; as neither Younghusband's brigade nor other reinforcements are available, a cautious strategy is imposed upon us. I recognise fully strategic importance of Kut al Amara, but please let me know how it is proposed to distribute troops after its capture. If Kut al Amara is held in force it seems unlikely enemy will take any further offensive on Euphrates side but will concentrate on Tigris line. Therefore we must be strong at Kut. Assuming that defeated Turks are retiring by Shatt al Hai, do you think that any advantage is gained by retaining troops in so unhealthy an outpost as Nasiriya, with which communications are difficult, especially when river falls. Have you considered advisability of withdrawing from there and concentration of strength on Tigris side. Bushire and Ahwaz must continue to be held as outposts for political reasons, but would it not be well that remainder of troops should be at Basra and along Tigris ? Please let me have your views before any decision is taken."

This telegram, with the exception of the first sentence,* was referred by India to General Nixon for his views. General Nixon wired at length on the 2nd August in reply. While he favoured a concentration on the Tigris, he deprecated strongly any idea of abandoning Nasiriya. He considered its occupation necessary for the effective control of the powerful surrounding Arab tribes and of the Basra *vilayet* ; and he thought that great political harm would result from a withdrawal from Nasiriya, whose climate was less unhealthy than that of Qurna or Basra. During the current low-water season, water communication was difficult, but the difficulties were not insuperable. The 18th Brigade was returning to join its division, and when this move had been completed the whole 6th Division would be concentrated near Amara. The Nasiriya detachment would be one brigade strong, there would be one brigade at Basra, and the third brigade of the 12th Division would be on the line of communication between Basra and Amara. After its occupation, General Nixon proposed to

---

* To avoid raising hopes that might not be fulfilled, General Nixon had been told nothing about the possibility of getting the 28th Brigade.

hold Kut with two brigades, leaving one brigade at Amara. Unless Kut were occupied, the reduction of the Nasiriya garrison would be impossible.

As regards Ahwaz, General Nixon considered that suitable arrangements with the local tribes would obviate the necessity for retaining troops in Arabistan; although, if hostility on the part of the Persian Government were expected and if it were necessary to hold the oil-fields against every possible combination of tribes, he would require very strong reinforcements.

On the 31st July, Lord Hardinge had sent a private telegram to Mr. Chamberlain, in which he said that the importance of Kut seemed to grow daily on account of its command of the Shatt al Hai, where the Turks were now re-forming—about twenty miles from Kut—the force that had been beaten at Nasiriya. Lord Hardinge considered that Nixon's main need was British drafts* to replace casualties which were occurring at an appalling rate, largely on account of the evil climate. He gave the fighting strengths of the 1/4th Hampshire as 115, the West Kents 289 and the Norfolks 389, while those of other units were, he said, little better. General Nixon was asking urgently for another Territorial battalion which India could not at that time see her way to provide, but, Lord Hardinge said, they had no choice but to send one thousand drafts from Territorial units, although they were very loth to do so.

On the 5th August the Viceroy sent the following telegram to the India Office:—

"Your telegram of 30th ultimo. These questions have been under close and constant consideration for months past, and Nixon's views, originally called for on June 19th, and furnished in his despatch of June 24th, have again been asked for on your above-mentioned telegram. His reply puts the case so clearly that we repeat it as our answer to your telegram. (Here followed General Nixon's telegram of 2nd August, summarised above.) We concur in Nixons views, and propose to authorise him to advance on Kut when he is ready. So far as we are aware, Nixon knows nothing about the proposal to reinforce him temporarily with the 28th Brigade, and has always believed his present force capable of effecting the occupation of Kut so long as he received drafts to fill up his British battalions and he was not required to disseminate troops along the pipe-line. We concur in his views."

---

* The War Office had been unable up to that time to send any drafts to India or Mesopotamia to replace the casualties in British units.

The Secretary of State replied to this telegram on the 6th :—

". . . . I concur in course of action proposed by Nixon and recommended by you unless you think fit to qualify it in view of Marling's telegram of August 3rd* and his surmise as to objective of Isfahan gathering. What is strength and distribution of troops on Karun line? I presume that there are sufficient with local arrangements at oil-fields for defence against raiders. . . ."

This telegram was repeated to General Nixon by India, who informed him on the 11th that they did not intend that the course of action he proposed should be modified.

It will be noticed in the above correspondence that H.M. Government, at the instance of the Admiralty, were specially insistent on the necessity of securing the safety of the oil supply. As a matter of fact, after the occupation of Amara the supply was never again seriously endangered and Arabistan remained quiet. But it will be convenient here to summarise further correspondence which took place at this period on the subject. On the 13th August, General Nixon telegraphed that, provided the Bakhtiaris held to the arrangement made with them to protect the oil-fields, the existing British garrison in Arabistan would suffice. But if circumstances developed adversely in Persia he could not undertake the responsibility for operations so far inland as the oil-fields, in addition to operations in Mesopotamia, with the force at his disposal. It was only on this understanding that he could undertake an advance on Kut; and he advocated strongly that arrangements should be made to subsidise the Bawi tribe to protect the pipe-line.

General Nixon concluded his telegram by giving it as his opinion that there was no better way of counteracting unrest in Persia than by advancing to Baghdad. This, he said, "would sever German communications with Persia, both road and telegraphic, and also the channel through which

---

*This telegram from the British Minister at Tehran to the Foreign Office referred to German activities at Isfahan. The British Consul-General there reported the existence of a force of some three hundred Germans and Austrian prisoners of war from Trans-Caspia in a camp outside Isfahan, with large quantities of rifles and ammunition, besides machine guns, bombs, and a wireless telegraph apparatus. The Germans had also subsidised and collected a considerable number of Mujahids (volunteers). It seemed likely, he said, that the Germans schemed, with Isfahan as their base and in communication with the Turks at Kermanshah, to throw all Persia into disorder, paralyse action by the Persian Government by destruction of the telegraph lines, and try to involve her in war against us. The Germans might, Mr. Marling thought, be contemplating an attack on the oil-fields or a threat to the British position at Basra.

money reaches them, enabling them to make lavish disbursements in support of intrigues in Persia." To enable him to hold Baghdad, however, he would need a division as reinforcements, and he suggested the withdrawal of the necessary Indian troops from Europe.

With the exception of the opinion regarding an advance to Baghdad, which did not meet with their approval, the Government of India agreed with the views expressed by General Nixon, and they telegraphed accordingly on the 18th to the India Office. They did not anticipate that the Bakhtiaris would repudiate their agreement, and if the Bawi were subsidised, as they recommended, they saw no undue risk in Nixon's proposed advance to Kut, which was strategically desirable and would have a quieting influence on Persia.

On the 20th August the India Office replied that, as their enquiries regarding the Arabistan garrison had reference to local disorders and not to the wider question of Persian hostilities, General Nixon's military arrangements under existing circumstances were accepted. Three weeks later a subsidy to the Bawi tribe was sanctioned, and a wireless installation was erected at the oil-fields and was in working order by the 19th September.

In the meantime the anti-British activities of German emissaries in Persia had brought about an attack, on the 12th and 13th July, by Persian tribesmen on the British troops sent to guard the British Residency at Bushire. The attack was unsuccessful; but the Persian Government failed to take steps to rectify matters either here or elsewhere in Persia; and at the end of July H.M. Government, seeing that their advice and warnings to the Persian Government were having no effect, decided to take action themselves. Instructions were issued for a combined naval and military force to seize and occupy the port and town of Bushire until the British demands were complied with, and punitive measures were to be carried out against Dilwar, the neighbouring headquarters* of the tribesmen who had made the attack on the 12th and 13th. At the same time, the Government of India despatched two squadrons of cavalry and three hundred infantry with six machine guns to Nasratabad in Seistan to prevent Turco-German parties from using that route to enter Afghanistan and Baluchistan.

---

* It was about twenty miles along the sea coast from Bushire.

The British garrison at Bushire was reinforced by a squadron of the 16th Cavalry and the 11th Rajputs from Basra, the 43rd Erinpura Regiment being sent from India to replace the Rajputs in Mesopotamia.

Bushire town and its administration having been taken over on the 8th August, a combined naval and military expedition was despatched against Dilwar.* Landing having been effected on the 13th in the face of considerable opposition, punitive operations† were carried out till the night of the 15th/16th, by which time Dilwar fort and village had been captured and destroyed. The force then returned to Bushire, where Brigadier-General Brooking, commanding the 33rd Brigade in Mesopotamia, was now sent by General Nixon to take command. Hostilities of a desultory nature against General Brooking's force at Bushire were carried out by Persian tribesmen until the 9th September, when an attack by some six hundred of them gave General Brooking the opportunity he desired. He counter-attacked and inflicted a severe defeat on them on that day, which, for the time being, put an end to enemy activity near Bushire. The operations were carried out in extreme heat, and cost the British over one hundred and fifty naval and military battle casualties, besides many due to the climate.

The Russians also were much concerned at the Persian Government's inaction in the face of the continued German hostile activities; and, in support of our common policy, Russian troops were landed at Enzeli on the Caspian at the beginning of September. This had the desired effect of bringing home to the Persian Government where the German action was likely to lead them; and they seemed at last inclined to consider the question seriously. The effect at the oil-fields was also almost immediate; and General Nixon reported on the 16th September that the situation had much improved, and that four leading Bawi Shaikhs had made formal submission to the Shaikh of Mohammerah.

During August the Indian authorities had many causes for anxiety. German schemes for landing arms in India, to assist the revolutionary plots already subsidised by them, had come to light; military precautions had to be taken on the North-West Frontier to meet a *Jahad* by Mohmands, Swatis and Bunerwals, which was expected to materialise at the end of

---

* H.M.S. *Juno, Pyramus, Lawrence* and *Dalhousie*, with half the 96th Infantry and two machine guns.

† It has been decided not to describe operations in Persia in any detail in this history.

the *Ramazan* fast, i.e., on the 15th August; and a German mission was approaching Kabul.

By the middle of September matters had improved a little. The German plots had been apparently discovered and overcome, but it seemed likely that the many complex factors at the root of the unrest in the country would continue to aggravate the situation as long as the war lasted; and our British military strength in the country was gradually decreasing owing to the lack of drafts from England. Attacks on the North-West Frontier by Bunerwals, Hindustani fanatics and Swatis on the 17th August and 3rd September had been successfully dealt with, but a further attack by Mohmands was anticipated. The Amir had again assured the Viceroy of his intention to maintain neutrality; but the German Mission had reached Kabul; the Amir's Anglophobe brother Nasrulla was found to be collecting unusual and detailed information regarding the British troops on the frontier,* and generally the situation in Afghanistan seemed precarious.

On the 13th August, in his weekly private letter to Lord Hardinge, Mr Chamberlain had mentioned that he was anxious to get the Indian infantry† divisions withdrawn from France before winter conditions set in, but that Lord Kitchener objected to their withdrawal. In answering this on the 10th September, Lord Hardinge entirely agreed as to the advisability of withdrawing these divisions from France before the winter, and he suggested that they should be sent to Egypt, where they could be used as a central reserve for use in Mesopotamia or elsewhere in the East as circumstances might require. He pointed out that India had no troops at all in hand to meet fresh possibilities in Persia or Mesopotamia, and owing to the many calls on India one of the three divisions which they had endeavoured to keep intact for the defence of the North-West Frontier was now diminishing gradually.

On the 25th August Mr. Chamberlain had written to Lord Hardinge that, owing to the failure of the Sulva operations, the situation in the Dardanelles was critical. In commenting on this situation in his letter of the 17th September, Lord Hardinge said that, in case of any partial failure in the Dardanelles, it seemed to him desirable to bear in mind that the capture by us of Baghdad would have as great an effect in the Middle

---

* The Amir was aware of this and took steps to watch Nasrulla's activities, apparently with a view to checking them if necessary.

† The cavalry had less duty in the trenches, and could consequently stand the climate better.

THE QUESTION OF BAGHDAD

East as success in the Dardanelles would have in the Balkans and the Near East. Few things, he said, would impress Afghans, Persians and Arabs so much as the fall of Baghdad. He went on to discuss the question of an advance on Baghdad, which would, he said, be facilitated by our occupation of Kut; but he concluded, "I hesitate even to consider such a policy (i.e., to take Baghdad) unless we could have a reserve of troops to draw from in Egypt, as I suggested in my last letter."

In offering the above opinion, Lord Hardinge was to some extent influenced by a memorandum on an advance to Baghdad written by General Nixon on the 30th August. This memorandum will be discussed in more detail in the next volume, and it will be sufficient here to summarise very briefly its contents. After referring to the military, political and commercial advantages of an occupation of Baghdad, discussing the question of possible Turkish reinforcement, and taking into consideration his impending advance on Kut, General Nixon came to the conclusion that, unless unfavourable contingencies intervened, an early advance on Baghdad was desirable. For this purpose he considered that the troops at his disposal would probably be sufficient, although to hold Baghdad he would require reinforcement.

The periodical appreciations written by the General Staff in India at this period show that the question as to how the Indian infantry divisions from France could best be utilised was receiving special attention; and also that it was fully realised that the occupation of Kut would place us in a very favourable position for an advance on Baghdad, if this should be ordered. It was even considered that it might be possible to carry out a raid from Kut on Baghdad to rescue the British women and children detained there, though more troops would be required if we were to hold Baghdad and to secure ourselves against Persian intervention, for it seemed likely that during the coming winter months the Turks would be able to spare troops to reinforce Mesopotamia.

In Mesopotamia itself, immediately after the capture of Nasiriya, orders were issued for the transfer to Amara of the 6th Division units which had taken part in the operations on the Euphrates. But owing to the shallowness of the Hammar lake the process was a slow one, and the movement was not completed till the 20th August. Great difficulty was also experienced in bringing back the river tugs, and it was only by removing their armour plates and their guns, and by lightening them otherwise in every way, that they could be towed across the lake by the light-draught stern-wheelers.

General Townshend reached Basra from India on the 21st August. He had spent some weeks at Simla, having stayed for part of the time with the Viceroy, and he had seen the Commander-in-Chief, who struck him as very much overworked and tired.* In his book General Townshend says that he had gathered in India that an advance on Baghdad was intended. This is not confirmed from other sources, though the question was undoubtedly under discussion, and it is not clear from his book on what grounds he based this opinion, for he goes on to say that he could not get anything out of the Viceroy as regards our policy in Mesopotamia; that a very important Foreign Department official informed him that he did not think there was any idea at the moment of an advance on Baghdad, and that the Foreign Department would strongly deprecate such a move unless made with adequate forces; and that the Commander-in-Chief, while assuring him that he should not go beyond Kut unless reinforced sufficiently, at the same time told him that he had no troops to spare for the purpose. In any case General Townshend himself, in a letter to General Wolfe-Murray (then Chief of the Imperial General Staff at the War Office), expressed the opinion that we ought to hold what we had got in Mesopotamia and not advance any more.

On the 22nd August General Nixon received from India a repetition of a telegram from the Secretary of State of the 20th, accepting the military arrangements proposed and during the next two days he talked over the advance to Kut with General Townshend. On the 23rd General Townshend received his instructions, which opened, " Your mission is the destruction and dispersal of the enemy, who, according to the intelligence already furnished you, are prepared to dispute your advance; and the occupation of Kut al Amara, thereby consolidating our control of the Basra *vilayet* ": the instructions then dealt with the troops allotted for the operations and other necessary details.†

Before leaving Basra for Amara on the 25th, General Townshend says in his book that he told Sir John Nixon that if he routed and stampeded the Turks in the coming battle he

---

* That Sir Beauchamp Duff was in bad health at this time is confirmed from other sources.

† They were somewhat modified before the battle, and are consequently not given here in full.

might follow them into Baghdad. That is, if they were well on the run, and no opposition was offered, he was willing to take the responsibility of entering Baghdad. He understood that the Government did not want us to enter Baghdad and then have to retreat before superior numbers. But he gathered that his orders gave him latitude to pursue, and if he found there was no one left in Baghdad he might proceed there in the gunboat flotilla with a battalion and bring away the European women detained there. Apparently General Nixon raised no objection and told General Townshend in such an event to telegraph, as he might be able to enter Baghdad with him. By the 28th General Townshend reached Amara and started his plans for the advance which General Nixon had instructed him to draw out and submit.

On the 6th September a wire from India informed General Nixon that the Turks refused to consider an exchange of the British women detained in Baghdad; and he was told on the same day, with reference to this information, that he must not undertake operations farther up the Tigris than those already authorised without reference to the Commander-in-Chief in India.

As regards the Turkish strength and dispositions in Mesopotamia and the possibility of reinforcements reaching the enemy, the War Office, on the 17th August, telegraphed a report from Athens that Jamal Pasha was said to be leaving Syria for Mesopotamia with two Army Corps. The War Office, however, considered that this force was not likely to exceed one Army Corps of trained men.

On the 3rd September General Nixon referred to a report of doubtful value, which he discredited, to the effect that six thousand Turkish infantry had recently arrived at Mosul on their way to Baghdad; but if this force existed, it might be that of Jamal Pasha.

At the beginning of September the British Intelligence Staff in Mesopotamia estimated that the Turkish position covering Kut was held by five to six thousand troops with twelve guns; that five hundred infantry with five guns were at Ctesiphon, where a strongly entrenched position was being constructed; that at Baghdad were eight battalions of recruits and possibly twelve guns, and that on the Euphrates line, about Kifl, were three thousand Turks. As possible reinforcements there might be, as mentioned above, six thousand infantry at Mosul; and there were three thousand infantry at Khaniqin whose withdrawal from there was probably dependent on the situation in Persia.

General Townshend completed his plan of operations on the 28th August. The main feature of this was his conclusion that he should take advantage of the enemy's dissemination of force on the two banks of the unfordable river, and carry out his own main attack against the enemy's left flank. A day or two later, in reply to a query on the subject from General Nixon, he stated that, if after the fight circumstances dictated a pursuit to Baghdad, he proposed to carry it out by river and by land, and that he might instal his main force in the Ctesiphon position while he reconnoitred into Baghdad in the naval flotilla.

On the 1st September he began to move his troops by river for their forward concentration at Ali Gharbi, and on the 2nd he was informed that, in consequence of his representations, the 30th Brigade (12th Division) would be allotted as line of communication troops between Amara and Kut, which would give him the whole of his own division for the battle. About the same time he was warned by General Nixon that the political situation in Persia rendered an early advance on Kut most desirable.

The Turks were at this period showing considerable activity by pushing detachments down to within a few miles of Ali Gharbi, and in consequence there were several minor engagements in this area until the 11th, by which date General Townshend had concentrated the whole of his force, except the 63rd Field and 1/5th Hants Howitzer Batteries, at Ali Gharbi. It is worthy of note that this was the first time in the campaign that the three infantry brigades of the 6th Division had been concentrated in one place.

General Gorringe now assumed command of the Line of Communication Defence Troops, with his headquarters at Amara; for the defence of the line above Amara he had at his disposal, in addition to the 30th Infantry Brigade, two 4-inch guns of the 104th Heavy Battery and six 15-pounder guns. India had sent twelve of these guns in response to a request from General Nixon, and they were now being manned by artillery volunteers from Burma and India, the first contingent having arrived in time to take part in the Nasiriya operations with four guns. On the 12th September General Nixon with his headquarters left Basra for Amara.

The naval flotilla accompanying General Townshend consisted of the *Comet, Shaitan, Sumana* and four 4·7-inch guns in horseboats towed by two small naval launches. Captain Nunn, R.N., was away in Ceylon with the *Espiègle* and his place as Senior Naval Officer was taken by other officers. On the 15th September the position was held by Lieutenant-Commander Cookson, R.N.

By the 16th General Townshend's force had reached Sannaiyat eight miles from Nur-ud-Din's position. The advance from Ali Gharbi had been carried out principally by marching along the river bank, accompanied by the naval flotilla and the river transport. The weather was still intensely hot by day, with temperatures varying from 110° to 120° in the shade; but the nights and early mornings were comparatively cool, and by marching only from daybreak to 8.30 a.m. the casualties from heat were kept as low as possible; nevertheless, on the 12th and 13th they amounted to 101. The march, especially the last stage, had been very trying to the troops owing to the heat, the rough ground to be traversed, and the trouble given by the heterogeneous second line transport. No fighting of any consequence, however, occurred, as the Turkish advanced troops fell back before the British advance without offering any real opposition. General Townshend had now to halt and send back all his shipping to Amara to bring up the 63rd Field and 1/5th Hants Howitzer Batteries and also the remaining supplies. The last ship did not reach Sannaiyat again till the night of the 25th.

On the 14th and 15th aerial and naval reconnaissances of the enemy's position had been carried out showing that the Turks were in strength and working hard at their entrenchments.* On the 16th further information was obtained by aerial reconnaissances supported by the naval flotilla; and by a cavalry reconnaissance particularly directed to ascertain the extent of dry land between the Suwada and Suwaikiya† marshes, and to investigate the truth of a report that the Turks were digging trenches between the Suwada and the Ataba marshes. General Townshend in his book describes the fine aerial reconnaissance work performed at this time by Major Reilly, who by the 17th had furnished him with a map and detailed information of the enemy position. There was sufficient dry land between the marshes for General Townshend to make the turning movement he desired; and the cavalry reconnaissance showed that the ground, some two miles wide, between the marshes was hard and good, and that the route

---

* It is of interest to note that the aerial reconnaissances of the 14th reported that the trenches were deserted, and that no guns could be seen. It required the action of the naval flotilla the next day to force the enemy to show their strength.

† See Map 7.

leading to this avenue from Nukhailat was equally good and was fit for the three arms. In the air reconnaissance of the 16th one of the British aeroplanes was forced to land within the enemy's lines and was captured with its pilot and observer.

On the 17th General Townshend wired the results of the reconnaissances to General Nixon. Nur-ud-Din, he said, had evidently received reinforcements and his position was much stronger than anything we had as yet encountered in the campaign. He asked, therefore, if he might use the two battalions of the 30th Brigade from the line of communications between his force and Ali Gharbi as a reinforcement. This was agreed to by General Nixon.

By the night of the 25th General Townshend's force had completed its concentration at Sunnaiyat. The headquarters of the 30th Infantry Brigade, with the 2/7th Gurkhas and 76th Punjabis, two armoured motor cars, each carrying a Maxim, and one and a half squadrons of the 16th Cavalry had joined him, and two naval seaplanes had also arrived.* The total combatant strength of the military portion of his force amounted to nearly 11,000, with 28 guns and 40 machine guns†.

On the 25th General Nixon arrived in the *Malamir*. He had announced his intention of being present at the battle, but had been careful to inform General Townshend that he did not intend to interfere with his arrangements. He said that he wished to be on the spot in case questions of general policy had to be settled as a result of the battle.

The Turkish position was astride the Tigris, about seven miles north-east of Kut, and after several months of preparation was a very formidable one. On the right or south bank the defences extended southwards for some five miles, lying along and in front of the remains of a former high-level canal known as the Es-Sinn banks.‡ Some twenty feet high, these provided an extensive view and field of fire and, except for a few low mounds on the river's edge—three thousand and six thousand yards distant to the east on the right bank—were the only outstanding

---

* Three seaplanes had arrived at Basra on the 5th September from East Africa.

† The troops consisted of : 6th Division Headquarters ; one flight of four aeroplanes ; three and a half squadrons of cavalry (7th Lancers and 16th Cavalry) ; 10th Brigade R.F.A. (eighteen guns) ; 1/5th Hants Howitzer Battery (four howitzers) ; 86th and half 104th Heavy Batteries (six guns) ; Maxim battery ; 17th and 22nd Companies Sappers and Miners ; 16th, 17th, 18th and half 30th Infantry Brigades ; and 48th Pioneers.

There were also the bridging train and signal, medical and administrative units.

‡ See Map 7.

THE TURKISH POSITION

feature in the flat and open plain. The Turkish extreme right flank rested on a large redoubt.* The Tigris itself was blocked close to the Turkish trenches by a boom, constructed of barges and wire cables and commanded at close range from both banks of the river by guns and fire trenches. On the left bank the entrenchments extended for seven miles northwards, separated into three sections by the Horse Shoe and Suwada marshes. The defences on the extreme left consisted of a chain of redoubts, connected by a maze of trenches, and reached to within two thousand yards of the Ataba marsh.†

The trenches themselves were very well constructed, with a thorough attention to detail. Well traversed and well concealed, they afforded a clear command over the ground in front of them, which was flat and devoid of cover. The front of the position was covered‡ by formidable barbed wire entanglements, military pits, and land mines, while behind were miles of communication trenches and underground chambers. Covered outlets had been made to the river banks, where ramps and landing stages facilitated the utilisation of river craft; and pumping engines and water channels carried water from the river to the trenches. Gun emplacements of brick and mortar had been constructed, offering alternative positions for batteries and connected with one another by broad communication trenches.

A bridge of boats some five miles upstream formed the only lateral communication between the two portions of the Turkish force, and its distance so far in rear constituted a grave defect in the Turkish position.

This position was believed to be occupied on the right bank by the 35th Turkish Division (six battalions) and on the left bank by the 38th Division (six battalions); four battalions formed a reserve near the Turkish bridge of boats, and the mounted troops§ consisted of two cavalry regiments and four hundred camelry, supplemented by a large number of Arab horsemen. It was estimated that the total strength of the two divisions did not exceed six thousand infantry, of whom one quarter were Turks and three quarters Arabs.

---

* In the operations for the relief of Kut, in March 1916, this was known as the Dujaila redoubt.
† It is probable that the Turkish left rested originally on the marsh which had recently receded in its due seasonal course.
‡ The entrenchments north of the Suwada marsh were not so completely covered by obstacles as elsewhere in the position.
§ During the battle most of these were absent on a raid against the British communications near Sannaiyat.

The *moral* of these troops was not considered to be high, and this conclusion was found after the battle to have been justified by the fact that the Turkish troops had been distributed among the Arabs as a stiffening. The enemy were thought not to have more than twenty-five guns, but this proved to be an under-estimate, for they were found to have possessed three heavy guns, two howitzers, eight Q.F. field guns, sixteen 15-pounders, two mountain guns and seven old muzzle-loaders, i.e., a total of thirty-eight.

On the 26th September General Townshend advanced from Sannaiyat to Nukhailat, about four miles from the Turkish position. The advance was carried out in two columns, known as "A" and "B" columns. Column "A," under General Delamain, marched along the right bank of the river, with a right flank guard on the left bank; it consisted of three and a half squadrons* and two machine gun sections 7th Lancers and 16th Cavalry, 76th and 82nd Field and one section 1/5th Hants Howitzer Batteries, 22nd Sapper Company, 16th, 17th and half 30th Infantry Brigades, Maxim Battery, and some signal and medical units. Column "B," under General Fry, consisted of the 63rd Field and one section 1/5th Hants Howitzer Batteries, 17th Sapper Company, 18th Infantry Brigade and 48th Pioneers. Excepting the 63rd Field Battery and 48th Pioneers, who marched along the left bank of the river, this column moved up the river in steamers, preceded by the naval flotilla, and disembarked on the left bank at Nukhailat. The two columns were organised thus early in accordance with the part each was to play in the forthcoming battle.

The Bridging Train, composed of eighteen pontoons and forty-two *danaks*,† was towed up in previously prepared sections, and a bridge across the Tigris was ready at Nukhailat soon after 4 p.m. on the 26th. The site was technically not an ideal one, as it was on a very sharp curve of the river, but it had the advantage of being screened from the view of the Turks and of being just out of range‡ of their shrapnel. The naval 4·7-inch guns, the four 5-inch guns of the 86th Battery and the two 4-inch guns of the 104th Battery moved up in barges on the river.

---

* The 7th Lancers were so weak in strength that they were formed in two squadrons and, with one and a half squadrons 16th Cavalry and the machine gun section of each regiment, were amalgamated temporarily into one command under Major Mears, 16th Cavalry.

† Thirty to forty feet long and somewhat similar to the *mahaila*, but not so low amidships.

‡ Sandes: "In Kut and Captivity."

PREPARATIONS FOR BATTLE 319

General Dalamain's column was provided with first and second line transport. The first line consisted of pack mules, but the second line was of a somewhat heterogeneous description, including a number of hired camels, bullocks and donkeys. General Fry's column had first line transport only, the second line baggage and stores being carried in steamers and barges. It had been found impossible without further delay to provide more land transport.

General Townshend having decided to make his main attack against the Turkish left, made all possible arrangements to deceive the Turks and to induce Nur-ud-Din to believe that the main attack would be carried out along both banks of the river, somewhat after the manner of the operations at Nasiriya in the previous July. It will be seen that he was entirely successful in this; and although some Indian trans-frontier sepoys deserted to the Turks the night before the battle and informed Nur-ud-Din that General Townshend intended to make his main attack against the Turkish left, Nur-ud-Din would not believe them, as he took their story as a ruse to mislead him.

General Townshend established his headquarters on the left bank of the river near Nukhailat, where an observation tower of scaffolding was erected for him, and here he was joined later by General Nixon. General Delamain's column camped at the Chahela mounds on the right bank and pitched all the available tents to give the Turks the impression that the main British force was in permanent camp there; and they also constructed entrenchments to cover the camp, the bridge and the shipping. During the afternoon the 103rd Mahrattas advanced some two miles up the right bank of the river and entrenched themselves there with much display to deceive the enemy. They remained there during the ensuing night and returned to the Chahela mounds at midday on the 27th. During the afternoon of the 26th the Turkish guns fired on the Chahela camp, on which they had evidently " registered," but without doing much harm.

General Fry's column moved during the night 26th/27th into a position in readiness on the left bank, and early on the 27th advanced to make their preparatory attack. This was directed against the enemy's centre or " horse-shoe " position and, until the decisive attack under General Delamain had taken the Turkish left, its rôle was to mislead the enemy, by advancing on a very extended front and " by display and ruse," into thinking that it was the British main attack. This advance, well supported by the British naval and military guns, was opposed by the Turkish guns—including for a time those in the Turkish armed steamer *Pioneer*—and led to a smart engagement. This terminated early in the afternoon, when the 18th Brigade had established themselves in trenches some two thousand yards from the Turkish position and had enabled the commander of the 63rd Field Battery to reconnoitre and establish a position to be entrenched for his battery some three thousand yards from the Turkish lines. Thanks to the cover obtained from some dry irrigation canals, the British casualties in this operation only amounted to one man killed and twenty-four wounded.

During the morning of the 27th General Delamain's force made a demonstration against the enemy's position on the right bank. This was carried out by the Oxfords, the 119th, one troop 7th Lancers and two field guns. They met with no opposition, and could discern few signs of the enemy in their right bank trenches. During the afternoon they returned to camp, and in the evening the 16th and part of the 30th Brigades made a further demonstration up the right bank, digging trenches to deceive the enemy. They failed to draw the enemy's fire, however, and after dusk the 16th Brigade withdrew to camp, leaving the 30th Brigade to hold these trenches and the bridgehead near Nukhailat. It has been said that these movements deceived Nur-ud-Din and caused him to reinforce his right from his reserve and to keep his reserve on the right bank of the river.

On the 26th General Delamain's right flank guard (one troop 7th Lancers, two field guns and 104th Rifles), under command of Lieutenant-Colonel Clery, 104th Rifles, had established itself at the south-eastern corner of the Suwada marsh, forming what was known as " Clery's Post." They met with no opposition, and the only enemy seen were a few mounted men to the north-west of the Suwada marsh.

The British 4-inch and 5-inch heavy guns were landed on the left bank on the evening of the 27th, and during the ensuing night were installed in positions about 5,000 and 6,700 yards, respectively, from the Turkish centre. It had been hoped to establish these guns farther forward but there was no possible landing place for them on the left bank between 6,700 and 2,500 yards from the enemy's trenches; and although the bullock teams of the 4-inch guns had been brought up the river, enabling them to advance about a mile, none were available for the 5-inch guns, which were thus immobile on land.

THE NIGHT ADVANCE

As in the case of transport animals, further and undesirable delay would have occurred if they had had to be brought up.

At dusk on the 27th, General Delamain's infantry, following the cavalry, artillery and transport, which had all passed over during the afternoon, crossed the boat bridge over the Tigris ; and by midnight 27th/28th his whole force was concentrated at Clery's Post, with the exception of the two battalions 30th Brigade remaining on the right bank. On the way to Clery's Post the column was joined by the other section of the 1/5th Hants Howitzer Battery from General Fry's column, and at Clery's Post the detachment there under Colonel Clery also joined the column. Half the 117th Mahrattas were, however, left to protect the second line transport and rations which remained there.

In accordance with the operation order for the battle, issued by General Townshend on the 26th, General Delamain's column was, on the 28th, to execute a turning attack against the enemy's left flank and rear. General Delamain was in the first place to attack and envelop the enemy's entrenchments north of the Suwada marsh ; he was then to sweep down in a south-easterly direction, leaving the Suwada marsh on his left, and attack the flank of the enemy's second position between the Suwada marsh and the Tigris ; this second position was supposed to be in rear of the trenches which were being engaged by the column under General Fry.

At 2 a.m. General Delamain left Clery's Post for his position of deployment, a point about 5,000 yards east of the northern section of the hostile position. It was marked by its position in relation to the south-west corner of the Suwaikiya marsh, of which the Royal Engineer officer who guided the column had obtained a compass bearing in a personal reconnaissance. In this, however, he had been prevented by hostile horsemen from traversing the whole route ; and had received orders to make no attempt to carry out further reconnaissance as it was considered undesirable to arouse the enemy's suspicions. The operation map prepared as a result of air reconnaissance gave a fair indication of the relative position of the different topographical features, but the wide variation of its magnetic bearings with those obtained by the Engineer officer made it inadvisable to include any compass bearing in the orders issued to the column.*

---

* At that time the Air Force in Mesopotamia had not got a really reliable compass for aeroplane work.

General Delamain's intention was to attack from the position of deployment " with a view to enveloping the left flank of the hostile position and sweeping round southwards on to the river."* The envelopment was to be carried out by General Hoghton, commanding 17th Brigade, with the four battalions of his own brigade and two battalions (20th Punjabis and 104th Rifles) of the 16th Brigade, besides four guns of the Maxim Battery. The frontal attack, under General Delamain's personal direction, was to be carried out by the remainder of the column, i.e., the Dorsets, half the 117th Mahrattas, the 22nd Sapper Company, and two guns of the Maxim Battery, supported by the 76th and 82nd Field and the 1/5th Hants Howitzer Batteries. The night march of the column was organised accordingly. The cavalry were to operate on the right, moving round between the Suwaikiya and Ataba marshes, and were to secure the right and rear of the attack from surprise and to be in readiness to pursue.

Only first line pack transport accompanied units beyond Clery's Post. Each infantry soldier carried two hundred rounds of ammunition, and another hundred rounds per rifle were carried in regimental and brigade reserve.

General Hoghton's force headed the column. Preceded by a small advanced guard of the 20th Punjabis, his six infantry battalions moved in column of route—two battalions abreast at close interval—with small left flank guards and the transport on their right flank. No. 2 Field Ambulance and four guns of the Maxim Battery then followed, and after them General Delamain's force in the following order :—Headquarters, Sappers, Artillery, Ammunition reserves, No. 1 Field Ambulance, two guns Maxim Battery, and half 117th Mahrattas, with the Dorsets on the left as flank guard.

The going was fairly easy, though soft and spongy in places. But the troops suffered considerably from the dust-laden atmosphere, which was at the same time heavy, damp, and close, causing the men to fall asleep immediately at every halt.

At 4.45 a.m. the advanced guard reported marsh on three sides, whereupon the column was halted and it was soon discovered that the force had been led with commendable accuracy into an indentation of the Suwaikiya marsh, some 200 yards to the east of its south-western corner. The position of deployment having thus been reached, the column deployed

---

* General Delamain's operation order.

for attack, the general direction ordered being west-south-west. General Delamain's own force on the left was deployed with the half battalion 117th Mahrattas in front, supported by the 22nd Sapper Company and the Dorsets echeloned on the left rear as reserve. General Hoghton, on the right, deployed his infantry in two lines on a 1,200 yards frontage; the leading line consisting, from the right, of the 20th Punjabis, Oxfords, and 22nd Punjabis, and the second line, from the right, of the 104th Rifles, 103rd Mahrattas, and 119th Infantry.

Between 5.15 and 5.30 a.m. General Hoghton and the cavalry moved off, the latter—who had been over the ground previously—proceeding correctly towards the passage between the Suwaikiya and Ataba marshes, in accordance with their instructions, while General Delamain's force remained in position in order to allow General Hoghton time to develop his turning movement.

When the sun rose just after 6 a.m., General Hoghton found marsh on his left. Being doubtful as to the accuracy of the sketch map issued to the troops, and thinking that the water on his left was probably an isolated swamp that had been omitted from the map, he continued for a short while without changing direction. The growing daylight, however, soon showed him that the water on his left was the Ataba marsh and it became apparent that his force, confused by the dim light at the start and attracted by the movement of the cavalry to their right, had lost direction and were marching through the passage between the Ataba and Suwaikiya marshes. When this change of direction was observed by General Delamain from the position of deployment, he sent orders (received by General Hoghton at 6.35 a.m.) not to go any farther northward, but to advance against the Turkish left. General Hoghton replied, however, that he was now so far to the north that he was committed to go round the Ataba marsh, and rather than retrace his steps in order to make a fresh start, he considered it more prudent to continue rapidly round the marsh, as this course would bring him out in rear of the enemy's position. General Delamain concurred and sent the 76th Field Battery to join General Hoghton.

The cavalry in advance of him, after driving back some hostile mounted troops, reached the northern end of the Ataba marsh by 7 a.m., and then moved westward.

Soon after 7 a.m. the officer commanding the 76th Field Battery reported to General Hoghton that his battery ran a great danger of being bogged if it continued to follow the infantry. This necessitated a short halt for reconnaissance before they could again proceed, at 7.30 a.m. The leading line of infantry were now well round the north corner of the Ataba marsh. Beyond a few shots fired at them from a long distance southward they had met no opposition, and they thought they could now discern the Turkish "Northern Redoubt."* At 7.40 a.m. General Hoghton received orders from General Delamain, based on the reports of reconnaissances, that he was not to halt on any account, that the enemy's position was very lightly held, and that he was at once to attack the enemy's main force, which was reported to be in a hollow behind their "Southern Redoubt."

In wheeling round the Ataba marsh, the infantry had maintained their deployment formation, and they still retained this, except that the 104th Rifles and brigaded machine guns† were now echeloned in rear of the right of the 20th Punjabis. The 22nd Punjabis with their left on the western edge of the Ataba marsh directed the movement, which was almost due south and intended to attack the enemy in the hollow, passing through the low ground immediately behind the trenches in rear of the Turkish "Centre Redoubt."

No sooner, however, had the advance started than reports from the cavalry and the 20th Punjabis showed that an enemy force of about a battalion was in occupation of a hitherto unlocated entrenchment to the westward. As it was necessary to capture this work to permit of the advance of his column, General Hoghton ordered the 104th Rifles, supported by the fire of the brigaded machine guns and two guns of the 76th Field Battery, to attack it. Well supported by these guns and with the cavalry watching their right, the 104th carried the work with great dash at the point of the bayonet at 9.10 a.m., and, suffering but few casualties themselves, they took prisoner one Turkish officer and 111 men. Shortly afterwards a body of about five hundred Turkish troops, advancing to the support of this outlying work, were caught in the open by the fire of the British machine guns and were driven back with heavy loss.

It will be convenient now to return to General Delamain. His original intention had been that General Hoghton's force should attack the Northern Redoubt at daybreak, whilst the

---

* The Turkish entrenchments between the Ataba and Suwada marshes consisted of three main redoubts, connected with one another and with the rear by a considerable system of trenches. These three redoubts will be referred to as the "Northern," "Centre," and "Southern" redoubts. (See Map 7.)

† The Maxim Battery followed in rear of the two lines of infantry.

force under his own command should attack on the rest of the enemy's front in co-operation. A check, however, had been imposed on his movements by the detour of General Hoghton's force. He therefore advanced deliberately from the position of deployment, effecting reconnaissances of the hostile position by means of a staff officer's patrol, as well as by an aeroplane and two light armoured cars which had been sent up to him from Force Headquarters.

By 8 a.m. he had established his force at a distance of some 2,000 yards north-east of the Northern Redoubt, there to await the development of the turning movement. At 8.20 a.m., when General Hoghton's nearest troops could be descried halted near the south-western corner of the Ataba marsh, and the sound of the subsidiary attack by the 104th Rifles on the unfinished redoubt could be heard, General Delamain, having gathered from his reconnaissances that Northern and Centre Redoubts were weakly held and expecting that reinforcements might arrive at any moment from the Turkish reserve, ordered an attack by the force under his immediate command.

Northern Redoubt was allotted as the objective of the half battalion 117th Mahrattas, supported by the 22nd Sapper Company; Centre Redoubt was assigned to half the Dorsets, while the other half was retained as reserve. The unexpectedly strong resistance of the Ottoman Turk garrison of Northern Redoubt, however, caused the Dorsets to be diverted later to the support of the 117th and Sappers. The 82nd Field and 1/5th Hants Howitzer Batteries were ordered to co-operate at a range of 2,200 yards.

While this attack on Northern Redoubt was being prepared, and that of the 104th Rifles on the unfinished redoubt was taking place, General Hoghton opened communication with, and informed General Delamain of the direction of his advance and asked for co-operation. General Delamain in reply informed General Hoghton of the impending attack on Northern Redoubt and urged him to push on. These were the last messages transmitted by cable, as General Hoghton had now reached the end of the seven miles of heavy telephone cable carried by his signal unit. Although all the reserve heavy cable with headquarters at Nukhailat had been placed at General Delamain's disposal, it only sufficed to provide him with three miles, and General Hoghton with seven miles, in advance of the position of deployment. Thereafter, communication became almost entirely lost, as owing to the flat nature of the country, the dust and the mirage, visual signalling was almost impossible ; and the flimsy light cable quickly got broken and useless.

The 104th Rifles having captured the outlying work at 9.10 a.m., General Hoghton pushed on his southward advance steadily, detaching first the 103rd Mahrattas to attack Northern Redoubt, then the 119th Infantry to attack Centre Redoubt, and finally the Oxfords to support the attack of the 119th. These three battalions, on reaching their objectives, passed under the command of General Delamain, leaving General Hoghton with the 76th Field Battery, the 20th Punjabis, the 22nd Punjabis, and the 104th Rifles to pursue his southward movement in rear of the Turkish position.

General Delamain's attack on Northern Redoubt started at 8.45 a.m. and met with stout resistance, but the advance was steadily pressed over the open and coverless plain ; being well supported by the two batteries. The infantry and sappers displayed great dash and determination though suffering considerable casualties—in the 117th Mahrattas amounting to 50 per cent. of the numbers engaged—and the whole of the Dorsets had gradually to be absorbed in the firing line. Pushing on, however, with great gallantry, the three units carried the Northern Redoubt at the point of the bayonet just after 10 a.m. In this achievement they were materially assisted by the action of the 103rd from General Hoghton's force, who—well supported by the 76th Field and Maxim Batteries—had taken the trenches to the north and northwest of the redoubt about 10 a.m. At this hour the 119th were nearing the trenches behind Centre Redoubt. One hundred and thirty-five Turkish soldiers surrendered to the British in Northern Redoubt, while many others retreated down the communication trenches.

After the capture of the Northern Redoubt, the 103rd joined hands with the Dorsets, Sappers and 117th, who at once pushed down and occupied the Centre Redoubt, which the enemy evacuated without much further resistance. By this time the 119th, supported by the Oxfords, had captured two lines of trenches west of the Centre Redoubt, but were checked by heavy fire from gunpits about a thousand yards away to the south of this redoubt.

Meanwhile, General Delamain had advanced his headquarters to the Northern Redoubt as soon as it was captured, and as, by that time, a strong wind had got up, raising clouds of dust which, combined with the usual mirage, was making artillery observation very difficult, he ordered the 82nd Field Battery, followed shortly by the 1/5th Hants Howitzers, up to a fresh position close to Northern Redoubt to co-operate with the infantry attacks southward.

The Turks put up a stout resistance from the communication and other trenches to the south-west and south of the Centre Redoubt and from the Southern Redoubt itself. A company of the 119th, supported by a company of the Oxfords, captured the two Turkish guns in the gunpits south of the Centre Redoubt, and a mixed party of 119th, Oxfords, and 103rd gained a footing in the trenches south of the Centre Redoubt, where General Delamain's portion of the force was reorganising. Heavy and confused fighting ensued, and the Turks, fighting well, started to counter-attack, with the result that the British attack was held up for some time about eight hundred yards short of the Southern Redoubt, the check being largely owing to the lack of close artillery support, which the dust and mirage had rendered so difficult. The deep communication trenches hampered reorganisation and reinforcement of the British front line, but it was gradually effected; the 82nd and Hampshire Batteries redoubled their efforts, and the Maxim Battery moved in to afford close support to the infantry attack, with the result that an assault by the Oxfords,* 119th, and 103rd carried the redoubt about 12.45 p.m., capturing three hundred Turkish soldiers.

After the Oxfords, 103rd, and 119th had been detached, soon after 9 a.m., from General Hoghton's force to join in General Delamain's attack on the three redoubts, the 22nd Punjabis continued their advance towards the low ground behind the Centre Redoubt. Beginning, however, to suffer from enfilade fire from the Turkish trenches behind this redoubt, they swung round a little to their left. This was before 10 a.m., and just then the 20th Punjabis reported an enemy force advancing from the south-south-west, and apparently directed against the right flank of General Hoghton's force. Ordering the 20th to remain in observation of this force, General Hoghton collected the 104th, 22nd and brigaded machine guns, which were all somewhat scattered, and advanced with them to attack the approaching enemy. This was in accordance with orders he had received shortly before from General Delamain to attack the enemy wherever encountered,

---

* In his report General Nixon describes the action of the Oxfords here as being " particularly fine."

and he decided on this even though, owing to the dust and the mirage, he could not discern how General Delamain's attack on the redoubts was progressing. The enemy opposed to him now appeared in considerable force to the southward, and his troops came under a sharp rifle and accurate quick-firing shrapnel fire, which caused many casualties. The 76th Field Battery now joined General Hoghton again, and with their effective support, the infantry carried out a spirited advance and forced the enemy to make a rapid retirement. Shortly afterwards they also drove off a body of hostile cavalry which threatened to attack them.

Just before noon General Delamain sent for General Hoghton and ordered him to press on with his attack southward. On returning to his force, General Hoghton found that the retiring enemy had been reinforced and had taken up a position at the south-eastern edge of the hollow to the south-west of the Southern Redoubt. General Hoghton's troops were by now considerably exhausted owing to their exertions and the lack of drinking water, and the ammunition carried by the men was running short. He halted, therefore, to reorganise and replenish ammunition.

At 12.45 p.m. the advance was resumed. The enemy did not stand and parties of them were continually moving across General Hoghton's front, being no doubt fugitives from the redoubts and trenches, which by this time had passed entirely into General Delamain's hands. Between 1 and 2.15 p.m. all communication between the two generals was interrupted and, owing to the dust and mirage, General Hoghton could see little of what was going on to his left rear. He slowly continued his advance, however, to the southward until 3.30 p.m. By this time the men's exhaustion had become complete. They had been marching or fighting, almost continuously, since 2 a.m.; and the heat, dust* and lack of drinking† water had all contributed to fatigue them. General Hoghton therefore halted for a short rest, having reached a point to the north-west of the Horse Shoe marsh, about two miles from the Tigris. Almost at once the force came under heavy and accurate artillery fire from Turkish guns due south. This not only caused many casualties among the troops but it also stampeded the water and ammunition mules,

---

* A strong wind blew all day and raised clouds of dust, which caused acute discomfort to the men and intensified their craving for water.

† General Townshend says in his book that the cavalry reconnaissance had reported the water in the marshes as "brackish, but drinkable." This, as he says, proved incorrect, as the men found that the water was undrinkable.

and the 76th Battery was unable to reply through lack of ammunition.* General Hoghton retired towards the Suwada marsh in the hope of getting water to revive his men, meeting near point " B " General Delamain, who—after reorganising the troops which had captured Southern Redoubt—was advancing in support of General Hoghton. General Delamain ordered him to halt and reorganise his force for a further advance.

The cavalry under Major Mears had left the position of deployment at 5.30 a.m. and, soon after, their advanced squadron (7th Lancers) found themselves opposed by about a squadron of Turkish and Arab cavalry entrenched to the northward of the Ataba marsh and between it and the Suwaikiya, which here takes a long sweep to the westward.† Aided by their machine guns the 7th Lancers squadron drove the enemy back and changed direction to the west. The whole of the cavalry then halted, north of the Ataba marsh, about 7 a.m., to cover the right of General Hoghton's approaching column.

About 8.30 a.m. the cavalry were joined by the two armoured cars with machine guns, and about the same time their patrols located the Turkish entrenchment, which was captured by the 104th Rifles at 9.10 a.m. Major Mears then informed General Hoghton that he would pursue enemy infantry retiring from this entrenchment and try to cut them off. Making a wide *détour*, the cavalry pushed right round the enemy's left flank and turned southward, finally taking up dismounted positions in dry irrigation cuts about twelve hundred yards from the Turkish camp near their boat bridge. From here they could see a Turkish battery drawn up about eight hundred yards off, with a Turkish battalion in close formation quite near to it, and they also sighted Turkish infantry retiring across their front in a southerly direction. The idea of attempting to capture the Turkish battery was first conceived, but the ground was so intersected with irrigation canals that mounted action was impossible, and Major Mears decided that, considering his isolated position, the enemy force was too strong for him to tackle with any chance of success. He therefore ordered as heavy rifle and machine gun fire as possible to be opened on the Turkish battery and the retiring enemy infantry. The Turkish battery, however, soon located them and replied vigorously and effectively, and some of the British artillery, who had sighted but not recognised them, also

---

* The ammunition column had altered its position, and the 76th wagons had gone astray.
† Not shown in Map 7.

shelled them and did some damage. The cavalry were thus forced to retire, which they did slowly and in good order under heavy shell fire. They had incurred several casualties among their men and a good many among their horses.

While retiring they received instructions to co-operate with General Hoghton, who was advancing southward. Moving in his supposed direction, they were diverted from their course by hostile shell fire and missed him, eventually reaching General Delamain's position about 2.30 p.m. From here the armoured cars were sent back to Clery's Post.*

The slow progress in the action of General Delamain's column had necessarily affected General Fry's attack south of the Suwada marsh. Leaving their trenches—some two thousand yards from the Horse Shoe marsh and fifteen hundred yards north of the Tigris—the infantry of the 18th Brigade commenced their advance at 6 a.m. Their front line consisted of the 7th Rajputs, 120th Infantry and 110th Mahrattas, with the Norfolks in local reserve. The 63rd Field and 86th and 104th Heavy Batteries supported the advance, having as their escort, and to assist them generally, the 48th Pioneers. As the attack was not to be pressed home till news of success in the north by General Delamain had been received, the advance was made slowly and methodically. The Turkish guns were well entrenched and concealed, and the British artillery found observation and communication very difficult, owing to the flatness of the country, the mirage, the dust and the strong wind.

The naval flotilla and the four 4·7-inch naval guns in barges were to keep up a bombardment of the enemy's position on the right bank of the river. The 4·7-inch guns, which were on the river near the position of the 104th Battery and had been placed for the operation under the fire control of the 6th Divisional Artillery Commander, opened fire at 6 a.m. and were at once replied to with considerable accuracy by hostile guns on the right bank.

By 8.30 a.m. the right of the 18th Infantry Brigade was fifteen hundred yards from the enemy's trenches north of the Horse Shoe marsh and their left was twelve hundred yards from the trenches south of that marsh. In the meantime, General Townshend had received a few reports from General Delamain. At 7.30 a.m. he was told that the 17th Brigade,

---

* They had done very good work, and proved the utility of motor cars in this country. They subsequently did useful work in conveying wounded back to the river. But being of too light a type, their axles got bent and put them out of action.

who were making the turning movement, had been obliged to march round the marsh to the north of the enemy's position and that this was delaying operations, and at 8.30 he received another report saying that the 17th Brigade was west of the Ataba marsh and north of the enemy's left, and that General Delamain's portion of the column was attacking the central and northern redoubts, which General Delamain expected to be in within half an hour. After receipt of this message General Townshend sent General Fry the news of the early success anticipated by General Delamain, and at the same time instructed him not to make his decisive attack till he saw that the enemy opposite him were being affected by General Delamain's march southwards.

At 10.40 a.m. an aeroplane flew over General Townshend's headquarters and fired a Very light, which was the agreed signal to show that General Delamain's assault had been successful. About the same time General Fry reported that a force of three hundred enemy troops had advanced along the right bank of the Tigris and taken up a position to enfilade the 18th Brigade lines. The naval flotilla, advancing to investigate this situation, fired on the Turkish force—whom they estimated at about one thousand—and forced them to retire again to their trenches. The Turks on this bank showed no further activity throughout the day.

Just after 11 a.m. telephone communication between Generals Townshend's and Delamain's headquarters was broken, owing to insufficiency of cable, and remained so throughout the day. Visual signalling being impossible, the only means of communication* was by aeroplane or seaplane, which rendered valuable service. The great majority of the personnel manning the seaplanes had recently returned from service in East Africa and suffered continuously from malaria. Really unfit to fly the seaplanes, which were mechanically ill-adapted for the work in Mesopotamia, these men showed a fine spirit in continuing to work, refusing to say when they were ill.

At 11.20 a.m. General Townshend received a message by aeroplane from General Delamain, saying that his column was advancing south on to the flank of the enemy position south of the Suwada marsh; and at 12 noon he received a further message saying that the column had arrived south of the marsh, but

---

* A wireless set could not be made available for General Delamain for this day's operations. The wireless sets available were with General Townshend's headquarters and on board the *Malamir* with General Nixon's headquarters.

that their progress was slow and hampered by many wounded, and asking that General Fry's attack should press in to assist them. On General Fry being requested to do so by General Townshend, he replied that he would do what he could, but that the enemy's opposition was still such that no decisive attack was yet possible. A comparison of the above timings with the movements of General Hoghton's force as given previously appear to show that the reports to General Townshend gave the situation of the flanking movement too optimistically.* At 1.45 p.m., however, General Townshend received a further report from General Delamain that he was then in possession of the whole of the enemy position north of the Suwada marsh. This showed him that the whole of General Delamain's force could not have been moving south at noon. At 3.30 p.m., having received no further reports, General Townshend sent orders to his aeroplanes to report on the situation of General Delamain's force, and at 5.30 p.m. they brought him a report, written at 4.50 by General Delamain, saying that he was about to attack the enemy position between the Suwada and Horse Shoe marshes and asking for the support of concentrated artillery fire by the guns with Generals Townshend and Fry.

By 4.30 p.m. General Fry's infantry had worked farther forward, the right of their firing line being within nine hundred yards of the hostile trenches between the Suwada and Horse Shoe marshes; but owing to heavy enfilade fire from the hostile trenches south of the Horse Shoe marsh their left had been echeloned back to face southward. In making this advance the infantry had received such effective support from the 63rd, 86th and 104th Batteries and from the naval guns, that the Turkish guns had been practically silenced.

Meanwhile, General Delamain, having rested his tired troops for an hour, left the 119th Infantry to hold the captured northern position and began a further advance at about 4.50 p.m. from point " B " round the south-western corner of the Suwada marsh, with the intention of assisting the attack of the 18th Brigade by taking in reverse the Turkish position between the Suwada and Horse Shoe marshes, as contemplated in the general plan of his divisional commander. The three battalions of the 17th Brigade led the advance. The 22nd Punjabis, on the left of the leading line, moved along

---

* Some margin must, however, be allowed in the timings given on both sides, as those given in the war diaries sometimes vary, and although the times given in this account have been arrived at with all possible care, their absolute accuracy cannot be guaranteed.

the western edge of the Suwada marsh, with the Oxfords on their right and the 103rd and Brigade machine guns following in support. The 16th Brigade, with the Maxim Battery on their right, moved in echelon on the right rear of the 17th Brigade—covering the guns, the Sapper company and the transport—and the cavalry were still further out to the right to cover that flank.

About 5.30 p.m. General Delamain reached a position some three thousand yards west of the Horse Shoe position and, having sent a message by aeroplane to inform General Fry of his intentions, was about to attack eastwards. But the appearance of strong hostile reinforcements, moving from the southwest towards the Horse Shoe marsh, forced him to change his intentions. He immediately changed front, to face and attack the advancing enemy, who appear to have come from the Turkish right bank position. Though dead beat and parched with thirst, General Delamain's men responded gallantly to the call upon them and carried out the necessary deployment and extension skilfully and rapidly. With the 16th Brigade on the right and the 17th on the left and well supported by the 76th, 82nd, 1/5th Hants and Maxim batteries, the successive lines of British infantry made straight for the enemy with fine dash and spirit. The Turks at once took up a defensive position* along a dry canal running north-west from the Tigris; and the British, whose advance led through long grass straight into the face of the setting sun, had some difficulty in discerning exactly where the enemy were.

The Turks opened a heavy rifle fire, supported by four field and two machine guns, but their guns were quickly silenced by the British artillery firing at ranges varying from 1,700 to 2,600 yards; and the British infantry, scarcely halting to fire, fixed bayonets at four hundred yards' distance and swept on, driving the enemy headlong from the canal. The Turkish losses were heavy, including their four guns, but they were saved from further destruction by the fall of night, which enabled the remnants of their force to make good their escape. General Delamain's force were now so exhausted as to be incapable of further movement†, so they occupied the enemy's position, where they passed a quiet night.

In the meanwhile, about 5.30 p.m., General Fry's brigade had renewed its efforts to close in on the enemy's position in

---
* See " C " in Map 7.

† Moreover, the ground was so cut up by deep nullahs that movement was practically impossible.

co-operation with the expected attack by General Delamain. In the absence of this attack, however, the 18th Brigade were unable to advance nearer than five hundred yards to the hostile trenches. In this situation they dug themselves in at nightfall.

Generals Townshend and Fry could hear that General Delamain's force was heavily engaged, but they were still out of communication with him and had no idea what was happening. About 6.40 p.m., when it was completely dark, General Delamain's guns ceased firing. But General Townshend received no further news till the next morning, when General Fry's patrols and the British aeroplanes found that during the night the Turkish force had evacuated all their positions east of Kut and were in full retreat up the Tigris towards Baghdad.

General Delamain's men, after their fine attack, passed a miserable night; stupefied with their exertions, hungry and parched with thirst, they suffered intensely from the bitter cold.* After they had had a few hours' rest, General Delamain sent Captain Cochran, of the Divisional General Staff, who had accompanied his force, with a small cavalry escort to inform General Townshend of what had happened, but all the horses of the party were killed on the way by enemy fire and the party had to lie out in the plain waiting for the dawn and could neither get the news through to General Townshend nor inform General Delamain that they had failed to do so. The cavalry, which had withdrawn from the final attack when darkness fell, spent several hours trying to find water and then General Delamain's column, in both of which they failed. They then settled down for the night in a separate bivouac. Early next morning the aeroplanes brought General Delamain the news of the Turkish flight and his force was at last able to get to the Tigris to obtain water.

Soon after General Delamain's successful attack the naval flotilla made a gallant attempt to break through the Turkish obstruction in the Tigris. While co-operating with General Fry's attack, the Senior Naval Officer (Lieutenant-Commander E. C. Cookson, R.N.) received a message from General Townshend, about 6 p.m., suggesting that he should make an effort to get through the obstruction, when it might be possible to capture the Turkish steamers. Knowing that General Delamain's force was in rear of the Turkish trenches, General

---

* The temperature dropped 50 degrees. Captain Birch Reynardson, in "Mesopotamia, 1914–1915," gives a graphic description of the men's condition.

Townshend was convinced that the Turks would retreat; so he was anxious to organise his pursuit as soon as possible.

Lieutenant-Commander Cookson decided to make the attempt, and started to do so as soon as it got dark. With all lights out, the three armed tugs crept upstream followed by a motor boat. But they were detected as they neared the obstruction and immediately came under a very heavy rifle and machine-gun fire from both banks of the river. It was found that the obstruction consisted of a *mahaila* and two iron lighters joined together by wire hawsers, and the only satisfactory method of clearing a way was to cut the moorings by which the craft were held together and thus release the *mahaila* —which was in the middle—to float downstream with the current.

Lieutenant-Commander Cookson ordered the *Comet*** to place herself alongside the *mahaila*. This having been done, under a hail of bullets at point-blank range, Lieutenant-Commander Cookson " found that he could not send a man over the ship's side to cut away the obstruction because it meant certain death, so he took an axe and went himself."† He fell between the *Comet* and the *mahaila* absolutely riddled with bullets; and he died ten minutes after some of his crew had extricated him. It may fitly be said of Commander Cookson, as it was of one of Wellington's Peninsular heroes: "no man died that night with more glory."

Fourteen of the small crew of the *Comet* had been wounded in this operation, and the commander decided that the very heavy fire of the enemy rendered it impossible to attempt more. He, therefore, retired and the flotilla moved downstream and anchored for the night near Nukhailat.

During the battle the majority of the Turkish mounted troops had been absent on a raid against the British communications. General Townshend heard on the 27th from his post at Sannaiyat that they were threatened with an attack from a Turco-Arab mounted force with at least four guns; and he also heard that the enemy had captured a telegraph launch and sunk fifteen *mahailas* (carrying oil and coal for his steamers), between Sannaiyat and Shaikh Sa'ad. Early in the afternoon the *Comet* was sent to Sannaiyat with a detachment of the 48th Pioneers, but they returned again in the evening as the post had not been attacked. Throughout the 28th, General

---
* Lieutenant-Commander Cookson was himself on board the *Comet*.
† General Townshend's special despatch on this exploit.
Lieutenant-Commander Cookson was awarded the V.C. (posthumously).

Townshend continued to receive reports from Sannaiyat of attacks and threatened attacks, but he steadily declined to detach troops from his main enterprise to go to that place till 6 p.m., when he sent there one company each of the 76th Punjabis and 2/7th Gurkhas. But the threatened attack did not materialise and the detachment rejoined headquarters early on the 29th.

By 10 a.m. on that day the naval flotilla, having passed the obstruction* in the Tigris, reached Kut—about forty-five minutes after the arrival there of General Delamain's cavalry—and pressed on in pursuit of the enemy's steamers. But the low state of the river rendered navigation very difficult, and it was not till the morning of the 30th that two of the enemy's steamers—the *Pioneer* and *Basra*—were overtaken. By this time the *Sumana* had run aground and broken both her rudders, the *Shaitan* had been hit by a shell from the Turkish rearguard guns and was also aground, and the *Comet* was alone. She at once engaged the enemy steamers and was soon joined by the *Shaitan*, who had managed to follow on. They appear to have hit the *Basra*, for she dropped two *mahailas*—full of ammunition—which she was towing and found safety in her superior speed.

About noon, when the British gunboats came under fire from the mountain guns of a Turkish force which had emerged from inland and was now behind them, the *Shaitan* again ran aground, and for a time the position appeared critical as the leading portion of General Townshend's pursuing force was far behind. Fortunately, however, she managed to get off again, and the S.N.O. (Lieut. Singleton), deciding that further pursuit was too risky, brought his two craft back to Kut.

General Townshend's orders for the pursuit had allotted General Fry's force, i.e., the 63rd Field Battery, half the 17th Sapper Company and the 18th Infantry Brigade to carry out the pursuit by river, moving in steamers behind the naval flotilla, while the cavalry were to pursue by land up the left bank of the Tigris. General Delamain's brigade was to march in and occupy Kut, while General Hoghton's brigade remained to clear up the battlefield and evacuate the wounded. In regard to the latter, the evidence given before the Mesopotamia Commission shows that the improvised arrangements for the reception and accommodation of the wounded proved inadequate.

---

* The Turks had left behind two men to fire an old muzzle-loading gun covering this obstruction. But this futile, though gallant, resistance was quickly disposed of.

General Townshend says in his book that he had told the senior medical officer with his division to make arrangements for six per cent. casualties, whereas they amounted to nearly double this number. Moreover, the fighting had been spread over many miles of country and did not cease till dark. Consequently the medical personnel were much overworked and it took them some time to cope with the situation.*

Considerable delay occurred in embarking General Fry's force. The steamers took some time to pass the obstruction, and ramps had to be constructed on the steep banks of the river to embark the artillery. They got off at last just before 6 p.m., but had to halt for the night two miles downstream of Kut. Further progress was much impeded by the difficult navigation, and the steamers took twenty-four hours to traverse two miles of river in the neighbourhood of Kut, off which they anchored for the night 30th September/1st October. General Townshend had decided to conduct the pursuit by river in person, and with his headquarters accompanied the river column on board the *Mejidieh*.

The cavalry, who to some extent were tied to the steamers for lack of land transport, overtook the enemy on the 1st October forty miles above Kut; but, finding that the Turkish force was making an orderly retreat, covered by a strong rearguard of all arms, they halted until the river column caught them up. This was not till the 3rd October. On that day General Townshend received news from his aeroplanes that the Turks had halted and were installed in the already entrenched position at Ctesiphon, where Major Reilly, of the Air Force, reported six miles of trenches on the left bank.

On the 5th October the river column reached Aziziya, 61 miles by land and 102 miles by river above Kut. It now seemed to General Townshend to be useless to continue the pursuit, so he decided to halt and land his force, while he communicated with General Nixon, who was at Kut, in regard to the future policy to be adopted.

The operations had been a complete success. The Turks had lost some 4,000 men in casualties, of whom 1,153 were prisoners in the hands of the 6th Division. The British had also captured fourteen of the Turkish guns, many rifles and a large quantity of stores and ammunition. That the Turks did not lose more heavily was due to the skill and rapidity with

---

* Some of the wounded were butchered by Arabs, of whom three were caught red-handed and publicly hanged.

which they extricated their forces south of the Suwada marsh on the night of the 28th/29th, and to the low state of the Tigris, which so hampered the pursuit.

The British casualties, from the 26th to 28th September, totalled 1,233, of whom only 94 were killed. The loopholes in the Turkish trenches seemed designed with a view to preventing their men firing too high, and this fact, when considered with the remarkable number of men who were wounded in their lower extremities, may have accounted for the low percentage of fatal casualties among the British. Five-sixths of the total casualties had been sustained by the seven and a half infantry battalions of General Delamain's column, and the largest proportion of these fell to the lot of the 117th Mahrattas. The half battalion of this regiment engaged on the 28th September went into action 225 strong and suffered 114 casualties.

In his report General Nixon expressed his appreciation of the ability and generalship displayed by General Townshend throughout the operations, and he considered that his scheme for turning the Turkish left was the manœuvre whereby the position could best be captured without incurring very heavy losses. He concluded: "The troops under the command of Major-General Townshend displayed the highest soldierly qualities and worthily upheld the reputation they have earned during this arduous campaign. The conduct of the infantry in the attack was particularly noteworthy. They were set a task involving prolonged exertion and endurance, and performed it with an alacrity and resolution which must have been most disconcerting to the enemy. The dash with which the Indian troops attacked a well-entrenched and stubborn foe I attribute largely to the confidence with which they have been inspired by the British battalions of the force."

Before concluding this chapter, it is desirable to refer briefly to certain developments in the organisation of General Nixon's force between June and October 1915.

Owing mainly to the critical situation on their North-West Frontier, the Government of India had felt themselves unable to comply with General Nixon's request or Mr. Chamberlain's suggestions to reinforce Mesopotamia with one or two British Territorial battalions from India. To supplement the greatly depleted numbers of General Nixon's five British battalions they had, however, sent about a thousand men from the Territorial units in India.

In July General Nixon asked for fifty-six additional machine-guns. Neither India nor the War Office could spare any, but,

AEROPLANES AND RIVER CRAFT

at the end of August, India sent seventeen old pattern Nordenfeldt machine-guns, which they hoped might be useful in ships or defensive posts.

It has already been explained that it was only due to the patriotic and prompt response of Australia and New Zealand that it had been possible to send any aeroplanes to Mesopotamia. At that time the War Office could give very little assistance, as the whole output available was insufficient to meet more important demands elsewhere; but in the middle of August they agreed to arrange in the near future for a complete air squadron of three flights for Mesopotamia. The first instalment, consisting of four Martinsyde* machines to make the second flight in the country, reached Basra on the 28th August. But, what with losses and breakdowns, there were only available for the battle of Kut three aeroplanes and two seaplanes.

Owing to the operations having so far been mainly carried out in inundated areas, no adequate opportunity had been given to test the suitability to the country of mechanical transport; and when the battle of Kut took place, this was still limited to two armoured cars, two lorries and one motor ambulance.

As already mentioned, General Nixon had been instructed to report to India on the adequacy and suitability of the river transport at his disposal. Before his arrival in Mesopotamia General Barrett had made certain demands for steamers and tugs, and these had arrived at Basra in May. During that month, as mentioned in a previous chapter, General Nixon had asked for six light-draught tugs and some motor launches, and these had been ordered from England. During June the number of river steamers and tugs at General Nixon's disposal was increased by six,† i.e., the Lynch steamer *Julnar* (which had completed its repairs), a tug transferred by the Navy, and four steamers and tugs captured during the Amara operations.

At this period the river craft in Mesopotamia were only just sufficient to keep the two divisions in the country supplied with their ordinary requirements and to provide for minor troop movements. Any troop movements other than the ordinary relief of units, and any unforeseen contingencies, such as an unexpected number of casualties, breakdown of vesssels, etc., at once put a strain on the river craft which they were unequal to; and, in this connection, it must be remembered that,

---

* These proved unsuitable for the climate and caused several accidents. They could not carry an observer, and required very skilled pilots to fly them.

† This brought his total up to twenty-seven, see p. 268.

owing to the floods, troops in Southern Mesopotamia were unable to march from May to August except in a very few areas for short distances.

During June, owing mainly to the Nasiriya operations, the hampering effect on the military operations of the lack of river craft made such an impression on Major-General Kemball (General Nixon's senior general staff officer), that he asked General Nixon's permission to intervene to take up himself the question of this shortage as a question of primary importance affecting the whole policy of the campaign. After personal investigation he assembled a conference in Mesopotamia of the senior administrative staff and corps officers on the 30th June, and as a result he submitted some days later to General Nixon a comprehensive memorandum on the subject.

General Nixon was thus able for the first time to give the Government of India a broad and clear view of the situation. On the 8th July, in a telegraphic report on the operations up the Euphrates, he stated that these operations had been hampered throughout by the type of river vessel at his disposal and that he was sending by post a letter explaining the need for the urgent supply of nine light-draught steamers. This letter, dated 10th July, forwarding General Kemball's memorandum, was received in India on the 21st, and was followed by a supplementary letter written on the 17th and received in India on the 27th July.

In his communication of the 10th General Nixon, referring to the attached memorandum and his previous reports, said that he trusted that it would be realised how much operations were dependent on an efficient and adequate river flotilla. He explained how he had from the first recognised that he must make the most of existing resources, owing to the difficulty of getting suitable craft from India or Burma—even if they existed there—across the sea in the monsoon. But he emphasised what a great source of anxiety to him the question had proved, and he pointed out how the course of events must inevitably tend to a steady diminution of his available craft. He urged most strongly that the six paddle-steamers and three stern-wheelers asked for in his telegram of the 8th should be provided.

General Kemball in his memorandum said that, as there was every sign that the war would be a protracted one, the time had come to take stock of our resources and to meet the demands of the future. He showed, from a review of the past operations in Mesopotamia, how urgent was the supply of nine river steamers, and he pointed out that the seven " P " steamers (sent to comply with General Barrett's demand) would during the period of low water be confined to certain reaches of the river, whereas, on the other hand, the length of our communications tended to increase. The " P " steamers were, in fact, not well suited to the Tigris at any time, and although the six tugs asked for in May would be useful for towing barges, they would never, he said, be as convenient for troop movements as the river steamers.

A detailed specification for the nine steamers asked for and a statement showing the available river craft in Mesopotamia were attached.

The supplementary letter of the 17th July asked for more craft, bringing General Nixon's total demand to six paddle steamers, three stern-wheelers, eight tugs (including six* asked for in May), forty-three barges and six launches.

The construction of the launches was at once put in hand in India, but the Viceroy telegraphed to the India Office on the 3rd August asking them to arrange in England for the construction of the remainder, saying that the specifications would follow by letter. This letter, which forwarded the whole of General Nixon's communications on the subject, and which recommended strongly the acceptance of his proposal, was despatched from India on the 5th August. On the 26th August the Viceroy again telegraphed to the India Office giving General Nixon's order of priority for the construction of these craft, but adding that, in view of the urgency of the case, he considered that the vessels should be constructed simultaneously, and that it was imperative that they should be supplied earlier than in from six to twelve months' time.

On the 25th September General Nixon telegraphed that everything possible should be done to expedite the delivery of these river craft, and he showed how the concentration of General Townshend's force for the advance on Kut had been delayed by the shortage of river transport. This telegram was at once repeated to the India Office, who replied on the 30th, saying that the vessels asked for by General Nixon would be supplied as early as possible. This reply was passed on to General Nixon.

The evidence given before the Mesopotamia Commission shows that there was some delay in England, owing to various reasons, and that orders were placed for the construction of

---

* The India Office had been asked by telegram on the 6th July to arrange for these in England.

the required vessels early in November. On the 3rd November a telegram from the India Office informed the Viceroy of the dates by which the various craft might be expected in Mesopotamia, i.e., from March to June 1916. Here we will leave the matter for the present.

The Admiralty sent out from England during July and August the materials for twelve shallow-draught gunboats for Mesopotamia, to be put together at the Anglo-Persian Oil Company's works at Abadan. On the 30th August the local Admiralty representative informed General Nixon that he hoped to have the first gunboat ready by the middle of November.

In October 1915 the sloop *Alert* arrived and berthed at Abadan, being fitted to provide a naval depôt, necessitated by the coming increase in the naval flotilla.

Improvements in the port facilities of Basra were also inaugurated at this period.

In March General Nixon had also been requested in his instructions to report as to the employment of a light railway. The incidence of the floods, however, prevented any adequate survey for this for several months. On the 14th August General Nixon recommended in a lengthy memorandum the construction of a railway from Basra to Nasiriya, not only on military, but also on political and commercial grounds.* He inserted the two last recommendations on the special advice of his political and civil advisers. In India the proposal was strongly supported by the General Staff on military grounds, but, in the usual course of official procedure, it had to be referred to other departments of the Government of India to be reviewed on its political and commercial aspects. On neither of these grounds did it find favour, and when it reached the Financial Member of the Viceroy's Executive Council he minuted: " .... If .... His Excellency the Commander-in-Chief and Army Member can definitely assure me that his project is absolutely necessary for the safeguarding of our military position ... I cannot, of course, resist a reference home on this basis." The reasons why the Commander-in-Chief felt unable to give the required assurance and the consequent rejection of the proposal will be dealt with in the next volume.

In order to counteract to some extent the evil effect of the Mesopotamian climate on the troops there, arrangements were made in July to send at a time eight hundred British and

---

* At that time a railway up the Tigris was not considered practicable.

HOSPITAL SHIPS

three hundred Indian soldiers to India for short periods of rest and recuperation, and to send the naval sloops in turn to Ceylon, where there was a naval hutted camp in the hills.

Until July only one regular hospital ship, the *Madras*, had been provided to evacuate sick and wounded from Mesopotamia and East Africa to Bombay; but as this proved insufficient a second ship was provided in July, and, of the two, one was allotted permanently for Mesopotamia.

In March a river hospital steamer, the *Bengali*, was prepared in India for Mesopotamia; but unfortunately she sank on the ocean voyage there. In June General Nixon, on being asked if he considered that fitted ambulance motor boats would be suitable to replace the *Bengali*, replied that he did not consider they would. He said that native boats could be fitted locally for the purpose, but that he would like four tugs with a draught of not more than three feet six inches and with a speed of ten knots in slack water, each to tow two of these native boats. As, however, no such tugs could be found in India, no immediate supply was possible.

The distribution of the force in Mesopotamia at the beginning of October is given in Appendix VII.

APPENDIX I.

Extracts from the diary of Dr. Zugmayer (one of the German emissaries) which was captured in Persia.

14/9/14.—" Telegraphic summons to appear at the Foreign Office, Berlin.

16/9/14 to 19/9/14.—Consultations at the Foreign Office. Zimmerman, Langvorth, Wesendank, Oppenheim, Heger, Neuhofer, Mueller, 3 Indians, Tafel, Niedermayer.

29/9/14.—Arrive at Constantinople.

30/9/14.—During the day made the acquaintance of my future colleagues. Dr. Consten, Fischer, Bischoffshausen, also Major von Bessert and others . . . . we approach the Great Perso-Afghan plan. Schuneman (Urmia 1904) is still expected. Others have already left and wait for us at Aleppo. Several members are already at Damascus. Special plans with Niedermayer. Enver Pasha confident of the Amir of Afghanistan. Idea of parallel columns, etc. . . .

8/10/14.—If all one hears here from Turkish sources about Persia and Afghanistan is only half true, our mission will not be needed any more. In any case, we're two months too late . . . . Our Ambassador here is an incapable ass and Enver can do with him what he likes. The only strong German is Liman. Turkey is to receive a large loan from Germany. One reckons therefore at the moment on an immediate declaration of war. Persia is to make an alliance with Turkey in order that the Turks may work there undisturbed against British and Russians.

9/10/14.—Inspect at Begsians a dagger and two fancy daggers which we ought to take to the Amir.

26/10/14.—Arrive Aleppo . . . . where the whole expedition is assembled."

(The next entries in the diary show much disagreement and discussion as to the relations between the German and Turkish members of the expedition.)

5/11/14.—" Order Turkish uniform. Military official with rank of Major. Wassmuss returns after a quarrel with the Turkish leader, he too is now convinced that we must not deliver ourselves into the hands of the Turks . . . . but he still insists on the South Persia route.

8/12/14.—12 men of the Hapag steamer *Ekbatana* arrive, which ship with four others was sunk in the Shatt al Arab to bar the passage to Basra to the British.

18/12/14.—Wassmuss intends to separate himself from the expedition for some time, work alone in South Persia . . . . He and Niedermayer want to leave soon for Baghdad, the rest of us first to Mosul, then to await further orders.

21/12/14.—Wassmuss and Niedermayer leave. One of the three Indians having been imprisoned has to be released.

22/12/14.—Cannot leave before Xmas. Our new Chief Turk, Khalil Bey is reported to be in Tarsus. British cruiser *Doris* partially destroys railway, Tarsus-Alexandretta.

28/12/14.—Khalil arrives. We receive order to go direct to Baghdad.

8/1/15.—Arrive Jerablus. Wagner is here. Winchelman, Dietrich and Spiegelmann arrive in the afternoon with the boats from Birejik.

APPENDIX I

9/1/15.—Depart in the afternoon, 10 boats, i.e., double boats, four of which for passengers. In our boat, in one half, 3 Turkish officers and the Pathan; in the other half, Von Versen, Berghausen and myself. Stop at sunset.

29/1/15.—Arrive Falluja. Wassmuss has already left on his expedition to the south.

31/1/15.—The Turks have retaken Basra [sic.]

5/2/15 to 7/2/15.—Arrive Baghdad. We find a surprising situation. Sulaiman Askari forbids for the present any activity of German expeditions in Iraq vicinity and Persia. Griesinger, W. Paschen and Wagner . . . . have been detained and disarmed at Qizil Robat . . . . arms and ammunition have been taken from us . . . . The Turks want to divide us, as we have too much sympathy for Persia . . . . Official communications with Afghanistan do not yet exist . . . . In a letter to Niedermayer, Sulaiman Askari orders that various appointments in the army be given to the members of the expedition . . . . The Turks on their part have officially given up entirely the expedition to Afghanistan. Thereupon the Embassy already before our arrival demanded rendering of accounts for the £ stg. 50,000 which have been paid. The Embassy orders the Consul to take energetic measures with Askari. The latter . . . . pretends to believe that the action and pressure of the Germans might upset the Arabs of South Persia because the British spread the report that the Germans intend to occupy Iraq . . . . The Turks prepare a Perso-Afghan expedition under the command of Rauf, which ought to be unknown to us."

10/2/15 to 26/2/15.—The entries in the diary show how the expedition is divided up. A small group to go via Mosul and Sauj Bulaq to Hamadan. Others to take the Maxims of the expedition to Basra. Officers to superintend the reserve organisations in Baghdad and Dr. Zugmayer and Griesinger to go to Isfahan, travelling as Acting Consul and Secretary respectively for Isfahan. Germans erect wireless station at Baghdad.

27/2/15.—" Start and reach Baquba.

3/3/15.—Arrive Qasr-i-Shirin.

5/3/15.—Do a great deal of political agitation.

* * * * * * * * *

13/3/15.—Kermanshah. One of the " mujahids " from Karbala has arrived. He has received £ stg. 2,000 from the German Government. He has to preach here; specially the disbanding of the Persian Cossacks ought to be effected by this means . . . . the gendarmerie is already entirely with us and is in German pay . . . . the Arabs begin an insurrection against the British."

14/3/15.—(The diary also explains how they rifle the British Consul's waste paper basket regularly).

28/3/15.—" Thirty sowars leave for the frontier to meet Prince Reuss, Count Bogothili and Niedermayer and company who are leaving Baghdad to-day."

(The diary then goes on to describe the journey to Isfahan (reached on 24/4/15), and his anti-British activities in Persia.)

1/6/15 to 3/6/15.—" Niedermayer in a long letter explains to me his, i.e., the Legation's policy. In Tehran they do not reckon any more on a Persian declaration of war but Niedermayer will begin his work in Afghanistan even if Persia remains neutral.

16/6/15.—Arrive Yezd.

4/7/15.—Arrive Kerman."

(The rest of the diary gives an account of the anti-British and anti-Russian propaganda and action taken by this expedition and other groups in Persia, and is no longer relevant to this history.)

APPENDIX II.

Embarkation Strength of General Delamain's Force.

Units.	British.		Indian.		Followers.	Animals.
	Officers.	Other Ranks.	Officers.	Other ranks.		
Brigade Headquarters ..	5	6	—	—	7	6
1st Indian Mountain Artillery Brigade.	12	—	11	606	55	359
22nd Company, Sappers and Miners.	4	2	4	209	13	62
2nd Dorsetshire Regiment	22	875	—	—	—	24
20th Punjabis ..	13	—	19	808	45	26
104th Rifles	13	—	19	809	43	26
117th Mahrattas ..	12	—	18	808	45	24
Section, 34th Divisional Signal Company.	1	13	—	23	4	4
125th Field Ambulance..	5	6	6	9	171	10
12th Mule Corps.. ..	—	—	—	48	—	81
13th Mule Corps.. ..	—	3	2	301	—	668
Supply Column .. .. (S. & T.C.)	1	4	3	—	50	—
Field Post Office ..	3	6	—	10	24	—
Ordnance Field Park ..	—	3	—	9	3	—
Total ..	91	918	82	3,640	460	1,290

APPENDIX II 347

Embarkation Strength of the Reinforcements under General Barrett.

Units.	B.O.	B.O.R.	I.O.	I.O.R.	Followers.	Horses.	Mules.	Camels.	Vehicles.
Divisional Headquarters (including headquarters Divisional Artillery and C.R.E. Staff).	29	38	1	33	51	43	—	—	
33rd Cavalry	4	—	6	216	30	236	—	8	18 ammn. carts, 1 G.S. wagon.
10th Brigade R.F.A.	17	525	—	36	107	547	—	—	
Divisional Ammunition Column	4	54	—	125	43	168	—	—	
No. 17 Company, 3rd Sappers and Miners.	4	2	4	193	29	5	18	—	
No. 3 Troop of No. 41 Wireless Telegraph Squadron.	1	24	—	8	2	32	—	—	
34th Divisional Signal Company	3	40	2	80	8	17	26	—	
18th Infantry Brigade Headquarters.	3	4	—	—	3	6	—	—	
2nd Norfolk Regiment	23	912	—	—	25	12	12	—	
110th Mahratta Light Infantry	12	—	19	802	39	12	12	—	
120th Rajputana Infantry	13	—	19	807	45	14	12	—	
7th Rajputs	12	—	18	808	40	14	12	—	
48th Pioneers	14	—	19	815	92	15	42	—	
Medical Units	23	31	24	39	450	11	42	—	
Supply and Transport Corps	11	38	—	77	269	14	8	—	5 carts.
10th Mule Corps	1	1	5	284	25	14	672	—	
12th Mule Corps	1	2	4	180	14	7	360	—	
Ordnance Field Park	—	2	—	—	—	—	—	—	
Field Veterinary Section	1	4	—	2	110	2	—	—	
Jaipur Imperial Service Transport Corps.	1	—	11	431	63	3	827	—	360 carts.
Military Accounts Department	5	14	13	51	51	—	—	—	
52nd Silladar Camel Corps	1	—	1	10	115	4	—	325	
Kalat Camel Corps }	1	—	12	16	255	3	—	839	
Las Bela Camel Corps									
Totals	184	1,691	158	5,013	1,866	1,179	2,049	1,172	383 carts and 1 G.S. wagon.

348 HISTORY OF THE WAR: MESOPOTAMIA

APPENDIX III.

Composition of Force " D " on 1st December 1914.

MILITARY.

Headquarters.
    General Officer Commanding—Lieutenant-General Sir A. A. Barrett, K.C.B., K.C.V.O., Indian Army.
    General Staff Branch :—
        General Staff Officer 1st Grade (Colonel R. N. Gamble, D.S.O., British Service).
        General Staff Officer, 2nd Grade.
        General Staff Officer, 3rd Grade.
        Two Special Service Officers (attached).
    Adjutant General's and Quarter-Master General's Branches :—
        Deputy Assistant Adjutant General.
        Assistant Quarter-Master General.
        Deputy Assistant Adjutant and Quarter-Master General.
    Attached :—
        Divisional Artillery Commander.
        Divisional Engineer Commander.
        Assistant Director of Medical Services.
        Deputy Assistant Director of Medical Services.
        Assistant Director of Supplies.
        Assistant Director of Transport.
        Deputy Assistant Director of Ordnance Services.
        Assistant Director of Veterinary Services.
        Deputy Judge Advocate General.
        Controller of Military Accounts and his assistants.
        Interpreter.
        Chaplain (C. of E.).

Divisional Troops.
    Cavalry :—
        33rd Queen Victoria's Own Light Cavalry.
    Artillery :—
        Headquarters Divisional Artillery—Divisional Artillery Commander, Brigadier-General C. T. Robinson.
        10th Brigade, Royal Field Artillery.
            76th Battery, R.F.A.
            82nd Battery, R.F.A.
            63rd Battery, R.F.A.
            6th Ammunition Column, R.F.A.
        1st Indian Mountain Artillery Brigade.
            No. 23 Indian Mountain Battery.
            No. 30 Indian Mountain Battery.
    Royal Engineers :—
        Headquarters, Divisional Engineers.
        No. 17 Company, 3rd Sappers and Miners.
        No. 22 Company, 3rd Sappers and Miners.
        No. 34 Divisional Signal Company.
        No. 3 Troop, Wireless Signal Squadron (afterwards termed No. 41 Wireless Signal Company).
    Pioneers :—
        48th Pioneers.

APPENDIX III

Infantry.
    16th Indian Infantry Brigade—Brigadier-General W. S. Delamain, C.B., D.S.O., Indian Army.
        2nd Battalion Dorsetshire Regiment.
        20th Duke of Cambridge's Own Infantry (Brownlow's Punjabis).
        104th Wellesley's Rifles.
        117th Mahrattas.
    17th Indian Infantry Brigade—Brigadier-General W. H. Dobbie, C.B., Indian Army.
        1st Battalion Oxfordshire and Buckinghamshire Light Infantry.
        119th Infantry (The Mooltan Regiment).
        103rd Mahratta Light Infantry.
        22nd Punjabis.
    18th Indian Infantry Brigade—Major-General C. I. Fry, Indian Army.
        2nd Battalion Norfolk Regiment.
        110th Mahratta Light Infantry.
        120th Rajputana Infantry.
        7th Duke of Connaught's Own Rajputs.

Medical Services.
    Assistant Director of Medical Services—Colonel P. Hehir, M.D., Indian Medical Service.
        No. 16 British Field Ambulance ⎫
        No. 17 British Field Ambulance ⎪
        No. 125 Indian Field Ambulance ⎬ Converted later into Combined Field Ambulances, numbered 1 to 4.
        No. 126 Indian Field Ambulance ⎪
        No. 127 Indian Field Ambulance ⎭
        No. 19 Combined Clearing Hospital.
        No. 57 Indian Stationary Hospital.
        No. 3 (*a*) British General Hospital. (2½ sections).
        No. 9 Indian General Hospital. (6 sections).
        No. 2 X-Ray Section.
        Advanced Depôt Medical Stores.

NAVAL.

    Senior Naval Officer—Captain A. Hayes-Sadler, R.N.

Armed Vessels.
    H.M.S. *Espiègle* (Sloop)—six 4-inch Q.F. and two 3-pounder guns and two maxims.
    H.M.S. *Odin* (Sloop)—four 4-inch Q.F. and two 3-pounder guns and two maxims.
    H.M.S. *Lawrence* (Paddle Steamer, Royal Indian Marine)—four 4-inch Q.F. and four 6-pounder guns.
    Comet (Steam Yacht)—one 3-pounder gun and three old Nordenfeldts.
    Lewis Pelly (Small Steam Yacht)—two 3-pounder Hotchkiss guns and one maxim.
    Miner (Small River Steamer)—one 12-pounder (8 cwt.) gun, one 3-pounder and one maxim.
    Shaitan (Steam Tug)—one 12-pounder (8 cwt.) gun and one maxim.
    Sirdar-i-Naphte (Steam Tug)—one 12-pounder (8 cwt.) gun and one maxim.
    Mashona (Steam Tug)—one 3-pounder gun.

    H.M.S. *Ocean* (pre-Dreadnought Battleship)—off bar of Shatt al Arab.

    H.M.S. *Dalhousie* (Royal Indian Marine)—four 6-pounder guns—off Bushire.

Unarmed Vessels.
    Mejidieh, Blosse Lynch and *Malamir* of the Euphrates and Tigris Steam Navigation Co. (Lynch Bros.).
    Sumana, Shihab and *Shurur* of the Société de Transports Fluviaux.
    The *Salimi* and six small launches taken up locally.

APPENDIX IV.

Reorganisation of Force " D " as decided upon by the Government of India on 1st April 1915.

G.O.C. Force.—General Sir J. E. Nixon, K.C.B.

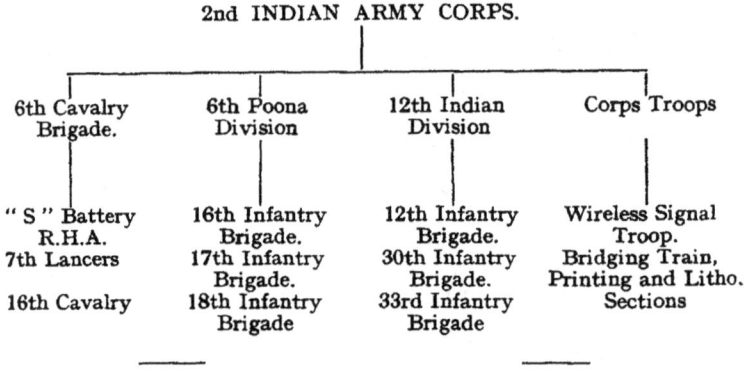

6th Divisional Troops

33rd Cavalry (less 2 squadrons)
10th Brigade R.F.A. (18 guns).
Divisional Ammunition Column.
1st Indian Mountain Artillery Brigade (12 guns).
17th Field Coy. ⎫ Sappers
22nd Field Coy. ⎬ and
                ⎭ Miners.
34 Divisional Signal Coy.
48th Pioneers.

12th Divisional Troops

2 squadrons 33rd Cavalry.
86th Heavy Battery R.G.A. (4 guns).
104th Heavy Battery R.G.A. (4 guns).
1/5th Hants Howitzer Battery R.F.A. (4 howitzers).
12th Field Coy. ⎫ Sappers
Sirmur Imperial ⎬ and
Service Coy.   ⎭ Miners.
12 Divisional Signal Coy.

The composition of Infantry brigades was as follows :—

16th.—2nd Dorsetshire Regiment, 20th Punjabis, 104th Rifles, 117th Mahrattas.

17th.—1st Oxfordshire and Buckinghamshire Light Infantry, 22nd Punjabis, 103rd Mahrattas, 119th Infantry.

18th.—2nd Norfolk Regiment, 7th Rajputs, 110th Mahrattas, 120th Rajputana Infantry.

12th.—2nd Queen's Own Royal West Kent Regiment, 4th Rajputs, 44th Merwara Infantry, 90th Punjabis.

30th.—24th Punjabis, 76th Punjabis, 2/7th Gurkhas.

33rd.—1/4 Hampshire Regiment, 11th Rajputs, 66th Punjabis, 67th Punjabis.

APPENDIX IV

Commanders and principal Staff Officers.

Army Corps Staff.

Senior General Staff Officer.— Major-General G. V. Kemball.
General Staff Officer (1st Grade).—Major G. R. Cassells, 35th Sikhs.
General Staff Officer (1st Grade).—Major W. H. Beach, R.E.
D.A. and Q.M.G.— Brigadier-General W. G. Hamilton.
A.Q.M.G.— Colonel J. A. Douglas, C.M.G.
Deputy Director Army Signals.—Major L. H. Queripel, R.A.
C.R.A.— Brigadier-General C. T. Robinson, R.A.
C.R.E.— Colonel J. P. Brewin, R.E.
I.G. Communications.— Major-General K. S. Davison, C.B.

G.O.C. 6th Poona Division.—Lieutenant-General Sir A. A. Barrett, K.C.B., K.C.V.O.
G.S.O. (1) 6th Poona Division.—Colonel R. N. Gamble, D.S.O.
A.Q.M.G. 6th Poona Division.—Colonel L. W. Shakespear.

G.O.C. 12th Indian Division.—Major-General G. F. Gorringe, C.B., C.M.G., D.S.O.
G.S.O. (1) 12th Indian Division.—Major H. F. J. Browne, 5th Gurkhas.
A.Q.M.G. 12th Indian Division.—Colonel C. E. Hendley.

G.O.C. 6th Cavalry Brigade.—Brigadier-General H. Kennedy.
G.O.C. 16th Infantry Brigade.—Brigadier-General W. S. Delamain, C.B., D.S.O.
G.O.C. 17th Infantry Brigade.—Brigadier-General W. H. Dobbie, C.B.
G.O.C. 18th Infantry Brigade.—Major-General C. I. Fry.
G.O.C. 12th Infantry Brigade.—Brigadier-General K. E. Lean, C.B.
G.O.C. 30th Infantry Brigade.—Major-General C. J. Melliss, V.C., C.B.
G.O.C. 33rd Infantry Brigade.—Brigadier-General R. Wapshare.

APPENDIX V.

British Forces in Arabistan on 1st May 1915, under the command of Major-General G. F. Gorringe.

6th Cavalry Brigade (Brigadier-General H. Kennedy) :—
   "S" Battery, R.H.A.
   7th Lancers.
   33rd Light Cavalry.
   No. 131 Cavalry Field Ambulance.
   Supply Column.

30th Infantry Brigade (Major-General C. J. Melliss) :—
   1/4th Hampshire Regiment.
   24th Punjabis.
   76th Punjabis.
   2/7th Gurkha Rifles.

12th Infantry Brigade (Brigadier-General K. E. Lean) :—
   2nd Queen's Own Royal West Kent Regiment.
   4th Rajputs.
   44th Merwara Infantry.
   90th Punjabis.
   67th Punjabis.

Divisional Troops :—
　　10th Brigade R.F.A. (less one gun 63rd Battery).
　　No. 6 Ammunition Column.
　　Maxim Gun Battery.
　　12th Company Sappers and Miners.
　　11th Rajputs.
　　66th Punjabis.
　　1 Company 48th Pioneers.
　　2 Sections No. 31 Signal Company.
　　2 Sections No. 34 Signal Company.
　　Wireless Signal Troop Company.
　　No. 3 Combined Field Ambulance.
　　No. 106 Combined Field Ambulance.
　　2 Sections No. 19 Combined Clearing Hospital.
　　Divisional Supply Column.

Approximate Total—12,500 of all ranks, including followers.

APPENDIX VI.

Summary of a pamphlet " The Turco-British Campaign in Mesopotamia and our mistakes," by Staff Bimbashi Muhammad Amin ; published by the Turkish General Staff.

(Translated for the Historical Section, Committee of Imperial Defence, by Brigadier-General U. W. Evans, C.B., C.M.G.)

　　Turkish Army Headquarters had allotted the 12th and 13th Army Corps of the 4th Army Inspectorate (i.e., the regular garrison of Mesopotamia) to the 3rd Erzerum and 4th Syrian Armies. They relied on local gendarmerie and locally raised volunteers and levies to maintain internal order in Mesopotamia, and to guard against foreign aggression. They also relied on raising the country and adjacent—and even distant—Musulman regions against an infidel invader. They did not realise that the tribes and people in Mesopotamia were too diverse in habits, race and religion, as well as disinclined through ignorance and maladministration, to give the necessary assistance. It was a long time before Turkish Army Headquarters gave up their hopes of extensive support from local levies and realised that the tribesmen of Lower Mesopotamia merely looked upon the war as a means of personal profit and were always ready to back the winning side.
　　When war broke out, the bulk of the 12th and 13th Army Corps had been withdrawn from Mesopotamia. The 12th Army Corps (comprising 35th and 36th Divisions) was sent to Syria and the 37th Division of the 13th Army Corps was despatched to Erzerum. Even the 38th Division was about to proceed to Erzerum when, as the writer says, the Turkish military headquarters at Constantinople suddenly realised that Mesopotamia might be invaded, and at the urgent instance of the 4th Army Inspectorate the order was countermanded.
　　Until the British invasion had almost begun, the Turkish Government thought such action to be a most unlikely contingency. How could England, with its little army, add aggressive action against the Turks to her contest with the German millions ?

APPENDIX VI

Thus, when the British descent upon Mesopotamia took place, the total Turkish forces in Mesopotamia comprised :—

Infantry.—38th Division .. 6 battalions.
    26th Regiment .. 1 battalion.
    Gendarmerie .. 9 battalions and 1 company.
    Frontier troops .. 6 battalions and 8 companies.

          22 battalions and 9 companies.

Artillery.—10 battalions.

Cavalry.—1 squadron.

This amounted in round numbers to 17,000 rifles, 380 sabres, 44 field guns and 3 machine guns.

The troops are described as being below establishment, ill-trained, ill-disciplined and badly equipped, with no proper organisation for supply and maintenance. Desertions were many and at one time, in Baghdad, they amounted to 1,200 in one day.

Of the total numbers mentioned above, the Turks concentrated in the vicinity of Basra to meet the British only 4,700 rifles, 18 guns and 3 machine guns. The writer criticises this strongly, saying that the Russian and Persian menace from the east could have been practically ignored and that 13,000 rifles, 360 sabres, 36 guns and 3 machine guns should have been concentrated at Basra. If this concentration could not have been effected sufficiently rapidly to meet the British below Basra, it should have been made further north.

With regard to the use made of the Turkish troops in the Basra area to meet the British invasion in 1914, the writer comments upon the inferior leadership and the piecemeal destruction of the small forces that were available.

Some 4,700 rifles and 18 guns were available; yet the Turkish strength which opposed the British landing at Fao was only 110 rifles and 4 guns. A great fault was made in not attributing sufficient importance to Fao—the gateway of Mesopotamia. Another line of attack—via Kuwait by land—might have been taken by the British, but it was not likely that a sea power would take that route unless it was forced to do so.

At the fight at Saihan, the Turks only put into action 2,000* rifles and 8 guns; and again at the next fight at Sahil the Turkish strength only amounted to 1,200* rifles and 8 guns.

The writer refers to the unduly precipitate retreat from Basra, whereby a detachment of three battalions and 8 guns was left in the lurch at Baljaniya and had to beat a hurried retreat, finally reaching Nasiriya after suffering great hardships. Had the Turkish leader kept his head, he could have arranged an orderly withdrawal and concentrated at Qurna a force of quite respectable dimensions.

As it was, the troops available after the capture of Basra were unduly dispersed in the Qurna vicinity. On the 4th December, the detachment actually in Qurna watched the discomfiture of the detachment in Muzaira'a without attempting to cross the river and help, which they had plenty of means of doing. At the same time, there was about Sakrikiya, a few miles above Qurna up the Tigris, another detachment of two or three battalions with some guns. These troops made no move whatever to assist. The Turkish Commander-in-Chief, still further up the Tigris at Ezra's Tomb, was too far away and failed to arrange for co-ordinated action against the British troops.

The detachment in Muzaira'a on the 4th December was under 900 rifles strong. It was reduced that day to little over 200 in strength. This tiny force was left to face General Fry on the 7th December,† and was afforded

---

* These are presumably exclusive of Arabs.
Footnote by Historical Section, Committee of Imperial Defence :—
† This is almost certainly inaccurate. There were without doubt considerably more than 200 Turkish troops facing General Fry at Muzaira'a on the 7th December.

no assistance by the troops holding Qurna on the opposite bank of the Tigris beyond a little artillery support. As for the troops in Qurna, the local commander there never discovered till too late that the enemy were crossing the Tigris, and had no one in observation to guard against his retreat being cut off. The writer thinks that the 1,000 men in Qurna might have broken through the 1,400 enemy on the right bank of the Tigris on the evening of the 8th December. The Turkish Commander-in-Chief at Ezra's Tomb and the troops at Sakrikiya, far from making any counter-attack, fled and took no advantage of General Fry's dangerous position with part of his force north of Qurna, separated by the Tigris from the rest at Muzaira'a.

The writer considers that a counter-attack from Sakrikiya would at least have enabled the Qurna garrison to be relieved and would have allowed the whole force to be withdrawn up the Tigris until reinforcements should enable the Turks to place a superior force against the enemy.

As it was, the actual strength employed against General Fry in Muzaira'a and Qurna on the 7th and 8th December comprised about 1,200* effectives, whilst the strength of the Turkish force withdrawing from Sakrikiya on the 10th December up the Tigris amounted to over 2,000 men, with 6 guns.

The Turkish War Office in December 1914 told their Mesopotamian General Headquarters " to avoid dispersion and, until the arrival of sufficient reserves warranted a counter-move, the enemy was to be afforded no opportunity of gaining a decisive result." But Mesopotamian Headquarters did not listen.

After the capture of Qurna, the same errors of dispersion were made—one detachment on the Euphrates, one on the Tigris and one in Arabistan. The different commanders were incapable and there was no co-operation. Each fraction was left to itself and felt too weak to do its allotted task. Cut off from one another by great swamps, what could they do against the English, who, using the Euphrates, Tigris and Karun rivers, could bring a superior force to any one of the three sectors?

The Turkish Commander-in-Chief was now Sulaiman Askari and for him the writer has scarcely a good word to say. At the outbreak of war, Sulaiman Askari had been in Constantinople and it was to him mainly that the Turkish Army Headquarters turned for advice regarding Mesopotamia. When he was made Commander-in-Chief in Mesopotamia, he was imbued with the idea of hurling the English into the Persian Gulf and of invading India. He actually refused the offer of reinforcement from Aleppo by a regular division and suggested that it should be sent to Kermanshah! The writer is of the opinion that, mainly due to the influence of Sulaiman Askari, the Turkish War Office in the early stages of the war was full of grandiose ideas of sweeping the East with hordes of Arab and Tartar horsemen and armies from Austria, etc. There was no question of capability of defence. Iraq could certainly look after herself.

The writer describes how the Turkish right wing, under the personal command of Sulaiman Askari, after long preparations, was defeated at Shaiba. The idea was for the three Turkish wings to attack simultaneously—the right wing to take Basra and all three to meet at Mohammerah.

The centre and left wings were too weak and badly commanded to produce any effect. As for the right wing, by great expenditure some thousands of Arabs had been induced to join, but these were a weakness rather than a help. The writer refers to the " accursed, mirage-ridden battle of Shaiba " as a " contest between knowledge and ignorance. On the one side ignorance and mediæval manœuvres, on the other the skill and experience of forty years' soldiering possessed by Fry, Melliss and Delamain. . . . Our troops were not equal in numbers or quality to their task."

Footnote by Historical Section, Committee of Imperial Defence :—
* The writer is almost certainly inaccurate in this figure, which seems to be much too low. On the 7th December, 1914, on the left bank of the Tigris about Muzaira'a the Turks lost, in addition to killed and wounded, about 130 prisoners and 3 field guns. The British estimate of Turkish numbers on the left bank was 2,000 (see Chapter VII., p. 148). The Qurna garrison, which surrendered on the 9th December, totalled 1,034 officers and men, and 4 guns.

APPENDIX VI 355

The writer says* that the Turkish forces under Sulaiman Askari at Shaiba totalled about 12,000 troops, 12 guns and 10,000 Arab auxiliaries. He overestimates the British force at 7,000 to 8,000 rifles, 21 guns and 2,000 cavalry.

Referring to the centre Turkish detachment on the Tigris, the writer says that " at first the position taken up near Sakrikiya was good, but when the Tigris floods converted the country into a sea dotted with islets it was most unsuitable for defence." Dotted about on islets in small groups without any means of communication or supply except Arab boats, the position of the troops was hopeless. About the 15th May, Nur-ud-Din, the new Commander-in-Chief in Mesopotamia, ordered the Tigris detachment to retire, but the local commander said that he had not the means to do so and remained !

In his description of General Townshend's attack on the 31st May, the writer acknowledges the decisive effect of the British gunfire. He gives the Turkish losses as 428 men and 3 guns. The strength of the Turkish centre is given as 7 battalions, 2 machine guns and one battery of artillery, besides some Arab auxiliaries. " The divisional commander should have withdrawn quickly and tried to save his three Kurd battalions. But he did nothing but watch the piecemeal destruction of his division through his glasses and send wires to Baghdad headquarters." In the retreat up the Tigris, the gunboat *Marmariss* and the Divisional Commander led the rout. Details of the *débacle* are given and how the erstwhile Arab allies stripped and murdered the Turks.

The writer refers to the " tragedy of Amara " ; how the Fire Brigade Regiment (850 strong), which had lost heavily at Shaiba, met the fleeing Turks and their commander south of Amara ; how the retreat to Amara was continued and the regiment ordered back there ; how the British opened fire on the regiment just as they finished a disorderly disembarkation ; how an immediate panic ensued both among the Turkish steamers and troops ; how the latter surrendered like a flock of sheep ; how the British " came boldly on, anchored at the wharf, sent one officer and eight or ten men ashore and captured Amara, although there were over 1,000 Turks there."

In referring to the Turkish left wing in Arabistan, the writer says that this detachment in February 1915 comprised two battalions (about 1,500 strong), two field guns, over 100 sabres and some 3,000 Arab auxiliaries. In March, it was increased by three battalions and two mountain guns. The object of the detachment was to attract enemy forces by descending the Karun river to Mohammerah and in this way assist the Shaiba enterprise. Ghazban, chief of the Bani Lam Arabs, was very keen on this enterprise—partly in hope of loot and partly to be avenged on his old enemy, the Shaikh of Mohammerah.

The Turkish commander, a brave old man of 70 years in age, was in a very difficult position. In front of him were the British in greatly superior strength, on his right impassable marshes, on his left tribesmen of doubtful attachment to the Turkish cause and to his rear the Bani Lam—a tribe whose only gods were gifts and success. On the 26th March, Sulaiman Askari ordered him to march on Mohammerah. On the 12th April, he started to advance against the British camp near Ahwaz, but after an hour's gunfire in the afternoon, finding the Arabs would not do anything, he broke off the fight.

After the Shaiba defeat, the Turkish left wing was ordered to withdraw to the Turkish frontier. The British pursuit was slow and the detachment got away, but so ill-disciplined and disorganised was it, that a vigorous pursuit would have destroyed it. On approaching Amara on the 4th June, a sudden Arab attack upon the advanced guard enlightened it as to the fate of that town. The movement of the detachment became a disorderly rout. Harassed by murderous Arabs, the remnants finally reached Kut al Amara in small groups.

---

* He is evidently doubtful, as he takes these figures from British sources.

APPENDIX VII.

Distribution of the Force in Mesopotamia at the beginning of October, 1915.

TIGRIS LINE.

At and above Kut al Amara.
  General Headquarters.
    6th Cavalry Brigade.*—7th Lancers, 3 squadrons; 16th Cavalry, 2 squadrons; 33rd Cavalry, 3 squadrons; "S" Battery, R.H.A. (6 guns).
    6th Division—Divisional Headquarters.
      16th Infantry Brigade.—2nd Dorsetshire, 20th Punjabis, 104th Rifles, 117th Mahrattas.
      17th Infantry Brigade.—1st Oxfordshire and Buckinghamshire Light Infantry, 22nd Punjabis, 103rd Mahrattas, 119th Infantry.
      18th Infantry Brigade.—2nd Norfolk, 7th Rajputs, 110th Mahrattas, 120th Infantry.
      10th Brigade R.F.A. (18 guns).—63rd Battery, 76th Battery, 82nd Battery.
      86th Heavy Battery R.G.A. (four 5-inch guns).
      One section, 104th Heavy Battery R.G.A. (two 4-inch guns).
      1/5th Hants Howitzer Battery (four howitzers).
      Maxim Battery (six machine guns).
      6th Divisional Ammunition Column.
      17th Company, Sappers and Miners.
      22nd Company, Sappers and Miners.
      48th Pioneers.
      34th Divisional Signal Company.
      One Flight, Royal Air Force.
      Mechanical Transport Section.
      One section, Army Corps Signal Company.
      One Wagon Wireless Station.
      Two Pack Wireless Stations.
      Bridging Train.
      Advanced Ordnance Depot.
      No. 106 Field Ambulance (four sections).
      No. 19 Clearing Hospital (two sections).

    30th Infantry Brigade.—Brigade Headquarters, 2/7th Gurkhas, 76th Punjabis. } For L. of C. duties.
    Detachment Volunteer Artillery Battery, with one 15-pounder gun.

Ali Gharbi.
  Half battalion 24th Punjabis (30th Brigade).
  Detachment Volunteer Artillery Battery (one gun).
  One Pack Wireless Station.

Amara.
  Headquarters, 12th Division.
  No. 12 Divisional Signal Company (less two brigade sections).
  One Pack Wireless Station.
  Headquarters, Heavy Brigade R.G.A.
  One section, 104th Heavy Battery, R.G.A. (two 4-inch guns).
  Headquarters, Volunteer Artillery Battery (four 15-pounder guns).
  1/4th Hampshire Regiment. } Of 30th Infantry Brigade.
  24th Punjabis (less half battalion).
  One section, No. 2 British General Hospital.
  Half section, No. 3A British General Hospital.

---
* Including some units *en route* from Basra to Kut, viz., 33rd Cavalry and "S" Battery, R.H.A.

APPENDIX VII

One section, No. 9 Indian General Hospital.
Bengal Stationary Hospital.
No. 9 Advanced Depot, Medical Stores.
No. 9 Field Veterinary Section.

Qala Salih.

One Indian Officer and 25 rifles, 24th Punjabis.

Qurna.

43rd Erinpura Regiment (less half battalion) [33rd Infantry Brigade].

EUPHRATES LINE.

Nasiriya.

12th Infantry Brigade (Brigadier-General Brooking).—2nd Royal West Kent Regiment, 67th Punjabis, 44th Infantry, 90th Punjabis.
One Squadron, 33rd Cavalry.
30th Mountain Battery (six guns).
Detachment Volunteer Artillery Battery (four guns).
One Brigade Section, No. 12 Divisional Signal Company.
One Pack Wireless Station.
12th Company, Sappers and Miners.
No. 3 Field Ambulance (five sections).

SHATT AL ARAB.

Basra.

Headquarters, Inspector-General of Communications.
23rd Mountain Battery (six guns).
Sirmur Sappers.
Headquarters, 33rd Infantry Brigade.—66th Punjabis, 4th Rajputs.
Brigade Section, No. 12 Divisional Signal Company.
Army Corps Signal Company (less one section).
Headquarters, Wireless Signal Squadron.
Aviation Depot.
Base Depots.
No. 4 Field Ambulance (three sections).
No. 3A British General Hospital (less half section).
No. 2 X-Ray Section.
No. 57 Indian Stationary Hospital.
No. 9 Indian General Hospital (less one section).
Sanitary Section.
No. 6 Field Veterinary Section.

Fao.

14 rifles, 4th Rajputs.

Abadan.

One Indian Officer and 25 rifles, 4th Rajputs.

ARABISTAN.

Ahwaz.

One squadron, 23rd Cavalry.
Half battalion, 43rd Erinpura Regiment.
No. 4 Field Ambulance (two sections).

Band-i-qir.

23rd Cavalry (less one squadron).

BUSHIRE.

One squadron, 16th Cavalry.
11th Rajputs.
96th Infantry.
Fifty rifles, 2/7th Gurkhas.

ABBREVIATIONS USED IN INDEX.

A.C.	Army Corps.
Bn.	Battalion.
C.G.S.I.	Chief of the General Staff, India.
C.I.G.S.	Chief of the Imperial General Staff.
C.-in-C.	Commander-in-Chief.
E.B.F.	Euphrates Blockade Force.
H.Q.	Headquarters.
I.A.	Indian Army.
I.E.F.	Indian Expeditionary Force.
I.O.	India Office.
M/T.	Mechanical Transport.
R.F.C.	Royal Flying Corps.
R.I.M.	Royal Indian Marine.
R.N.A.S.	Royal Naval Air Service.
S. & M.	Sappers and Miners.
S. of S.	Secretary of State.
S.N.O.	Senior Naval Officer.
T.F.	Territorial Force.
W.O.	War Office.
W/T.	Wireless Telegraphy.

Note.—For divisions, brigades, regiments, battalions, etc., *see under* " Artillery " ; " Cavalry " ; " Infantry."

INDEX.

A.

Abadan.
    Oil works at, 78, 80–1, 85 ; suggested diversion of Force " B " to, 81 ; *Lawrence* arrives at, 85 ; question of occupation of, 94–5 ; right of access to, 96 ; wireless station at, 103 *n* ; Brit. garrison posted at, 179 ; Brit. force at, (11 April 1915), 197, (beginning October), Appendix VII., 357 ; *Alert* arrives at, 342. See also " Anglo-Persian Oilfields " ; " Shatt al Arab."

Abdul Hamid II., (Sultan of Turkey).
    Administration under, (1876–1908), 17–8 ; relations of, with German Emperor, 37 ; deposition of, (1909), 37.

Abu Aran.
    Turkish position at, 243 ; capture of, 258 ; intense heat of, 267 *n*.

Aden.
    Turkish attack on, anticipated, 160 ; anxiety of Govt. of India, regarding, 177 ; troops for, to be found by India, 187 ; Turkish threat to, 240 ; situation in, (June 1915), 270 ; Brit. force at, 304.

Administration.
    Turkish neglect of river conservancy, 4–5 ; Turkish system of, 13 ; under Abdul Hamid II., (1876–1908), 17–8 ; Arab opposition to, 19 ; Young Turks policy, (1908–12), 21.

Admiralty.
    Asked to provide river gunboats, 158 *n*, 169, arranges to send twelve, 236 *n*, despatched (July–August 1915), 342 ; attach great importance to oil supply, 237, 303, 307.

Afghanistan.
    Russian activity against, (1885), 51, 54 ; Durand Frontier Agreement, (1893), 51 ; relations of, with India, 60–1, 79, 160 ; Brit. abstention from *espionage*, 61 ; relation of Mesopotamia to, 71 ; enemy emissaries in, 77, 89–90, 159, 192 ; German officers reported on their way to, 186, 240 *n*, 274 ; measures to prevent Germans reaching, 274 ; German Mission at Kabul, 310 ; situation in, (September 1915), 310.

————, Amir of.
    Consults Govt. of India *re* Russian menace, 52 ; relations of, with India, 60–1, 79, 160, 304, 310 ; declines to subscribe to Anglo-Russian Convention, 60 ; pro-Afghan agencies of, 61 ; refusal of, to proclaim a *Jahad*, 304.

————, Army.
    Trained under Turkish instructors, 60 ; equipment and strength of, 61.

Afghan War, (1878–9).
    Effect of, on Indian military resources, 50 ; assistance in, by Ruling Indian Princes, 51.

Africa, British East.
    Govt. of India agree to employment of troops in, 81.

————, German East.
    Govt. of India agree to employment of I.E.F. " B " in, 80 ; despatch of I.E.F. " B " to, 82–3.

Agriculture.
    Dependence of Iraq on irrigation, and of Up. Mesopotamia on rainfall, 9.

Ahmed Bey.
    Strength of force under, (24 July 1915), 297.

Ahwaz.
  Probable Turkish raid on, 166; disquieting news from, 167; *Comet* leaves for, 168; Europeans leave, 168; Gen. Barrett reinforces, 168, 174, 185; moral effect of Turkish occupation of, 168 n; defensive force at, 169-70, 179, 196-7, strength of, 174; strength of Turkish force advancing on, (4 February 1915), 170, (10 February), 174; action near, (3 March 1915), 183-5, results of, 188; Sir P. Cox on importance of, 187-8; Brit. force at, (11 April), 197; Turkish activity at, during battle of Shaiba 219; Brit. camp at, attacked, (15-19 April), 221; Brit. force at, (end April), 223-4, (20 June), 234, (end of July), 301, (beginning October), Appendix VII., 357.

Aircraft.
  Lack of, 134 n, 158, 165; W.O. agree to send two, 188, arrive Basra (14 May 1915) and first flight of, (27 May), 255; advance on Amara, 255, 258, 261; Gen. Nixon asks for more, 269; in preparations for Nasiriya advance, 275-6; affected by heat, 275, 289 n, 339 n; two " Caudron " aeroplanes arrive Basra (14 July), 289 n; advance to Nasiriya, 290-8; advance to Kut, 315-38; three seaplanes arrive Basra (5 September), 316 n; W.O. agree to send air squadron to Mesopotamia, 339, four machines arrive Basra (28 August), 339; number available for battle of Kut, 339. See also " Air Services, Indian Army "; " Royal Flying Corps "; " Royal Naval Air Service."

Air Services, Indian Army.
  Strength of, at outbreak of war, 63; personnel surrendered to W.O. at outbreak of war, 68, 158; aviators from Australia and New Zealand, 188, 339.

Ajab Khan, Subadar-Major (76th Punjabis).
  Gallantry of, 230.

Ajaimi, Shaikh of Muntafik. *See* " Shaikh Ajaimi of Muntafik."

Akaika channel.
  Mined by Turks, 241, 279; navigation of, 275; dammed by Turks, 275, 277; dam breached, 277-8; description of, 278-9; action in, (5 July 1915), 280-2.

Aleppo.
  Turkish XIIth A.C. reported to have left, 156.

Alert, H.M.S. (sloop).
  Arrives Abadan (October 1915), 342.

Alexandretta.
  View of Gen. Staff on occupation of, 71; Turkish intentions against, 86.

Al Hasa.
  Province of, 14; Turkish garrisons ejected from, (1913), 14, 25.

Al Huwair creek.
  Reconnaissance of, 245.

Ali Bey.
  In command of Fire Brig. Regt., 127, 170 n; in command of Turkish right wing at Nasiriya, 170 n; battle of Shaiba, 208 n.

Ali Gharbi.
  Brit. occupy, 300; force at, (end July 1915), 301, (beginning October), Appendix VII., 356; minor engagements near, 314; concentration at, (11 September), 314.

Ali Ibn Husain (Arabistan).
  Concentration at, (4 May 1915), 227.

INDEX 361

Allawi.
  Hostile force dispersed at, (6 January 1915), 158 ; E.B.F. operate against, 192.

Amara.
  Turks retire on, 126-7, 154 ; Gen. Barrett advocates occupation of, 155 ; Sir P. Cox urges advance to, 161, 168 ; Govt. of India's policy (January 1915) *re* advance to, 161 ; Turkish force at, 165, 223, moves to Bisaitin from, 166 ; views of S. of S. and Viceroy on advance to, 180 ; preparations for advance on, by Arabistan force, 231-3 ; units of Arabistan force reach, 233 ; strategic importance of, 237 ; the advance to, and capture of, (31 May-4 June 1915), 244-66 ; description of, 264-5 ; Brit. force at, (13 June), 267, (end July), 301, (beginning October), Appendix VII., 356-7 ; Brit. force *en route* to, (end July), 300 ; force from Nasiriya arrives at, 311 ; Gen. Nixon and H.Q. leave Basra for, (12 September), 314.

Ammunition.
  Factory at Kabul, 61 ; in India, at outbreak of war, 63.

————, Supply of.
  Turkish.
    Mainly dependent on German, 30.
  British.
    During battle of Kut, 328-9.

Anaiza (Arab tribe).
  Turkish plan for co-operation of, 162.

Anatolia.
  Absence of communications in, 71.

Anderson, Major M. H., (33rd Cavalry).
  Killed (29 April 1915), 226.

Anglo-Persian Oilfields.
  Communications with, 2, 14 ; protection of, in Bakhtiari territory, 14 ; effect on, of Turkish operations in Mesopotamia, 71 ; defence of, 73-4 ; *Lawrence* arrives Abadan to protect, 85 ; responsibility for protection of, 93 *n* ; probable Turkish raid on, 166 ; protection of, (January 1915), 167-8 ; moral effect of Turkish raid on, 168 *n* ; Bakhtiaris ordered to defend, 169, arrive at, (5 February), 173 ; pipe line breached and oil stores looted (5 February), 173 ; operations for repair and security of, 222, 224 ; pipe line repaired by 13 June, 233 ; Mr. Chamberlain on protection of, (12 July), 303 ; Lord Hardinge on protection of, 304 ; rendered secure by occupation of Amara, 307 ; W/T station erected at the, 308. *See also* " Abadan " ; " Ahwaz " ; " Shatt al Arab."

Anglo-Russian Convention of 1907. *See* " Treaties."

Apa Bagwe, Lance-Naick, (110th Mahratta L.I.).
  Specially mentioned for gallantry at Muzaira'a, 142 *n*.

Aqaba.
  Turkish intentions against, 86.

Arab Committee in Mesopotamia. *See under* " Committees."

Arabia.
  Responsibility for, divided between Gen. Staffs, W.O. and India, 70 ; enemy emissaries in, 77 ; effect in Central, of capture of Basra and Qurna, 162.

Arabistan.
  Communications with, 214 ; Turco-Arab intentions against, 166 ; intention of Bakhtiaris to oppose Turkish advance into, 167 ; effect of German propoganda in, 179 ; reports on situation in, (6-7 March 1915), 188 ; operations in, (24 April-10 June 1915), 224-34 ; Brit. force in, (beginning October), Appendix VII., 357.

Arabs.
   Spheres of tribes, 1 ; in Mesopotamia, 10–11 ; characteristics of, 11–13 ; opposition to Turkish Govt., 19, 25 ; operations of Pasha of Baghdad against 43 ; lawlessness of, in Persian Gulf, 45–6 ; establishment of, treaty relations with, 46 ; menace of, against Egypt and the Suez Canal, 71 ; Turkey prepares Chiefs for intervention, 75, 89 ; co-operation of, 83–4, 94, 95 n, 134, 138–9, attitude of, 188, 126, 154–5, 271 ; in Turkish force at action of Sahil, 124 ; loot Basra, 127–8 ; Gen. Barrett on co-operation of, 138–9 ; Turkish plan for using, 162 ; constant minor hostilities with, 170 ; mobility of, 185 ; disheartened by activity of E.B.F., 192 ; turn against retreating Turks, 216, 218, 220, 299 ; change of attitude of, in Arabistan, 225 ; treachery of, 226, 230–1, 299 ; Brit. wounded mutilated by, 228, 337 n ; minor operations against, (5 and 8 May 1915), 244–5 ; attempt to loot Amara, 263 ; hostility of, during advance to Nasiriya, 278, 279.

Armenia.
   Situation in, (June 1915), 270.

Armoured cars.
   At battle of Kut, 329–30, 330 n, 339.

Army Corps, Indian.
   2nd.—I.E.F. "D" reorganised as, (1 April 1915), Appendix IV., 350–1.

————, Turkish.
   IVth.—Reported moving from Syria, 155, 156 n ; strength of, 155 ; German officers with, 155.
   IXth.—⎤
   Xth.— ⎬ Possibility of reinforcements from, 101.
   XIth.—⎦
   XIIth. (Mosul).—Two divisions of, move westward, 103 ; reported making for Baghdad, 156 ; strength of, 156 ; reported diverted to the Caucasus, (January 1915), 165 ;
   XIIIth.—Mobilization of, 77 ; one div. of, at Mosul, 103–4.

Army Bearer Corps. *See* "Medical Services, Indian Army."

Army in India. *See* "Indian Army."

"Army in India Committee," 1912. *See under* "Committees."

Artillery, British.
   Brigade, Field :
      10th.—With 6th Div., 113 ; Shaiba, 197 ; Arabistan operations, 225–34, Appendix V., 352 ; battle of Kut, 314–38.
   Batteries, Field :
      63rd.—With 6th Div., 113 ; disembarkation of, 115 ; action of Sahil, 119–24 ; action near Ruta, 163–5 ; with E.B.F., 191, 197 ; battle of Shaiba, 201–19 ; Arabistan operations, 225–31, Appendix V., 352 ; advance to Amara, 251–64 ; advance to Nasiriya, 276–98 ; Nasiriya, 300 ; battle of Kut, 314–38.
      76th.—With 6th Div., 113 ; disembarkation of, 122 ; action of Sahil, 122 ; advance on, and capture of Qurna, 144–51 ; action at Ruta, 163–5 ; Ahwaz 174 ; ordered to Shaiba, 178 ; action near Shaiba, (3 March 1915), 181–3 ; battle of Shaiba, 201–19 ; Arabistan operations, 225–33, Appendix V., 352 ; Ahwaz, 234 ; Amara, 301 ; battle of Kut, 318–38.
      82nd.—With 6th Div., 113 ; advance on, and capture of Qurna, 141–51 ; action near Ahwaz, 183–5 ; Ahwaz, 197, 224 ; Arabistan operations, 225–33, Appendix V., 352 ; arrives Amara, 233 ; Ali Gharbi, 301 ; battle of Kut, 318–38.

INDEX 363

Artillery, British—*cont*.
  Batteries, Field, (T.F.) :
    1st/5th Hampshire (How.).—Under orders to reinforce I.E.F. " D," 188 ; arrives Basra, 193 ; Basra, 197 ; joins Qurna garrison, 242 ; Nuhairat, 245 ; advance to Amara, 251-64 ; advance to Nasiriya, 286-98 ; battle of Kut, 314-38.
  ————, Garrison (Heavy) :
    86th.—Under orders to leave India for Basra, (2 March 1915), 185 ; with E.B.F., 191, 197 ; Qurna and Basra, 197 ; advance to Amara, 251-64 ; advance to Nasiriya, 289-98 ; Amara, 301 ; battle of Kut, 314-38.
    104th.—Under orders to join I.E.F. " D," 157 ; with E.B.F., 191 ; Qurna and Kurmat Ali, 197 ; advance to Amara, 251-64 ; Ali Gharbi and Amara, 301, 314 ; battle of Kut, 314-38.
  ————, Horse :
    " S,"—*En route* to Basra, 170 ; in 6th Cav. Brig., 178 *n* ; action near Shaiba, 181-3 ; battle of Shaiba, 201-19 ; Arabistan operations, 224-33, Appendix V., 351 ; Ahwaz, 234, 301.
  ————, in India.
  Batteries reduced to four guns, 90 *n* ; 15-pounder guns manned by volunteers, 289-98, 300, 314.
  ————, ————, Madras Artillery Volunteers.
  Advance to Nasiriya, 289-98 ; Nasiriya, 300.
  ————, ————, Mountain Brigade.
    1st.—In I.E.F. " D," 99.
  ————, ————, Mountain Batteries.
    23rd Peshawar.—Ordered to Persian Gulf, 92 ; with 16th Inf. Brig., 99 ; night of 10-11 November 1914, 109 ; action of Saihan, 115-8 ; action of Sahil, 119-24 ; Ahwaz, 174, action near Ahwaz, 183-5 ; Shaiba, 197 ; battle of Shaiba, 201-19 ; Fort George, 241, 301.
    30th.—Ordered to Persian Gulf, 92 ; with 16th Inf. Brig., 99 ; action of Saihan, 115-8 ; action of Sahil, 119-24 ; advance on, and capture of Qurna, 145-51 ; action at Ruta, 163-5 ; Basra, 197 ; ordered to Shaiba 199 ; battle of Shaiba, 204-5 ; Qurna, 248 ; advance to Amara, 249-64 ; advance to Nasiriya, 276-98 ; Nasiriya, 300.
  ————, Turkish.
  Strength of, 29-30 ; captured at Qurna, 151 ; German officers with, 158 ; Sahil, 124 ; Ruta, 165 ; battle of Shaiba, 201 *n* ; advance to Amara, 256-7.

Asani bend.
  Brit. camp at, 283.

Asia Minor.
  Difficulty of operations in, 71.

Astara (Azerbaijan).
  Russian landing at, force Turkish retirement from Tabriz, 167.

Ati's House.
  Description of, 278-9 ; Brit. occupy position at, 279 ; signalling station and report centre at, 280.

At Tuba mounds.
  Turkish line extends to, 176.

Australia.
  Govt. of India borrow aviators from, 188, 339.

Aziziya.
  Brit. force reaches, (5 October 1915), 337.

B.

Baghdad.
Martial law proclaimed in, and violation of Brit. domicile rights, 77; movement of Turkish troops from, 84; evacuation of Brit. subjects from, 79, 84; effect of Turkish confiscation of coal at, 84; conditions in, (11 September 1914), 85; Turkish artillery at, 104; Sir P. Cox suggests advance to, 133–4; views of India and I.O. on suggested advance to, 135–7, 272 *n*; advance to, vetoed, 137; views of Gen. Barrett on advance to, 138–9; Turkish force at, (November), 140, (December), 154; Turkish reinforcements for, 155 *n*, 156, 169; Turkish force at or near, (June 1915), 269, (end July), 301, (beginning September), 313; question of occupation of, 272, 272 *n*; views of Gen. Nixon on advance to, 307–8, 311; Govt. of India disapprove of proposed advance to, 308; political importance of occupation of, 310–1.

———— railway.
Development of, and effect of gaps in, on operations, 23–4; strategic effect of, 35, (1871–1914), 40–3; House of Commons Committee on, 40; Committee of Imperial Defence and the, 40; Brit. policy *re*, 40–3.

————, *Vali* of.
Operations of, against Arabs, 43, and assistance of, in navigation of Euphrates, 44; promises to protect Brit. subjects, 85.

Bahmanshir river.
Comet in, 118 *n*.

Bahrein.
Landing at, 94–5; I.E.F. " D " arrives at, (23 October 1914), but disembarkation suspended, 103; difficulties of water supply at, 103; I.E.F. " D " leaves, for Shatt al Arab, (2 November), 104–5, 105 *n*.

Bahrein (launch).
As reserve mine-sweeper, 255 *n*.

Bakhtiaris.
Intention of, to oppose Turkish advance into Arabistan, 167; ordered to defend oilfields, 169; reach oilfields (5 February 1915), 173; Khans of, informed of Turkish intention not to invade territory of, 179; attitude of, 240.

Baljaniya.
Turkish forces at, 119, 125; Gen. Barrett decides to advance on, 125–6; Turks evacuate, 127; Turkish battery at, dismantled, 128.

Bandar Nasiri.
Brit. camp opposite, 183.

Band-i-qir (Arabistan).
Brit. force in, (beginning October 1915), Appendix VII., 357.

Bani Lam tribes.
Hostile to Great Britain, 15; with Turkish force moving to Bisaitin, 166. *See also* " Shaikh Ghazban of the Bani Lam."

Bani Tamin tribe.
Operations against, (8–9 June 1915), 233.

Bani Turuf tribesmen.
Join Turkish force moving to Bisaitin, 166; join Turks at Ghadir, 183; desire of, to negotiate, 225.

Barbukh creek.
Minor action at, (30 January 1915), 168; Turkish advanced positions near, 243.

INDEX 365

Barjisiya wood (Battle of Shaiba).
  Enemy concentration at, 209–11; attack on Turkish position near, 212–5.
Barrett, Lieut-Gen. Sir A. A., K.C.B., K.C.V.O.
  Arrives off Shatt al Arab, (13 November 1914), 110, 114; assumes command (14 November), 110, 114–5; receives orders (31 October) to reinforce Gen. Delamain, 112; orders to, (2 November), 113; force under, sails from Bombay and Karachi, (7–9 November), 113; orders to, (14 November), 115; decision to advance, 118–9; plan for move on Sahil, 119–20; reports on situation (20 November), 125–6; decides to advance on Baljaniya, 125–6; decides to move on Basra, 128; reaches Basra (21 November), 128; ceremonial entry of, into Basra (23 November), 130; appreciation of, (29 November), 138–9; orders of, (30 November) for advance on Qurna (3 December), 141, 144–5; advocates occupation of Amara, 155; on suggested occupation of Nasiriya, 155; *re* advance to Suq ash Shuyukh and Nasiriya, 156; strengthens garrison at Qurna, 157, 159; asks for additional river craft and aeroplanes, 158, 165, 169, 339; decides to attack Turkish position near Ruta creek, 163; asks for reinforcements (26 January), 165; organises *Bellum* squadron, 167; reinforces Ahwaz (30 January), 168; Lord Hardinge discusses situation with, 172; reinforces Ahwaz (10 February), 174; reports to India (17 February), intention to withdraw troops to Basra owing to floods, 175; reinforces Shaiba, 178, 181; reports on land transport and future intentions, 180–1; report on action near Ahwaz (3 March), 185; authorises disembarkation of troops at Bushire, 193; informed (31 March) Turkish force had left Nasiriya, 193; leaves Mesopotamia (12 April), 196.
Barrow, Gen. Sir E. G., G.C.B. (Military Secretary, I.O.).
  On measures for security of Persian Gulf, 78–9, 81; and employment of Indian troops outside India, 80–1; suggests diverting Force " B" to Persian Gulf, 81, 84; appreciation of, (26 September 1914), and action taken upon, 86–9; views of, on suggested advance to Baghdad, 136–7; averse to proposed advance to Kut, 271.
Basidu.
  Landing at, considered, 94–5.
Basra.
  In 1914, 4; as terminus of Baghdad railway, 42; East India Company in, 43; Gen. Staff, India, responsible for, 70; plan for occupation of, drawn up, 70 *n*; Turks requisition coal at, 78, effect of, 84; movement of Turkish troops to, 79, 84; sailings to, resumed, 91; reported intention of *Emden* to make for, 97; operations leading to occupation of, 99–126; Turkish force in, (October 1914), 100, 100 *n*; objective of I.E.F. " D," 102, 115, 125, 168–9; Turks evacuate, 126–7; the occupation of, 127–133; Brit. residents from, seek assistance, 127–8; Capt. Hayes-Sadler in *Espiègle* reaches, (20 November), 128; Gen. Barrett's force reaches, (21 November), 128; description of, 129; port facilities, 129–30, 342; Major Brownlow appointed Mil. Gov. of 130; ceremonial entry into, (23 November), 130–1; relations between inhabitants of and Brit. troops, 132; suggested announcement of permanent occupation of, 139–40; reported Turkish advance on, 158, 165–6; Turkish plan for defence of, 162; Gen. Barrett asks for reinforcements for protection of, 165; Turkish intention to attack, 166, 168; strength of Brit. garrison in, (end January 1915), 168, 170, (March), 181; Lord Hardinge on security of, 170; Lord Hardinge's visit to, 171; Lord Hardinge's memorandum of 3 March on future of, 171 *n*; floods affect situation at, 175, 198; views of C.G.S.I. on probable Turkish attack on, 180; Brit. reserve force in, (March 1915), 181; Brit. force at, (11 April), 197, 197 *n*, (beginning October), Appendix VII., 357; attitude of population during battle of Shaiba, 204 *n*; Brit. force and Force H.Q. at, (13 June), 267, (end July), 301.

Basra, *Vali* of. *See* " Subhi Bey."
———— *Vilayet.*
Correspondence *re* occupation of, 154-6, 186, 234-41, 270, 302.
Basra (Turkish steamer).
Overtaken, but escapes, 336.
Bawi tribe.
Refuses to obey Shaikh of Mohammerah, 169 ; loot oil stores and breach pipe line (5 February 1915), 173 ; wavering attitude of, 174 ; joined by Cha'ab tribe, 174, 221 ; defeat of, by Shaikh of Mohammerah's force, 179 ; defeat of, (15 April), 221 ; concentrated near Ahwaz, 221, 224 ; offer guarantee of safety of caravan routes, 225 ; assist at repair of pipe line, 233 ; subsided, 308 ; submission of Shaikhs of the, 309.
Bedouins.
Turks endeavour to enlist sympathies of, 96. *See also* " Arabs."
Bellum squadron.
Formation and purposes of, 167, 244 ; affair of 8 May, 1915, 245 ; offensive up Tigris, 244-264.
Bellums (native craft), 2 ;
Description of, 130 ; battle of Shaiba, 205 ; advance to Nasiriya, 277-98.
Bengali (hospital ship).
Sinks on voyage to Mesopotamia, 343.
Bennett, Mr. Thomas Jewell.
Paper on Persian Gulf *quoted*, 46-7.
Bieberstein, Baron Marschall von.
German Ambassador to Turkey (1897-1912), 38 *n.*
Bisaitin.
Turkish force moves from Amara to, 166 ; Brit. reconnaissance to, 229 ; Brit. force at, 229, 232, leaves for Amara, 233.
Black Sea.
Goeben and *Breslau* bombard Russian ports in, 98.
Blockade of Euphrates. *See* " Euphrates Blockade Force."
Blockships.
Sunk in Shatt al Arab, 105, 127 ; passed, 128 ; buoyed and regulated, 140 ; below Qurna, 140, 148-9 ; below Ruta, 157-8 ; sunk in Euphrates, 283 ; across Tigris, 317, and attempt to breach, 335.
Blois-Johnson, Lt.-Col. T. G., (22nd Punjabis).
In advance to Amara, 251-64.
Blosse Lynch (river steamer).
Requisitioned, 125 ; reaches Basra, 128 ; advance on and capture of Qurna, 141-51 ; attack at Muzaibila, 157 ; takes 76th Battery section to Ahwaz, 174 ; advance to Amara, 252-64 ; advance to Nasiriya, 277-98.
Bombay.
Embarkation of I.E.F. " D " at, 97, 103, 113. *See also* " Karachi."
Boom defence.
Across Tigris at Qurna, 242 ; during operations 257 ; near Kut, 317.
Boundaries of Mesopotamia, 1.
Braika.
Arabistan force at, 225-6.
Breslau (German light cruiser.)
Effect of arrival of, with *Goeben*, at Constantinople, 75 ; retention of crew of, 77, 97 ; in Black Sea, 91, 98.

INDEX 367

Bridges.
    Types of, 7; at Basra, 128, 132; constructed for attack on Qurna. 149–50; at Qurna, 175, 242, damaged, 219; constructed across Karkha, 227–9; in Turkish Kut position, 317; at Nukhailat, 318.

Bridging train.
    Qurna, 197, 241; advance to Amara, 251–64; Amara, 301; battle of Kut, 314–38.

British India Steamship Navigation Company.
    Diversion of ships of, 80; resume sailings to Basra, 91.

Britten, Lt.-Col. T. X. (110th Mahratta L.I.).
    In attack on Qurna, 150.

Brooking, Brig.-Gen. H. T., C.B.
    Commander of 33rd Brig. in command at Bushire, 309; defeats Persian tribesmen (9 September 1915), 309.

Browne, Lt.-Col. A. J. Wogan (33rd Cavalry).
    In command at action near Shaiba (3 March 1915), 181–3.

Brownlow, Major d'A. C. (Deputy Judge Advocate-Gen. to I. E. F. " D ").
    Appointed Mil. Gov. of Basra, 130.

Buildings and houses.
    Generally unsuitable for military use, 8.

Bulbul (Turkish river steamer).
    Sunk by *Shaitan*, 259, 265.

Bullard, Mr. R. W., C.I.E.
    Civil Adviser to Mil. Gov. of Basra, 130.

Bushire.
    Brit. Resident at, 46, 47, 77–8; W/T station at, 103 *n*; hostility against Brit. consulate, 192; German Consul at, arrested and deported, 192; *Clio* despatched to, and disembarkation of troops at, 193; Gen. Nixon arrives at (5 April 1915), 196; activities of Turco-German agents in, 196; Gen. Nixon made responsible for defence of, 274; Brit. force at, 274, 301; unsuccessful attack on Brit. Residency at, (12–13 July), 308; occupied (8 August), and Brit. garrison reinforced, 309; action at, (9 September), 309.

C.

Calcutta.
    Riot near, 90 *n*.

Campbell, Lieut. M. G. G., R.E. (17th S. and M.).
    Gallantry of, 150.

Camps, British.
    Sanniya, 108; Sahil, 124; Maqil, 140; on Shwaiyib, 141; Muzaira'a, 148–9; on Karun, opposite Bandar Nasiri, 183; at Shaiba, 200; near Zubair, 220; Ahwaz, 221; Khafajiya, 231; Asani bend, 283.

———, Turkish.
    Sakrikiya, 157; Ruta, 164; Nukhaila, 176; on Karkha, 179; Ghadir, 183, 221.

Candler, Edmund.
    " The Long Road to Baghdad," *quoted*, 117–8, referred to 234 *n*.

Casualties, British and Indian.
    Night 10–11 November 1914, Sanniya, 109; Saihan, 117; Sahil, 124; Muzaira'a, 144, 146, 148; on *Shaitan*, 148; in crossing the Tigris (8 December), 151; Ruta creek, 164; action near Shaiba, 183; action near Ahwaz, 185; on *Espiègle*, 193; battle of Shaiba, 203, 205–6, 208, 216; Arabistan force, 226, 230–1, 233–4; reconnaissance of Al Huwair creek, 245; advance to, and capture of Amara, 254–6, 265; advance to, and capture of Nasiriya, 280, 282, 285–7, 289–90, 293, 296–7; Bushire, 309; during the advance to, and battle of Kut, 315–6, 320, 324, 326, 328, 330, 335, 338.

Casualties, Turkish.
  Fao, 108; night 10–11 November 1914, Sanniya, 109; Saihan, 117; Sahil, 124; Muzaira'a 144, 148; Ruta creek, 165; night 29–30 January 1915, Muzaira'a, 166; action near Shaiba, 183; action near Ahwaz, 185; battle of Shaiba, 206, 208, 217; Arabistan operations, 230–1; advance to, and capture of Amara, 254–6, 265; advance to, and capture of Nasiriya, 281–2, 297; battle of Kut, 324, 326–7, 337.

Cato, Conrad.
  " The Navy in Mesopotamia," *quoted*, 276 *n*.

Caucasus.
  Turkish hopes of Moslem rising in the, 77; Turkish Pan-Islamic propaganda in, 86; effect in Mesopotamia of Turkish defeat in, 159; Turkish 37th Div. reported in, and XIIth A.C. diverted to, 165; Turkish divisions in, 178; not likely to provide Turkish reinforcements for Mesopotamia, 180; Russian intentions in, 272, 272 *n*.

" Caudron " aeroplanes.
  Two arrive Basra (14 July 1915), 289 *n*. *See also* " Aircraft."

Cavalry.
  Unable to penetrate marshes, 163.
  ———, Indian, Brigade.
    6th.—Organised and ordered to Shaiba, 178; composition of, 178 *n*; Shaiba, 197; battle of Shaiba, 201–19; Arabistan operations, 225–33, Appendix V., 351; Ahwaz, 234, 301.
  ———, ———, Regiments.
    7*th Hariana Lancers*.—Under orders to reinforce I.E.F. " D," 170–1, 173, 178; in 6th Cav. Brig., 178 *n*; battle of Shaiba, 201–19, casualties, 203, 206; Arabistan operations, 224–33, Appendix V., 351; arrive Amara, 233; Ali Gharbi and Amara, 301; battle of Kut, 314–38, casualties, 330.
    16*th Cavalry*.—*En route* to Basra, 170; disembarks at Basra (14 February 1915), 176 *n*; with Basra Movable Column, 176; in 6th Cav. Brig., 178 *n*; action near Shaiba, 181–3; battle of Shaiba, 201–19; Fort George, 241, 301; Bushire, 301, 309; battle of Kut, 314–38.
    23*rd Cavalry (Frontier Force)*.—Ahwaz, 234, 268, 301.
    33*rd Queen Victoria's Own Light Cavalry*.—With 6th Div., 113; action of Sahil, 119–24; sent to Shaiba, 141 *n*; action at Ruta, 163–5; Ahwaz, 174, 197, 224; in 6th Cav. Brig., 178 *n*; action near Shaiba, 181–3; action near Ahwaz, 183–5; Basra, 197; Arabistan operations, 225–33, Appendix V., 351; Ahwaz, 234, 301.
  ———, Turkish.
    Strength of, 29.

Cha'ab tribe.
  Join Bawi insurgents, 174, 221; exhorted to remain loyal to Mohammerah 179; concentrated near Ahwaz, 221, 224.

Chahela mounds.
  Brit. at, during battle of Kut, 319.

Chamberlain, The Rt. Hon. J. Austen, P.C., M.P. (S. of S. for India, May, 1915–July 1917).
  On I.O. organisation, 72; succeeds Lord Crewe (27 May 1915), telegram of 28 May, 239; correspondence *re* advance to Nasiriya, 270; proposed advance to Kut, 271, 273, 301–7; telegram of 12 July *re* protection of oil interests, 303; withdrawal of Indian divisions from France, 310.

Churchill, The Rt. Hon. Winston S., P.C., M.P. (First Lord of the Admiralty).
  On defence of oil works and employment of Indian army, 81.

Clery, Lt.-Col. C.B. (104th Rifles).
  In battle of Kut, 320.

INDEX 369

"Clery's Post" (Battle of Kut), 320-2.

Climatic conditions.
: In Mesopotamia, 7–8; effect of, on operations, 10; measures to counteract effect of, on Brit. force, 342–3. *See also* "Rainfall"; "Sandstorms"; "Weather"; "Wind."

Climo, Lt.-Col. S. H., D.S.O. (24th Punjabis).
: Succeeds Gen. Dobbie in command of 17th Inf. Brig. (21 May 1915), 248; advance to Amara, 251–64; advance to Nasiriya, 276–98.

Clio, H.M.S. (sloop).
: Arrangements for despatch of, to Basra, 169; despatched to Bushire, 193; affair of 8 May 1915, 245; advance to Amara, 251–64; refitting, 268.

Coal.
: Confiscation of, by Turks, 78, effect of, 84

Cochran, Capt. G. W. (81st Pioneers).
: In battle of Kut, 334.

Comet (R.I.M. Paddle Yacht).
: At Mohammerah, 107, 118; down Bahmanshir river, 118 *n*; Karun, 166, 168; arrives Ahwaz (1 February 1915), 169; damaged by shell, 219; supports advance to Amara, 251–7; advance to, and capture of Amara, 260–4; in the "River Column," 300; Ali Gharbi, 301; advance to Kut, 314–38; attempt to breach boom across Tigris, 335.

Commander-in-Chief, India.
: H.Q. of, at Simla, 56. *See also* "Creagh, Gen. Sir O'Moore"; "Duff, Gen. Sir B."; "Kitchener of Khartoum, Lord"; "Palmer, Gen. Sir Power."

Committee of Imperial Defence. *See under* "Committees."

Committees.
: House of Commons, on railway communications in Middle East, 40; Imperial Defence and Baghdad railway, 40; Indian Army Organisation, of 1879, 50–1; "Army in India Committee" of 1912, 54, 57–9, constitution of, 58; War Committee, and co-ordination of operations in Mesopotamia, 72; Arab, in Mesopotamia, 83.

Communications.
: From the sea, 1; by river with Arabistan and the Anglo-Persian Oilfields, 2; waterways best means of travel, 6; absence of, in Thrace and Anatolia, 71; menace to Turkish, with Mesopotamia, 71; Suez Canal, 71; at Basra, 132; improvement in, 140.

Communications, field.
: Difficulty of, at action of Sahil, 121, 124; Turkish menace to, 174; telephonic, difficulties of, during advance to Nasiriya, 291, 295 *n*; at battle of Kut, 325–6, 331.

Conferences, British.
: On board *Varela* (28 October 1914), 103, (2 November), 105, (16 November), 118–9; on board *Lawrence* (6 December), 145; on river transport (30 June 1915), 340.

———, Turkish.
: At Ruta (10 February 1915), 174–5.

Connaught, H.R.H. The Duke of.
: At Delhi, on services of I.A. in Great War, 66 *n*.

Conventions. *See* "Treaties."

Conscription.
: Never imposed in India, 65.

Cookson, Lt.-Com. E. C. (*Shushan*).
: Wounded Al Huwair creek, 245; temporary S.N.O. in advance to Kut, 315, 334–5; killed, 335; awarded posthumous V.C., 335 *n*.

Cox, Lt.-Col. Sir P. Z., K.C.I.E., C.S.I. (Chief Political Officer).
Persian Gulf question referred to, in 1911, 73; reports on Turkish preparations, 77–8; as chief political adviser to Gen. Delamain, 94, 102; reads Proclamation in Basra (23 November 1914), 130; reports on situation and suggests, (23 November), advance to Baghdad, 133–4; suggests announcing permanent occupation of Basra, 139–40; reports of 25 November, 140; at surrender of Qurna, 151; views of, on political effect of inactivity after capture of Qurna, 161; urges advance to Nasiriya and Amara, 161, 168; Ibn Saud reports to, 171, 178; reports situation (4 March 1915), 187–8; reports of 6 and 7 March, 188; in advance to Amara, 260; in advance to Nasiriya, 283.

Creagh, Gen. Sir G. O'Moore, V.C., G.C.B., G.C.S.I.
Indian Army system (evidence before Mesopotamia Commission), 55, 59, 73.

Crewe, Lord (S. of S. for India, to May 1915).
On employment of I.A., 82; action taken on Gen. Barrow's appreciation of 26 September 1914, 89; telegram of 5 October, 93; evidence of, before Mesopotamia Commission, 95 *n*, 235; views of, on suggested occupation of Nasiriya and Amara, 154, 186, 235–7; and reinforcing of I.E.F. " D," 165, 167–8, 177, 186–9; urges despatch of troops to protect oilfields (29 January 1915), 167; on main objective of I.E.F. " D," 169; telegrams to India of 3, 4, and 5 March, 187–8; telegram to India of 19 April, 222; telegram of 24 April, 235, 239; sanctions advance to Amara, 237; telegram of 24 May, 237; succeeded by Mr. Austen Chamberlain, 239.

Ctesiphon.
Turkish force at, (beginning of September 1915), 313; Turks retire to, after battle of Kut, 337.

Curzon of Kedleston, Lord (Viceroy of India, 1899–1905).
On railways in Turkish territory, 40–1; Viceroy (1899), 52; the " Curzon Policy," 52–4; extension of office as Viceroy, 55; resignation of, 55.

D.

Dabba island.
Turkish guns at, 100; Turkish obstruction at, 126–7, passed, 128, buoyed and regulated, 140.

Daghistani.
In command of force retiring towards Amara, 261, 263–4.

Dalhousie (R.I.M.S.).
Escorts I.E.F. " D," 103; operations at Dilwar, 309.

Damascus.
Reported move of Turkish troops from, 155 *n*.

Danaks (native craft).
Description of, 318 *n*.

Dardanelles.
Operations against, considered, 71; *Goeben* and *Breslau* enter, 75; closing of, 90; exploited by Germans, 91; Govt. of India informed of intention to bombard the, 177; operations against, likely to affect Turkish reinforcements for Mesopotamia, 180; results at, likely to affect Eastern situation, 241, 310; situation in, (June 1915), 270.

Date plantations.
Impede operations, 124, 279, 281.

Davison, Maj.-Gen., K.S., C.B.
In command of 12th Inf. Brig., 166; arrives Qurna, 174; at Ahwaz (11 April 1915), 197, 221; appointed Inspector-Gen. of Communications, 222, 267.

INDEX 371

Declarations of war.
On Turkey, by Russia, France, and Great Britain, 98.

Delamain, Brig.-Gen. W. S., C.B., D.S.O.
In command of 16th Inf. Brig., 92; composition of force under, 99; instructions to, 99–102; ordered to commence hostilities against Turkey, 104–5; orders to, (2 November 1914), 105 *n*; force under, lands at Sanniya, 108; W/T communication from India interrupted, 109, 113–4; delayed by bad weather, 109–10; report on situation (13 November), 114; Operation Order for attack on Saihan, (15 November), 115; despatched to attack Shaikh Ajaimi, 176; returns to Basra, 177; ordered to Shaiba (24 February 1915), with reinforcements, 178; orders to, for action of 3 March near Shaiba, 181; battle of Shaiba, 206–19; advance to Amara, 251–64; in temporary command of 6th Div., 299; occupies Ali Gharbi, 300, in command at, (end July), 301; battle of Kut, 318–38.

Dexter, Mr. Tom
Personal Asst. to Mil. Gov. of Basra, 130.

Dilke, Sir Charles.
Statement of policy of, *re* Baghdad railway, 40–1.

Dilwar.
Operation against, (13–16 August 1915), 309.

Diseases.
Prevalence of, 8, 129.

Djavid Pasha.
Turkish force under, moves south, 156.

Djemal Pasha (Turkish Minister of Marine).
"Memories of a Turkish Statesman," referred to, 75 *n*; Francophile sentiments of, 76.

Dobbie, Brig.-Gen. W. H., C.B.
Arrives in Shatt al Arab (end November 1914), 140–1; activity of force under, (1 January 1915), 157; in command at Qurna, 197, 242 invalided (21 May), 248.

Doha.
Turkish garrison in, (1871), 25.

Ducat, Major R. (20th Punjabis).
Dies of wounds received night 10–11 November 1914 at Sanniya, 109.

Duff, Gen. Sir B., G.C.B., K.C.S.I., K.C.V.O., C.I.E.
Indian Army system, 55, 59, 63; evidence of, before Mesopotamia Committee, 55, 59, 62, 133, 196; informs Gen. Barrett that no more troops could be sent to Mesopotamia, 155; reinforcements for I.E.F. "D," 160, 173; opinion of (January 1915), on strength of I.E.F. "D," 161; agrees with Gen. Nixon's views, 239, 271; averse to proposed advance to Kut, 271.

Dunlop, Lt.-Col. H. H. (44th Merwaras).
In advance to Nasiriya, 287–98.

Durand Frontier Agreement.
With Afghanistan, (1893), 51.

Dust.
Impedes operations in Arabistan, 227; effect of, in battle of Kut, 322, 327–8, 330.

E.

East India Company.
Activity of, 43, 46; agreement of, with Shah of Persia, 45; military forces of, till 1858, 49, 64–5.

East Persia Cordon.
Inception of, 274.

Education.
  System of, in Turkish army, 30-1; spread of, affects pre-war internal situation in India, 62; of I.A. recruits, 65.

Egypt.
  Defence of, and Arab menace against, 71; enemy emissaries in, 77; Govt. of India agree to employment of troops in, 80-1; Turkish preparations against, 86, 162; Govt. of India's views on return of troops from, 177; reinforcements from, 189.

Ekbatana (German liner).
  Activity of, 78; Turkish blockship in Shatt al Arab, 127.

Elkes, Lt.-Com. F. J. G. M. (R.N.R.).
  In command of *Shaitan*, killed in attack on Qurna (7 December 1914), 148.

Emden (German light cruiser).
  Retards despatch of troopships from India, 91; effect of reported intention to make for Basra, 97.

Emigration.
  From India affects pre-war internal situation, 62.

Engineers.
  Strength of, in Turkish army at outbreak of war, 30.

Enver Pasha (Turkish Minister for War).
  Minister for War, 27 *n*; causes, with Talaat Pasha, downfall of Turkish Cabinet (1913), 38; sketch of, 39; influence of Germans over, 75; knowledge of German intentions, 75; becomes supreme authority after mobilization, 76; reported intrigues of, with Ibn Saud, 89; ambitious schemes of, in Arabia and Egypt, 96; resolves to drive Brit. from Mesopotamia, 127.

Equipment.
  Deficiency of, in I.A. at outbreak of war, 63; dependencies of I.A. upon U.K. for, 64, 68.

Erzerum.
  Treaty of 1847, 24.

Espiègle, H.M.S. (sloop).
  Ordered to Shatt al Arab, 84; arrives Mohammerah, 91; armament of, 97 *n*; movement of, (3–6 November 1914), 106–7; action opposite Abadan, 107–8; sinks enemy launches, 108–9, 126; action at Saihan, 116; action at Sahil, 119–24; reconnoitres Turkish obstruction in Shatt al Arab, 125; passes obstruction and reaches Basra, 128; reconnoitres towards Qurna, 140; attack on Qurna, 141–51; attack at Muzaibila, 157; attack at Ruta, 163–5; visits Mashur (24 February 1915), 179; reconnoitres up Karun (26 February), 179; activity of, north of Qurna (3 March), 193; assistance at Qurna (11–13 April), 219; in affairs of 5 and 8 May, 1915, 245; advance to Amara, 251–64; advance to Nasiriya, 276–98; at Ceylon, 314.

Espionage.
  Brit. abstention from, in Afghanistan, 61; easy conditions for, at Qurna, 242.

Euphrates and Tigris Steam Navigation Company. *See* "Lynch & Co."

Euphrates Blockade Force.
  Interferes with Turkish advance against Shaiba, 190; organisation (March 1915), 191, and operations of, 192; activity of, (15–16 April), 219; blockade of Euphrates by, 220; reinforced, 220; reconnoitres approaches to Hammar lake, 220, 223; duties of, taken over by navy, 241.

INDEX 373

Euphrates, river.
    Description and navigation of, 1–3 ; Brit. navigation rights, 43–4 ; reconnaissances of, 175, 220, 223, 241, 278–9, 281–3 ; Turkish main force on, 180 ; blockade of, 220 ; fairway of, blocked by Turks, 241, 283 ; navigation of, near Hammar lake, 275 ; mines in, 278 ; description of, from Akaika channel to Nasiriya, 282–3.

Europe.
    I.A. not equipped for war in, 63 ; Govt. of India agree to employment of I.E.F. " A " in, 80.

Evans, Brig.-Gen. U. W., C.B., C.M.G., 352.

Ezra's Tomb.
    Turkish force at, 138, 156–8, 165–6 ; *Marmariss* near, 141 ; Brit. reach, 259 ; L. of C. post at, 265, 267 *n*.

F.

Fao.
    Telegraph station at, 85 ; Turkish batteries at, 100 ; attack on, 106–7 ; capture of, (6 November 1914), 107–8 ; Brit. force at, (11 April 1915), 197, (beginning of October), Appendix VII., 357.

Farman aeroplanes.
    Affected by heat, 275, 289 *n*. *See also* " Aircraft."

Farmar, Major W. C. R. (R.G.A.)
    In command of E.B.F., 191.

Fars.
    Persian Gov.-Gen. of, supports German propaganda, 192 ; activities of Turco-German agents in, 196.

Finance.
    Pre-war conditions of military, in India, 54, 57.

Flags.
    Use of, at Muzaira'a, 142 *n* ; captured at battle of Shaiba, 208 ; white, enemy, at battle of Shaiba, 215 ; Arab villages display white, 260 ; white, displayed by Turks in action in Akaika channel, 281 ; white displayed at Suq ash Shuyukh, 283.

Floods.
    Effect of, on navigation, 3 ; neglect of dams, 4–5 ; effect of, on operations, 5–6, 340 ; render reconnaissance difficult, 158 ; cause discomfort, 159–190 ; near Qurna and west of Basra, impede Turkish advance, 174 ; affect situation, 174–6 ; cause withdrawal of Brit. troops to Basra, 175 ; effect of, on Basra Movable Column, 176 ; at Qurna, 190, 242 ; at Basra, 198 ; at Fort George, 241 ; at Nasiriya, 298 ; delay survey for railway, 342.

Fort George (near Old Basra).
    Brit. force at, 241, 267, 301.

Fort Snipe.
    British advanced post north of Qurna, 174, 242, flooded out, 174 ; advance to Amara to start from, 249.

France.
    Supports Turkey in Crimean War, 36 ; Baghdad railway, 42 ; declares war on Turkey (5 November 1914), 98.

Frat (Turkish steamer).
    Sunk in Euphrates, 283.

Frazer, Lt.-Col. G. S. (110th Mahratta L.I.).
    In command of force to attack Qurna, and Gen. Barrett's orders to, 141 ; orders retirement to camp at Shwaiyab, 144 ; Gen. Barrett's report on action of, 144 *n* ; force under, crosses Tigris, 150, advance to Nasiriya, 296.

374 HISTORY OF THE WAR: MESOPOTAMIA

Frontiers.
  Of Arab tribes, indefinite, 1 ; Turco-Persian, 1, 43, 96 ; Indian-Afghan (Durand Frontier Agreement), 51.

Fry, Major-Gen. C. I., C.B.
  In command of 18th Inf. Brig., 119 *n* ; ordered to, and reaches Basra, 128 ; ordered to reinforce Col. Frazer's force, 144–5 ; reaches Shwaiyab camp and holds conference, 145 ; plan of attack on Muzaira'a, 145–6 ; at surrender of Qurna, 151 ; in command at Shaiba, 197 ; in temporary command of 6th Div., 198–9, 205 ; battle of Shaiba, 201–19 ; in command at Zubair, 220, Fort George, 241, Amara, 300 ; ordered to send reinforcements to the " River Column," 300 ; battle of Kut, 318–38.

G.

Garrisons.
  Turkish, expelled from Al Hasa in 1913, 14, 25, in Doha (1871), 25, expelled from Nejd in 1831, 25.

Gendarmerie.
  Captured at Qurna, 151.

George V., H.M. The King-Emperor.
  Message from, on services of I.A. in Great War, 66 *n* ; message from, to Gen. Nixon, 298.

Germans.
  With Turkish IVth A.C., 155 ; Turkish guns handled by, 158 ; reported, on way to Afghanistan, 186, 240 *n*, 274 ; with Turks, 223, 236.

Germany.
  Influence of, in Turkish policy, 21–3, 37–9 ; Turco-German plans of operations, 32–4 ; and railways in Turkish territory, 40–3 ; value of Turkey to, as an ally, 70 ; domination of, in Turkey, 75 ; exploits Brit. retention of Turkish battleships, 76 ; sends emissaries to Egypt, India, etc., 77, 89–90, 179, 186 ; Turkish Govt. prepared to support, 89 ; exploits neutral situation of Persia, 159, 192 ; subsidises plots in India, 309.

————, Ambassador. *See* " Bieberstein, Baron Marschall von."

————, Military Mission in Turkey. *See under* " Turkey."

————, Minister for Foreign Affairs. *See* " Jagow, Herr von."

————, Navy. *See* " *Breslau* " ; " *Goeben*."

Ghabishiya.
  Turkish supply *mahailas* stopped at, 192.

Ghadir.
  Turkish force at, 183, 221, inactivity of, 190, 224 ; Turks leave, for Illa, 225 ; Brit. post at, 228.

Ghazban. *See* " Shaikh Ghazban of the Bani Lam."

Ghulam Haidar, Sapper (17th S. & M.).
  Gallantry of, 149–50.

Ghulam Nabi, Havildar (17th S. & M.).
  Gallantry of, 149–50.

Gladstone, Mr. W. E.
  Anti-Turkish policy of, 36.

Goeben (German battle cruiser).
  Effect of arrival of, with *Breslau*, at Constantinople, 75 ; retention of crew of, 77, 97 ; in Black Sea, 98.
Goltz, Field-Marshal von der.
  Reorganises Turkish army (1883 and 1911), 26.
Gorringe, Major-Gen. G. F., C.B., C.M.G., D.S.O.
  In command of 33rd Inf. Brig., 188, 193 ; in command at Basra, 197 ; conducts operations in Arabistan, 224–34, force under, (1 May), Appendix V., 351–2 ; demonstration towards Amara, 231 ; leaves Ahwaz for Basra (15 June), 233 ; in command of advance to Nasiriya, 275–98 ; Gen. Nixon's instructions to, (23 June), 275 ; Operation Orders, 286–7, 291–2 ; Nasiriya, 300 ; in command of L. of C. troops at Amara, 314.
Grand Vizier of Turkey. *See* " Sa'id Halim."
Great Britain.
  Influence of Brit. interests on Turco-German plans of operation, 33–4 ; pre-war policy, 35–48 ; Agreement of 1907 with Russia, 36, 38, 53 ; relations of, with Turkey (1878), 36–7 ; decline of influence of, in Turkey, 37–9 ; Baghdad railway, policy of, 40–3 ; rights of, on waterways, 43–5 ; relations of, with Persian Gulf (from 1622), 45–7 ; results of intervention of, in Persian Gulf, 46 ; relations of, with Persia, 47–8 ; pre-war military policy of, in India, 49–74 ; Durand Frontier Agreement of 1893 with Afghanistan, 51 ; I.A. dependent upon, 64, 68 ; Turkey opposed to war with, 76 ; effect of retention by, of Turkish battleships, 76 ; preparations for defence of Persian Gulf, 78–80 ; asked to support formation of a United Arabian State, 83 ; Govt. of, orders a force to Persian Gulf, 91–2 ; declares war on Turkey, 98 ; *communiqué* of, *re* outbreak of war with Turkey, and assurance of respect for Holy Places, 110–2.

——————— ———————, Ambassador. *See* " Mallet, Sir Louis."
Greek Minister at Berlin.
  Informed by German Emperor of alliance with Turkey, 75.
Grey, Sir Edward (S. of S. for Foreign Affairs).
  Telegram to, of 27 August 1914, from Sir Louis Mallet, *cited*, 77 ; and closing of Dardanelles, 91.
Gunboats, river.
  Lack of, contributes to keep I.E.F. " D " on defensive, 134 *n* ; Admiralty asked to provide, 158 *n*, 169, two sink on passage in Red Sea, 236 *n* ; Admiralty arrange to send twelve, 236 *n*, despatched (July–August 1915), 342.
Gun Hill.
  Turkish position at, 190 ; capture of, 256.

H.

Haig, Lt.-Gen. Sir Douglas, K.C.B., K.C.I.E., K.C.V.O.
  On Indian assistance in event of war, 73.
Hallett, Lieut. C. G. (R.I.M.).
  Succeeds Lt.-Com. Seymour as S.N.O., E.B.F., 191.
Hamilton, Com. A. (R.I.M.).
  Marine Transport Officer with force, 102.
Hammar lake.
  Description and navigation of, 2 ; navigation difficulties affect reconnaissance, 158 ; impassable by steamers of over 3-ft. draught, 158 ; Turkish patrol boat on, 175 ; E.B.F. reconnoitres approaches to, 220, 223, 241 ; shallowness of, 276, 285, 311–2.

Hardinge of Penshurst, Lord (Viceroy of India, November 1910–April 1916).
   Views of, on strength of I.A., 73 ; and defence of Persian Gulf, 78–80, 83 ; telegram of 5 October 1914, 93–4 ; report of Sir P. Cox to, (23 November), 133–4 ; views of, (January 1915), on reinforcements, 161 ; visits Persian Gulf and Mesopotamia, 167–8, 170–2 ; views of, on increasing strength of I.E.F. " D," 168, 177, 186 ; evidence of, before Mesopotamia Commission, 170 ; visits Basra, 171 ; Memorandum of 3 March on future of Basra, 171 n ; discusses situation with Gen. Barrett and S.N.O., 172 ; impressions on, and results of visit to I.E.F. " D," 173 ; views of, on advance to Nasiriya and Amara, 186 ; relieved of responsibility for possible consequences of depletion of force in India, 188 ; Lord Crewe's telegram to, of 19 April, 222 ; correspondence *re* policy governing operations, 234–41 ; correspondence *re* advance to Nasiriya, 270 ; and proposed advance to Kut, 271, 273, 303–7 ; and Baghdad as probable ultimate objective, 272 n ; telegram of 27 July seeking I.O. sanction for advance to Kut, 303–4 ; letters of, on general situation, 304–5, 310–1 ; and withdrawal of Indian divisions from France, 310 ; and question of river transport, 340–2.

Harris, Lieut. W. V. H., R.N. (*Sumana*).
   In advance to Nasiriya, 293.

Hawiza.
   German agents in, 179.

Hayes-Sadler, Capt. A., R.N., (S.N.O., Persian Gulf).
   Ordered to commence hostilities against Turkey, 104 ; confers with Gen. Delamain (2 November 1914), 105 ; reaches Basra, 128 ; attends conference (6 December), 145 ; at surrender of Qurna, 151 ; hands over duties of S.N.O. to Com. Nunn (11 December), 157.

Heat. *See* " Weather."

Hejaz.
   Turkish plan for defence of, 162.

———— railway.
   Political importance of, 37.

Hewett, Capt. G. (48th Pioneers).
   In advance to Nasiriya, 293.

Hindiya barrage, 2.

Hirtzel, Sir F. A., K.C.B. (Political Secretary, I.O.).
   On measures for security of Persian Gulf, 80.

Hoghton, Brig.-Gen. F. A.
   In command of 17th Inf. Brig. at battle of Kut, 322–28.

Holderness, Sir T. W., K.C.B.
   Lord Hardinge's letter to, of 20 January 1915, on reinforcements, 161.

Holy Places of Islam.
   Statement in India (1 November 1914) as to immunity of from Brit. hostile action, 112, effect of, 162 ; Brit. control of, welcomed, 167.

Hong Kong.
   Reduction of Indian garrison in, 161.

Hor Bahmanshir river.
   As alternative to Shatt al Arab, 101.

Hor Musa.
   Espiègle on, 179.

Hospital ships.
   Provision of, 343. *See also* " *Bengali* " ; " *Madras*."

Houses. *See* " Buildings and houses."

INDEX

I.

Ibn Rashid.
 Hostility of, 15, 25; Turkish plan for co-operation of, 162; Ibn Saud claims to have defeated, 178.

Ibn Saud, Emir of Nejd.
 Ejects Turkish garrisons from Al Hasa in 1913, 14, 25; friendly attitude of, 14–5, 25; assistance of, 83, 156, 162, 171, 178; Major Shakespear's knowledge of, 86; reported intrigues of, with Enver Pasha, 89; Major Shakespear instructed to communicate with, 93–4; Major Shakespear reports on, (4 January 1915), 161–2, (19 January), 171; asks for treaty with Great Britain, 162; letters of, to Sir P. Cox (19 January), 171, (16 February), 178; effective assistance of, not to be expected, 178. *See also* "Nejd."

Illa (Arabistan).
 Turco-Arab force at, (end April 1915), 223, 225; Turkish force crosses Karkha at, 227; Brit. advance on, 227–8; Brit. force at, 231–2.

Imam Yahya.
 Turkish plan for co-operation of, 162.

Imperial Service Troops.
 Organisation of, 51–2; strength of, at outbreak of war, 63; employment of, outside India, 80–1.

India.
 The army in, and pre-war military policy, 49–74; Durand Frontier Agreement (1893), 51; effect of famine of 1896, on military estimates, 54; relations of, with Afghanistan, 60–1; pre-war internal situation in, 62, 64; population of, 62; pre-war output of military material, 68; arrangements for assistance of, in the event of war, 68–9, 73; effect on, of Turkish operations in Mesopotamia, 72; enemy emissaries in, 77–8, 86, 89–90; disquieting news from Mesopotamia received in, 77–8; employment of army of, outside, 80–1; Musalman feeling in, 82; Gen. Barrow, on "The rôle of India in a Turkish war," 86–8; internal situation in, affects reinforcements for I.E.F. "D," 134 *n*, 160, 177, 222; internal situation in, (February–March 1915), 179, 186, (April), 222, (May), 240, (August–September), 309–10; inception of the "East Persia Cordon," 274. *See also* "North-West Frontier of India."

——, General Staff.
 Responsibilities of, 69–70; views of, *re* advance to Nasiriya, 271; appreciations on question of advance to Kut and Baghdad, 271–3, 311.

——, Government of.
 Relations with the Persian Gulf mainly controlled by, 47; responsible for conduct of operations in Persian Gulf, 72, 93; refers preparations for defence of Persian Gulf to H.M. Govt., 78; agree to employment of troops outside India, 80–1; appreciation of 7 October 1914, 94; *communiqué re* outbreak of war with Turkey, and assurance as to British respect for Holy Places, 110–2; views of, on suggested advance to Baghdad, 135–7; Gen. Barrett not to advance without previous reference to, 156; policy of, in Mesopotamia (January 1915), 161; and reinforcing of I.E.F. "D," 165, 167–8, 177, 222; views of, on protection of oilfields, 167–8, 222; views of, on situation in Mesopotamia (2 March), 186; informed by S. of S. that troops for Aden or Mesopotamia must be found from India, 187; to send a brigade to Mesopotamia, 187–8; borrows aviators from Australia and New Zealand, 188; decides (18 March) to organise I.E.F. "D" as an A.C. under Gen. Nixon, 193; correspondence *re* policy governing operations, 234–41; arranges to reinforce medical services, 269; consideration of advance to Kut, 301–8; disapprove of proposed advance to Baghdad, 308; proposed withdrawal of Indian divisions from France, 310; reinforces I.E.F. "D" with Territorials, 338; and question of river transport, 340–2.

India, Viceroy of. *See* "Curzon of Kedleston, Lord"; "Hardinge of Penshurst, Lord."

Indian Army and Army in India.
Pre-war policy of, 49–74; formation of Staff Corps, 50; Organisation Committee of 1879, 50–1; division of, into four A.Cs. (1895), 51, reorganisation of, (1900–8), 53–7; "Army in India Committee" of 1912, 54, 57–9, 62, 67–8; pre-war military finance, 54, 57, 59; Lord Kitchener's scheme of reorganisation, 55–7; organisation criticised in Mesopotamia Commission Report, 55–6; Gen. Sir Power Palmer's scheme for reorganisation of, 56; "Army in India Committee" of 1912 and Lord Kitchener's scheme for reorganisation of, 58 n; effect of economy on, 59; strength of, 59; factors governing pre-war employment of, 60–2; attempts to corrupt the, 62, 192; strength and organisation of, on outbreak of war, 62–4; dependent for expansion upon the U.K., 64, 68; recruitment for, after 1858, 65; languages in, 65; military qualities of native soldiery, 65–6; services of, in Great War (message from H.M. The King Emperor), 66 n; value to, of Brit. officers, 66; W.O. demands upon, at outbreak of war, 66; qualifications of native officers, 66–7; Staff College and possible operations in Mesopotamia, 70 n; employment of, in Mesopotamia, considered, 72–3; Lord Hardinge's views on strength of, 73; employment of, outside India, 80–2; difficulty of sending a third inf. div. to Europe, 86; demands upon, by Home Govt., 90; replaced by Brit. Territorials, 90, 167; shortage of Brit. officers in, 160; uncertain attitude of Mahomedan troops, 186. *See also* "Conscription"; "Imperial Service Troops"; "Man-power"; "Sappers and Miners."

Indian Expeditionary Force "A."
Govt. of India agree to employment of, in Europe, 80; dates of embarkation of, 82, 90, 103; composition of, 80, 90; replaced by Territorials, 90; strength of drafts from India for, 160 n.

——— ——— ——— "B."
Govt. of India agree to employment of, in East Africa, 80; suggested diversion of, to Persian Gulf, 81; despatch of, to German East Africa, 82–3,103.

——— ——— ——— "D." *See under separate headings.*

Indian Marine. *See* "Royal Indian Marine."

India Office.
Control of operations in Persian Gulf by, 72; Mr. Chamberlain on organisation of, 72; views of, on suggested advance to Baghdad, 135–7; vetoes advance to Baghdad, but sanctions advance to Qurna, 137; correspondence *re* occupation of the Basra *vilayet*, 234–41; considerations on advance to Kut, 303–7. *See also* "Barrow, Gen."; "Chamberlain, The Rt. Hon. J. Austen"; "Crewe, Lord"; "Hirtzel, Sir A."

Infantry, British, Regiments.
Norfolk, 2nd Bn.—In 18th Inf. Brig., 113; action of Sahil, 119–24; advance to Basra, 128 n; advance on, and capture of Qurna, 141–51; action at Ruta, 163–5, with E.B.F., 191, Shaiba, 197; battle of Shaiba, 201–19; Zubair, 220; advance to Amara, 251–64; reach Amara, 263; advance to Nasiriya, 289–98; battle of Kut, 314–38.
Hampshire, 1st/4th.—In 33rd Inf. Brig., 188, 193 n; with E.B.F. 191, 197 n; Basra, 197; Arabistan operations with 30th Inf. Brig., 225–33, Appendix V., 351; ordered to Basra, 231; advance to, and capture of Amara, 262; sickness in, 269, 276; advance to Nasiriya, 276–98, casualties, 293, 297; Nasiriya, 300; battle of Kut, 314–38.

INDEX 379

Infantry, British, Regiments—*cont.*

Dorsetshire, 2nd Bn.—In 16th Inf. Brig., 99 ; capture of Fao, 106–8 ; action of Saihan, 115–8 ; action of Sahil, 119–24 ; casualties of, at Sahil, 124 *n* ; Ahwaz, 169, 174, action near Ahwaz, 183–5 ; action near Shaiba, 181–3 ; Shaiba, 197 ; battle of Shaiba, 201–19, casualties, 216 ; advance to Amara, 251–64 ; Ali Gharbi, 301 ; battle of Kut, 314–38.

Oxfordshire and Buckinghamshire Light Infantry, 1st Bn.—In 17th Inf. Brig. 140 ; action at Ruta, 163–5 ; Qurna, 197, 241 ; with E.B.F., 220 ; in *Shushan*, 245 ; advance to Amara, 251–64 ; Amara, 301 ; battle of Kut, 314–38.

Queen's Own Royal West Kent, 2nd Bn.—In 12th Inf. Brig., 166 ; Ahwaz, 197, 224 ; Arabistan operations, 225–33, Appendix V., 351 ; advance to, and capture of Amara, 262 ; advance to Nasiriya, 286–98, casualties, 297 ; Nasiriya, 300 ; battle of Kut, 314–38.

———, Indian, Divisions.

6th (Poona).—Probable employment of, in Persian Gulf, 89 ; mobilization of, 99 ; held in readiness to reinforce I.E.F. " D," 99 ; first portion of, (16th Inf. Brig.), lands at Sanniya (8–10 November 1914), 108 ; 18th Inf. Brig. arrives off Shatt al Arab (13 November), 110–4 ; 17th Inf. Brig. arrives off Shatt al Arab (end November), 140–1 ; success of first phase of operations of, 153 ; disposition of, (4 February 1915), 170 ; commanded temporarily by Gen. Fry, 199 ; in battle of Kut as a complete formation, 314.

12th.—Gen. Gorringe in command of, 223 *n*, 224 ; three bns. ordered to Basra, 233, battle of Kut, 314–38.

———, ———, Brigades.

12th.—Held in readiness to reinforce I.E.F. " D," 165 ; composition of, 166 ; arrangements made to leave India by 1 February 1915, 166, 170 ; arrive Basra, 173 ; two bns. arrive Qurna (10 February), 174 ; Ahwaz, 197, 224 ; Arabistan operations, 225–34 ; Appendix V., 351 ; advance to Nasiriya, 286–98 ; Nasiriya, 300 ; battle of Kut, 314–38.

16th.—Ordered to Persian Gulf, 92 ; composition of, 99, 197 *n*, Appendix II., 346 ; armament and equipment of, 102 ; capture of Fao, 106–8 ; action of Saihan, 115–8 ; action of Sahil, 120–4 ; reinforces Shaiba, 178 ; Shaiba, 197 ; battle of Shaiba, 201–19 ; advance to Amara, 251–64 ; Ali Gharbi, 301 ; battle of Kut, 314–38 ; embarkation strength of, Appendix II., 346.

17th.—Arrangements made for despatch of, 113 ; composition of, 140, 197 ; arrives in Shatt al Arab, 140 ; action at Ruta, 163–5 ; Qurna, 197, 241 ; advance to Amara, 249–64 ; to lead advance of 1 June 1915, 258 *n* ; Amara, 301 ; battle of Kut, 314–38.

18th.—Under orders to reinforce I.E.F. " D," 112 ; composition of, 113 ; action of Sahil, 120–4 ; Shaiba, 197 ; one bn. (7th Rajputs) at Basra, 197 ; battle of Shaiba, 201–19 ; Zubair, 220 ; Fort George, 241 ; advance to Nasiriya, 289–98 ; battle of Kut, 314–38.

28th.—Proposed reinforcements of I.E.F. " D " by, 303–5 ; Aden, 304.

30th.—From Egypt to reinforce I.E.F. " D," 189, 193 ; composition of, 196 ; arrives Basra (6 April 1915), 196 ; ordered to Shaiba, 199 ; battle of Shaiba, 204–5 ; Arabistan operations, 225–31, Appendix V., 351 ; ordered to Basra, 231 ; advance to Nasiriya, 276–98 ; sickness in, 276 ; Nasiriya, 300 ; battle of Kut, 314–38.

33rd.—Under orders to reinforce I.E.F. " D," 188 ; bulk of, arrives Basra (17–25 March 1915), 193 ; remainder arrive Basra (9 April), 193 *n*, 196 ; dispositions of, (11 April), 197 ; Ahwaz, 197, 224 ; Arabistan force, 225, Appendix V., 352 ; composition of, at Ahwaz (20 June), 234 ; sickness in, 269, 276 ; Basra, 301 ; battle of Kut, 314–38.

Infantry, Indian, Regiments.
- *4th Prince Albert Victor's Rajputs.*—In 12th Inf. Brig., 166; Ahwaz, 174, 197, 224; action near Ahwaz, 183–5; Arabistan operations, 225–33, Appendix V., 351; in 33rd Inf. Brig. at Ahwaz, 234; Basra, 301; battle of Kut, 314–38.
- *7th Duke of Connaught's Own Rajputs.*—In 18th Inf. Brig., 113; action of Sahil, 119–24; attack on, and capture of Qurna, 144–51; action at Ruta, 163–5; ordered to Ahwaz, 168–9; Ahwaz, 174; action near Ahwaz, 183–5; Basra, 197; Zubair, 220; Fort George, 241; battle of Kut, 314–38.
- *11th Rajputs.*—In 33rd Inf. Brig., 188, 193 n; arrive Basra (9 April 1915), 196; Basra, 197, 301; Arabistan operations, 225–33, Appendix V., 352; Ahwaz, 234; Bushire, 309.
- *20th Duke of Cambridge's Own Infantry (Brownlow's Punjabis).*—In 16th Inf. Brig., 99; capture of Fao, 106–8; successful counter-attack by, night 10–11 November 1914, 109; action of Saihan, 115–8; action of Sahil, 119–24; Shaiba, 141 n; Basra, 197, 197 n; volunteers from, propel *bellums* to Shaiba, 205, casualties, 205; Qala Salih, 301; battle of Kut, 314–38.
- *22nd Punjabis.*—In 17th Inf. Brig., 140; action at Ruta, 163–5; Qurna, 197, 241–2; advance to Amara, 251–64; the " River Column," 300; Ali Gharbi, 301; battle of Kut, 314–38.
- *24th Punjabis.*—In 30th Inf. Brig., 196; Basra, 197; ordered to Shaiba, 199; battle of Shaiba, 204–19, casualties, 216; Arabistan operations, 225–31, Appendix V., 351; ordered to Basra, 231; advance to Nasiriya, 276–98, casualties, 289–90; Nasiriya, 300; battle of Kut, 314–38.
- *43rd Erinpura Regiment.*—Replace 11th Rajputs, 309.
- *44th Merwara Infantry.*—In 12th Inf. Brig., 166; Ahwaz, 197, 224; Arabistan operations, 225–34, Appendix V., 351; Ghadir, 228; advance to Nasiriya, 286–98; Nasiriya, 300; battle of Kut, 314–38.
- *48th Pioneers.*—In 6th (Poona) Division, 113; action of Sahil, 119–24‡; Shaiba, 197; battle of Shaiba, 201–19; Arabistan operations, 225–34, Appendix V., 352; advance to Amara, 251–64; advance to Nasiriya, 276–98; battle of Kut, 314–38.
- *66th Punjabis.*—In 33rd Inf. Brig., 188, 193 n; with E.B.F., 191–197; disposition of, (11 April, 1915), 197; Arabistan operations, 225–33, Appendix V., 352; Ahwaz, 234; Qurna and Basra, 301.
- *67th Punjabis.*—In 33rd Inf. Brig., 188, 193 n; Ahwaz, 197, 224; Arabistan operations, 225–33, Appendix V., 351; arrive Amara, 233; advance to Nasiriya, 286–98, casualties, 290; in 12th Inf. Brig., 286 n; Nasiriya, 300.
- *76th Punjabis.*—In 30th Inf. Brig., 196; Basra, 197; ordered to Shaiba, 199; battle of Shaiba, 204–19; Arabistan operations, 225–31, Appendix V., 351, gallantry of, 230, casualties, 230–1; ordered to Basra, 231; advance to Nasiriya, 276–98, casualties, 282, 290; Nasiriya, 300; battle of Kut, 314–38.
- *90th Punjabis.*—In 12th Inf. Brig., 166; ordered to reinforce Ahwaz, 185; Ahwaz, 197, 224; Arabistan operations, 225–33, Appendix V., 351; arrive Amara, 233; advance to Nasiriya, 286, casualties, 290; Nasiriya, 300.
- *96th Berar Infantry.*—Bushire, 274, 301; operations at Dilwar, 309.
- *103rd Mahratta Light Infantry.*—In 17th Inf. Brig., 140; action at Ruta, 163–5; Qurna, 197, 241; with E.B.F., 220; advance to Amara, 251–64; Amara, 301; battle of Kut, 314–38.
- *104th Wellesley's Rifles.*—In 16th Inf. Brig., 99; action of Saihan, 115–8; action of Sahil, 119–24; advance on, and capture of Qurna, 141–51; Shaiba, 197; battle of Shaiba, 201–19; advance to Amara, 251–64; Ali Gharbi, 301; battle of Kut, 314–38.

INDEX 381

Infantry, Indian, Regiments—*cont.*

110th Mahratta Light Infantry.—In 18th Inf. Brig., 113 ; action of Sahil, 119–24 ; Basra, 128 *n* ; advance on, and capture of Qurna, 141–51 ; Shaiba, 197 ; battle of Shaiba, 201–19 ; Zubair, 220 ; Fort George, 241 ; advance to Nasiriya, 289–98 ; battle of Kut, 314–38.

117th Mahrattas.—In 16th Inf. Brig., 99 ; capture of Fao, 106–8 ; repels Turkish night attack, 10–11 November 1914, 109 ; action of Sahil, 119–24 ; Kurmat Ali, 175, 178 ; Shaiba, 197 ; battle of Shaiba, 201–19 ; Qurna, 248 ; Ali Gharbi, 301 ; battle of Kut, 314–38, casualties, 326, 338.

119th Infantry (The Mooltan Regiment).—In 17th Inf. Brig., 140 ; action at Ruta, 163–5 ; posted to 16th Inf. Brig. at Shaiba, 197 *n* ; battle of Shaiba, 201–19 ; Qurna, 247 ; advance to Amara, 251–64 ; Amara, 301 ; battle of Kut, 314–38.

120th Rajputana Infantry.—In 18th Inf. Brig., 113 ; action of Sahil, 119–24 ; advance on, and capture of Qurna, 144–51 ; Shaiba, 197 ; battle of Shaiba, 201–19, casualties, 216 ; Zubair, 220 ; advance to Nasiriya, 289–98 ; battle of Kut, 314–38.

2nd Bn. 7th Gurkha Rifles.—In 30th Inf. Brig., 196 ; Basra, 197 ; ordered to Shaiba, 199 ; battle of Shaiba, 204–19 ; Arabistan operations, 225–31, Appendix V., 351 ; ordered to Basra, 231 ; advance to Nasiriya, 276–98 ; Nasiriya, 300 ; battle of Kut, 314–38.

Infantry, Turkish.
Strength of, 29–30.

————, ————, Divisions.

35th.—In XIIth A.C., 156 ; ordered to Mesopotamia, 170 *n* ; location of, 178, 180 ; retires on Kut (end July 1915), 301 ; battle of Kut, 317.

36th.—In XIIth A.C., 156 ; reported in the Caucasus, 177.

37th.—Reported at Mosul moving towards Erzerum, 103–4 ; reported in Caucasus, 165, 177 ; at or near Baghdad (end July 1915), 301.

38th.—Only regular division in Mesopotamia at end of October 1914, 104 ; located after capture of Qurna, 154 ; in Turkish force at Nasiriya, 170 *n*, 180 ; at or near Kut (end July 1915), 301 ; battle of Kut, 317.

————, ————, Regiments.

11th Depôt.—Sent to Mosul, 32.

26th.—One bn. of, Basra (October 1914), 100 ; action of Sahil, 124 ; a number of, captured at Qurna, 151 ; *en route* for Nasiriya, 170 *n*.

112th.—Two bns. of, Basra and Zubair (October 1914), 100 ; action of Sahil, 124.

113th.—Locality of, (October 1914), 100 ; action of Sahil, 124.

114th.—Locality of, (October 1914), 100, 104 ; action of Sahil, 124.

Fire Brigade.—Mobilization and despatch of, under Ali Bey, 127, 170 *n* ; reach Nasiriya, 170 *n* ; surrender of, at Amara, 262.

Murattab.—A number of, captured at Qurna, 151.

————, ————, Battalion.

Osmanjik.—Under orders for Mesopotamia, 170 *n*.

Information.
Obtained from prisoners, 109, 116, 154 ; from G.O.C. Egypt as to movements of IVth Turkish A.C., 155 ; Turkish movements (January, 1915), 165 ; obtained by aircraft, 258, 261.

Irrigation.
Hindiya barrage, 2 ; agriculture in Iraq dependent upon, 9 ; Akaika channel dam, 277–8.

Isfahan (Persia).
German activities in, 274, 307 *n*.

J.

Jagow, Herr von (German Minister for Foreign Affairs).
Asks Turkey to declare war on Russia (4 August 1914), 75.

Jahad.
Possibility of a, 72, 82, 90, 160, 174 ; Arab co-operation, means of preventing, 84 ; preaching of, at Nasiriya, 158 ; possibility of a, assisted by Brit. inactivity, 161 ; receiving no support in S. Nejd, 162 ; Bani Turuf join Turks on call of, 166 ; effect of, at Ahwaz, 167 ; effect of, at Basra, 170 ; Turks press Sharif of Mecca to proclaim, 171 ; on N.W. Frontier of India, 186–7 ; decrease of enthusiasm for, at Ghadir, 190 ; refusal of Amir of Afghanistan to proclaim, 304 ; expected on 15 August 1915 on N.W. Frontier of India, 309–10.

Jaipur Imperial Service Transport Corps.
In 6th Div., 113.

Jamal Pasha.
Reported leaving Syria for Mesopotamia with Turkish reinforcements, 313.

Jask.
W/T station at, 103 *n*.

John O'Scott, s.s.
Turkish blockship in Shatt al Arab, 127.

Julnar (river steamer).
With I.E.F. " D," 339.

Juno, H.M.S. (light cruiser).
Operations at Dilwar, 309.

K.

Kabul.
Arms factory at, 61.

Kaiser, The. *See* " Wilhelm II, Emperor of Germany."

Karachi.
Embarkation of I.E.F. " D " at, 102–3, 113. *See also* " Bombay."

Karka river.
Turkish force reaches, (10 February 1915), 174 ; strength of Turkish force in camp on, 179 ; operations of Arabistan force, 225–34 ; flying bridges across, 227–9 ; description of, 227, 228 *n*.

Karun river.
Description and navigation of, 1 ; Turkish threat to intern Brit. warship lying in, 97 ; movements of *Comet* in, 166 ; naval reconnaissance of, 179.

Kemball, Major-Gen. G. V., C.B., D.S.O.
Memorandum on river transport by, 340–2.

Kennedy, Brig.-Gen. H.
Commands 6th Cav. Brig., 178 *n* ; battle of Shaiba, 205–19 ; Arabistan operations, 225–34, Appendix V., 351 ; instructions to, for advance on Amara, 232.

Khafajiya (Arabistan).
Turks retire beyond, 228 ; Brit. advance to, 228–31 ; fighting at, (14–16 May 1915), 229–31 ; Brit. force at, 231–2.

Khamisiya.
Turks retire to, after battle of Shaiba, 218 ; E.B.F. to operate against Turks at, 220 ; Turkish force at, 223.

Khaniqin.
Turkish force at, 313.

INDEX

Kifl.
   Turkish force at, 313.
Kiln Post.
   H.Q. established at, 205.
Kitchener of Khartoum, Lord.
   I.A. reorganisation, scheme of, 55–7, criticised by "Army in India Committee" of 1912, 58 n; agrees to scheme for operations against Turkey, 71; Sir B. Duff's telegram to, of 5 January 1915 *re* reinforcements, 160; informs Sir B. Duff of intention to bombard Dardanelles, 177; movements of 28th Inf. Brig., 304–5; withdrawal of Indian divisions from France, 310.
Köhler, Colonel.
   Reorganisation of Turkish army under, (1882–3), 26.
Kumait.
   Brit. advanced post at, 299, evacuated, 300.
Kurma Safha channel.   See "Akaika channel."
Kurmat Ali.
   Confluence of Euphrates and Tigris at, 1; Brit. post established at, 175, 178; detachment from, attacks Turkish *mahailas*, 181, 191; E.B.F. despatched from, (11 March 1915), 191, returns to, 192; Brit. force at, (11 April), 197.
Kut al Amara.
   Turkish force at, (June 1915), 269; Gen. Nixon's views on occupation of, 270–1, 273, 301–7; India and I.O. averse to proposed advance to, 271, 304; route from, to Nasiriya, 271; considerations on advance to, 272–3, 301–7; strategic importance of, 272, 303; Turks retire towards, 300; Turkish force at or near, (end July), 301, (beginning September), 313; Govt. of India agree (5 August) with Gen. Nixon's views on advance to, 306; advance to, sanctioned, 307; battle of, (28 September 1915), 314–38; Brit. force enters, (29 September), 336; Gen. Nixon at, 337.
Kuwait.
   Arab State of, 14.   *See also* "Shaikh of Kuwait."

L.

Lake, Lt.-Gen. Sir P. H. N., K.C.B., K.C.M.G. (C.G.S. India).
   Member of "Army in India Committee" of 1912, 58; Persian Gulf question referred to in 1911, 73; asks C.I.G.S. for an appreciation of Turkish intentions, 179; views of, on probable Turkish attack on Basra, 180; appreciation of situation in Mesopotamia, (31 March 1915), 195–6.
Language, English.
   Extended use of, in India, 62.
Languages.
   In I.A., 65, 65 n.
Lawrence (R.I.M. paddle steamer).
   Preparations for despatch of, to Shatt al Arab, 79; ordered to Shatt al Arab, 84; arrives Abadan, 85; passes obstruction in Shatt al Arab, 128; attack on Qurna, 141–51; conference held on, 145; advance to Amara, 251–64; sent to Bushire, 268; operations at Dilwar, 309.
Lean, Brig.-Gen. K. E., C.B.
   In command of 12th Inf. Brig. at Ahwaz, 222, 224; Arabistan operations, 225–32, Appendix V., 351; on sick list, 232.
Lewis Pelly (armed launch).
   Action at Sahil, 119–24; advance on, and capture of Qurna, 141–51; Qurna, 219; as reserve mine-sweeper, 255 n.

Looting.
>By Arabs, of Basra, 127–8, at Amara, 263.

Loring, Capt. E. J., R.E. (17th S. & M.).
>In advance to Nasiriya, 293.

Lynch, Capt. (Indian Marine), 44.

Lynch & Co.
>Rights of navigation of, 44 ; coal belonging to, at Basra, requisitioned by Turks, 78 ; steamers of, held up, 78, 84, requisitioned, 125.

M.

Machine gun companies.
>Turkish strength of, 30.

Madras (hospital ship), 343.

Mahailas (native craft).
>Description of, 2 *n*, 130 ; Qurna, 149 ; Turkish supply, action against, (3 March 1915), 181, 191 ; (12 March) Nukhaila, 192 ; battle of Shaiba, 202 ; sunk and captured by E.B.F. (15–16 April), 219 ; use of, in offensive up Tigris, 246–7 ; enemy, captured, etc., in advance to Amara, 259–60, 265 ; use of, in advance to Nasiriya, 277–98.

Mahomedans, Indian. *See* " Musalmans."

Mahsoudi (sternwheel river steamer).
>Advance to Nasiriya, 276–98 ; armament of, 276–7.

Maiyadiya creek.
>Turkish position at, 292 ; captured, 293.

Majinina creek.
>Turkish position near, 283–4 ; barge grounded across and position captured, 293–4.

Malamir (river steamer).
>Requisitioned, 125 ; advance on, and capture of Qurna, 141–51 ; advance on Nasiriya, 277–98 ; arrives Sannaiyat with Gen. Nixon, 316 ; Gen. Nixon's H.Q. in, battle of Kut, 331 *n*.

Mallet, Sir Louis, G.C.M.G., C.B. (Brit. Ambassador to Turkey).
>Statement of Grand Vizier to, 77 ; accurately gauges situation in Turkey, 77 ; reports on conditions in Baghdad, 85 ; report of, (29 September 1914), 91 ; report on Turkish military preparations, 96, 98.

Man-power.
>In India of Europeans and Anglo-Indians in 1914, 62 ; of native population, 64 ; full exploitation of, not considered before great war, 65. *See also* " Afghan Army " ; " Indian Army " ; "Turkish Army" ; " Population."

Maps, charts.
>Of Arabistan, inaccurate, 226 *n* ; of Tigris, 259 ; aerial, of enemy position at Kut, 315, 321 ; sketch, battle of Kut, 323.

Maqil.
>Port facilities at, 129, 342 ; camp formed at, 140.

Marches.
>From Sahil to Basra, 128–9 ; from Basra to Shwaibda, 176 ; Arabistan force, 225 ; from Bisaitin to Amara (9–14 June 1915), 233 ; Brit. force in advance to Kut, 315.

Marid.
>Brit. garrison posted at, 179 ; Ahwaz reinforced from, 185.

Marling, Mr. C. M., C.B., C.M.G. (Brit. Minister at Tehran).
>Reports on situation in Persia, 274, 307 *n*.

INDEX 385

Marmariss (Turkish gunboat).
    In Mesopotamian waters, 31 ; early preparation of, 78 ; *Odin* ordered to watch, 79 ; retires on Qurna, 140 ; near Ezra's Tomb, 141 ; driven up Tigris during action at Qurna, 152 ; near Peardrop Bend, 190–1 ; near Qurna, 223 ; shelled during advance to Amara, 259 ; overtaken and captured, 260, 265.

Marshes.
    Cavalry unable to penetrate, 163.

Martinsyde aeroplanes.
    Four arrive Basra (28 August 1915), 339 ; unsuited for Mesopotamia, 339 *n*. *See also* " Aircraft."

Mashona (armed launch).
    Armed by *Ocean*, 105 ; attack on Fao, 107–8.

Mashuf (native craft).
    Description of, 152 *n*.

Mauritius.
    Govt. of India agree to employment of troops in, 81.

Mazliq channel.
    Navigation of, 275.

Maxim Battery.
    Arabistan operations, 225, Appendix V., 352 ; Nasiriya operations, 289 ; battle of Kut, 314–38.

McMahon, Lt.-Col. Sir A. H., G.C.V.O., K.C.I.E., C.S.I.
    Persian Gulf question referred to, in 1911, 73.

Mears, Major C. D., M.V.O. (16th Cavalry).
    In battle of Kut, 318 *n*, 329–38.

Mechanical transport. *See* " Transport, mechanical."

Medical Services, Indian Army.
    Brit. officers with, at outbreak of war, 64 ; pre-war organisation, and dependance of, upon Great Britain, 67–8 ; in Basra, 132 ; Lord Hardinge's visit to, in Mesopotamia, 172 ; with Arabistan force, 232, 234 ; India unable to send sufficient units, 232 ; Gen. Nixon asks for more, (18 June 1915), 269 ; battle of Kut, 336–7.

———— ————, Turkish Army.
    State of, at outbreak of war, 30.

Mejidieh (river steamer).
    Requisitioned, 125 ; reaches Basra, 128 ; advance on, and capture of Qurna, 141–51 ; attack at Ruta, 163–5 ; advance to Amara, 252–64 ; advance to Nasiriya, 277–98 ; pursuit after battle of Kut, 337.

Melliss, Major-Gen. C. J., V.C., C.B.
    In command of 30th Inf. Brig., 196 ; assumes command of 6th Div., 199, 205 ; battle of Shaiba, 203–19 ; Arabistan operations, 225–31, Appendix V., 351 ; ordered to Basra, 231 ; advance to Nasiriya, 276–98.

Mesopotamia Commission.
    Criticism of I.A. system, 55–6 ; Lord Hardinge's evidence, 73 ; Lord Crewe's evidence, 95 *n*, 235 ; Sir B. Duff's evidence, 55, 59, 63, 133, 196 ; Sir J. Nixon's evidence, 196 ; report *quoted*, 220 ; Gen. Barrow's evidence, 237 ; river transport, 269, 341–2 ; arrangements for evacuation of wounded after battle of Kut, 336–7.

———— ————, Naval forces in. *See* " Navy, The Royal, co-operation of."

Meyer, Sir W. S., K.C.I.E., K.C.S.I.
    Member of " Army in India Committee " of 1912, 58.

Miner (armed launch).
    Advance on, and capture of Qurna, 141–51 ; damaged, 143–4 ; attack at Ruta, 163–5 ; Qurna (11–13 April 1915), 219 ; advance to Amara, 251–64 ; advance to Nasiriya, 276–98.

Mines, Turkish.
   In Tigris, 179, 191, 219, 256 ; damages bridge of boats near Qurna, 219; Germans assist Turks with, 236 ; in Akaika channel, 241, 279.
Mirage.
   At Saihan, 117 ; effects of, 117–8, at action of Sahil, 123, at Muzaira'a, 142, 146–7, at action near Shaiba, 182, at battle of Shaiba, 202, 207, 211, 213–4, 216, at battle of Kut, 326–8, 330.
Mobilization, Turkish.
   Effect of, on civil population, 31 ; ordered on 31 July 1914 to commence on 3 August, 76 ; initiated and carried out by Germans, 76 ; in Mesopotamia, 77.
Mohmands (N.W. Frontier tribe).
   Activity of, (18 April 1915), affects reinforcements for Mesopotamia, 222 ; activity of, (June), 270.
Mohammerah.
   Confluence of Karun river with Shatt al Arab at, 1 ; suggested diversion of Force " B " to, 81 ; Lynch & Co's steamers sent to, 84 ; *Odin* arrives at, 85 ; *Espiègle* arrives at, 91 ; right of access to, 96 ; Gen. Barrett asks for reinforcements for protection of, (26 January 1915), 165 ; Brit. troops sent to, 166. *See also* " Shaikh of Mohammerah " ; " Shatt al Arab."
Molesworth, Lt.-Col., R.P. (R.G.A.).
   Succeeds Major Farmar in command of E.B.F., 191.
Morley of Blackburn, Lord.
   On railways in Turkish territory, 40–2.
Moslems.
   Anti-Brit. sentiments of, 78 ; uncertainty of, in India, 82 ; immunity of Holy Places of, 112.
Mosul.
   Turkish force probably at, 313.
Mosul (Turkish river steamer).
   Shelled during advance to Amara, 259 ; captured, 260.
Mud.
   Impedes operations at Sahil, 121, of Basra Movable Column, 176.
Muhaisin tribe.
   Remains loyal to Shaikh of Mohammerah, 187.
Muhammad Amin, Staff Bimbashi (Turkish Historian).
   Pamphlet, Appendix VI., 352–5.
Mule Corps, 10th.
   In 6th Div., 113.
———   ———, 12th.
   In 6th Div., 113.
Muntafik (Arab Confederation).
   Hostile to Great Britain, 15 ; force of Shaikh Ajaimi located at Nasiriya, 154, 170 *n* ; attitude of, 155 ; area occupied by, 155 *n* ; Nasiriya, H.Q. of the, 270. *See also* " Shaikh Ajaimi of Muntafik."
Murray, Lt.-Gen. Sir J. Wolfe, K.C.B. (C.I.G.S.).
   Asked by C.G.S., India, for an appreciation of Turkish intentions, 179 ; reply sent (1 March 1915), 180 ; letter from Gen. Townshend to, on advance to Baghdad, 312.
Musalmans.
   Feeling of, in India, 82, 90 *n* ; Holy Places of, statement as to immunity of, from Brit. hostile action, 112.
Muzaffari (sternwheel river steamer).
   With E.B.F., 191 ; advance to Amara, 257–64 ; advance to Nasiriya, 276–98 ; armament of, 277 ; damaged, 294.

INDEX 387

Muzaibila.
  Minor operations near, (1 January 1915), 157 ; Turkish troops move from on Ahwaz, 174 ; Turkish position at, 243 ; evacuated, 258.

Muzaira'a.
  Strength of Turkish force at, 141-2, 145, 148 ; action at, and retirement from, (4 December 1914), 141-4 ; Turks reoccupy, (6 December), 145 ; action at, and capture of, (7-8 December), 145-7 ; Turks retreat from, 147 ; Brit. troops withdrawn to camp near, 148, 151 ; casualties at, (7 December), 148 ; Turkish night attack on, (29-30 January 1915), 166 ; Brit. force at, (4 February), 170 ; strength of Turkish force near, (4 February), 170 ; Brit. withdraw from owing to floods, 175,179.

N.

Nasiriya.
  Turkish force at, 138, 154, 170, 170 n, 178, 190, 223, 269 ; occupation of, mooted, 154-5 ; Shaikh Ajaimi located at, 154, 158 ; Gen. Barrett recommends advance to, 156 ; strategic importance of, 156, 271 ; reported Turkish advance from, to Basra, 158 ; Sir P. Cox urges advance to, 161, 168 ; Govt. of India's policy, (January 1915), *re* advance to, 161 ; Arab force reported to have left, 168 ; views of S. of S. and Viceroy on advance to, 186 ; Turkish force advance from, 193 ; advance to, by water, impossible, 223 ; Turks retire from, 241 ; advance to, sanctioned (22 June), 270 ; H.Q. of Muntafik tribes, 270 ; route from, to Kut, 271 ; the advance to, and occupation of, (27 June-25 July), 274-98 ; description of, 298 ; Brit. force at, (end July), 300 ; considerations of withdrawal from, 305-6 ; units of 6th Div. at, transferred to Amara, 311.

Nasratabad (Seistan).
  Force despatched to, from India, 308.

Nasrulla.
  Anti-Brit. influence of, 60 ; controls pro-Afghan agencies, 61 ; activity of, 310.

Navigation.
  Shatt al Arab, 1-2 ; Karun, 1 ; Euphrates, 2-3, 223 ; Hammar lake, 2, 158 ; Tigris, 3-4, 259 n ; Shatt al Hai, 4, 178 n ; difficulties in 1914, 4 ; Brit. rights of, 43-5 ; difficulties of, during advance to Amara, 259-60.

Navy, The Royal.
  In Mesopotamia (1 December 1914), Appendix III., 349.

———, ———, Co-operation of.
  Fao, 106-8 ; Saihan, 116 ; Sahil, 119-24 ; advance on, and capture of, Qurna, 141-51 ; Muzaibila, 157 ; Ruta, 163-5 ; action near Nukhaila, 181 ; Qurna, (11-13 April 1915), 219 ; against Bawi tribesmen, 221 ; takes over duties of E.B.F., 241 ; advance on, and capture of Amara, 251-64 ; advance to Nasiriya, 275-98 ; advance to Kut, 314-38. See also " *Alert* " ; " *Bahrein* " ; " *Clio* " ; " *Comet* " ; " *Dalhousie* " ; " *Espiègle* " ; " *Julnar* " ; " *Juno* " ; " *Lawrence* " ; " *Lewis Polly* " ; " *Mashona* " ; " *Miner* " ; " *Muzaffari* " ; " *Ocean* " ; " *Odin* " ; " *Pyramus* " ; " *Salimi* " ; " *Shaitan* " ; " *Shirin* " ; " *Shuhrur* " ; " *Shushan* " ; " *Sirdar-i-Naphte* " ; " *Sumana* " ; " *Varela.* "

———, Turkish.
  In Mesopotamia, 31 ; controlled by Germans, 91 ; raid in Black Sea, 98 ; losses, of armed launches, 108-9, 126, 152, capture of Amara, 265, advance to Nasiriya, 296. See also " *Basra* " ; " *Breslau* " ; " *Bulbul* " ; " *Frat* " ; " *Goeben* " ; " *Marmariss* " ; " *Mosul* " ; " *Pioneer* " ; " *Risafa.* "

HISTORY OF THE WAR: MESOPOTAMIA

Nejd.
   System of government, 15; Turkish garrisons expelled from, (1831), 25; attitude of, towards a *Jahad*, 162. *See also* " Ibn Saud."

Nepal Durbar.
   Gives a Gurkhar contingent for service in India, 160.

Neutrality.
   Of Turkey, 76–7, 84–6; of Afghanistan, 79, 310; alleged violation of, by *Odin*, 85; of Persia, 93, 159, 192.

New Zealand.
   Govt. of India borrow aviators from, 188, 339.

Nicholson of Roundhay, Field-Marshal Lord.
   President of " Army in India Committee " of 1912, 58, 67.

Night operations.
   10–11 November 1914, Sanniya, 109; 29–30 January 1915, Muzaira'a, 166; battle of Shaiba, 203; in Arabistan, 227, 232–3; advance to Amara, 253, 259; advance to Nasiriya, 285–7; advance to Kut, 319, 321–2.

Nixon, Gen. Sir John E., K.C.B.
   To command I.E.F. " D," 193; arrives Basra (9 April 1915), 194, 196; instructions to, 194–6; evidence of, before Mesopotamia Commission, 196; arrives Bushire (5 April), 196; Shaiba, 199, 203–4; decides to reduce force at Shaiba (17 April), 219; demands for river transport, 220, 268, 339; orders blockade of Euphrates, 220; decides on operations in Arabistan, 221–2, 224; asks for reinforcements (19 April), and India's refusal (22 April), 222; sends Gen. Townshend to report on situation at Qurna, 223; orders to Gen. Gorringe, 224, 231; appreciation of 17 May, 235–6, 247; assures India no reinforcements required for advance to Amara, 236; informed (23 May) no more troops could be sent him, 237; importance of protecting oil pipe-line impressed upon, 237; asks for definite orders *re* occupation of Amara and Nasiriya, 237; views of, on advance to Amara and Nasiriya, 238; instructions to, (27 May), 238–9; C.-in-C., India, agrees with views of, 239, 271; Gen. Townshend reports to, (27 April), 243; informs India (27 April) no urgency for operations on Tigris, 244; issues definite orders for offensive up Tigris (11 May), 245–6; approves Gen. Townshend's plan of operations, 246; visits Qurna (12 May), 247; decides against postponing attack, 248; at Qurna (30 May), 249; arrives Amara (4 June), 263; on success of operations up Tigris, 265; leaves Amara (8 June), for Basra, 266; asks for more aeroplanes (12 June), 269; asks for more medical personnel (18 June), 269; given sanction for advance to Nasiriya, 270; informed (10 June) must not expect any reinforcements, 270; views on advance to Kut, 270–1, 273, 301–6; made responsible for defence of Bushire, 274; instructions to Gen. Gorringe (23 June), 275; report on advance to Nasiriya, 297–8; message to, from H.M. The King, 298; Memo. of 24 June, 301–3; telegram of 2 August, 305–6; Govt. of India (5 August) agree with views of, on advance to Kut, 306; advance to Kut sanctioned, 307; views on advance to Baghdad, 307–8, 311, Govt. of India disapprove, 308; instructions to Gen. Townshend (23 August), 312; informed (6 September) not to advance beyond Kut without reference to India, 313; present at Battle of Kut, 316; H.Q. in *Malamir*, 331 *n*; at Kut al Amara, 337; asks for additional machine guns, 338; report of, on river transport, 340–2; views of, on hospital ships, 343.

Norfolk Hill.
   Capture of, 253–5.

INDEX 389

North mound (Battle of Shaiba).
  Arabs occupy, 202 ; Major Wheeler's squadron attacks, 202–3 ; Gen. Kennedy attacks, 205–6 ; Gen. Delamain attacks and captures, 206.

North-West Frontier of India.
  Durand Frontier Agreement of 1893, 51 ; rising of 1897 on, 52 ; the "Curzon Policy," 52–4 ; effect of expeditions of 1895–8, on military estimates, 54 ; pre-war tribal aggression on, 60 ; demands of, on I.A., 60–2, 90 ; pre-war fighting strength of tribes on, 61 ; relation of Mesopotamia to, 71 ; situation on, (18 September 1914), 86, (23 July 1915), 304 ; extent of, 90 n ; reinforcements for, 135 ; unrest on, 160, 186, 222, 270, 310, 338.

Nuhairat.
  Brit. artillery position at, 245.

Nukhaila.
  Cavalry skirmish near, (9 February 1915), 176 ; Turkish force at, 176, 178, 190, attacked by E.B.F., 192 ; action near, (3 March), 181–3, 191 ; Turkish concentration and strength near (6 April), 193.

Nukhailat.
  Brit. force advancing on Kut reaches, 318 ; bridge across Tigris at, 318 ; Gen. Townshend establishes H.Q. near, 319.

Nunn, Capt. W., D.S.O., R.N.
  Takes over duties of S.N.O. (11 December 1914), 157 ; Lord Hardinge discusses situation with, 172 ; advance to Amara, 251–64 ; transfers to *Comet*, 260 ; advance to Nasiriya on *Shushan*, 275–98 ; at Ceylon, 314.

Nur Dad, Lance-Naick (17th S. & M.).
  Gallantry of, 149–50.

Nur-ud-Din.
  In command of Turkish forces, 302 ; battle of Kut, 314–38 ; deceived by Brit. ruse, 319–20.

O.

Observation towers.
  Constructed at Qurna, 242 ; " Ati's House," 278 ; erected at Nukhailat, 319.

Ocean, H.M.S. (battleship).
  Escorts I.E.F. " D," 103 ; Fao, 105–8 ; leaves Persian Gulf for Egypt (11 December 1914), 157.

Odin, H.M.S. (sloop).
  Preparations for despatch of, to Shatt al Arab, 79 ; ordered to Shatt al Arab, 84 ; arrives Mohammerah, 85 ; alleged violation of neutrality by, 85 ; leaves Shatt al Arab for Bushire, 91 ; armament of, 97 n ; attack on Fao, 106–8 ; action at Saihan, 116 ; action at Sahil, 119–24 ; passes obstruction in Shatt al Arab, 128 ; reaches Basra, 128 ; reconnoitres towards Qurna, 140 ; attack on Qurna, 141–51 ; leaves for repairs, 157 ; moves to engage *Marmariss*, 190–1 ; Qurna, 219 ; affair of 5 May 1915, 245 ; advance to Amara, 251–64 ; advance to Nasiriya, 276–98.

Oilfields. . *See* " Anglo-Persian Oilfields."

Oil, supply of.
  Mr. Churchill on, 82 ; Admiralty attach great importance to, 237, 303 ; secured, by occupation of Amara, 307.

One Tower Hill.
  Turkish position at, shelled from Nuhairat, 245 ; capture of, 253–5.

One Tree Hill.
   Turkish advanced post at, 243; shelled from Nuhairat, 245; capture of, 253–4.
Operation orders.
   Gen. Delamain's, for attack on Saihan (15 November 1914), 115; at Sahil (17 November), 120–1; Gen. Barrett's, of 16 November, 119; Gen. Barrett to Col. Frazer (30 November), 141; Gen. Barrett to Gen. Fry to reinforce Col. Frazer, 144–5; Gen. Barrett for action of 3 March 1915, near Shaiba, 181; to Gen. Gorringe for operations in Arabistan, 224; Gen. Gorringe's, for operations in Arabistan, 227–31; to Gen. Gorringe for advance on Amara, 231–3; Gen. Townshend's (28 May) for advance to Amara, 250–2; Gen. Gorringe's, for advance on Nasiriya, 280, 286–7, 291–2; Gen. Townshend's (26 September) for battle of Kut, 321; Gen. Delamain in battle of Kut, *quoted*, 322; Gen. Townshend's, for the pursuit after battle of Kut, 336.
Operations.
   Effect of climatic conditions on, 10. *See also* " Plans of Operation."
Orders.
   To Gen. Barrett (31 October 1914) to reinforce Gen. Delamain, 112; (2 November), 113; (14 November), 115; (4 January 1915), 156.
———.
   To Gen. Delamain (3 and 5 October 1914), 92–3; (10 October), 99–102; (31 October), to commence hostilities, 104–5; (2 November), 105 *n*.
———.
   To Capt. Hayes-Sadler, R.N. (31 October 1914), to commence hostilities, 104.
———.
   To. Gen. Nixon (24, 30 and 31 March 1915), 194–6.
———.
   To Admiral Peirse (31 October 1914), to commence hostilities, 104.
Orders in Council.
   Persian Coast and Islands, 47.
Outram, Sir James.
   Expedition of 1857, referred to, 139.

P.

P 1; *P 3*; *P 4*. (river steamers).
   In advance to Amara, 252–64.
Palmer, Gen. Sir Power.
   Army in India reorganisation scheme of, 56.
Palmer, Lieut. I. M., R.N. (*Comet*).
   In advance to Amara, 262.
Pan-Islamic movement.
   Brief *résumé* of, 19–20; exploitation of, by Young Turks, 60; Turkish arrangements to spread, 86; effect of propaganda of, in India, 90 *n*.
Pan-Turanian movement.
   Brief *résumé* of, 20–1; exploitation of, by Young Turks, 60.
Parr, Lt.-Col. H. O. (7th Rajputs).
   Severely wounded in action near Ahwaz (3 March 1915), 184.
Parsons, Capt. B. E. T. (1st/4th Hants).
   In advance to Nasiriya, 293.
Peardrop Bend.
   Marmariss at, 190.

INDEX 391

Peebles, Lt.-Col. E. C., D.S.O. (Norfolks).
> In advance to Amara, 251–64.

Peirse, Rear-Ad. R. H. (C.-in-C., East Indies).
> Ordered to commence hostilities against Turkey, 104.

Perrin, Major C. L. (76th Punjabis).
> In Arabistan operations, 230.

Persia.
> Relations of, with Turkey in 1842, 24 ; attitude of, at outbreak of war, 24–5 ; relations of, with Great Britain, 47–8 ; independence of, little affected by operations in Mesopotamia, 48 ; relation of Mesopotamia to, 77, 86, 192 ; enemy emissaries in, 77, 86, 192 ; probable violation of neutrality of, by I. E. F. " D," 93–4 ; violation of neutrality of, by Russian and Turkish forces, 159, 179 ; protection of Brit. subjects, 167 ; protests against Turkish aggression, 169 ; protests against arrest of German agents, 192 ; German breaches of neutrality, 192 ; German influence in, 240, 270, 273–4, 307–8 ; deterioration of situation in, 273–4 ; situation in, (3 August 1915), 307 n ; situation in, improved by Russo-Brit. activity, 309. *See also* " Shah of Persia " ; " Persian Gulf " ; " East India Company."

————, Southern.
> Situation in, (March 1915), 192 ; (June), 274.

Persian Gulf.
> Political relations of Great Britain with, from 1622, 45–7 ; lawlessness of Arabs in, 45–6 ; results of Brit. intervention in, 46 ; Mr. T. J. Bennett's paper on, *quoted*, 46–7 ; Brit. Consular organisation, 47 ; I.A., Gen. Staff, responsible for, 70 ; relations of Mesopotamia to, 71 ; effect on, of Turkish operations in Mesopotamia, 71–2 ; assistance of India in, 73 ; Brit. measures for security of, 78–81, 83–4 ; situation in, (September 1914), 85–6 ; Gen. Barrow's appreciation, 26 September, 86–8 ; Brit. Govt. order a force to the, 91–2 ; Sir P. Cox to control political matters in, 94 ; Lord Crewe's views on effect of force in, 95 n ; position in the, secured, 153 ; operations at Bushire (12–13 July 1915), 308 ; operations against Dilwar (13–16 August), 309 ; action at Bushire (9 September), 309. *See also* " Persia " ; " East India Company " ; " Cox, Sir P."

Pioneer (Turkish armed steamer).
> Engagement with, (27 September 1915), 320 ; overtaken, 336.

Pioneers.
> Work of, in Basra, 132.

Pipe-line. *See* " Anglo-Persian Oilfields."

Plans of operation.
> Turco-German, 32–4 ; division of responsibility between Gen. Staffs at W.O. and India, 69–70 ; no pre-war plan for Mesopotamia, 70, 72 ; for occupation of Basra drawn up, 70 n ; against Turkey, 71 ; for I.E.F. " D," (10 October 1914), 99–102 ; for landing at Fao issued (28 October 1915), 103 ; Gen. Barrett's, for advance from Sanniya, 119–20 ; Turco-Arab, 161–2, 166 ; Turkish, for utilising Arab tribes, 162 ; Gen. Barrett's, for attack near Ruta, 163 ; Turkish, against Basra, 179 ; Turkish against Shaiba, 190–1 ; in Arabistan, 224, 231 ; for occupation of the Basra *Vilayet*, 234–41 ; Gen. Townshend's, for offensive up Tigris, 246 ; Gen. Gorringe's, during advance to Nasiriya (14 July 1915), 286–7 ; (24 July), 291–2 ; Gen. Townshend's, for advance to Kut (28 August), 314.

Population.
> Of Mesopotamia, 10 ; effect of mobilization on civil, 31 ; of India, 62, 64 ; of Basra, 129. *See also* " Man-power."

Port facilities. *See* " Basra " ; " Maqil."

Press, The.
  Increase of newspapers affects pre-war internal situation in India, 62.
Prisoners of war, captured by British.
  At Sanniya, night (10–11 November 1914), 109; information obtained from, 109, 116, 154; action of Saihan, 117; action of Sahil, 124; Muzaira'a, 142, 144; Qurna, 151; Muzaira'a night (29–30 January 1915), 166; battle of Shaiba, 207–8, 217; Arabistan operations, 231; advance to Amara, 256, 259–63, 265; advance to Nasiriya, 281–2, 294, 297; battle of Kut, 324, 326–7, 337.
———, captured by Turks.
  Advance to Kut, 316, 319.
Proclamations, British.
  Regarding immunity of Moslem Holy Places, 110–2; in Basra (23 November 1914), 130–1; in Amara, 263.
Products.
  Staple, 9; principal areas of, 9.
Propaganda.
  Enemy in Middle East and India, etc., 77, 89–90, 159; effect of German, in Arabistan, 179; enemy, in S. Persia, 192.
Punjab.
  Unrest in, necessitates military precautions, 160; plot for a general rising in, discovered, 177; arrests of leaders ease internal situation, 179.
Pyramus, H.M.S. (light cruiser).
  Operations at Dilwar, 309.

Q.

Qala Salih.
  L. of C. post at, 265, 267 *n*, 301.
Qurainat.
  Shaikh Ajaimi's force at, 176.
Qurna.
  Euphrates Old Channel joins Tigris at, 2; the advance on, and capture of, (4–8 December 1914), 139–53; Gen. Barrow advocates advance to, 136–7; description of, 152; strategic importance of, 152, 156; Brit. garrison at, 156–7, 159, 170, 196, 301; difficulties of reconnaissance, 158; defensive strength of, 158–9; not to be considered as limit of Brit. advance, 161; Turkish activity near, 162; probable Turkish advance on, 166; Turkish night attack on, (29–30 January 1915), 166; strength of Turkish force located near, (4 February), 170, (end April), 223; reduction Brit. force, owing to floods, 175, 179; pontoon bridge at, 175, 242, damaged, 219; reserve force for, 181; floods at, 190, 242; Turkish force reduced opposite, 191; Brit. force at, (11 April), 197; Turks bombard Brit. position at, (11–13 April), 219; measures to prevent reinforcement of Turks before, 231; Gen. Townshend arrives at, (24 April), 241, 243; strength of Brit. force at, (24 April), 241–2; boom defence across Tigris and observation tower at, 242; conditions in, 242–3; force from, in affair of 8 May, 245; Gen. Nixon at, (12 May), 247; Brit. force at, (13 June), 267.

———.
  First action of, (4–8 December 1914), 139–53.

———.
  Second action of, (31 May 1915), 253–7.

INDEX 393

R.

Radcliffe, Major F. W. (Dorsets).
 Landing arrangements near Fao, 105–6.
Rafts.
 Use of, down Tigris by Turkish reinforcements, 24.
Railways.
 Smyrna-Aidin, in 1914, 22–3 ; German interests predominant, 23 ; Baghdad, 23–4, 35, 40–3 ; Hejaz, 37.
 ———, light.
 Proposed construction of a, from Basra to Nasiriya, 180 ; floods delay survey for, 342 ; proposal for, rejected, 342.
Rainfall.
 Effect on navigation of Tigris, 3 ; annual average, 5 ; agriculture in Up. Mesopotamia dependent upon, 9 ; retards operations, 114 ; delays movement of Arabistan force, 225, 227.
Ramuz (Ram Hormuz).
 Rising at, 187, 187 n.
Reconnaissance, British.
 Of Fao, 105–6 ; of Shatt al Arab, 108, 125 ; naval, of Qurna, 140, 145 ; difficulties of, 158 ; (5–6 January 1915) from Qurna, 158 ; means of, improved by a *Bellum* squadron, 167 ; up Euphrates (15 February), 175, (April), 220, (May), 241 ; up Karun (26 February), 179 ; of Arabistan force, 226–34 ; by Gen. Townshend, 243 ; of Al Huwair creek, 245 ; in vicinity of Amara, 265 ; during advance to Nasiriya, 278–9, 281–4, 290 ; during advance to, and battle of Kut, 315, 321, 324–5.
 ———, Turkish.
 Towards Shaiba (1 April 1915), 193.
Reeds.
 Prevalence of, 243 n ; afford good cover, 245 ; obstruct operations, 256, 287.
Reilly, Flight Commander, Major H. L. (R.F.C.).
 Aerial reconnaissances by, 315, 337.
Risafa (Turkish steamer).
 Sunk in Euphrates, 283.
Reinforcements, British.
 In November 1914, 110, Appendix II., 347, 113–5, 118 ; internal situation in India, likely to interfere with, 134 n, 160, 177, 222 ; (December), 157 ; (January 1915), 157–8 ; inf. brig. mobilized in India (January), 161, 165 ; Gen. Barrett informs India (22 January) no urgent necessity for, 165 ; Gen. Barrett asks for, (26 January), 165 ; (February), 170–1 ; another inf. brig. being prepared in India, 171 ; ordered not to be sent, 173 ; Govt. of India ordered to reinforce I.E.F. " D " 187–8 ; (March), 188 ; (June), 234 n ; of I.E.F. " D " by Territorials from India, 338.
 ———, Turkish.
 Delayed by gaps in Baghdad railway, 24 ; (December 1914), 127, 155 n ; (January 1915), 158 ; effect on, of Turkish defeat in Caucasus, 159 ; (February), 169–70, 178 ; likely effect on, of operations against Dardanelles, 180.
Religions.
 In Mesopotamia, 13 ; effect of, on policy, 36.
Reserves, Indian Army.
 Inefficiency of, at outbreak of war, 63, 65 ; number of Brit. officers in, at outbreak of war, 63, 69.

Reserves, Turkish Army.
> System of, 31-2 ; number of, in Baghdad, 104.

Reynardson, Capt. H. Birch (Oxfords).
> " Mesopotamia 1914–1915," referred to 334 *n*.

" River Column."
> Formation, and reinforcement of, 300.

River system.
> Best means of communication, 6 ; Brit. navigation nights, 43–5. *See also* " Euphrates " ; " Karum " ; " Shatt al Arab " ; " Shatt at Hai " ; " Tigris."

Roads.
> Condition in 1914, 6 ; main routes, 6–7 ; condition of, at Basra, 132 ; from Shatrat al Muntafik to Nasiriya, 271.

Robertson, Gen. Sir W. R., K.C.B., K.C.V.O., D.S.O.
> Recommendations of, to co-ordinate operations in Mesopotamia, 72.

Robinson, Brig.-Gen. C. T. (R.A.).
> Ordered to defend Ahwaz and strength of force under, 174 ; effect of presence in Ahwaz, 179 ; action near Ahwaz, 183–5 ; advance to Amara, 251–64.

Rosher, Lt.-Col. H. L. (Dorsets).
> Capture of Fao, 106–8 ; action near Shaiba, 181–3.

Royal Flying Corps.
> W.O. agree to send two flights of, from Egypt, 269 ; advance to Nasiriya, 290–8 ; advance to Kut, 315–38, 339. *See also* " Aircraft."

Royal Indian Marine.
> And navigation rights, 44. *See also* " Dalhousie " ; " Hamilton, Cdr." ; " Lawrence."

Royal Marines.
> At capture of Fao, 106–8.

Royal Naval Air Service.
> Arrive Basra (5 September 1915) from East Africa, 316 *n* ; advance to Kut, 316–38.

Russia.
> Agreement of 1907 with Great Britain, 36, 38, 53, 57, 60 ; attack on Afghans (1885), 51, 54 ; railway to Afghan border, 52 ; best means of helping, 71 ; Germany asks Turkey to declare war on, 75 ; declares war on Turkey (2 November 1914), 98 ; inception of the " East Persia Cordon," 274.

Russo-Japanese war.
> Effect of, on Indian military situation, 57 ; internal situation in India affected by Japanese victories in Manchuria, 62.

Ruta.
> Turks block Tigris near, 157–8 ; action at, 20 January 1915, 162–5 ; Turkish force at, 164, 236, 243 ; Turks move from, owing to floods, 174, 179 ; Turkish bns. leave, 175 ; Turks lay mines in Tigris near, 179, 258 ; evacuated by Turks, 258.

S.

Saba (Arabistan).
> Arabistan force concentrates at, 225.

Sadanawiya creek.
> Attack on, and capture of Turkish position at, 295–6.

Sa'id Halim, (Grand Vizier of Turkey).
> Opposed to war with Great Britain, 76 ; statement of, *re* neutrality, 76–7 ; anxious to reopen Dardanelles, 91.

INDEX 395

Sahil.
 Action of, (17 November 1914), 119–24 ; site for Brit. camp selected at, 124 ; unsuitable for disembarkation at, 125, 128 *n* ; the advance from, (20 November), 128.

Saihan, action of, (15 November 1914), 115–8.

Sakrikiya.
 Turkish camp at, 157.

Salimi (river steamer).
 Advance to, and capture of Qurna, 141–51 ; with E.B.F., 191.

Sami Bey.
 In command of Turkish attack (night 10–11 November 1914), 109.

Sandes, Major E. W. C., R.E. (S. & M.).
 " In Kut and Captivity," referred to, 318 *n*.

Sanders, Gen. Liman von.
 Head of German Mil. Mission to Turkey, 27.

Sandstorms.
 Impede operations at Sahil, 124.

Sanitation.
 General lack of, in Mesopotamia, 8 ; absence of, in Basra, 129.

Sannaiyat.
 Brit. force in advance to Kut reaches, 315 ; Brit. concentrate at, 316, advance from, 318.

Sanniya.
 Gen. Delamain's force lands at, (8–10 November 1914), 108 ; Turks attack Brit. camp at, (night 10–11 November), 109 ; Gen. Delamain reports on position at, 114 ; Gen. Barrett arrives at, (14 November), 110, 114–5 ; the advance from, 119.

Sappers and Miners.
 Work of, in Basra, 132 ; with E.B.F., 191, with the " River Column," 300.

———, *2nd Queen Victoria's Own, 12th Company*.
 Arrive Basra, 193 ; Arabistan operations, 225–33, Appendix V., 352 ; Ahwaz, 234 ; advance to Nasiriya, 276–98 ; Nasiriya, 300, Appendix VII., 357.

———, *3rd, 17th Company*.
 In 6th Div., 113 ; disembarkation of, 115 ; action of Sahil, 119–24 ; advance to, and capture of Qurna, 141–51 ; construct flying bridge, 149–50 ; action at Ruta, 163–5 ; Shaiba, 197 ; battle of Shaiba, 201–19 ; advance to Nasiriya, 289–98, casualties, 293 ; battle of Kut, 314–38.

———, *3rd, 22nd Company*.
 In I.E.F. " D," 99 ; action of Sahil, 119–24 ; Ahwaz, 174, 197 ; Shaiba, 197 ; battle of Shaiba, 201–19 ; advance to Amara, 251–64 ; Ali Gharbi and Amara, 301 ; battle of Kut, 314–38.

———, *Sirmur Company, Imperial Service Troops*.
 Joins I.E.F. " D," 157 ; Qurna, 197–241 ; advance to Amara, 249–64 ; Basra, 301.

———, *12th (Divisional Signal) Company*.
 Ahwaz, 197 ; advance to Nasiriya, 276–98, casualties, 297.

———, *31st (Divisional Signal) Company*.
 Arabistan operations, 225–34, Appendix V., 352.

———, *34th (Divisional Signal) Company*.
 Qurna and Shaiba, 197 ; Arabistan operations, 225–34, Appendix V., 352 ; battle of Kut, 314–38.

Sappers and Miners, *Wireless Troop*.
    Ahwaz, 197 ; Shaiba, 197 ; Arabistan operations, 225-34, Appendix V., 352 ; advance to Nasiriya, 276 ; battle of Kut, 314-38.
Sardinia.
    Supports Turkey in Crimean war, 36.
Sayad Idrisi.
    Turkish plan for co-operation of, 162.
Scallon, Lt.-Gen. Sir R. I., K.C.B., K.C.I.E., D.S.O.
    Member of " Army in India Committee " of 1912, 58.
Secretary of State for India. *See* " Chamberlain, The Rt. Hon. J. Austen, P.C., M.P." ; " Crewe, Lord."
Senior Naval Officer. *See* " Cookson, Lt.-Com. E." ; " Hallett, Lieut. C. G." ; " Hayes-Sadler, Capt. A." ; " Nunn, Capt. W." ; " Seymour, Lieut. A. G." ; " Singleton, Lieut. M."
Seymour, Lt.-Com. A. G., R.N.
    S.N.O. with E.B.F., 191 ; wounded in advance to Nasiriya, 296.
Shah of Persia.
    Agreement between, and East India Company, 45 ; seeks naval aid against Arabs, 46.
Shaiba.
    Brit. force sent to hold, 141, 168, 170 ; difficulties of transport to, owing to floods, 175-6, 198-9 ; Gen. Barrett reinforces, 178, 181 ; reserve force for, 181 ; Turkish intention to advance against, 190-1 ; Brit. force at, (11 April 1915), 197 ; strategic importance of, 198 ; Gen. Nixon decides to reduce force at, (17 April), 219.

————, action near, (3rd March 1915), 181-3.

————, battle of, (12-14 April 1915), 201-19.

Shaikh Ajaimi of Muntafik.
    Emissary from, arrives Basra to convey submission of, 133-4 ; remained on side of Turkey throughout war, 138 *n* ; located about Nasiriya, 154, 158, 170 *n* ; attitude of, 156 ; with Turkish force to attack Basra, 166, 170 *n* ; activity of, (9-19 February 1915), 176.
Shaikh Ghazban of the Bani Lam.
    With Turkish force moving to Bisaitin, 166, 169 ; moves with the Bani Turuf to join Turks at Ghadir, 183 ; vacillating attitude of, 299.
Shaikh of Kuwait.
    Under Brit. protection, 14, 25-6 ; assistance of, 83 ; estimated military strength of, 101 ; friendly attitude of, 138.
Shaikh of Mohammerah.
    Oil pipe-line through territory of, 14 ; friendly attitude of, 25, 45, 83 ; responsibility of, for policing oilfields, 93 *n* ; estimated military strength of, 101 ; apprehensions of, 118, 161 ; measures to protect the, 119, 166 ; reports Turkish evacuation of Baljaniya and Basra, 127 ; gives use of palace as hospital, 132 ; loses control of Ahwaz, 167 ; forces of, at Ahwaz, 169 ; unreliability of tribes under, 169, 173 ; advisability of supporting the, 169 ; presses for reinforcements, 173 ; defeats Bawi tribesmen, 179, 221 ; Cha'ab Shaikhs exhorted to remain loyal to, 179 ; deserted by all but one of his tribes, 187 ; submission of Bawi Shaikhs to, 309.
Shaikh Sa'ad.
    Turkish force at, 300.
Shaitan (H.M. armed launch).
    Advance to, and capture of Qurna, 141-51 ; commander of, killed (7 December 1914), 148 ; Ahwaz (1 February 1915), 169 ; engages Bawi tribesmen (15 April), 221 ; advance to Amara, 251-64 ; sinks *Bulbul*, 259 ; the " River Column," 300 ; Ali Gharbi, 301 ; advance to Kut, 314-38.

INDEX 397

Shakespear, Major W. H. I., C.I.E.
  Knowledge of, of Ibn Saud, 86 ; movements of, and instructions to, 93–4 ; reports situation with Ibn Saud (4 January 1915), 161–2, (19 January), 171 ; death of, 178.
Shakturs (native craft).
  Description and use of, 3.
Shamshamiya (Shatt al Arab).
  Turkish guns at, 84, 100 ; Turkish obstruction at, 105, 127.
Sharif of Mecca.
  Turkish plan for co-operation of, 162 ; Turks press, to proclaim *Jahad*, 171.
Shatrat al Muntafik.
  Turks reported moving to, 178.
Shatt al Arab.
  Description and navigation of, 1 ; conservancy of, 43, 45 ; Turkish preparation to block, 78 ; Brit. measures for security of, 78–9, 84 ; Turkish defence of, 78, 84–5, 100 ; Brit. warships arrive in, 85 ; Turkey protests against *Odin* remaining in, 85 ; *Odin* leaves, for Bushire, 91 ; Brit. Govt. decide to send a force to, 91–2 ; right of access to Abadan and Mohammerah, 96 ; Turks block, 105 ; Gen. Delamain arrives off, (3 November 1914), 106 ; Turkish attempt to block, 125–7 ; Brit. ships pass obstruction, 128 ; blocked below Qurna, 140, 148–9 ; obstruction buoyed and regulated, 140 ; depth of, at Qurna, 143 n.
Shatt al Hai.
  Description and navigation of, 4 ; reported move of Turkish troops down, 178 ; not passable by steamers below Shatrat al Muntafik, 178 n, 301 n ; Turks retire up, 241 ; importance of holding both ends of, 270–1 ; use of, seasonal, 271.
Shipping, British.
  Warned to avoid Turkish ports, 80 ; effect on, of Turkish preparations, 78, 80, 84 ; sailings to Basra resumed, 91.
Shiraz (in Fars).
  German agents in, 179, 192 ; hostility against Brit. Consulate, 192.
Shirin ; *Shuhrur* (tugs).
  Advance to Nasiriya, 277–98.
Shushan (sternwheel river steamer).
  With E.B.F., 191 ; reconnaissance of Al Huwair creek, 245, casualties, 245 ; advance to Amara, 251–64 ; advance to Nasiriya, 276–98 ; armament and age of, 276 ; flies pendant of S.N.O., 277 ; casualties, 296.
Shwaibda.
  Basra Movable Column reaches, and returns from, 176–7.
Shwaiyib river.
  Base camp on, for attack on Qurna, 141–51 ; retirement to, 144 ; Gen. Fry reaches, 145 ; too narrow for navigation, 158 ; overflows, 175.
Sickness.
  In Arabistan force, 232, 234 ; due to heat, 249, 269 ; in 30th and 33rd Inf. Brig., 269, 276 ; during advance to Nasiriya, 289, 297, 297 n ; of aircraft personnel during battle of Kut, 331.
Signalling. *See* " Communications, field."
Simla.
  H.Q. of C.-in-C., India, 56.
Sinai peninsula.
  Turkish plan for advance on, 162.

Singleton, Lieut. M., R.N. (*Shaitan*).
  Gallantry of, at Amara, 262 ; succeeds Lt.-Com. Cookson as temporary S.N.O., 336.
Sirdar-i-Naphte (armed tug).
  In Shatt al Arab, 105 ; attack on Fao, 106–8 ; action at Sahil, 119–24.
Slade, Adm. Sir E. J. W., K.C.I.E., K.C.V.O.
  Persian Gulf question referred to, in 1911, 73 ; measures for security of Persian Gulf, 78–80.
South mound (Battle of Shaiba).
  Enemy concentrate at, 208 ; captured, 210–1 ; Gen. Melliss's H.Q. on, 211.
Southern Persia. *See* " Persia, Southern."
Stack, Lt.-Col. C. S. (33rd Cavalry).
  Severely wounded in action near Shaiba (3 March 1915), 182.
Stone.
  Scarcity of, 6.
Subhi Bey, *Vali* of Basra.
  Threatens to commandeer coal and oil, 78 ; hostile attitude of, 96 ; surrenders Qurna, 151.
Subsidies.
  To the Bawi tribe, 308 ; German, in India, 309.
Sudhan Singh, Jemadar (7th Lancers).
  Killed at battle of Shaiba, 206.
Suez Canal.
  Defence of, 71 ; Arab menace against, 71 ; defeat of Turks at, referred to, 177.
Sulaiman Askari Bey.
  Commands Turkish reinforcements, 158, 165 ; wounded at action at Ruta, 165 ; assumes command of Turkish right wing, 190, Appendix VI., 354–5 ; battle of Shaiba, 208 *n* ; commits suicide, 218–9.
Sultan of Turkey.
  Supreme head of army, 27. *See also* " Abdul Hamid II."
Sumana (armed launch).
  In Shatt al Arab, 105 ; with E.B.F., 191 ; advance to Amara, 251–64 ; advance to Nasiriya, 276–81, 291–8, put out of action, 281 ; refitting 284 ; grounds barge across Majinina creek, 293 ; advance to Kut, 314–38.
Supplies.
  Difficulties of, 9 ; difficulties of landing, at Sahil, 125 ; sufficient only for inhabitants, 138. *See also* " Transport, Land ; River."
Suq ash Shuyukh.
  Remnants of 38th Turkish Div. located at, 154 ; Gen. Barrett recommends advance to, 156 ; E.B.F. ordered to blockade Euphrates at, 220 ; waterways to, unnavigable, 223 ; Turks obstruct Euphrates near, 241 ; occupation of, (6 July 1915), 283.
Swedish officers.
  In Persian Gendarmerie, 159, 192, 274.
Syria.
  Reported move of Turkish troops from, 155–6.

T.

T. 1 ; *T. 4*. (Tugs.)
  Advance to Nasiriya, 277–98.
Tabriz.
  Turks retire from, 167.

INDEX 399

Tactics.
  Affected by climatic conditions, 10.

Talaat Pasha (Turkish Minister of the Interior).
  Causes, with Enver Pasha, downfall of Turkish Cabinet (1913), 38; knowledge of German intentions, 75; waning power of, 76.

Telephones, telephoning. *See* " Equipment "; " Communications, field."

Territorial Force.
  Replace Indian troops sent to Europe and Egypt, 90; condition of, in India, 160; to reinforce I.E.F. " D," 187-8; sent from India to reinforce I.E.F. " D," 338.

Territorial waters.
  Six miles limit claimed by Turkey, 97.

" Thornycroft Point."
  Turkish position at, 283; captured, 292.

Thrace.
  Absence of communications in, 71.

Tigris, river.
  Confluence with Euphrates at Kurmat Ali, 1; confluence with Euphrates (Old Channel) at Qurna, 2; description and navigation of, 3-5; Brit. navigation rights, 43-4; flying bridge constructed across, for attack on Qurna, 149-50; Turkish obstruction below Ruta, 157-8; controlling banks of, broken, 175; Turkish mines in, 179; boom defence across, at Qurna, 242; Turkish boom across, near Kut, 317, attempt to breach, 335; shallowness of, hampers operations, 336, 338.

Timber.
  All imported, 6.

Townshend, Major-Gen. C. V. F., C.B., D.S.O.
  Arrives Basra (22 April 1915) to command 6th Div., 223; sent to Qurna to report on situation, 223; arrives Qurna (24 April), 241, 243, returns to Basra (26th), and suggests turning movement from Ahwaz, 243; in command of offensive up Tigris, 244-65; plan of operations for offensive up Tigris, 246; at Qurna with Gen. Nixon (12 May), 247; " My Campaign in Mesopotamia," *cited*, 247, 260, 321-3, 315, 328 *n*; favours postponing attack, 247-8; instructions to units for advance on Amara, 248-9; Operation Order (28 May) for advance to Amara, 250-2; H.Q. of, in advance to Amara, 252; Operation Order (31 May) for advance to Amara, 257; tranships to *Comet* with S.N.O., 260; receives surrender of Amara, 262; proceeds to India on sick leave, 299; returns to Mesopotamia (21 August); 312; letter to C.I.G.S., 312; in command at battle of Kut, 312-38; instructions to, (23 August), 312; arrives Amara (28 August), 313; plan of operations for advance to Kut (28 August), 314; Operation Order (26 September) for battle of Kut, 321; special despatch on Com. Cookson's exploit, *quoted*, 335; orders for pursuit after battle of Kut, 336; at Aziziya (5 October), 337.

Townley, Sir W. B., K.C.M.G. (Brit. Minister at Tehran).
  Reports on effect of enemy propaganda, 159.

Tracks.
  Across marshes, unsuitable for military purposes, 7; in Arabistan, to oilfields, 14.

Transport, Animal.
  Suffers from heat, 103; camels returned to India, 153 *n*, 157; hindered by floods, 175-6; with I.E.F. " D " (March 1915), 180; with Gen. Gorringe in Arabistan, 225.

Transport, Land.
   Wheeled, use of, 6 ; principal means of, 6 ; collection of local supplies by, 9 ; local, sufficient only for inhabitants, 138 ; floods affect, 175–6, 198 ; with I.E.F. " D " (March 1915), 180 ; work of, with Arabistan force, 234.
———, mechanical.
   Nucleus of service started, 267 ; numbers of, (end September 1915), 339,
———, River.
   Importance of, to I.E.F. " D," 118 ; insufficient for advance beyond Qurna 138, 158 ; local, sufficient only for inhabitants, 138 ; Gen. Barrett asks for additional, 158, 165, 169, 339 ; shortage of, 169, 186, 221, 236, 299, 339–42 ; *bellums* used to supply Shaiba, 198 ; Gen. Nixon's demand for, 220, 268, 339, 341 ; with Arabistan force, 224–34, 248 ; use of, limited, 243 ; in offensive up Tigris, 246–64 ; number of, (June 1915), 268, (September), 339 ; general remarks on, 268–9 ; Gen. Kemball's Memorandum, and Gen. Nixon's report to India on, 340–2.
———, Turkish.
   Difficulties of, intensified by E.B.F., 192.
———, ———, Land.
   Difficulties of, 180–1.
———, ———, River.
   Probable use of, to move on Qurna and Kurmat Ali, 181.
Transports   See " *Umaria* " ; " *Varela*."
Treaties.
   Turco-British, (1913–4), 21 ; Erzerum, (1847), 24 ; Anglo-Russian, (1907), 36, 38, 53, 57, 60 ; Persian, with East India Company, 45 ; Durand Frontier Agreement, (1893), 51 ; Anglo-Japanese, 57 ; German-Austrian alliance, 60 ; Turco-German alliance, (1914), signed 2 August, 75 *n*.
Trenches, Turkish.
   Battle of Shaiba, 213–4, 218 ; Norfolk Hill, 255 ; Majinina position, 294 ; Kut position, 317, 324 *n*, 327, 338.
Turco-German alliance. *See under* " Treaties."
Turco-Italian War of 1911.
   Effect of, in Mesopotamia, 19.
Turco-Persian frontier. *See* " Frontiers."
Turkey.
   Effect on Mesopotamia, of 1908 revolution in, 18–9 ; relations with Persia in 1842, 24 ; value of, as an ally, 32, 37 ; Turco-German plans of operation, 32–4 ; relations of, with Great Britain (1878), 36–7 ; support of, in Crimean War, 36 ; policy of Mr. W. E. Gladstone, 36 ; counter-revolution of 1909, 37 ; decline of Brit. and rise of German influence in, 37–9 ; downfall of Cabinet in 1913, 38 ; German Ambassador to, (1897–1912), 38 *n* ; Brit. policy *re* railways in territory of, 40–3 ; navigation agreement with, 44 ; possibility of hostilities with, 70 ; value of, to Germany, 70 ; difficulty of operations against, 71 ; possible results of military action of, in Mesopotamia, 71–2 ; asked by Germany to declare war on Russia, 75 ; domination of Germans in, 75 ; prepares Arab Chiefs and Governors in Mesopotamia for intervention, 75–6 ; pro-Brit. sentiments of, 76 ; effect in, of retention by Great Britain on battleships of, 76 ; statement of Grand Vizier as to neutrality of, 76–7 ; violation of International obligations by, 77 ; situation in, accurately gauged by Brit. Ambassador, 77 ; sends emissaries to Egypt, India, etc., 77–8, 89–90 ; question of Arab support in event of war with, 83–4 ; Govt. of, prepared to assist Germany, 89 ; Musalman sympathy with, 90 *n* ; military preparedness of, 96 ; Allies declare war on, 98 ; Brit. *communiqué re* outbreak of war with, 110–12 ; effect in, of action at Sahil, 127. *See also* " Sultan of Turkey " ; " Turkey Army."

INDEX 401

Turkey, Army.
German reorganisation of, (1882–1911), 26 ; administrative system, 27 ; strength of, at outbreak of war, 27–8 ; organisation and distribution, 28–32 ; maximum strength, reached in May 1916, 29 ; system of education in, 30–1 ; reserve system, 31–2 ; strength of, in Mesopotamia, maintained by local recruitment, 32 ; Afghan army trained by instructors of, 60 ; movement of troops to Basra, 79, 84 ; strength and distribution of, in Mesopotamia (October 1914), 100–1, 103–4, (action of Saihan), 116 n, (first action of Qurna), 140, 145, 148, (action at Ruta), 164, (January 1915), 165, (4 February), 170, (late February), 178, 180, (March), 190, (battle of Shaiba), 208–9, 217, 217 n, 218, Turco-Arab force in Arabistan (end April), 223–4, (14 June), 273, (retiring from Amara), 269, (at Nasiriya), 297, (end July), 301, (battle of Kut), 316–8, 324.

————, ————, Air services.
State of, at outbreak of war, 30.

————, Cabinet.
Downfall of, (1913), 38 ; opposed to war with Great Britain, 76.

————, German Military Mission in, 27, 76.

U.

Umaria (transport).
Attack on Fao, 106–8.

Umm Chir (Arabistan).
Reconnaissance to, 231–2.

Umm as Sabiyan.
Brit. outpost at, 284–5, 287.

Umm, Qasr.
Suggested as best base for main operations, 101 ; idea of landing at abandoned, 114.

V.

Vale, 1st Class Petty Officer W. (*Shaitan*).
Gallantry of, action at Qurna, (7 December 1914), 148.

Vali of Pusht-i-Kuh.
Agrees to join Turks, 173.

Varela (Transport).
Conference on, (28 October 1914), 103, (2nd November), 105 ; attack on Fao, 106–8.

Viceroy of India. *See* " Curzon of Kedleston, Lord " ; " Hardinge, Lord."

Volunteers.
Calcutta Engineers, with I.E.F. " D," 157 ; from India and Burma, 289–98, 300, 314.

W.

Wapshare, Major-Gen. R., C.B.
In command at Ahwaz (20 June 1915), 234.

War Committee. *See* under " Committees."

War, Declarations of. *See* " Declarations of War."

—— Office.
Demands of, upon I.A., at outbreak of war, 66, 68 ; on forcing of Dardanelles, 71 ; urged to send reinforcements, 177 ; agree to send two aeroplanes, 188 ; agree to send two flights of the R.F.C. from Egypt, 269 ; arranges to send an air squadron to Mesopotamia, 339. *See also* " Murray, Lt.-Gen. Sir J. Wolfe."

War Office, General Staff.
> Pre-occupation of, at outbreak of war with Turkey, 69; allocation of responsibility between Gen. Staff, India, and, 69–70; views of, regarding occupation of Alexandretta, 71.

Wassmuss (German agent).
> Movements of, 179; arrested, but escapes, 192; activity of, 273–4, Appendix I., 344–5.

Water supply.
> Difficulties of, 10; at Bahrein, limited, 103; at Basra, 132; in Arabistan, 226–7, 232; during battle of Kut, 328, 328 n, 334.

Waterways. *See* " River system."

Weather.
> Influence of, on operations at Sanniya, 109–10; W/T interrupted by bad, 109, 113–4; influence of, on operations at Sahil, 121; experienced by Basra Movable Column (19–20 February 1915), 176–7; effect of heat at battle of Shaiba, 214, 214 n, 215–6; during operations in Arabistan, 225, 227–9, 231–4; during advance to Amara, 249, 257, 265; in June, 269; during advance to Nasiriya, 278, 284 n, 289–90, 292, 295; during action of 9 September, at Bushire, 309; during advance to, and battle of Kut, 315, 322, 326–8, 330, 334. *See also* " Dust "; " Floods "; " Mud "; " Rainfall "; " Sandstorms "; " Wind."

Wheeler, Major G. G. M. (7th Lancers).
> In battle of Shaiba, 202–6, killed, 206.

Wilhelm II (Emperor of Germany).
> Relations of, with Sultan of Turkey, 37; informs Greek minister of conclusion of alliance with Turkey, 75.

Wind.
> Gale impedes march of Basra Movable Column, 176; impedes operations in Arabistan, 227; delays passage of Akaika channel (30 June 1915), 278; effect of, during battle of Kut, 326–7, 328 n, 330.

Wireless telegraphy.
> Turkish protests against, on *Odin*, 85; arrangements for stations at Bushire and Abadan, 103 n; interrupted by bad weather, 109, 113–4; station erected at oilfields, 308. *See also* " Equipment."

Wonckhaus (German firm).
> Head of, in Basra, acts as German consul, 129 n; employé of, arrested at Ahwaz, 168.

Wounded.
> Mutilated by Arabs, 228, 337 n; evidence as to arrangements for, before Mesopotamia Commission, 336–7.

Y.

Yemen.
> Turkish plan for defence of, 162.

Younghusband, Major-Gen. Sir G. J., K.C.I.E., C.B.
> In command of 28th Inf. Brig., 304–5.

Young Turks, The.
> Rise of, 18; policy of, 21; counter-revolution of 1909, 37; exploitation of Pan-Islamic and Pan-Turanian movements by, 60.

Z.

Zubair.
> Turkish force at, (October 1914), 100; Turks reported in strength south of, (1 April 1915), 193; floods at, 198; Brit. camp near, 220, 241; reduction of Brit. force near, 241.

Zugmayer, Dr. (German emissary in Persia).
> Extracts from diary of, Appendix I., 344–5.

www.ingramcontent.com/pod-product-compliance
Lightning Source LLC
Chambersburg PA
CBHW070804300426
44111CB00014B/2426